D0761310

HEIDEGGER AND LANGUAGE

STUDIES IN CONTINENTAL THOUGHT

John Sallis, editor

CONSULTING EDITORS

Robert Bernasconi
Rudolph Bernet
John D. Caputo
David Carr
Edward S. Casey
Hubert Dreyfus
Don Ihde
David Farrell Krell
Lenore Langsdorf
Alphonso Lingis
William L. McBride
J. N. Mohanty
Mary Rawlinson
Tom Rockmore
Calvin O. Schrag
† *Reiner Schürmann*
Charles E. Scott
Thomas Sheehan
Robert Sokolowski
Bruce W. Wilshire
David Wood

Heidegger and Language

EDITED BY JEFFREY POWELL

Indiana University Press
Bloomington & Indianapolis

b13990007
i9
B
3279
.H49
H3417
2013
.i 14292099
#805506255

Françoise Dastur's essay was originally published in French under the title "Heidegger et la question de 'l'essence' du langage" in *Alter: Revue de phénoménologie* 19 (2011).

This book is a publication of

Indiana University Press
601 North Morton Street
Bloomington, Indiana 47404-3797 USA

iupress.indiana.edu

Telephone orders 800-842-6796
Fax orders 812-855-7931

© 2013 by Indiana University Press

All rights reserved
No part of this book may be reproduced or utilized in any form or by any means, electronic or mechanical, including photocopying and recording, or by any information storage and retrieval system, without permission in writing from the publisher. The Association of American University Presses' Resolution on Permissions constitutes the only exception to this prohibition.

⊗The paper used in this publication meets the minimum requirements of the American National Standard for Information Sciences—Permanence of Paper for Printed Library Materials, ANSI Z39.48-1992.

Manufactured in the United States of America

Library of Congress Cataloging-in-Publication Data

Heidegger and language / edited by Jeffrey Powell.
p. cm. — (Studies in Continental thought)
Includes index.
ISBN 978-0-253-00740-7 (cloth : alk. paper) — ISBN 978-0-253-00748-3 (pbk. : alk. paper) — ISBN 978-0-253-00760-5 (electronic book) 1. Heidegger, Martin, 1889–1976. 2. Language and languages—Philosophy. I. Powell, Jeffrey, [date]
B3279.H49H3417 2013
193—dc23

2012031187

1 2 3 4 5 18 17 16 15 14 13

CONTENTS

HEIDEGGER AND LANGUAGE

Introduction

It is well known in many quarters that Martin Heidegger's long encounter with the question of language was not restricted to a kind of linguistics or a traditional philosophy of language. This is not to say, however, that Heidegger's writings concerning language had nothing to contribute to those approaches to language and many others. Quite the contrary; Heidegger's influence on those interested in the question of language has been far and wide. To that end, the essays in this collection speak to many disciplines and many concerns, including but not limited to metaphysics, poetry, the political, logic, and the very possibility of philosophy.

Many of the above concerns and more have been joined to the question of language for the simple reason that the twentieth century has been characterized as the century of language. The beginning of the century was especially fruitful in this regard. Linguistics in its contemporary form, as well as a proliferation of French discourses with different yet related concerns, began with Saussure. The analytic tradition was particularly intense as evidenced by Russell, Frege, and Wittgenstein. Within the continental tradition, the question of language occupied the center of debate beginning with Husserl's *Logical Investigations,* and it remains either at the center or in the background of virtually every debate today. Granted the importance of Husserl, it is nevertheless Martin Heidegger who has shaped and given force to the question of language throughout the twentieth century and now into the twenty-first. The power of this question, as launched by Heidegger, was first formally introduced with the publication of *Being and Time* in 1927, although it was already present in a number of the earlier lecture-courses that served as its trial grounds. In *Being and Time,* the role of language is absolutely crucial for each and every analysis. As preparatory for raising the question of being, language exists as one of the three constituent moments in the analysis of the being of the *da* in Dasein, along with understanding (*Verstehen*) and attunement (*Befindlichkeit*). What makes the question of language even more important is that both understanding and attunement are determined through the being of language, which is discourse, says Heidegger: "Attunement and understanding are equiprimordially determined by *discourse.*"[1] Six sections later, in section 34, Heidegger addresses language in a more straightforward way. However, despite much that is exciting in the discussion—the grounding of language in discourse, the grounding of discourse in silence, discourse and the outside, and so forth—it leaves one wishing for more, much more. To satisfy that wish, and to round out *Being and Time* a bit more, one must come to terms with what Heidegger has to say about language *after Being and Time.* To do so is to both inform our understanding of *Being and Time,* to fill in the gaps, as it were, as do the essays by Walter Brogan and Dan Dahlstrom, and to radicalize the thinking that begins with *Being and Time.* This collection attempts to make some modest progress in that direction.

It is difficult to attribute a singular meaning to the question of language in the thought of Martin Heidegger. From the very beginning, the idea of a consistent view has been secondary to the manner in which whatever shows itself does indeed show itself, and language is no exception. That this is the case is certainly contrary to all philosophical method, and it is even contrary to the appearance of a consistent view of language by Heidegger. While Heidegger was indeed a philosopher, and in many regards a very traditional one, he does not, in the end, offer a philosophy of language, even in the midst of a sustained treatment of the question of language. Despite the inconsistency, however, the importance of the question of language was for Heidegger never in doubt, an importance that might well account for the attempt to collect all the many meanings of language into one consistent view. This is not an attempt to insert a strategical trick to avoid any possible critique of Heidegger. Quite the contrary; it is simply to highlight two phenomena encountered in the reading of Heidegger. First, while Heidegger engages in a relatively consistent deconstruction of the history of the concern for language, and this from at least two angles—the apophantical-as and the proposition on the one hand, and the content of what is said by the "they" in *Gerede*—language as a, so to speak, positive phenomenon does not show the same consistency. Second, from early on, Heidegger was engaged in a slightly different deconstruction, one that attempted to overcome the obsession with method and system, both of which were comprised from out of the demand for consistency. This began with his critique of Husserl's obsession with phenomenological method and continued through the 1930s with a concerted critique and abandonment of all need for system, especially with regard to German Idealism. While both method and system might guarantee or validate a kind of certainty—more specifically, that achieved through calculation (*Rechnung*)—the certainty guaranteed is limited to method and system. That is, what is not guaranteed is the ontological value that the method or system sets out to represent. In the case of language, it does not serve to represent the objects of the world or beings as a whole, but rather it is a means through which the world reveals itself. Thus, language is not reducible to a propositional logic or theory of judgment concerning beings as a whole, "Speaking is being with the world, it is something primordial, and is in place prior to judgments."[2]

This insight regarding language occurs amidst an encounter with a text to which Heidegger returned again and again when confronting the question of language. That is, it was frequently the case that when Heidegger directly treated the question of language, the treatment occurred in the midst of an analysis of Aristotle's Περὶ ἑρμηνείας.[3] Indeed, one might even track the changes in Heidegger's treatment of language through his treatment of this little Aristotle treatise, perhaps even through the various manners in which Heidegger translated the treatise. It is indeed remarkable that the encounter with Aristotle's treatise both begins and ends or fulfills the thinking of language, beginning in the early 1920s and ending in the very last reflection on language in 1959. All the more reason to address Heidegger's encounter with language in the years in between, as this collection attempts to do. Heidegger's analysis of Aristotle establishes a certain determination of language from which Heidegger would never depart. Heidegger: "Language is the being and becoming of the human being himself" (GA 17, 17/12). The very next semester, the summer semester of 1924, Heidegger narrowed his attention to Aristotle's rhetoric, and the formulation resembled what would become *Being and Time*. In 1924, Heidegger wrote with emphasis the following: "*The being-in-the-world of human beings is fundamentally determined through speaking.*"[4] While the assertion from 1924 is never challenged in the succeeding years, Heidegger's thinking nevertheless remains restless, even if its more startling moments will always be traced back to *Being and Time.* That restlessness begins immediately following *Being and Time* with the introduction of the ontological difference in the 1927 lecture-course, *Basic Problems of Phenomenology.* This is followed by the first delivery of "What Is Metaphysics?" in 1929 and the astounding 1929/1930 lecture-course, *The Fundamental Concepts of Metaphysics: World—Finitude—Solitude.* Much is going on in the theater that is the mind of one Martin Heidegger. In 1931, Heidegger returns to Aristotle and in that return language is again figured. However, language has now been figured differently, for as Will McNeill demonstrates, it has now been put into relation with a number of other concerns with which it will be populated for much of the remainder of his career.

Shortly after the 1931 Aristotle course, Heidegger's gaze becomes distracted. The year of distraction is April 21, 1933, to late February 1934. Readers of Heidegger, as well as readers of some of the more popular presses, are aware of some of the details of that year. Despite the distraction, or perhaps even aligned with it, Heidegger pressed on in two lecture-courses from the same period, now published in translation as *Being and Truth,* which Richard Polt addresses in his contribution.

Beginning in 1934, the question of language was posed differently. While language remained a worldly phenomenon, it also began to be posed not simply in relation to art but essentially adjoined to the question of art. This reconfiguration is inseparable from Heidegger's encounter with Friedrich Hölderlin, which formally begins with the lecture-course from the winter semester of 1934/1935. This lecture-course treats the hymns "Germanien" and "Der Rhein" and is of note for several reasons. It is the first real treatment of Hölderlin by Heidegger. The Heideggerian vocabulary, so to speak, undergoes a radical transformation, much of which should be attributed to the encounter with Hölderlin. It is through this encounter that world is brought into strife with earth, *Sein* becomes displaced into *Seyn* (or some approximation to this), the half-gods are persistently present, and so forth. Language, as a question to be addressed, is provided its own section and title, §7, "The Language Character of Poetry."[5] If the being of humankind is distinctively linguistic, a distinction that is decisive for the power of humankind over plants and animals, this is not a distinction without danger. Quite the contrary. In the reading of Hölderlin, it is because "humankind *is* in language" (p. 62) that he or she faces the greatest danger, the danger of danger even. But this danger, in a sense, is the danger of *Seyn*, for beyng is brought into the open, revealed (even in its concealment) through language. And yet, it is for the same reason that *Seyn* can be relegated to not-being, *nichtsein*.

If danger is immanent in 1934, it is also imminent in contrast to earlier in the very same year. None of its danger is apparent in the course concerning language and logic in the warmer months of that year, despite the heat that had been earlier stoked in the preceding year.

In the summer of 1934, in the immediate aftermath of April 1934, the lecture-course *Logic as the Question of the Essence of Language* was delivered. This relation, the relation of logic to language, was a concern for Heidegger from very early on, as can be gleaned from a simple survey of some of the lecture-courses: *Logic: The Question of Truth* (1925–1926), *The Metaphysical Foundations of Logic* (1928), *Logic as the Question of the Essence of Language* (1934), *Basic Questions of Philosophy: Selected "Problems" of Logic* (1937–1938). That Heidegger is critical of what we typically mean by logic and what that means for thinking and language is addressed in the collection by John Sallis. The 1934 lecture-course is a diverse text in its published form, an amalgamation of well-known Heideggerian themes—especially care, world, attunement, and temporality—along with markers of the then present political situation—national socialism is mentioned, the *Volk*, the mission and program of the *Volk*—and themes that will be seized in the immediate future. Section 29 of the course appears to be something of a synthesis of the 1924 Aristotle course and *Being and Time*: "Language is the prevailing of the world-forming and safe-keeping middle of the historical Dasein of the people. Only where temporality is temporalized does language happen; only where language happens is temporality temporalized."[6] This is followed, only two sections later, by the final section of the book, titled "Poetry as Primordial Language." There Heidegger writes: "The essence of language essences (*west*) there where it happens as world-forming force, i.e., where it first pre-forms in advance the being of beings and brings them into structural articulation (*Gefüge*). This primordial language is the language of poetry" (GA 38: 170). Approximately ten weeks later, the long encounter with Hölderlin begins with the course concerning "Germanien" and "Der Rhein." The instruction of that encounter is finalized in the summer semester of 1942 with the lecture-course on Hölderlin's "Ister," although the encounter seemingly continues through today. Robert Bernasconi offers an original reading of the context of this relation between Heidegger and Hölderlin, a context that emphasizes Heidegger's placement within the Hölderlin scholarship of his own day.

Between the first and final Hölderlin courses, Heidegger engaged in one of the most astounding research programs ever conducted under the name of philosophy: *An Introduction to Metaphysics* (not published until 1953) and "The Origin of the Work of Art" (published in *Holzwege* in 1950) from 1935, the course on Schelling's freedom essay in 1936 (published in 1971), the Nietzsche courses from 1936–1940, and still other lesser known courses. At the same time, Heidegger was busy in the hut. There he penned a number of manuscripts that are still appearing: *Contributions to Philosophy (From Enowning)* (1936–1940), *Besinnung* (1938/1939), *Die Geschichte des Seyns* (1938/1940), *Über den Anfang* (1941), and *Das Ereignis* (1942). The consensus, at this point, would seem to indicate that *Contributions* is the *Being and Time* of the period, although such a judgment might well be emended over time. The importance of this period for Heidegger studies cannot be overstated. Likewise, the reader will notice that most of the essays in this collection concern Heidegger texts from this period forward. The essays by Daniela Vallega-Neu and Krzysztof Ziarek address this period specifically, while my own and Françoise Dastur's draw from those years, and Dennis Schmidt's essay concerning Heidegger's engagement with Homer is drawn from the *Parmenides* lecture-course of 1942–1943.

Regardless of the future status of *Contributions* relative to the other works of the period, it is noteworthy that language serves an absolutely crucial function in *Contributions,* just as it did for *Being and Time.* In fact, the entire text of *Contributions* is sandwiched between the concern for language. Beginning in an act of self-reflection on the work that is to ensue, Heidegger provides an account of the humdrum nature of the title, an account that also serves to re-situate or place the text at the edges of history. Heidegger assesses the title in the following manner, but it must be borne in mind that such an assessment extends well beyond the title to include not only the work that follows but all of philosophy: "Philosophy can be officially announced in no other way, since all essential titles have become impossible on account of the exhaustion of all fundamental words and the destruction of the genuine relation to the word."[7] Two hundred eighty-one sections later the text closes with the following section title: "*Language* (Its Origin)" (GA 65: 510). In the pages between the beginning of the text (which is an unnumbered section) and its final section, only a little ink is spilled on the question of language. However, at the same time, it is clear that language is always at issue. That is, if *Contributions* is true to its word, then it is only ever an interminable attempt to say beyng from out of the language of beings. This saying would require a transition from the language of beings, the language we speak, to becoming a language for the speaking of beyng. Such a transition, to play upon the word *Übergang*, attempts to cross over, go over, or venture over in the sense of adventure, from metaphysics (the language of beings), to an other saying, the saying of beyng. As such, the word of beings is bound to the saying of beyng, and each is bound to the other in the crossing from one to the other. Further, then, the saying of beyng will look like the language of being. To enter into the saying of beyng thus requires a transformation of language, a transformation that is nothing less than a transformation of humankind. Although Heidegger will continue to be interpreted in such manner, this is not the tomfoolery of words, and Heidegger knew this. Rather, the saying of beyng in the language of beings "is not a 'formal' trick in mere words, whereby their meaning is turned around; on the contrary, it is *the transformation of humankind itself*" (GA 65: 84). Gregor Samsa would be proud.

And yet, this transformation and its correspondent speech is not so much a transcending of *Being and Time* as its continuation and expansion, for this transformation is founded in the everyday language of humankind. We should recall that while *Being and Time* attempts to retrieve an understanding of the meaning of being to which the forgetting of being attests, a forgetting upon which the history of metaphysics is erected, it is nevertheless the case that humankind always already operates in such an understanding. Such an understanding, vague and concealed as it might be, is preserved in the language spoken. As much as *Contributions* calls for a transformation of Dasein and the relation to language enjoyed by humankind, it is also the case that this transformation can only occur within the language spoken. "Every saying of beyng is held in words and namings which are understandable in the view of everyday references of beings, and are exclusively thought in that view, but which as expressions of beyng, are misunderstood . . . the words themselves already reveal something

(something familiar) and thereby conceal what should be brought into the open in thoughtful saying" (GA 65: 83). That is to say, the transformation of humankind occurs in the transformed relation to language that would also reveal the language of beings as the thoughtful saying of beyng. If, then, the language of *Being and Time* suffers from the metaphysical tradition (or an anthropological terminology, which is the same thing), the cure for this suffering, a cure that does not go in the absence of danger, would be provided in a relation to language capable of hearing the language as the saying of beyng rather than simply the language of metaphysics.

The decade beginning in 1950 shows a more concentrated focus than ever regarding the question of language. Whereas virtually all of the earlier writings positioned language at the most penetrating level of the analyses, the series of language essays from the 1950s give it center stage. This series of meditations begins in 1950 with the essay simply titled "Language" and closes with the 1959 essay, one of Heidegger's most far-reaching, "The Way to Language." Between the two are the essays ". . . Poetically Man Dwells . . ." (1951); the Trakl essay, "Language in the Poem" (1953); "A Dialogue on Language" (1953/1954); "The Essence of Language" (1957); and "The Word" (1958). To these could also be added the three essays on the pre-Socratics from the third volume of *Vorträge und Aufsätze* and "The Anaximander Fragment" from *Holzwege.* The essays from David Farrell Krell, Peter Hanly, and Christopher Fynsk are all concerned with this material.

It is strange indeed that Heidegger embarks on such a terse, arduous, and seemingly unaccessible journey at this stage in his career. It was not until 1951 that his professional situation was resolved, the final chapter of which was an assessment of the importance of his philosophical work. Having received the endorsement of the Faculty of Philosophy due to the perceived importance of philosophical writings, Heidegger next had to receive the approval of the Faculty Senate. According to Ott, Heidegger's reinstatement as an emeritus member of the faculty with teaching privileges was achieved through the narrowest of margins (7:5), and that "Those opposed to the motion expressed serious doubts about the quality of Heidegger's philosophical work. It was claimed that the Faculty was vastly overrating Heidegger's intellectual importance; he was at best a vogue figure, at worst a charlatan."[8] If the stature of his philosophical importance is the final hurdle to overcome, which did appear to be the case in 1950, what is odd is that Heidegger initiates the decade with an essay that can hardly be characterized as a typical philosophical essay. Its most traditional component resides in the element of critique, a gesture that is sweeping in its nature in that Heidegger once again dispels "the representation of language that has prevailed for thousands of years."[9] That representation, according to Heidegger, views language as the expression of what is internal to the speaker, a subjectivity that at once combines what is most internal to the speaker—feelings and the like—and a kind of externality that serves to shape what is internal, which is a world-view (*Weltansicht*). Rather than this historical representation of language, Heidegger offers as the essence of language "neither expression, nor the activity of humankind," but instead what must have sounded strange to his listeners, especially those of a more philosophical ilk, "Language speaks" (US, 19/197). What is more, when Heidegger does turn to others for a kind of support to his thoughtful encounter with language, he turns not to the philosophers but the poets. In this particular case, he turns to Trakl. Why the poets? Because "What is spoken purely is the poem" (US, 16/194). By the end of the essay, we discover what has since become something like a refrain for all who have attempted to think with Heidegger about the nature of language:

Language speaks.

Man speaks insofar as he responds to language.

Strange. But not as strange as when Heidegger turns again to Trakl three years later, this time in earnest. Here, the strangeness of Heidegger's meditation on language meets with the strangeness that is Trakl's poetry, an encounter of strangeness that does not flinch in the face of strangeness. Rather than become distracted by different, more proper philosophical issues, Heidegger engages the strangeness, locates it and hovers around its most essential site, lingering awhile there, perhaps even compounding the strangeness. As he forecasts at the beginning of the essay: "The discussion (*Erörterung*), as it corresponds to a way of thinking (*Denkweg*), ends in a question. The question asks after the place of the site (*Ortschaft des Ortes*)" (US, 37). We would seem to be far from the philosophical tradition.

While the remaining language essays from the 1950s offer a respite from the strange attempt to situate Trakl, such a respite is an appearance only. This is especially the case for the series of essays "The Essence of Language," "The Word," and "The Way to Language." The first two essays might be viewed as companion pieces insofar as they share a concern for the Stefan George poem "The Word." No longer concerned with a kind of philosophical knowledge of the poem, Heidegger is more attuned to a listening to the site that would grant both poetry and thinking. However, such a characterization sounds strange, admits Heidegger. That is, to characterize thinking as listening is a far cry from the positing of claims about something, for example, a poem. And yet, if thinking is to address something other, if it is to address something other than itself, it must first be attuned to what is other. In this case, thinking must be attuned to the site from which the poem is issued, which is nothing short of the site of language, the essence of language. It will only be from out of a listening to what language grants from out of this strange site that thinking might respond to the essence of language as the language of essence, and likewise for poetry. As such, this situates poetry in the closest proximity to thinking, for they are both situated in the site of language. In either case, what is demanded of each is that it, in its own distinctive way, listen to the saying grant of language. "Poetizing moves in the element of saying, and so does thinking," writes Heidegger. And further, "We cannot here confidently decide whether poetizing is properly a thinking, or whether thinking is properly a poetizing" (US, 188–189). What we can decide, however, is that we are no longer engaged in a philosophical discourse.

If poetry and thinking reside in the same region or neighborhood, it is because the site of both would appear to be the site of language, the site that grants to each its distinctive way of speaking. This site is given the most concentrated attention and addressed in numerous ways in "The Way to Language." One of the most persistent of ways is a kind of web of ways, what Heidegger calls an *Aufriß*. There, Heidegger writes that "Language speaks by saying; that is, by showing. Its saying wells up from the once spoken yet long since unspoken saying that permeates the rift-design (*Aufriß*) in the essence of language."[10] Such a design of ways and paths must be permeated by a sketching or writing through which what is shown is capable of being shown. Thus a worldly language. This might be said in a different way, in a questioning way: "Is it an accident that proximally and for the most part significations are 'worldly,' sketched out beforehand (*vorgezeichnete*) by the significance of the world, that they are indeed often predominantly 'spatial'?"[11]

The later essays on language are at once the most exciting and most problematic of all of Heidegger's writings. They are exciting for those willing to go all the way with them, in that they offer an entirely different way of engaging in the act of thinking, a way that is not confined by any historical method, while still remaining attached to the history of the West. They remain problematic in at least two ways. First, because they attempt a new way of thinking, they require the development of a whole new set of critical tools. Very simply, how do we assess these writings without turning them into another example of philosophical method through the use of philosophical method? But, this particular problem assumes a radical distinction between the later writings and the earlier ones, a distinction the previous citation, as well as the work of numerous others concerning an "early" and "late" Heidegger or Heidegger I and Heidegger II, calls into question. More specifically, if the later essays are the realization of what was already contained in the texts of *Being and Time* and its preceding lecture-courses and seminars, then the need for the development of new modes of analysis applies to the early writings just as much as for the later ones. In this regard, Krell's essay examines a certain concern of Heidegger's that preoccupied Jacques Derrida and informed Jacques Lacan; and Fynsk's essay examines the relation between Heidegger and one of his most inventive readers, Maurice Blanchot. What is more, the essays in the present volume set out to be, then, not simply commentaries concerning Heidegger's thinking of language, but a step toward a new way of thinking.

NOTES

1. Martin Heidegger, *Sein und Zeit* (Tübingen: Max Niemayer Verlag, 1979), 133. In English, *Being and Time*, trans. Joan Stambaugh (Albany: SUNY Press, 1996), 126.

2. Martin Heidegger, *Einführung in die phänomenologische Forschung, Gesamtausgabe*, vol. 17 (Frankfurt am Main: Klostermann, 1994), 20. In English, *Introduction to Phenomenological Research*, trans. Daniel O. Dahlstrom (Bloomington: Indiana University Press, 2005), 15.

3. The passage from Aristotle, and its corresponding translation, most under consideration occurs at 16a. For the treatment and translation of the passage, as well as some of the material surrounding the passage, see the volume noted, as well as the following: *Logik: Die Frage nach der Wahrheit* (GA 21), 166–167; *Die Grundbegriffe der Metaphysik. Welt-Endlichkeit-Einsamkeit* (GA 29/30), §72; "Das Wesen der Sprache" from *Unterwegs zur Sprache*, 203–204; "Der Weg zur Sprache" from *Unterwegs zur Sprache*, 244.

4. Martin Heidegger, *Grundbegriffe der aristotelischen Philosophie, Gesamtausgabe*, vol. 18 (Frankfurt am Main: Klostermann, 2002), 18. In English, *Basic*

Concepts of Aristotelian Philosophy, trans. Robert D. Metcalf and Mark B. Tanzer (Bloomington: Indiana University Press, 2009).

5. Martin Heidegger, *Hölderlins Hymnen "Germanien" und "Der Rhein,"* Gesamtausgabe, vol. 39 (Frankfurt am Main: Klostermann, 1980), 59–77.

6. Martin Heidegger, *Logik als die Frage nach dem Wesen der Sprache,* Gesamtausgabe, vol. 38 (Frankfurt am Main: Klostermann, 1998), 169.

7. Martin Heidegger, *Beiträge zur Philosophie (Vom Ereignis),* Gesamtausgabe, vol. 65 (Frankfurt am Main: Klostermann, 1989), 3.

8. Hugo Ott, *Martin Heidegger: A Political Life,* trans. Allan Blunden (New York: HarperCollins, 1993), 362.

9. Martin Heidegger, "Die Sprache," in *Unterwegs zur Sprache,* 6th ed. (Pfullingen: Verlag Günther Neske, 1979), 19. In English, "Language," in *Poetry, Language, Thought,* trans. Albert Hofstadter (New York: HarperCollins, 1971), 196.

10. Martin Heidegger, *Basic Writings,* rev. ed., ed. and trans. David Farrell Krell (New York: HarperCollins, 1993), 411.

11. Martin Heidegger, *Being and Time,* trans. John Macquarrie and Edward Robinson (New York: HarperCollins, 1962), 209.

ONE

Heidegger's Ontological Analysis of Language

Daniel O. Dahlstrom

Language occupies a central position in Heidegger's later thinking, from his controversial yet telling pronouncements that "language speaks" and "language is the house of being" to his insistence on thinking through the language of poets, sensitive to how our very access to things hangs on our words.[1] Much attention is thus rightly devoted to the interpretation of Heidegger's mature views of language. Yet already in *Sein und Zeit* Heidegger gives a complex and compelling if frustratingly truncated account of language. On the one hand, it is possible to see if not the anticipation then at least the seeds of his mature views in that account. On the other hand, the early account is abbreviated to a fault, a sure sign that his views at the time are less than full formed. Precisely in this respect, interpretation is faced here with the familiar Herculean task of being generous, critical, and reflexive. The interpretation must find its own words to supplement Heidegger's remarks, with a view to examining the meaning of language for his thinking, both early and late. In other words, the interpretation must think and speak for itself as it attempts to say not simply what is unsaid by Heidegger himself about language but what he was or, better, should have been trying to say.

By no means do I have any pretensions of accomplishing this task in the following essay. Its aim is simply to make a start in this direction by presenting some central themes of Heidegger's discussion of language in *Sein und Zeit*, with a requisite supplementation where necessary and with an occasional sidelong glance at the bearing of that early account on his later formal treatments of language. The first section is a sketch of Heidegger's early ontology of language, that is, his account of language in the context of the project of fundamental ontology. The sketch is made with a view to motivating the question of what differentiates discourse from language. In the second section I look to his accounts of assertions and discursive meaning for part of an answer to that question.[2] By way of conclusion, I briefly address two relatively underdetermined senses of "equiprimordiality" with respect to discourse, namely, the equiprimordial status of communication within the constitution of discourse and the equiprimordial status of discourse as a basic existential.[3]

Discourse and the Use of Language

In *Sein und Zeit,* Heidegger famously distinguishes language (*Sprache*) from discourse (*Rede*). The distinction falls neatly into the ontological economy that he uses to navigate his existential analysis, namely, the difference between being on hand, being handy, and being-here (*Vorhanden-, Zuhanden- and Da-sein*). Discourse pertains only to being-here and vice versa; that is to say, discursiveness and being-here are not identical but they are equivalent. In Heidegger's terminology, discourse is an existential, a constitutive way of being-here that is disclosive of our being-here. To say that we exist as discursive beings is to say that, in and through our discursiveness, the meaning of being (i.e., being this or that, including ourselves) discloses itself to us, no less fundamentally than it does in the ways we find ourselves emotionally disposed in the world and in the ways we understand (project and work on) possibilities in our everyday lives. Indeed, Heidegger characterizes discourse as a basic existential, that is, the sort of existential that, like our disposed understanding (*befindliches Verstehen*) or mindless absorption in our world (*Verfallensein*), underlies and inflects being-in-the-world in its entirety, including its ontic comportments, that is, its concrete, empirical ways of behaving.[4]

By contrast, again according to *Sein und Zeit,* language is discourse that has been voiced (*hinausgesprochen*). Language is not a way of being-here (*da-seiendes*) but something encountered within the world as ready-to-hand (*ein Zuhandenes*). It can then be broken down in turn into word-things on hand (*vorhanden*) in nature and culture, something that we find in other species and in other cultures, open for inspection like any other cultural artifacts, from ancient hieroglyphics to contemporary texting, fertile soil for sciences of language such as philology, linguistics, psycholinguistics. Whether these sciences study the remains of dead languages or the objectifiable patterns of living forms of communication, they suppose the use of language by its users. Language as used is not simply on hand but handy (*zuhanden*), and this use of language as ready-to-hand supposes discourse or, as Heidegger also puts it, flouting his own distinction, "existential language" (SZ 161).

In this way Heidegger differentiates three distinct ontological levels or aspects of language: existential language, language as use, and language as something on hand.[5] To appreciate the difference between language as use and as something on hand, consider the difference between reading a poem and analyzing the language of the poem. The analysis dissects the linguistic parts of the text (juxtapositions, word-choices, grammar, and the like). By contrast, when we read or recite the text, we use those parts, configured as they are, without paying any more attention to them than we do to the page on which they are printed or the glasses on our face. To be sure, the uses of words are multifarious and highly context- and user-dependent and adults sometimes clumsily try to teach children how to use them by breaking with normal usage and calling attention to the words themselves (e.g., saying "ball" while holding the ball in front of her or pointing to it). But the endgame, of course, is mastery of usage, and children learn very early the art of adroitly moving back and forth between attending to the words themselves and simply using them (aping the behavior of other users).

There is much more to be said about this difference between language as an object or cultural artifact on hand in our environment and language as a handy means of manipulating things in that environment. Indeed, there is something uncanny about the difference since these modes of being and their phenomenologies, that is, the ways they afford themselves to us, are so radically distinct. We experience something like a gestalt shift when we stop to examine our use of a word, often leaving us more than a little uneasy about the success of capturing through such analysis the significance of that use. Yet this very uneasiness underscores the difference between the use of language and the analysis of it as something already used and simply on hand.

The difference between discourse and language use is not as perspicuous as that between the use of language and its objective presence in nature and culture. The former distinction is perhaps the more elusive one because both discourse and language use alike are something that we do (in contrast to something we find on hand in nature and culture). What precisely is the existential character of discourse that distinguishes it not merely from language as something on hand but from language as use? In other words, how are we to distinguish discourse as a fundamental way of being-here from the handiness of language?

It should be evident how much rides for Heidegger on this distinction. If discourse proves to be nothing but use of language, then the very distinctiveness of being-here, over against things on hand and handy, is called into question.[6] Moreover, if that distinctiveness becomes questionable, then so does the very project of fundamental ontology that the existential analysis is supposed to yield. Thus, any ontology, that is, any examination of what it means for entities to be is said to rest upon fundamental ontology, the foregoing analysis of what it means for us to be-here (*da zu sein*). Accordingly, on Heidegger's account, inasmuch as discourse is one of the basic, constitutive ways for us to be here, it both underlies and limits our ability to understand and use language as a cultural artifact. So the question becomes all the more pressing: what is it about discourse's difference from language in use that explains how it grounds that use (and thereby the objectifiable remnants of that use, the stuff of sciences such as linguistics, psycholinguistics, and linguistic anthropology)?

From one interpretive vantage point, the question of the difference between discourse and language use may seem trivial. Trivial because, on this interpretation, the difference between language use and discourse amounts simply to the difference between a description of the actual use of language and the ascription of it to its user (in this case, *Dasein*). Just as we can distinguish the practice of medicine from its practice qua ascribed to the doctor engaged in the practice, so we can distinguish the actual use of language from its use by a particular speaker or from a particular speaker's experience of using it. On this interpretation, discourse just is language insofar as it is in actual use *and attributable to Dasein, the user of the language.*

But this way of interpreting the difference between discourse and language use takes its bearings from the handiness (*Zuhandenheit*) of language, that is, language in use or, as we might also put it, from the pragmatics of language, rather than from the allegedly existential distinctiveness of discourse. Moreover, far from understanding discourse as constitutive of Dasein's manner of being, this line of interpretation takes discourse to be a tool, distinct from Dasein, that Dasein can pick up and put down at will (hence, my coupling of language use with the pragmatics of language in the previous sentence). Such an interpretation also runs the risk of smuggling into the account a substantialist ontological framework whereby Dasein is defined as the substance who has and uses language (ζῷον ἔχον λόγον), a theme against which Heidegger repeatedly rails in his later writings (though he gives it a positive spin in his early lecture on Aristotle's *Rhetoric*). So construed, discourse is not only conflated with language use, but in traditional terms is also reduced to an accident—not even a property—of Dasein, one that hardly defines what it means for Dasein to be.[7]

The Truthfulness of Discourse

There is more to discourse than the use of language precisely because the use of language presupposes the disclosiveness of discourse, that is, the way discourse qua existential opens up Dasein's world. We may use language as a tool—something ready-to-hand—to persuade others (or ourselves) of something but only because existential language, that is, discourse—as a manner of being-here—reveals the world and our way of being in it to us. Thus, to take a plain example, we are able to use the words in the sentence "The water's rising" to convince people in a flood plain to evacuate, but the words are persuasive because they make plain the state of affairs.[8] In general terms then, it is the disclosiveness or, as we might also put it, the truthfulness of discourse that distinguishes it (existential language) from the use of language, even while grounding that use. In *Sein und Zeit* Heidegger specifies this existential distinctiveness of discourse through analyses of (1) assertions as a form of discourse, (2) discursive meanings and sense, and (3) discourse's communicative dimension.

ASSERTIONS, ABOUTNESS (REFERENCE), AND PREDICATION

The very theme of Heidegger's existential analysis, namely, being-in-the-world, undermines traditional modern, epistemological debates over realism and idealism. Both emotions and practical know-how, Heidegger maintains, testify to ways of relating to things in the world and not to mere mental representations of them. In similar fashion, his account of discourse as a basic existential thwarts any attempt to motivate quandaries over the referentiality of our discourse. Our being-in-the-world means, among other things, that any analysis or self-analysis must take its bearings from the fact that we are always already with things and others. The same underlying phenomenon holds for discourse generally and assertions in particular. It is not, however, as though assertions piggyback on some foregoing phenomenon of being exposed and evolved with things within the world. Rather, as forms of discourse, assertions are themselves essential to the very fabric of our being-in-the-world, constituting at once both how we are with others and things within the world and how they are with us.[9] In other words, assertions are part of the existential status of discourse.

This observation helps explain the early Heidegger's confidence in the scientific and theoretical character of fundamental ontology. At least in *Sein und Zeit,* he did not think that a theoretical assertion necessarily overdetermines the ontological status of its reference, such that, by virtue of being the object of an assertion, it is something simply on hand, available for observation. Were this the case, there could be no assertions about being handy (ready-to-hand), let alone being-here (*Da-sein*).[10] Yet, while he lost his confidence in the appropriateness of scientific assertions for his thinking, he arguably never surrenders the idea that language is, in the terminology of *Sein und Zeit,* fundamentally discursive. That is to say, in the terminology of his later work, that language is an essential part of the revealing ground (*Seyn*) of the relation between being and being-here, between the world and human beings. "Language is the house of being" is, after all, an assertion, an assertion that he makes because it *reveals* something *about* being.[11]

In the present section, I have been suggesting that the import of Heidegger's account of discourse for a philosophy of language significantly parallels the import of existential analysis for a philosophy of knowledge. Left to its own devices or taken as foundational, epistemology can generate the pseudo-problem of knowledge of the external world or the irresolvable problem of putting subject and object together, the moment it abstracts from the underlying phenomenon of being-in-the-world. Analogously, a philosophy of language can concoct hopeless riddles of reconciling meanings and references, words and things, language and the world, the moment it abstracts from discourse as a fundamental way of being-in-the-world.

Heidegger's early views of the fundamentally revelatory character of assertions is, he would be the first to acknowledge, hardly novel. He draws extensively upon Aristotle's account of assertions, signaling this source by identifying this character with the apophantic nature of assertions.[12] The correspondence theory of truth, where truth is taken to be a property of an assertion, is derivative of the originally apophantic character of assertions, that is, their capacity to enable things to reveal themselves to us for what they are (a capacity that is in turn ontologically grounded, as discussed more below). As Heidegger puts it in *Sein und Zeit,* glossing this capacity of assertion:

> Asserting is a being towards a thing itself insofar as it is. . . .The very entity that is meant shows itself *just as* it is in itself, that is to say, that *it* is in the same way as *it* is pointed out, uncovered as being in the assertion . . .
>
> The assertion *is true* means: it uncovers the entity in itself. It asserts, points out, "lets be seen" (ἀπόφανσις) the entity in its uncoveredness.[13]

Assertions may mislead or even deceive, but these possibilities rest upon their fundamental function of letting something show itself from itself (*apo*), that is to say, as it is or as it presents itself on its own terms. Typically, if a friend says: "You look pale today," the friend is calling attention to your appearance, not to be confused or conflated with how you look to her specifically. Similarly, the weatherman's report "The skies are clear today" states a fact and not a belief about the skies. To be sure, very early on we learn how to manipulate such statements, justifying a certain amount of healthy skepticism about factual statements. But those manipulations (including exaggerations, tendentiousness, lies, and so on) live off that fundamentally apophantic character, namely, off the fact that assertions consist in acknowledging and calling attention to the way things present themselves for what they are.[14]

At the same time, it is important to note that Heidegger places assertions squarely within understanding and interpretation. We understand, that is to say, we meaningfully employ implements as part of our understanding of our world. Interpretation elaborates this understanding, bringing the ready-to-hand implement explicitly into view. Thus, we ask what something is "for" (*Wozu?*), precisely because it is "always already" accessible in such a way that what it is taken "as" can be set in relief. This "as" character constitutes the interpretation. For example, on the basis of what wheels are for, namely, for turning the axle, we interpret them as devices for turning. Assertions build precisely on this as-structure. That is to say, they are ways of making explicit what something is taken (interpreted) as, which in turn is based upon what it is for, that is, how it is understood. For example, the assertion "The wheels turn" is a way of making more explicit the interpretation of them *as* (*als*) turning, based upon the understanding that they are *for* (*zum*) turning.[15]

While assertions are forms of interpretation, they have their own distinctive structure. Assertions are about something and, by way of predication, they determine it as such and such, allowing us to communicate as much to one another. Heidegger discusses assertions before discourse in *Sein und Zeit,* despite the fact that assertions, particularly in view of these three functions—aboutness, predication, and communication—are essential to discourse. He stresses this same threefold character of assertions in other lectures as well. At the same time, sounding very much like Wittgenstein, Heidegger emphasizes that assertions are only one form of discourse and, in another striking similarity with the Austrian, he asserts that discourse underlies the phenomenon of assertion.

Inasmuch as predication seems to suppose aboutness, one might take Heidegger's way of listing these functions as somehow ordinal (as if aboutness were first, predication second, communication third). But this order of priority is highly questionable. To be sure, linguistic reference may build upon non-linguistic references, for example, in the way that "Look!" builds upon the gesture of pointing, but the mere exhortation "Look!" is no more informative about its reference than pointing, without sufficient learning and cues from the context. We have to already know from the context what sorts of things are normally pointed out, what sorts of things we are normally supposed to look at, if an assertion or, in this case, an exhortation is to have any chance of success. Predication is a way of registering or calling attention to those sorts of things, by way of describing and thus classifying them. In other words, it makes explicit the ways we carve up the world for our purposes, picking out certain items over others.[16] Since the capacity of an assertion to be about something, to refer to something, depends upon the descriptions embedded in predication, there is reason to think that predication is no less basic to assertions than aboutness, their function of being about something. Reference and meaning, what discourse is about and how discourse is about it, are inextricably joined, like human beings and the world they inhabit (and, just as importantly, inhabit together, so that communication is no less fundamental to assertions, despite its placement as the third function of assertions).

The foregoing interpretation of the joint importance of aboutness and predication for assertions suggests a parallel gloss on Heidegger's claim that the apophantic "as" builds upon the hermeneutic "as" (SZ 223). Just as predication typically co-constitutes how an assertion is about something yet also presupposes that aboutness, so the apophantic "as" supposes but also enters into the composition of the hermeneutic "as." The claim that the apophantic "as" builds upon the hermeneutic "as" still stands inasmuch as, for example, I refer to something *as* a lever, asserting "This is a lever" (the apophantic "as"), because I understand-and-use it as such (the hermeneutic "as").[17] But while such instances of the apophantic "as" suppose a use, that is, an interpretation, of things in a certain way within a certain context, they are also co-constitutive of it. Moreover, they are co-constitutive of it in two senses, already glossed above. On the one hand, the assertion as an instance of the sentences in a particular language is no less a ready-to-hand tool than the lever is. On the other hand, the assertion is apophantic precisely because it presents things as they are, allowing us to see them as they present themselves. From this vantage point, to assert that ordinary assertions (as part of the everyday workworld) are derivative of the hermeneutic "as" is precisely to assert their embeddedness in the disclosures, uses, and interpretations of things as such-and-such (the hermeneutic "as").[18]

On the basis of the foregoing considerations, we can conclude that assertions, like language generally, can function as something merely on hand, as something handy or ready-to-hand, or as an essential component of *Da-sein* (being-here). This last function is, to be sure, fundamental. Assertions are, after all, existential in the sense that Dasein makes assertions (asserting is something that Dasein does), disclosing its world by doing so. But there is also a sense in which assertions are tools that we use and in that respect they are handy (ready-to-hand). Once used or, better, holding their use at arm's length, assertions can also be examined as entities within the world and so become the stuff of linguistics or even logic. These latter two ontological senses of assertions, that is, as something used and as objects of investigation, suppose the existential and thus disclosive sense of an assertion.

DISCURSIVE MEANING AND SENSE

The notion of meaning is of singular importance to Heidegger's account of discourse and, indeed, his analysis of meanings reinforces the necessity of distinguishing discourse from language. In a fashion very much akin to Grice's well-known distinction between natural and non-natural (conventional) senses of meaning, Heidegger allows for both broad and narrow construals of meaning.[19] As we shall see, the broad construal applies to discourse (among other things), the narrow sense only to language. At the same time, Heidegger grounds meaning, under any construal, in Dasein's being-in-the-world and foregoing disclosure of its worldliness. Dasein's self-disclosiveness makes possible a meaningful engagement with implements as something handy (*Zuhandenes*). By virtue of this engagement, implements generally have meaning, broadly construed, and words as well as other linguistic complexes, too, come to have meaning as implements themselves (meaning narrowly construed). Meaning in the broad sense is meaning-in-use, of which "discursive meaning" is a prime example; meaning in the narrow sense is the meaning of a word or word-complex, taken "out of circulation" but with a view to capturing or cataloguing that circulating significance lexically.

For Heidegger, as noted above, both discursive meanings and linguistic meanings are grounded in being-in-the-world as a meaningful whole. To explain this grounding of meanings generally, Heidegger exploits notions of relevance and referredness, key features of the ready-to-hand. The pivotal distinction in this regard is the distinction between the *lateral relevance* of implements to one another and their *ultimate relevance* to Dasein's being-in-the-world. The ontological makeup of implements, that is, their handiness, rests upon their lateral relevance, that is, their referredness to one another. A tool's lateral relevance is what it respectively is for (*Wozu*), relative to one or more other implements. The entire set of such relevances cannot be itself relevant in that lateral sense, that is, there is nothing handy that these implements altogether are for. But that set of relevances, taken in its entirety, is in place for the sake of and because of Dasein. Hence, their ultimate relevance is their relevance to Dasein's being-in-the-world.[20] For example, a paved road is for vehicles, roads and vehicles are for transporting people and goods, and the entire set of implements included in processes of transportation is for the sake of our being-here

(*Da-sein*). The relevance of the parts of the transportation system, moreover, is based upon its "suitedness to the world" (*Weltmäßigkeit*), which in turn supposes Dasein's self-disclosure, that is, its "understanding of the world, towards which Dasein as an entity always already comports itself" (SZ 86). Consider, for example, cases where ferries are better suited than bridges as elements of transportation or descriptions are better suited than exhortations as elements of communication. The respective suitability is relative to Dasein's understanding of its world.[21]

Heidegger introduces the verb "mean" (i.e., *X means Y*) to characterize implements' lateral significance, that is, the way that they relate and refer to one another. Thus, a paved road *means* vehicles, just as housing *means* shelter. Such lateral relevance stands in the service of an ultimate relevance, that is, its relevance (meaning) for Dasein. But beyond any such relevance, there is a further way of construing meaning, a way that applies to Dasein itself. "In the trust-and-familiarity with these [relevant] relations, Dasein 'means' [something] to or for itself, it primordially gives itself its being and its potential-to-be to understand with respect to its being-in-the-world" (SZ 87). Here the meaning is not simply the lateral relevance of one implement to another, nor is it the relevance of the system of complexes to Dasein. Instead, the meaning is existential in the sense that Dasein gives itself meaning, not in an explicit or self-conscious way, but precisely in the way that it is at home with referential relations, lateral and ultimate, among the implements that make up its world.

Tools, implements, and the systems and complexes they form are meaningful by virtue of being for the sake of Dasein's being-in-the-world. Only on the basis of this ultimate relevance (meaning) are implements laterally relevant (*Um-zu*) to another. At the same time, *Dasein's* existential meaning, as described above, is distinct from an implement's lateral and ultimate relevance. In this way, these three meanings—the lateral and ultimate meaning of what is ready-to-hand as well as the existential meaning of being-here—are intimately linked to one another, constituting a meaningful whole. On the basis of this analysis of meanings, broadly construed, Heidegger speaks of Dasein's meaningfulness (*Bedeutsamkeit*) and "the relational whole of this meaning" (*das Bezugsganze dieses Bedeutens*) (SZ 87).

Note that the three sorts of meaning unpacked here—lateral, ultimate, and existential—are all meanings broadly construed, grounded in the meaningfulness of Dasein and its being-in-the-world. But, then, how does this broad construal of meaning relate to meaning in the context of discourse and language, that is, to the previous distinction between discursive and linguistic meanings? In making that distinction, I suggested that discursive meaning, in contrast to linguistic meaning, is an example of meaning broadly construed. While Heidegger's account is exasperatingly short on details in this connection, he contends that the meaningfulness of being-in-the-world discloses meanings that make "word and language" possible.

The meaningfulness itself, however, with which Dasein is in each case already deeply familiar (*vertraut*), contains in itself the ontological condition of the possibility for the fact that Dasein, in its interpretive understanding, can disclose something like "meanings" that for their part in turn found the possible being of word and language (SZ 87). One straightforward way of glossing this founding relation or, better, Heidegger's understanding of it is by enlisting his initial introduction of the notion of meaning in the context of elaborating the meanings (lateral and ultimate relevance) of implements. Our engagement with implements rests upon a foregoing disclosure of the meaningfulness of our being-in-the-world, that is, the existential meaning glossed earlier. That same meaningfulness underlies the lateral and ultimate meanings of implements, also described above. Implements have meaning, in the broad sense of the term. Discourse supposes and contributes to these meanings. We talk about and specify things in terms of meanings with which we are already acquainted, meanings that have taken shape (laterally, ultimately, or existentially) in the course of our being-in-the-world. Discourse, not to be confused with language, contributes to the constitution of this meaningful whole (existential meaning) since discourse is no less basic an existential than understanding or disposedness.[22] Meanings narrowly construed, that is, the lexical (linguistic) meanings of words, take shape in the meaning-in-use (discursive meaning) that is co-extensive with an interpretive understanding of the meaningful whole.

Given this reconstruction of Heidegger's account of meaning and how it relates to linguistic meaning, discursive meaning turns out to have a peculiarly amphibious character, straddling the sorts of non-linguistic meaning unpacked above. That is to say, precisely as meaning-in-use, discursive meaning can be understood, on the one hand, as the lateral or ultimate significance of an implement and, on the other, as the existential meaning of Dasein. In other words, the prima facie paradoxical conclusion of my interpretation is that, while discourse itself is an existential, discursive meanings can be used and re-used as well as self-disclosively enacted and re-enacted. While I do not think that this air of paradox can be easily dispelled (if it can be dispelled at all), it mirrors the distinction between existential and existentiel, two co-incident but distinguishable ways of being-here. (It also suggests a way of understanding Heidegger's own use of language in *Sein und Zeit,* where discursive meanings are both *used* and *disclosed,* i.e., both *handy* and *existential.*)

Like the concept of meaning, the concept of sense (*Sinn*) plays an important role in Heidegger's conception of discourse. Moreover, he construes sense—again like meaning—differently in different contexts, only one of which concerns language directly. But just as Heidegger ties straightforwardly linguistic meanings to non-linguistic meanings, so, too, it is possible to identify a basic connection between the contexts in which he finds it necessary to speak of and, indeed, address the significance of "sense." Though Heidegger tells his readers from the beginning of *Sein und Zeit* that the work's theme is the question of the sense of being (*Seinssinn*), he first introduces the notion of sense as such in his discussion of understanding and interpretation (SZ §32). We "understand" things, in Heidegger's distinctive sense of skillfully manipulating them, by projecting them onto an entire complex of meaningfulness (*ein Ganzes der Bedeutsamkeit*). This complex of meaningfulness encompasses the sets of referential relations—their lateral and ultimate relevance, discussed above, in which Dasein as being-in-the-world establishes itself from the outset. As noted earlier, we interpret something as something on the basis of these relevancies, that is, what they respectively are for.

Following this gloss of understanding, Heidegger introduces his first thematic discussion of *sense.* It is noteworthy that he immediately flags the fact that he uses the term in a more restrictive way than it is normally used. Thus, if something within the world comes to be understood, that is, if it is discovered by Dasein, then we say that "it makes *sense*" (*es hat Sinn*). Heidegger adds (translated loosely):

> But what is understood, taken strictly, is not the sense but the entity or even being. Sense is that within which the intelligibility of something maintains itself. What can be articulated in the disclosing, by way of understanding, we call sense. The *concept of sense* encompasses the formal

> framework of what necessarily belongs to what the interpretation, in understanding, articulates. [For every projection, there is something upon which it projects itself.] That *"upon-which" the projection projects is structured by what Dasein in advance has before it, by its preview of that, and by its preconception of that. Sense is that "upon-which" the projection, so structured, projects, on the basis of which something becomes intelligible as something.* (SZ 151, Heidegger's emphasis)

Hence, as Heidegger uses the term, "sense" does not apply to entities or even being; it is rather what the understanding projects the entities or being upon, such that their intelligibility is sustained. Heidegger invokes precisely this meaning of "sense" in making his case that time is the sense of being. Sense is thus, in a certain respect, the tacit "as" or the unthematized backdrop for any interpretation that takes something explicitly as this or that. As Heidegger puts it, he understands sense as the "existential phenomenon in which the formal framework of what is disclosable in understanding and articulable in interpretation becomes visible."[23]

Yet, while tacit or unthematized at one level, sense neither is without structure nor does it defy articulation. Its structure is the so-called "circle-structure" of interpretive understanding that is the expression of the "fore-structure" of Dasein itself (SZ 153). The interpretation moves within the ambit of what is already understood, albeit in an undeveloped way. Sense thus at once makes possible and sets limits to any interpretation. Or, to put this thought more paradoxically, in a certain respect, the sense of any interpretation—and its meaning—always lies necessarily beyond it.[24]

Heidegger invokes this account of sense at the outset of his discussion of discourse. After characterizing discourse as "the articulation of intelligibility," he recalls that what can be articulated in interpretation, more primordially in discourse, is "what we called the sense" (SZ 161). He refers to what is sorted out in the discursive articulation as a "whole of meaning" (*Bedeutungsganze*) that can in turn be resolved or analyzed into meanings. If we take these statements quite literally, then sense is a whole of meaning, that is, a meaningful context capable of being broken down into meanings. While there is presumably no meaning without a sense, meanings, discursively articulated, are our means of access to sense. Sense is the context of meaning, the horizon out of which meaning takes shape, albeit not without the interpreter.[25]

Conclusion

After relating that he regards disposedness and understanding as "equiprimordially constitutive manners of being-here," Heidegger adds that these two fundamental existentials are "equiprimordially determined by discourse."[26] This claim underscores the central role he accords it in the constitution of our being-here. By identifying it as "equiprimordial," he means to call attention to, among other things, the fact that the everyday intelligibility of things for us is always already sorted out ("*gegliedert*"). Just as we always already find ourselves in a situation, disposed in various ways to ourselves and others (others like and unlike ourselves), and just as we are always already projecting ourselves onto some possibility or another, so we are always already speaking with ourselves or others, articulating the intelligibility of our dispositions-and-projections. Stressing this equiprimordial character, Heidegger adds that discourse, precisely as the articulation of that intelligibility, underlies interpretation and assertion.

In this respect the communicative dimension of discourse can no longer be suppressed. The ways we find ourselves in the world together and thereby project our being-in-the-world constitute in a determinate way the intelligibility of our existence and our world, sorting out various determinations. Discourse articulates this sorting out. By virtue of growing up in a specific language, we are thrown into a sorting out that we re-enact, more or less creatively, in communicating. So viewed, communication is no less primordial an aspect of discourse than its capacity to be about something and specify it (the aboutness and predication discussed above). Indeed, as Jeffrey Powell aptly observes, communication fails in a certain sense when it becomes focused solely on its reference, on what it is about. Rather, in communicating, one maintains "the site or space of the openness toward the other with whom one speaks, and in speaking one shares a world," all the while keeping "open the possibility of a relation to what emerges in the world, things."[27]

It is important to emphasize that, as glossed in the foregoing paragraphs, the equiprimordiality of communication within discourse and the equiprimordiality of discourse itself (relative to other basic existentials) are existential, not existentiel. Heidegger is not claiming that there are no ontic instances of communicating nonsense or speaking without communicating. Nor is he claiming that there is no ontic instance of disposedness or understanding; for example, no fear or no exercise of know-how that is wordless. The equiprimordiality of discourse signifies that it is no less fundamental than our dispositions and understanding, not that some explicit verbalization enters into each concrete form, that is, each ontic expression or manifestation of disposed understanding. If I fear, it is because, existentially, I find myself in this mood in light of some understanding and *can* say so (regardless of whether I ontically do so). Both the ways that I am disposed to things or others and the possibilities that I am projecting are determined by my capacity to make sense of all these phenomena and articulate their meanings in words.

NOTES

1. *Unterwegs zur Sprache* (Pfullingen: Neske, 1959), 32–33: "Die Sprache spricht"; 191ff. (paraphrasing Stefan Georg): "Kein Ding ist, wo das Wort fehlt"; see, too, 196 and 216; *Erläuterungen zu Hölderlins Dichtung,* vierte, erweiterte Auflage (Frankfurt am Main: Klostermann, 1971), 38: "Nur wo Sprache, da ist Welt. . . ."; "Brief über den Humanismus" in *Wegmarken,* zweite, erweiterte Auflage (Frankfurt am Main: Klostermann, 1978), 357. I am grateful to Bryan Norwood for his comments on an earlier version of this paper.

2. But these considerations, if valid, provide only a part of the answer. My interpretation provisionally sets aside a further element of discourse as basic as its "aboutness" (or, in the case of assertions, their referential and predicative character), namely, the communicative dimension of discourse. A full *Auseinandersetzung* with Heidegger's account must come to terms with the significance of this communicative dimension, integrating it with the others. Heidegger places discussions of the communicative dimension *after* discussions of aboutness, even as he insists on the unity of both themes; see SZ 155 and 162. Not surprisingly, he endorses a sense of that communicative dimension that coincides with the referentiality and, indeed, the existential truth of discourse. In this regard, see his explanation for his appropriation of the premodern sense of hermeneutics as communicating *(Mitteilen)* in *Ontologie (Hermeneutik der Faktizität), Gesamtausgabe,* vol. 63, ed. Käte Bröcker-Oltmanns (Frankfurt am Main: Klostermann, 1988), 9–10, 15–20, as well as his interpretation of λόγος in connection with speaking, being-with-one-another, and ἀγαθόν in *Grundbegriffe der aristotelischen Philosophie, Gesamtausgabe,* vol. 18, ed. Mark Michalski (Frankfurt am Main: Klostermann, 2002), 50, 55–64.

3. Heidegger's placement of discourse on a par with the disposedness and understanding by no means entails, I argue, that Dasein's every mood or exhibition of know-how is an instance of language use.

4. Thomas Sheehan, "Heidegger's New Aspect: On *In-Sein, Zeitlichkeit,* and *The Genesis of Being and Time,*" *Research in Phenomenology* 25 (1995): 211–212.

5. We might regard these three aspects as three ways for language to be, as long as this way of speaking does not mislead us into thinking that language *is* in some determinable sense apart from them.

6. The issue here is obviously but nonetheless tellingly reflexive; if *Sein und Zeit* itself exemplifies only language in use, that is to say, if *Sein und Zeit* is not discourse (existential language), then its language is rhetorical rather than hermeneutical.

7. My use of "property" here follows the traditional Scholastic renditions of property as a distinct predicable that—in contrast to an accident—is *omni, soli, et semper* predicated of a species.

8. SZ 32: "Λόγος als Rede besagt vielmehr soviel wie δηλοῦν, offenbar machen das, wovon in der Rede 'die Rede' ist. Aristoteles hat diese Funktion der Rede schärfer expliziert als ἀποφαίνεσθαι. Der λόγος läßt etwas sehen (φαίνεσθαι), nämlich das, worüber die Rede ist und zwar für den Redenden (Medium), bzw. Für die miteinander Redenden." See, too, GA 18: 19–20. For a discussion of Rede as "a worldly phenomenon" (charged with the power of manifesting the world to and among those speaking with one another) and its relation to self-showing, see Jeffrey Powell, "Heidegger and the Communicative World," *Research in Phenomenology* 40 (2010): 55–71, esp. 60–63.

9. These considerations help explain why some scholars see Heidegger's views dovetailing with Wittgenstein's insistence on the inexpressibility of semantics, that is, the futility of appeals to metalanguage, given the assumption that the relation between words and things can only be shown and not said. According to Hintikka, this convergence can be traced to the fact that Wittgenstein and Heidegger alike view language as a universal medium and not merely as a tool or calculus. See Martin Kusch, *Language as Calculus vs. Language as Universal Medium: A Study In Husserl, Heidegger and Gadamer* (Dordrecht, the Netherlands: Kluwer Academic Press, 1989) and Jaakko Hintikka, *Lingua Universalis vs. Calculus Ratiocinator: An Ultimate Presupposition of Twentieth-Century Philosophy* (Dordrecht, the Netherlands: Kluwer, 1997), 162–190.

10. Heidegger himself calls attention to his own assertions; see, for example, SZ 221: "*Dasein ist 'in der Wahrheit'*. Diese Aussage hat ontologischen Sinn"; see, too, Heidegger's remark that "faktisch unsere Verhaltungen durchgängig von Aussagen durchgesetzt sind" in *Prolegomena zur Geschichte des Zeitbegriffs, Gesamtausgabe*, vol. 20, ed. Petra Jaeger, zweite, durchgesehene Auflage (Frankfurt am Main: Klostermann, 1988), 75.

11. See n. 1 above.

12. See in §§7 and 44 of *Sein und Zeit* (on λόγος and truth, respectively) as well as in his study of deception (ψεῦδος) in the first Marburg lectures (GA 17) and in his lectures on Aristotle's *Rhetoric* (GA 18) the following semester.

13. SZ 218. In the entire passage Heidegger himself links up referring with knowing and he does so by explicitly acknowledging the Husserlian legacy of this approach; see SZ 218n1.

14. Martin Heidegger, *Einführung in die phänomenologische Forschung, Gesamtausgabe*, vol. 17, ed. Friedrich-Wilhelm von Herrmann (Frankfurt am Main: Klostermann, 1994), 19: "Der λόγος ist nicht in der Weise eines Werkzeugs, sondern historisch und erwächst aus freien Stücken, d.h. einem jeweiligen Stande der

Sachentdeckung." See, too, ibid., 21: "Der λόγος ἀποφαντικός ist ein solches Reden mit der Welt, durch das die daseiende Welt als daseiende aufgezeigt wird." See, too, n. 9 above.

15. Should we infer from this embeddedness of the as-structure in the for-structure, that is, the fact that what we take something as is based upon what we take it for, that discourse is pragmatic or rhetorical *all the way down*, as we might put it? This inference is compelling if we limit the for-structure (what things, beings are for) to what, as part of our designs and intentions, they are for. But just as our being-here is not something we designed or intended, so not every sense of what entities are for, that is, how they are to be interpreted, is reducible to those designs or intentions.

16. GA 20: 75: "Faktisch ist es auch so, daß unsere schlichtesten Wahrnehmungen und Verfassungen schon *ausgedrückte*, mehr noch, in bestimmter Weise *interpretierte* sind. Wir sehen nicht so sehr primär und ursprünglich die Gegenstände und Dinge, sondern zunächst sprechen wir darüber, genauer sprechen wir nicht das aus, was wir sehen, sondern umgekehrt, wir sehen, was man über die Sache spricht."

17. Heidegger actually works with four levels of "as" constructions: existentiel and existential forms of the hermeneutic "as" and the apophantic "as," respectively. When I take something as a lever (existientiel hermeneutic "as"), I also take it as being handy or ready-to-hand (existential hermeneutic "as"). Derivatively, I assert "it is a lever" (existentiel apophantic "as") or "it is handy" (existential apophantic "as"); see my *Heidegger's Concept of Truth* (Cambridge: Cambridge University Press, 2001), 195.

18. This claim holds *mutatis mutandis* for exhortations ("Pull the lever") and questions ("Is that the lever?").

19. Paul Grice, "Meaning" in *Studies in the Way of Words* (Cambridge, Mass.: Harvard University Press, 1989), 214–215.

20. SZ 84: "Das primäre 'Wozu' ist ein Worum-willen. Das 'Um-willen' betrifft aber immer das Sein des *Daseins*, . . ."

21. At the same time, insofar as this worldliness is part of Dasein's essential makeup (its being-in-the-world), Dasein in each case already refers to and understands itself as in this world. By no means requiring some sort of theoretical transparency, this self-referential understanding is a primordial sense of trust-and-familiarity (*Vertrautheit*), and it is precisely in view of Dasein's primordial trust in that world and familiarity with it that implements can be encountered for what they are, namely, relevant, referring to one another, and that Dasein in *Angst* can experience their utter irrelevance.

22. My reconstruction of the ways in which Heidegger uses and construes meanings is derived from his account of meanings generally. He does not present such an explicit account himself. Note, however, that he takes issue with restricting *Bedeutung* to the ideal content of a judgment or with the "categories of meaning" of a linguistic science, oriented to assertions and grounded in an ontology of the present-at-hand; see SZ 156 and 165–166. See also his remark about the rootedness of *Bedeutungslehre* in the ontology of Dasein (SZ 166); see the following claim: "Aus der Zeitlichkeit der Rede, das heißt des Daseins überhaupt, kann erst die 'Entstehung' der 'Bedeutung' aufgeklärt . . . werden" (SZ 349); see, too, my essay "Husserl and Heidegger on Meaning," *Heidegger Jahrbuch* 6 (2012): 200–217.

23. SZ 156; see, too, SZ 324. Because sense is an existential, Heidegger notes that only Dasein can make sense (*sinnvoll*) or be senseless (*sinnlos*) and that all other sorts of entities are, strictly speaking, non-sensical (*unsinnig*) or even—as in the case of natural catastrophes—sense-defying (*widersinnig*). SZ 151: "Sinn 'hat' nur das Dasein, sofern die Erschlossenheit des In-der-Welt-seins durch das in ihr entdeckbare Seiende 'erfüllbar' ist."

24. Inasmuch as assertions are grounded in an interpretation, they have a sense, not to be confused with meaning; see SZ 153–154 and 156.

25. There is, in Heidegger's account of sense, a kind of verificationism since sense and existential truth coincide. But here several qualifications are in order. This coincidence is not to be confused with an identity since the sense that coincides with truth is also always partly false. Nor is Heidegger supposing that the senses or even the meanings of assertions or words as handy or on hand coincide with *their* truth, that is, correspondence with other things. Moreover, what we mean by what we say—even where what we mean is the sense of our being or existential truth—is only one factor in the constitution of that meaning. The coincidence of sense and existential truth anticipates Heidegger's later characterization of truth as "*Lichtung* des Seyns" and "Grund . . . für die Gründung des schaffenden Da-seins"; see *Beiträge zur Philosophie (Vom Ereignis), Gesamtausgabe*, vol. 65 (Frankfurt am Main: Klostermann, 1989), 327, 331.

26. SZ 133; see also SZ 161. Heidegger is even more emphatic about the determining role of language in his lectures on Aristotle's *Rhetoric;* see GA 18: 18: "*Das In-der-Welt-sein des Menschen ist im Grunde bestimmt durch das Sprechen*" (Heidegger's italics). For a gloss on Friedrich-Wilhelm von Herrmann's discussion of the structural difference between discourse and other basic existentials, see Powell, "Heidegger and the Communicative World," 67–69.

27. Powell, "Heidegger and the Communicative World," 69. Powell's emphasis on communication's equiprimordial role in constituting the phenomenon of discourses is richly corroborated by new theories of usage-based language acquisition that emphasize the social and cognitive skills children gain from communication prior to learning a symbolic language. See, for example, Michael Tomasello, *Constructing a Language: A Usage-Based Theory of Language Acquisition* (Cambridge, Mass.: Harvard University Press, 2003); for a review of the significance of these theories in the context of contemporary philosophy of language, see my forthcoming "The Explanation of Language," *Philosophy and Language*, Proceedings of the American Catholic Philosophical Association, vol. 84 (2010): 33–46.

TWO

Listening to the Silence: Reticence and the Call of Conscience in Heidegger's Philosophy

Walter Brogan

In the sections of Martin Heidegger's *Sein und Zeit* on being-towards-death that seem more and more to me to speak of mortal community, the passages on anticipation (*Vorlaufen*) are particularly telling. Heidegger says: "Anticipation discloses to existence that its extreme inmost possibility lies in *giving itself up*, and thus it shatters all one's clinging to whatever existence one has reached."[1] Being-towards-death teaches us not to hold on to ourselves. But in doing so, Heidegger says, it also frees us from the grasp of others and frees others from our grasp. Not holding on to others does not mean being out of touch with them. Thus Heidegger continues: "As the non-relational possibility, death individualizes, but only, as the possibility not-to-be-bypassed, in order to make Dasein as being-with understand the potentialities-of-being of the others."[2] Dasein is not a reified or pre-fixed subject who in being-towards-death isolates itself within itself. In fact, at least according to this statement, it is quite the opposite. The character of Dasein's self is such that it is for itself always apart from itself, ahead of itself in such a way that it shatters any possibility of closing itself off from what is other than itself, even from its own otherness.

Heidegger's analysis makes evident that there is the possibility of an existential foundation for community, despite the claim that being-towards-death is Dasein's extreme, non-relational possibility. In fact, he says in the above quote that it is precisely this manner of staying with itself that opens up the possibility of a being-with that understands the existentiality of the other. Yet, it is not a community that rests comfortably in its association with others, as might be said of the earlier analysis of being-with as a mode of inauthenticity and everydayness. In his analysis of the indefiniteness (*Unbestimmtheit,* indeterminateness) of death, Heidegger says:

> In anticipating (*Vorlaufen*) the indefinite certainty of death, Dasein opens itself to a constant *threat* (*Bedrohung*) arising from its own there. Being-towards-the-end must hold itself in this very threat, and can so little phase it out that it rather has to cultivate the indefiniteness of the certainty.[3]

Far from an isolated, protected space of self-enclosure, the singularity of Dasein is always and absolutely contested. The wholeness of Dasein is always, as its way of being-a-whole, in jeopardy. To the ground of Dasein, Heidegger says, belongs *Angst,* that is, Dasein is a ground that is fundamentally ungrounded.

Heidegger summarizes the analysis of existential being-towards-death in striking terms that on the surface seem to indicate a withdrawal from involvement with others:

> *Anticipation reveals to Dasein its lostness in the they-self, and brings it face to face with the possibility to be itself, primarily unsupported by concern that takes care of things, but to be itself in passionate (leidenschaftlichen) anxious freedom toward death which is free of the illusions of the they, factical, and certain of itself.*[4]

What I find most intriguing in this sentence is the word *leidenschaftlich,* passionate. Dasein has become passionate, affective, able to suffer. In anxious anticipation, the neutrality of Dasein is beginning to vanish. To me this is essential to Heidegger's analysis—that its recoil upon itself in being-towards-death disentangles it from the tendency within itself to let itself be determined by what it finds around itself, and that this is precisely the moment of freedom. But this freedom does not preclude the possibility that Dasein is still very much in touch with the other, existentially in touch, that is, in a free relation.

Heidegger begins section 54 of *Sein und Zeit* by reminding us of the they-self (*Das Man*) and the lostness to itself that characterizes Dasein in this mode. Dasein finds itself as lost to itself; its being is essentially split. This twofold structure of lostness and recovery is now exposed in a slightly different way. Heidegger asks whether there is any phenomenological evidence, any attestation, wherein this possibility of authentically and existentially encountering oneself in one's everyday self-abandonment can be disclosed. In this disclosure, is there any phenomenological evidence that the they-self is touched by the existential self, to which it is, nevertheless, opposed? Neglect (*Versäumnis*) of self, a dis-owing of self, a not choosing itself, belongs to Dasein in its inauthenticity. Can this process of disburdening (*Entlassen*) oneself from oneself be reversed? In a sense, this is a very Platonic question. Is a turning around, a return to oneself possible? Heidegger declares that this reversal would imply choosing to choose oneself (as opposed to the choosing not to choose that characterizes inauthenticity). This choosing to choose is what Heidegger will eventually call resoluteness (*Entschlossenheit*). Choosing to make a choice, of course, is not an actual choice in the specific sense of choosing this or that thing. It is rather a matter of recovering our capacity for choosing. For Heidegger, this amounts to the question of whether and how we can act freely. Heidegger is asking not about acting in one way as opposed to another or about the question of what one is to do, but about the ontology of action.

I think this is what Heidegger has in mind when, in his analysis of *Nichomachean Ethics* VI, he associates conscience (*Gewissen*) with *phronesis*.[5] For the phenomenon that Heidegger appeals to as the way the authentic self shows itself to the inauthentic self and chooses to be it is conscience and having a conscience. Heidegger claims we are familiar with conscience in the form of "the voice (*Stimme*) of conscience."[6] As something we hear, conscience is calling to us. It is summoning us back to ourselves from out of the lostness in the they-self. Once again, as was the case in his analysis of discourse, the focus here is on listening and hearing as an intrinsic characteristic of a being who is able to speak. Speaking and listening co-constitute the discourse (*Rede*) of Dasein. Heidegger says: "The call of conscience has the character of summoning (*Anruf*) Dasein to its ownmost potentiality of being a self."[7] But then he adds that this summoning that occurs in the call of conscience is a call back to ourselves as constituted by a lack.

In a sense what is involved here in the call of conscience is a return of the existential self to the very site of the they-self, the experience of oneself as not being oneself. Dasein is called to understand itself as itself in its thereness, in its thrownness. Heidegger makes this point through an analysis of hearing and listening:

> If Dasein is to be brought back from the lostness of failing to hear itself, and if this is to be done through itself, it must first be able to find itself, to find itself as something that has failed to hear itself and continues to do so in *listening* to the they. This listening must be stopped, that is, the possibility of another kind of hearing that interrupts that listening must be given by Dasein to itself. The possibility of such a breach lies in being summoned immediately. Dasein fails to hear itself, and listens to the they, and this listening gets broken by the call if that call, in accordance with its character as call, arouses another kind of hearing which, in relation to the hearing that is lost, has a character in every way opposite. If this lost hearing is numbed by the "noise" of the manifold ambiguity of everyday "new" idle talk, the call must call silently, unambiguously, with no foothold for curiosity. *What this gives us to understand in calling is conscience.*[8]

Authentic Dasein has a special kind of listening that calls itself back from both a failure to listen to itself and from a listening to the they-self, which it cuts off. This special call of self to itself is a kind of jolting of everydayness and the stupor of absorption and evasion. But this rupture or rift (*Bruch*) is a modality of Dasein's being. That means in a sense that all communication and idle talk, all everydayness, is haunted by this disruption, at least as an existential possibility; that is, at least inasmuch as our thrownness can never completely throw away who we are. To do so would be to no longer be Dasein. Even in the most sedimentary and vacuous forms of language, a poetic listening can retrieve the possibilities that lie frozen and hidden, that speak silently through the leveled down and trivializing speech of *Das Man*. But the hearing for the repressed voice of being in what is passed down and passed on in ordinary speech requires an existential attunement and often a certain degree of hermeneutic violence and excavation. Heidegger says that in the call of conscience the they-self is robbed of its refuge and subterfuge.

In addressing this issue of existential attunement to the unvoiced dimension of inauthentic speech, Heidegger says:

> Authentic silence is possible only in genuine discourse. In order to be silent, Dasein must have something to say, that is, must be in command of an authentic and rich disclosedness of itself. Then reticence makes manifest and puts down "idle talk." As a mode of discourse, reticence articulates the intelligibility of Dasein so primordially that it gives rise to a genuine potentiality for hearing and to a being-with-one-another that is transparent.[9]

Far from cutting us off from others, Heidegger says that being struck dumb in the face of the numbing effect of idle talk, authentic silence, opens up a space for communication that is transparent in the face of the other. Most of all, Heidegger says, hearing the "call" and the voice of conscience requires the gift of hearing the silence of the authentic word. Since this poetic listening is a listening, it is not something that can be imposed upon ordinary language from outside. We cannot decide to bring the voice of conscience to bear on inauthenticity, although we can want (*Wollen*) to have a conscience in the sense that we can stand ready for it and resolutely prepared for it. Authentic speaking has to be made room for and allowed to be made manifest. It is not a matter, either, of going looking for it in the form of curiosity. It comes suddenly for one who is prepared. It speaks to us.

The call of conscience is the return of phenomenological language, letting what is speak of and from out of itself. The site of the call of conscience is the they-self, and yet the idle chatter of the they-self closes off and covers over conscience. It cannot actually be heard by the they-self. Or rather, it can only be heard silently. It is a call back to oneself and at the same time a call away from the they. For this reason there is a double sense to Heidegger's statement that the call of conscience calls from afar. "It calls from afar to afar [*Ferne*]."[10] In this doubling of distance, Dasein is open to the estrangement of its own being as its most proper way of being. Dasein is a stranger to itself. It is clear that this sense of not being at home with oneself is more than the discomfort of *Das Man* in its evasion, though it is certainly the source of this. More so, I think, this call from afar, this voice of conscience, is the horizon of Dasein's being that is never to be overcome or surpassed. When one says this, one must at the same time acknowledge that this uncanniness and distance is also precisely the ground for all going beyond oneself and all forms of self-overcoming. Heidegger says in the marginal note: "He who has distanced himself from his own self."[11] So in a sense, conscience involves both Dasein's estrangement from itself, the strangeness that belongs to its very being in relation to itself, and also, in the call of conscience as a call back, Dasein's closeness to itself when it first encounters its own intrinsic, existential distantiality.

What is interesting to me is the notion of a breach with idle talk that is central to conscience. The listening to others that is part of the idle talk of the they-self is brought to a halt. The call of conscience cuts through the chatter and gossip of the everyday. Heidegger says the call discloses something else that is missing by stopping us in our tracks, so to speak, by jolting us out of the stupor of everydayness. It inserts precisely into the rupture of our absorption in everydayness another kind of hearing: the hearing of silence. In the call of conscience one can hear what is not being said and not being addressed in everyday discourse.

In section 56, it becomes even clearer that conscience belongs to the existential of discourse. Inasmuch as language has to do with *Mitdasein*, discourse is the site of communication with others. Yet we already know that conscience is the call of the self back to the self. Thus, conscience provides the ontological ground for an understanding of speaking to oneself, but it is not self-evident that it is also the basis for an ontology of communication in general. Nevertheless, I think this is the case. Conscience is not an alternative to everyday discourse that has nothing to do with this form of communication. Heidegger says: "The call reaches Dasein in this always-already-understanding-itself in everyday, average taking care of things. The call reaches the they-self of heedful being-with others."[12] This is a way of saying that conscience is the site or moment of the coming together of facticity and existence. If this is the case, then it is not a matter of eliminating everyday contact with others in the world of our concerns. Rather, the question is, how is average everydayness and our encounter with others in the world transformed in this moment of conscience? How does conscience function to expose us more authentically to the concreticity of our being and our openness to the being of others?

In being called back to itself, the self of Dasein analyzed in Division One, the self of everyday being-in-the-world is passed over (*übergangen*); Dasein goes beyond its being in the world. *Das Man* is passed by and passed over in the call of conscience. The they-self collapses (*zusammensinken*). It is very dramatic language. Stripped of the cover of the they-self, Dasein faces itself in its nakedness. Thus that which is talked about in the call of conscience is Dasein's self apart from the they-self; that which is summoned is Dasein's own self. But this does not mean Dasein is bereft of contact with others. Rather the possessive, dominating, gossipy talk of the everyday is suspended and a genuine existential opening for communication is prepared.

The call of conscience does not say anything. It says nothing. It speaks solely in silence (*Schweigen*), what Heidegger calls reticence (*Verschwiegenheit*). As silent speaking, conscience is a form of authentic discourse, and thus of communication. First and foremost, it is a way of speaking to oneself. But Heidegger insists that it also pervades our way of being with others. And he does so precisely because the call reaches profoundly into the they-self, and thus transforms our way of taking care of things and our way of being-with other Dasein. Conscience is a way of being. The distance to itself that conscience opens up is disturbing to Dasein. The call of conscience is not something with which we can feel familiar or to which we can become accustomed. It insists on being heard. One could call this an intensity of hearing, I suppose, but it also needs to be described as something like an existential hearing. This section is really about the existentiality of hearing, owning our receptivity, being open to and ready for the address.

Heidegger says: "The call without doubt does not come from someone else who is with me in the world. The call comes *from* me, and yet *over* me."[13] On the surface at least, this call is not the Levinasian call of the other. Perhaps it is also not the daimonic voice of Socrates. Yet it does come over me (*Überkommen*). I do receive it and it is handed down to me and overcomes me. It comes over me from beyond, yet it comes from me. So, what we have here is something like the self-transcendence of Dasein. If we were to claim that *Being and Time* offers something like a transcendental phenomenology, it would have to be in this sense. The twofoldness of Dasein's being—its equiprimordial existential facticity—is uncovered phenomenologically in the call of conscience. Heidegger says that "a thin wall" separates the "they" from the uncannniness of its being.[14] The wall presumably is the avoidance of silence and of listening existentially to what is not being spoken. He goes on to warn us again not to reduce what is being said here. The fact that the call is the call of self back to self does not make it merely subjective. But it does free Dasein, that is, it frees Dasein from the dominance of the they-self. In this regard, it is more than a critical voice (the daimon) that warns us what not to do if we want to have a good conscience.

Heidegger draws the discussion of conscience back into the discussion of the three overriding existentials that were first explicitly analyzed at the end of Division One and then made thematically explicit in the discussion of being-towards-death, namely understanding, attunement, and discourse. Conscience as an existential can never be authentically attained as something in which we somehow can dwell and thus achieve authentic existence. Conscience (*Gewissen*) is always encountered as a call, a summons, and what is called for is that we attune ourselves to the summons rather than to what is summoned. Another way of saying this is to say that understanding the call is a matter of holding ourselves ready for and open to the call. The call of conscience can only be heard in holding ourselves out toward having a conscience as a possibility for being. That is, it is a matter of choosing to have a conscience, wanting to have a conscience rather than possessing it. Conscience is never able to be counted on; nor is it ever closed off for us as something we can attain. It always calls us to be more than what we are. But in understanding, I *am* this possibility, this reaching out toward. What we might notice here is that in concretizing our understanding as being toward the call, and suggesting that understanding-conscience is nothing other than wanting to have a conscience, Heidegger has introduced wanting and thus desire into understanding. Aristotle does the same thing at one point in the *Nichomachean Ethics* when he speaks of desireful reason or reasonable desire (*orexis*). Wanting to have a conscience is the desire to **be**. But we are this desire. I think it could even be argued that the recovery of desire is what occurs when conscience calls us back from the lostness to ourselves of the they-self. If this were the case, then desireful understanding is what Heidegger means by authenticity or authentic existence. But what the call provokes us toward is the uncanniness of our being, that is, our not being at home with ourselves. Homelessness is the disposition that accompanies desire in authentic existential being. The attunement that, along with understanding and discourse, co-constitutes the existentiality of Dasein is, first and foremost, *Angst*. Heidegger says: "Wanting to have a conscience becomes a readiness for Angst."[15] Understanding as the possibility of being stands face to face with Angst as the possibility of not-being.

The whole treatment of discourse at this point in the development of the treatise centers on the call and thus around hearing as the primordial meaning of discourse. Conscience does not speak about anything. The language of assertion, propositional language that says something about something, is left behind by one who hears the call. There is nothing to talk about or explain. That's why this mode of discourse is so often parodied as nonsense and being dumb. In fact, existential discourse that occurs in the space of the withdrawal from the idle chatter of the they has nothing to say or add to that conversation. Kierkegaard makes this same point about the fact that the existential individual does not stand out and goes unnoticed as an existential individual in the public domain. He is still a tax collector. He still participates in the exchange economy, and so forth. The word Heidegger chooses to convey this notion of existential discourse is *reticence* (*Verschwiegenheit*). The discourse of conscience never comes to utterance. Dasein is summoned back to the stillness of itself.

"Resolute Dasein," Heidegger says, "frees itself for its world."[16] He makes clear in his analysis that the content of the world, being-in, concernful taking care of what is, and being-with others does not get altered in terms of its content. We do not abandon the others we meet in inauthentic everydayness and take on a new set of friends. Heidegger says:

> The circle of the others is not exchanged for a new one, and yet the being towards things at hand which understands and takes care of things, and the concerned being-with with the others is now defined in terms of **their** ownmost potentiality of being-a-self. . . . Resoluteness brings the self right into its being together with things at hand, actually taking care of them, and pushes it toward concerned being-with the others . . . freeing itself for its world . . . leaping ahead and freeing.[17]

Not only does Dasein get free from its determination by its entanglement and absorption in the world; along with this freedom comes the freedom of others. Heidegger reinforces the point about existential authenticity and its intractable, yet free, connection to inauthenticity in the following passage: "Resoluteness appropriates untruth authentically . . . Resoluteness means letting oneself be summoned out of one's lostness in the they; the irresoluteness of the they remains in dominance, but it cannot attack resolute existence."[18] It is this impermeability of the there of authentic Dasein that Heidegger calls being-in-a-situation.

What I find most remarkable in Heidegger's account of anticipatory resoluteness is the statement: "Dasein *holds* itself open for its constant lostness in the irresoluteness of the they—a lostness which is possible from the very ground of its being."[19] Being-towards-death becomes, in anticipatory resoluteness, becoming free for death, free for our mortality. Heidegger says: "Anticipatory resoluteness is the understanding that follows the call of conscience and that frees for death the possibility of gaining power over the existence of Dasein and of basically dispersing every fugitive self-covering-over."[20]

The Shift in the Role of Silence and the Call in Heidegger's *Beiträge*

In the *Beiträge*, Dasein has shed to a large extent the vestiges of subjectivity and self-consciousness that are arguably still present in *Sein und Zeit*. Here Heidegger says that thinking needs to "go under," that is, to enact its own unthinking of itself, so as to leave open a space in the interstices for *Ereignis*, the originary enowning event. This is a work that wants to think out of the "empty" spaces between words. For this reason, Heidegger's frequent discussions of language and the unsaying of language, and his constant allusions to the reticence and silence of words are important. It is as if Heidegger is working toward the possibility of becoming silent before the event. So the standpoint of phenomenology as engaged in a project of uncovering and disclosure also shifts in this text. One might be tempted to say that Dasein becomes passive in the face of the disclosive event, except that the very terms "active" and "passive" will have to be re-negotiated. To put it in other, perhaps better, terms, Dasein is no longer defined as anxious in the face of its own possibility of not-being.

The most complex analysis of Heidegger's new delineation of Dasein is found in chapter V, the section of the text on grounding. I only want to mention two points: Dasein is presented even more explicitly as the quintessential case of the between (*das Zwischenfall*) and Dasein is said to be "owned over to." At one point, Heidegger says Dasein is experienced, and by that he means, he says, enacted by a *verrückende Einrückung*, a displacing shifting-into.[21] Clearly Heidegger is further removing his understanding of Dasein from his earlier characterization of Dasein as thereness and presence (albeit ecstatic presence). He is situating Dasein more squarely in the space of transition.

The echo of be-ing (*Seyn*) occurs as refusal in the *Seinsverlassenheit*, the abandonment of being. Why is this refusal characterized as an echo, a sounding (*Anklang*)? No doubt there is a residue here of the early Greek notion of the cosmos as resonating with the song of the gods. And no doubt also, Heidegger's notion of attunement (*Stimmung*) in this text carries even more strongly than in *Sein und Zeit* the sense of a *Stimme* or voice. It is also important to recognize here the thematic from *Sein und Zeit* of a call, but here it is not the call of conscience but rather the call of the god, perhaps that of the last god, only faintly heard in the peal of stillness.[22] This would be especially important since there is a turn that is at issue here, and the turn is clearly one that requires a shifting from seeking and looking for to attentiveness and responsiveness. It is certainly the case that seeing and any form of eidetic philosophy is here necessarily left behind, since such can only be a philosophy that represents beings in the presence of its stare. The metaphorics of the eye (*Augen*) that were still prevalent in *Sein und Zeit* have disappeared in this text. But hearing still preserves a sensitivity for the other in beings, and thus still, at least faintly, may be able to enjoy the resonance of be-ing's refusal. Heidegger even calls this hearing and listening a kind of thinking (*Er-denken*).[23]

In section 13 of the *Beiträge*, in a discussion of reservedness (*Verhaltenheit*) and silence, Heidegger addresses one of the central themes of his meditations. He says: "*Es verschlägt einem das Wort.*"[24] The word fails. In this context, used in the passive with the dative, the phrase means: he was dumbfounded or struck dumb. But Heidegger warns that he does not mean this in the sense that we sometimes are at a loss for words. What is indicated here is an originary condition with regard to language. Heidegger's thinking in the *Beiträge*, from the point of view of ordinary discourse, is paradoxical. He argues that a being who is language-bound is one whose ability to speak is beholden to a fundamental condition of speechlessness. "The word fails one" not accidentally or on a particular occasion; the failure here is catastrophic, an absolute loss of the word. Yet, it is precisely through this dumbfoundedness, ironically, that the word first emerges. The genesis of speaking is the powerlessness before speaking.

In the pre-view of the *Beiträge*, Heidegger addresses the connection between ordinary language and the failure of the originary word.[25] The failure of the originary word is not accidental but the condition for the language of beings. Yet, the ordinary language of beings contains and preserves a trace of the saying of be-ing. The difficulty of the gifting of language and its connection to the failure of original saying cannot be avoided or overcome. Rather than overcoming the difficulty of the difference between ordinary language and the stillness of be-ing, we are asked to enter into it so deeply and concretely as to occasion a transformation, a displacement of language, where ordinary words regain their poetic force. Stillness is the preserve of the truth of be-ing. It is of course also a word intrinsically related to language. In a sense only one who can speak can be attuned to the stillness.

In section 36, Heidegger emphatically rejects any call for a new language, even though our language is the language of metaphysics, the language of beings. What is needed is not a new way of speaking but a new way of listening. What he calls for is that we say the language of beings as the language of be-ing. This would be what he calls a transformation of language. For now, in the age of machination (*Machenschaft*), the domain, the truth of be-ing, is closed off. So what is required is the hearing of the refusal; in a sense we must learn to speak this refusal and preserve this word in its refusal to speak. This saying of the withdrawal of be-ing is what Heidegger is attempting and why he focuses on reticence in silence (*Erschweigung*). In Greek *sigan* means silence, but in the sense of keeping silent, that is, holding a secret. In referring to sigetic language, Heidegger is speaking in these sections not only of silence but also of the secret. What is called for is a speaking that holds the secret of be-ing. He calls this the logic of genuine philosophy, a philosophy that is attentive to the other beginning in its way of speaking, attentive to the situation of authentic philosophical language at the end of metaphysics. It is not a reticence that wishes it could develop its own set of signs and its own logic. It does not speak in symbols as substitutes for what cannot be said. So how does the logic of the secret work? It shelters and safeguards the stillness by practicing attentive listening and thinking and by letting language belong to reservedness.

This whole text of the *Beiträge* is a sustained meditation on origin, *Ursprung* and *Anfang*. The origin occurs in the juncture of non-saying/saying. Heidegger is especially interested here in the origin of the poetic word. In a sense, these are the archical words through which the strife of world and earth gains expression in the appearance of beings. But this *archē*-language is experienced as the nullity of language, the absence of language. The *archē* of language is a profound negation of the word. But this negation, this saying that holds back archical language, is the source of language's most poetic ability to affirm beings. Heidegger goes so far as to call this loss of the word, this being-dumbfounded (*das Verschlagende*), *Ereignis*, namely, the hint and onset of be-ing. Heidegger, in this same passage, calls this failure of the word an inceptual condition for poetic naming. It is interesting that he calls this kind of non-saying saying a naming. Perhaps it is akin to Hesiod's naming of the gods. Heidegger goes on in the next paragraph to call this moment of poetic naming the time of language, when the word again works, is *poiesis*, that is, productive.

In his discussion of "the ones to come," Heidegger says they will be reticent and silent. They will care for the singularity of being. In section 248, Heidegger says the future ones give witness to the stillest stillness in which an imperceptible *Ruck*, an imperceptible tug turns the truth back from machination to *Ereignis*. He calls this reservedness and silence the innermost feast of the last god.[26] The ones to come are the listeners, in mourning and birth, grief and joy, to the hint of the last god. "How this hint is preserved as hint in the reserved reticence in silence, and how such preserving always resides in taking-leave and arriving, particularly in mourning (*Trauer*) *and* joy (*Freude*) . . ."[27]

The last god is tied closely to the double movement of flight and arrival. Both of these notions imply something removed, held apart from and beyond what is, something futural. Heidegger grasps the truth of be-ing as this event that appropriates the refusal (*Verweigerung*) and hint that belongs to the last god. This truth is not defined in terms of what is not there but as itself a fullness, the fullness of a granting that occurs as refusal, as holding back in reservedness. Holding back and refusing is, Heidegger insists, the highest form of gifting. In this sense be-ing is the passing (*Vorbeigang*—departure, going away) of the last god, the gift of refusal. And then Heidegger says it is as the passing of the last god that be-ing becomes the estrangement (*Befremdung*) and the stillness. That is, be-ing is, because of its belonging to the departure of the last god, what is estranged and other and is thus able to grant by way of a stillness that does not control or determine.

Dasein belongs to be-ing as the one who guards and preserves this strangeness and stillness. Dasein is the one who belongs to what is apart and other and what cannot be spoken or addressed. Only the one who stands in the turning of *Ereignis* can prepare for listening to the stillness of the beckoning hint of the last god in the draw of its withdrawal. Dasein belongs to the between of the event of be-ing and in its thrownness becomes itself. And the event of be-ing in turn needs Dasein.

NOTES

It is an honor to dedicate this essay to Anatoli Mikhailov, who more than anyone I know has responded to the call of conscience with the reticence and reserve of which Heidegger speaks.

1. Martin Heidegger, *Sein und Zeit* (Tübingen: Max Niemeyer Verlag, 1972), 264; *Being and Time,* trans. Joan Stambaugh (Albany: SUNY Press, 1996), 244.

2. *Sein und Zeit* 265/244.

3. *Sein und Zeit* 265/245.

4. *Sein und Zeit* 266/245.

5. Martin Heidegger, *Platon: Sophistes* 56 (Plato's *Sophist* 39), *Gesamtausgabe* 19 (Frankfurt am Main: Klostermann, 1992).

6. *Sein und Zeit,* 292/269.

7. *Sein und Zeit* 269/249.

8. *Sein und Zeit* 271/250.

9. *Sein und Zeit* 165/154.

10. *Sein und Zeit* 271/250.

11. *Sein und Zeit* 271/251.

12. *Sein und Zeit* 273/252.

13. *Sein und Zeit* 275/254.

14. *Sein und Zeit* 278/256.

15. *Sein und Zeit* 296/272.

16. *Sein und Zeit* 298/274.

17. *Sein und Zeit* 298/274.

18. *Sein und Zeit* 299/275.

19. *Sein und Zeit* 308/285.

20. *Sein und Zeit* 310/286.

21. Martin Heidegger, *Beiträge zur Philosophie* (Frankfurt am Main: Klostermann, 1989), 309; *Contributions to Philosophy (From Enowning),* trans. Parvis Emad and Kenneth Maly (Bloomington: Indiana University Press, 1999), 217.

22. "It is important to recognize that selfhood first springs forth out of the grounding of Da-sein and that this grounding is enacted as enownment of belonging to the call." *Beiträge* 67/47.

23. *Beiträge* 108/75.

24. *Beiträge* 36/26.

25. *Beiträge* 83/58.

26. *Beiträge* 399/280.

27. *Beiträge* 400/280.

THREE

In Force of Language: Language and Desire in Heidegger's Reading of Aristotle's *Metaphysics* Θ

William McNeill

In the summer semester of 1931, Heidegger presented a lecture course devoted to an intensive and textually focused reading of Aristotle's *Metaphysics* Θ, dealing with the essence and actuality of force, or *dunamis.* Not only does this course limit itself to what appears to be a restricted and localized textual question, of interest perhaps mainly to Aristotle specialists; it also appears that Heidegger's reading did not get very far: his interpretation barely makes it to the end of chapter 3 of *Metaphysics* Θ, and thus does not even approach the decisive chapters 6 through 10, where *dunamis* and *energeia* are most incisively analyzed in their own right. Nevertheless, the significance of this interpretation should not be underestimated, for it marks, I would argue, the beginnings of a transition to the focus on *technē*—on art, poetizing, and technicity—that would dominate the work of the 1930s and beyond; it provides the resources for the critical engagement with Nietzsche's thought of will to power in the mid-1930s, and for the analyses of power and technicity in the *Beiträge;* and it prepares the way both for the later thought of a destining of Being and for the question of "the way to language," a phrase that appears in this course perhaps for the first time.

Before broaching the nexus of language and desire in Heidegger's reading, which emerges in his interpretation of *technē* as a distinctive *dunamis meta logou,* I should first like to accompany his interpretation of Aristotle in its initial delimitation of the essence of *dunamis* or "force." The word "force," in German *Kraft*, it should be noted, is deliberately chosen by Heidegger over a number of other possible candidates for the translation of *dunamis*, such as *Macht* ("power"); *Können* ("ability" or "potentiality"); *Fähigkeit* ("capacity"); *Vermögen* ("capability"); *Möglichkeit* ("possibility"); or *Gewalt* ("sovereign force" or "might"). Yet *Kraft* does not have exactly the same semantic resonance as the English "force": in particular, it does not have the sense of violence that is often suggested by our use of the word "force" but implies rather intrinsic or inner strength, a quiet and unobtrusive resourcefulness: something that emerges—if indeed it emerges at all—from the concealed depths of Being. In this regard, Heidegger's choice of the word *Kraft* here to translate *dunamis* is significant not merely with respect to his interpretation of *Metaphysics* Θ, for it inscribes that interpretation within the overarching project of a destructuring (*Destruktion*) of the history of ontology, that is, within an attempt to recover and preserve what *Being and Time* called "the quiet force of the possible" (*die stille Kraft des Möglichen*)—a phrase to which Heidegger would return in his later, 1946 essay, the "Letter on 'Humanism.'" In *Being and Time*, the "quiet force of the possible" is invoked by Heidegger as that which is to be disclosed by authentic historical inquiry, and indeed in such a way that, as he expresses it there, "the 'force' of the possible penetrates into factical existence" (SZ 395). Philosophy itself, conceived under the auspices of a destructuring of the history of ontology, is indeed, in *Being and Time*, said to be motivated by nothing other than the desire to preserve "the *force of the most elementary words*" in which Dasein expresses itself, and to preserve such force from being leveled to incomprehensibility by the common understanding, a leveling that then gives rise to pseudo-problems (SZ 220). In *Being and Time*, however, the sense of *Kraft*, while clearly associated with possibility, was not developed in its own right, and these mentions remain suggestive at best. Furthermore, the relation between force and language likewise remained underdeveloped there.[1] It is not until the 1931 course that this very relation becomes thematic, occupying the center of Heidegger's attention.

On the Essence of Force

In his initial delimitation of *dunamis* in *Metaphysics* Θ, Aristotle indicates that while the usual sense of *dunamis* as *dunamis kata kinēsin* (*dunamis* with respect to movement) has multiple meanings, all are understood with reference to one and the same *eidos,* or form. All such forces are kinds of *archē,* kinds of origin, but all are understood with regard to one primary sense of *archē:* being an *archē* of *metabolē,* an origin of change, or of movement, *kinēsis.* Even though, as Aristotle tells us, this understanding of *dunamis* with respect to movement does not directly disclose the innermost essence of *dunamis,* it is nevertheless important to start from here in uncovering the properly ontological essence of force. Thus, what this most common sense tells us is of crucial significance: firstly, that *dunamis* is an *archē;* and second, that it is an *archē* of *metabolē* or *kinēsis,* where *metabolē* implies change in the sense of an overturning in which something turns over into something else, as the stone turns into and thus becomes a statue. Furthermore, Aristotle outlines, such an *archē* may be either in something other than that which changes, as in this example of the *technē* that originates or gives rise to the statue; or it may lie within one and the same being but in a different respect, as in the case of a doctor who heals himself: it is not qua patient that he heals himself; the *archē,* rather, lies in the healing art or *technē* that the patient happens also to have. Aristotle further stipulates two different kinds of force, both of which are grounded in the primary delimitation of force as an *archē metabolēs:* one is the power to be affected, *dunamis tou pathein,* a power to suffer, to undergo—where the *archē* is in the patient itself, in the entity undergoing change. (Heidegger translates this as *Ertragsamkeit,* "bearance," meaning the power to bear and sustain being changed.) In its very constitution, it implies a *dunamis tou poiein,* a force that can act upon it and bring forth that very change. The other kind of force is what Aristotle calls a *hexis apatheia:* a power to resist undergoing deterioration or annihilation in certain respects.

Now to every *dunamis kata kinēsin* there belongs the manner of its accomplishment, of its very unfolding: the "how" or way of its being, and thereby, as Heidegger puts it, a claim to the possible fulfillment of whatever the force directs itself toward. Because every force is intrinsically constituted as this very being under way toward possible fulfillment, there belongs to force the "how" of its unfolding, which may go well or go badly. In each case there is a going, a proceeding, a being under way, constitutive of force itself. But these considerations also tell us, Heidegger indicates, what it means to be an *archē* or origin in this context: an *archē* is not a thing, not some entity, but the being under way of force, a directional self-surpassing toward something other. The "how" belongs to the very essence of force (GA 33: 100–101; E 85).

Only following these considerations does Heidegger take up Aristotle's question of whether the forces of acting and being acted upon are one, or whether two distinct forces are meant. In a certain sense, as Aristotle tells us, they are one: the ability of material to be affected is, as Heidegger puts it, "implicated in the essence of the *dunamis tou poiein*" (GA 33: 105; E 89). The production or *poiēsis* of an axe is directed toward stone, bronze, iron, and the like, and not toward sand or water. And, conversely, the material to be acted upon must be suited to, must carry latent within itself a reference to particular kinds of actions that can be undertaken with it. Such, Heidegger remarks, is the ontological conception of *dunamis:* force itself is the relation of the *poiein* to *paschein.* The *archē tou poiein* and *archē tou paschein* are not two present-at-hand forces; nor does one force simply split into two independent, present-at-hand forces; rather, the very being of force entails "an outwardly directed implication," an originary divergence into two forces such that each implicates the other. On the other hand, it is equally possible to see the forces of acting and being acted upon as not one but two, namely, insofar as each is regarded as an independent, present-at-hand force. Here we mean not the Being of force itself, but the entity, the *subjectum,* that it is attributed to in each case: the patient acted upon and the agent that acts: this is the ontic conception. What Heidegger stresses here, however, is that Aristotle wants to make known "the inner cohesiveness of the ontological and ontic concept of force," the "ambiguity" that belongs to the essence of force (GA 33: 106; E 90). As Heidegger forcefully puts it, in a quite remarkable and altogether astonishing claim: the ontological unity of the Being of force, as "a unity of reflexive and inclusive relational being [*als Einheit des rück- und einbezüglichen Bezogenseins*], demands precisely the ontic discreteness and difference of beings, which always persist with the character of force-being, that is, are the 'subject' of force." If the Being of force is in a being, then that being is "split [*gespalten*] into two forces" (GA 33: 107; E 91). The ambiguity of force is thus, more carefully formulated, nothing other than the "simple, divisive essence" (*das zwiespältige, einfache Wesen*) of the Being of force. Yet what does this say but that force as such, when thought originarily—that is, as origin and origination itself—is not a regional phenomenon at all, but nothing less than Being itself? The Being of force is not a topic of regional inquiry: the Being of force is the force of Being.

I will come back to this most remarkable claim of Heidegger's later. For now, I shall round off this initial delimitation of force with a few words concerning the decisive phenomenon of *sterēsis,* or withdrawal, that pertains to the very essence of force and that must also, therefore, be latently at work within the Being of force. The question concerning the discordant and yet unitary Being of force as the relationship of *poiein* and *paschein,* acting and bearing, provides insight into the nature of the metabolic change, the overturning in and through beings themselves that may occur in the midst of this reciprocal relationship of forces. Force as *archē,* as the from-out-of-which that implicates into its own realm that which is intrinsically able to bear, "first provides a possible site for a turning over [*Umschlag*] from something to something" (GA 33: 115; E 97). Change, *metabolē,* belongs within this reciprocal relation: it is not to be understood one-sidedly as active transforming, nor with passive bearing simply added on, but as the reciprocal relation of both. The reciprocal relation of *poiein* and *paschein,* moreover, further illuminates the essence of force itself: that that which is in some way able to bear belongs to the domain of a force of producing means, first, that every such force delineates a realm for itself, within which it can be what it is (Heidegger characterizes this delineation as a kind of drawing: *Verzeichnung, Umzeichnung:* GA 33: 113; E 96). But this means, second, that every such force governs or dominates itself "in a peculiar sense," as Heidegger notes. And this implies, third, that force thus has a character of (self-)possession, one that is "difficult to grasp with sufficient generality." This character of possession is nothing other than the "implicating delineation" of force's proper domain in each instance. Yet that force has this character of possession means, fourthly, that force is thus intrinsically, in itself, exposed to the possibility of loss as a distinctive kind of withdrawal—distinctive because here unforce, *adunamia,* as *sterēsis,* is not simply the negation of force but a manner of being that belongs to that of which it is the withdrawal: the force itself. What is decisive here is that unforce remains bound to the realm of force that remains withdrawn from it—bound in and through the withdrawal itself (GA 33: 111; E 94). Thus, if a being does not have a power that, in accordance with its own essence, it ought to have—if, for example, a human being has lost the power to see (whether from being blind from birth, temporarily disabled, or simply because it is dark)—the inability to see is not a negation of the ability to see, but a steretic privation thereof, a withdrawal that, as withdrawal, is implicated in and takes its ownmost character from the ability to see *of* which it is the withdrawal. Every *sterēsis* brings with it a corresponding positive mode of Being. Inability, as withdrawal, as "standing in a withdrawal" (thus: as a standing that is still a kind of having, a not-having in being able to have[2]) is therefore quite different from a mere not-having, such as a rock's not having the ability to see. The modification from having to *sterēsis* is thus, Heidegger notes, "more essential" in the field of force than in other phenomena: "*dunamis* is in a preeminent sense bound and exposed to *sterēsis*" (GA 33: 112; E 95). When Aristotle says, then, that every force has a corresponding unforce in relation to and in accordance with the same phenomenon (1046 a30), he does not mean that on the one hand there is force and on the other hand its contrary, as though the two were phenomena independently present at hand. Rather, as Heidegger puts it, he means that "every force is, if it becomes unforce, the loss of its possession. It is unforce by virtue of one and the same thing by which force is forceful" (GA 33: 113; E 96). Heidegger here thinks *to auto*, "the same," ontologically: as the force of Being that is intrinsically bound and exposed to withdrawal.

Force and Logos

At this point I want to turn to Heidegger's account of a distinctive kind of force of change, a distinctive *dunamis* as *archē metabolēs:* that of *technē* as a *dunamis meta logou:* a force that occurs through and as *logos,* which Heidegger translates as *Kundschaft,* "notice" or "conversance," a making known and letting be manifest of beings as such. *Technē,* as a *dunamis meta logou,* is *archē metabolēs.* But what is the essential relation of force to *logos* here? And what is the relation of *logos* to the work to be produced by *technē*?

In a *dunamis meta logou,* the force in question belongs to an open, relational realm in which contraries are disclosed (*dēloi,* 1046 b8ff.): in doctoring, health and sickness, for example. In the case of forces without *logos,* such a realm is not given. Heat, for example, can produce only heat: its power does not stand within, or accomplish itself as, the possibility of contrary effects, of heat or cold. Yet in the case of a force that occurs through *logos*, the disclosure of contraries is not merely possible, but necessary, and thus constitutive of the force and of the accomplishment of force itself. To elucidate this, Heidegger first considers how, in *technē*, a work comes to be produced. All producing is directed toward a single end, the work or *ergon* to be produced, yet in such a way that every moment of the process of producing is interspersed with alternatives: this material, and not that; in this way, and not that. The process of bringing a material into its finished look is guided in advance by the anticipated *eidos* or look of the thing to be produced: the *eidos* is *telos* of the deliberative process that discloses it, but also, as such, *peras:* that which circumscribes and delimits. All production is, Heidegger remarks, a forging something into its boundaries (*in die Grenzen schlagen*), thus an enclosing that at the same time excludes; and this being-enclosed "is already in view in advance along with all that it includes *and* excludes" (GA 33: 138; E 118). In this sense, every work is in its essence "exclusive." Heidegger here speaks of a mutual enjoining of form and material: from the perspective of the *eidos,* the material, *hulē,* is as yet *apeiron,* unbounded; the *eidos,* by contrast, is boundary. "Both are directed away from one another *and yet* toward one another"; their lying opposite and facing one another is a "neighborhood"—a neighborhood, therefore, that is first enabled by the accomplishment of this force that is *dunamis meta logou* (GA 33: 139; E 118–119).

Yet Aristotle claims that *logos* is, as such, the ground of such givenness of contraries; thus, the inner connection between *eidos* and *logos,* the way in which *eidos* is *logos,* must be made visible. The *archē* of *technē* is an antecedent taking into view the outward appearance, the *eidos,* that will henceforth guide the process of production. Yet this *eidos* that is *logos* is not something independently present or already given. It must first be brought to appearance, come into view. This taking into view can occur only as the forming of a view or aspect, as the formation of a model that entails a "bringing into bounds" of what belongs to the model—thus, as a "selecting, a selective gathering of what belongs together, a *legein*" (GA 33: 142; E 121). All *logos,* as *legomenon,* is the *work* of this originary gathering or *legein,* an antecedent gathering of something into its bounds as this and not that, a selecting that is intrinsically an addressing of something as this and not that.

The *eidos,* as what has thus been selected, "assumes leadership in the entire process of production." It says what is to be produced and does so in such a way that it excludes whatever lies outside its bounds—yet in such a way that, nevertheless, "this other is constantly present along with it." But this means, indeed, that it includes the contrary with it, as its neighbor, so to speak: "the contrary is there and manifest in a peculiar way in the very fact of avoiding it and getting out of its way" (*ihm aus dem Weg gehen:* GA 33: 142–143; E 122). It is manifest, not directly or in itself, but incidentally—but this means: not by chance, but in the sense of "necessarily following along with something else." Getting out of the way of the contrary is at once a removal, a "taking away" or "carrying away" (*Wegbringen, Wegtrag:* GA 33: 135; E 115) of the contrary, and thereby, at the same time, the opening up of a way, of another way or path along which force itself can strike out or proceed.

In this way, we can understand how and why *logos* is, as Heidegger puts it, "the ground of the fact that the *enantia* announce themselves as such in every process of production." All *logos* is what it is only in and for a *legein,* a selective addressing as . . . that gathers a being into presence in advance of its actuality, that is, into and in the possibility of its Being. As intrinsically gathering and selective, *legein* is, however, thoroughly divisive, *zwiespältig:* it is a separating off and separating out of whatever can enter the neighborhood of the force it enables, the force that follows in its wake. In making manifest a possibility, Heidegger insists, the essence of *logos* is a giving notice (*Kundgabe*), a giving of something as something, indeed, necessarily so, and this because all giving is a response to a "receptive not-having." The not-having is primary: a not-having (not yet, never yet) in nevertheless being open for what could be had, but never can be. Why not? Because in every saying, in every giving of something as something,

> This receptive taking, as not-having, is only partially a taking into possession of something, because that which is to be possessed always remains other. Partially [*teil-weise*] means: always in this or that respect, always as this or that. With this "as" it is always a this or that which is decided upon and separated out. (GA 33: 144–145; E 123)

A book manifests itself to me as heavy, it gives notice of itself, of its own accord, and in this announcement the book's being heavy is separated out from its being grey, German, philosophical, and so forth (this does not preclude, of course, that these aspects may well belong together in one and the same book). This inaugural separating out, or *Teilung*, is also the ground of the possibility of my communicating this property of the book to others, of *Mit-teilung*. Yet in this initial separating out, the book remains itself: it is taken into possession only partially (*teil-weise*), in this one aspect—and, we might add, only temporarily, only for a time. What is thus taken into possession always remains other in its very Being: the otherness pertains to the happening of Being in beings, not to something like a physical alterity: for physicality is itself in turn only one aspect of the thing's self-showing. This partial taking into possession, is, however, for its part, grounded in an antecedent not-having. This antecedent and receptive not-having, as an openness for receiving the gift of Being is, however, in no way overcome by such partial taking into possession but must remain the not-having that it is: a not-having that is, nevertheless, directed toward the possibility of taking into possession. Yet this very directedness can accomplish itself and be the directedness that it is only by being *zwiespältig*, only by itself undergoing decision, a scission that, at a single stroke (*Schlag*), both opens and closes it, a stroke by which it enables itself—as force—by first relinquishing an indeterminate possibility of its own Being. Heidegger gestures toward this in asking why the "as" belongs to *logos*. It is, he says, because all giving notice belongs to notification (*Kundschaft*), and notification is originally a response to exploring or inquiring (*Erkunden*). "To explore, however, is necessarily to strike out on a way [*Weg-einschlagen*]. It is always the choice of one way *by* giving up others . . . the assuming of one position *and* the relinquishing of others" (GA 33: 145; E 124, emphasis added).

This thought is difficult. Yet what is of decisive importance here, Heidegger quietly indicates, is that this relinquishing of other paths is not only the opening up and thus already the venturing forth upon one particular path of human existence on the part of this *dunamis meta logou*, this force that human existence itself is. What is of decisive importance, rather, is that what is thereby relinquished is not simply abandoned. It is neither entirely lost nor forgotten: it does not disappear into utter concealment or sheer non-being. Rather, Heidegger suggests, what is thus relinquished or foregone, in all its indeterminacy, thereby first comes into Being and is precisely thereby preserved as such. It first enters, quietly accompanies, the neighborhood of force. Heidegger indeed here writes of a "birth":

> This *inner boundary* belongs to notification. The adopting of one course of exploring *and thus* the *simultaneous birth* of other courses that remain unexplored. This inner boundary is also the ownmost power [*Macht*] of notification. Therein lies the potential assurance of greatness in the venture of human existence. (GA 33: 145; E 124, emphasis added)

Striking out upon one particular path, venturing forth into the unknown, indirectly and altogether inconspicuously gives birth, in its wake, so to speak, to other possible courses. These unexplored other paths or courses in this way come to constitute the reserve of Being as such, through which the force of Being comes to pass. *Dunamis meta logou:* the *meta* here means, says Heidegger: "following in the wake of something, going after it and guided by it—by *logos*" (GA 33: 146–147; E 125, translation modified). The receptive not-having that directs itself toward the possibility of an (always partial) taking into possession constitutes itself (as possibility, ever indeterminate) only by submitting itself to decision, only in and through a submission to *logos*. But how can it submit itself before it has been constituted? It must, rather, first find itself thrown into this possibility: find itself by first coming to itself in the wake of its very thrownness. And this is its submission to language, its letting itself be spoken, as the instituting of a trace of itself—of what never will have been entirely determinate, of a force that follows in the wake of *logos*. Letting oneself be spoken, Heidegger notes—as *Sichsagenlassen:* letting something be said to oneself, that is, to the self that is not yet, the phenomenon of hearing as such—letting oneself be spoken does not mean "making words" but "desiring to proceed in this way or that, that is, already proceeding [*vorgehen*]" (GA 33: 146; E 124).

Logos and Desire

The gathering that is at work within the force of *technē*—a gathering that occurs as the silent dialogue of the self with itself, of the force of Being with itself, guiding the path of production—this gathering thus first springs from the inner divisiveness of *legein* as such.[3] What precedes, what leads the way as the very striking out upon a way (a way that always will have been a determinate way) is this divisiveness itself. Indeed, "the gatheredness of producing springs forth [*entspringt*] out of the essence of *logos* as gathering" (GA 33: 153; E 131), yet this gatheredness, the unity of conversance, is always, as Heidegger puts it, "a winning back" (GA 33: 145; E 124).

The "inner divisiveness of *logos*" is, therefore, "the origin and root of a proliferation into individual *logoi*" (GA 33: 153; E 131); the clarification of this divisive essence of *logos* for its part first shows "how and why it is that *logos,* at one with its divisiveness, must be dispersed into a *multiplicity* [*Vielfältigkeit*] of expository sayings and assertions, or better: why it is always already found split up and scattered in this way" (GA 33: 145; E 124). The unity of the self, of the force of Being that proceeds, that ventures forth and forges a path, proceeding as a dialogue or "taking counsel" with itself, is thus only ever a retrogressive unity, the desire to recover or retrieve that which has always already undergone division and dispersion. All gathering presupposes, answers to, an antecedent splitting. When Heidegger writes of *logos* as a conversant gathering and gatheredness of beings in One, that is, in the unity of the force of Being that is Dasein itself, he thus places this "One" in scare-quotes: it means, he adds, "Dasein that is at the same time dispersion [*Zerstreuung*]"[4] (GA 33: 128; E 109, translation modified).

The force of Being that is *dunamis meta logou* can thus come to itself and so *be* itself only by letting itself undergo such divisiveness. It can actualize itself as potentiality, as *dunamis,* and thus be a never entirely actual force, only in becoming the other of itself—of the self that it never yet was (since Being, or the "not yet," is constituted only in and through this originary closure). Yet this is possible only if force has already struck out upon a path, seeking to surpass and thereby preserve "itself" as this very self-surpassing, as "this" force, where the "this" will always be an aftereffect, consequent upon the originary work of force. Force can come to possess "itself" only as desire.[5]

Every *dunamis meta logou* thus occurs through and as a conversance (*logos*) that is orientated toward contraries, yet in such a way that the soul, according to Aristotle, in "having" *logos* also "has" within it an *archē* for movement (GA 33: 149; E 127). How is it possible for a *dunamis meta logou* to be an *archē* of movement? There is a strange double having here, a doubling within the very Being of being an *archē,* such that there are, as Heidegger puts it, "two *archai,* so to speak, and then again, only one." What is at stake in this doubling within the Being of force itself? "Having" *logos* means, as we have seen, being directed and guided by *logos.* The soul's "having" an *archē* of movement means, as Heidegger translates it, that the soul within itself holds and "holds before itself" such an *archē* (GA 33: 149–150; E 127–128). The "soul" or *psuchē* is nothing other than the Being of force itself, the primary *entelecheia* (being toward an end: a gathering that "has" and thus is, itself before itself, in advance of itself) of a natural body that "has" life in the manner of *dunamis*, of potentiality or force.[6]

The soul's being an *archē* of movement entails that it be able to move itself in relation to an other—whether a being that is other than itself, or that being that, within itself, is the other of itself. All self-moving, however, is a fleeing or pursuit (*phugē* or *diōxis*), protecting oneself from . . . or taking into possession . . . , and is always *heneka tinos*, for the sake of something, such that the *telos*, what is to be accomplished (the *prakton*) is there, is given, as something striven after, as an object of desire: the *orekton* (GA 33: 150; E 128). This, the *orekton*, is the *archē* of *kinēsis* that the soul "has": has not as a property but as "a holding itself in relation to" in which comportment the *orekton* is made known as such. "This having, *echein*," as Heidegger elucidates, "does not simply mean having in itself, as some sort of property, but having something in the manner of a holding itself in relation to [*Sich-dazu-verhalten*], of a comportment—whereby that at which the comportment is directed is made known somehow in and through this comportment itself" (GA 33: 151; E 129), Thus, the *archē* of *poiēsis* in *technē*, as an *epistēmē poiētikē*, a knowing that is directed toward production, is not only or primarily the *logos* as *eidos*, but—"even prior to this"—an *orekton*, an object of desire, as "yet another *archē*." As Aristotle explains in the *De Anima*, it is the *orekton* that properly moves, and not just the *eidos* (433 a28). In this sense, then, "there are, as it were, two *archai*, and yet, then again, only one": as with all force, production is directed toward one single *telos*, and yet this *telos* is given only in and through a separating out of the *archē* that manifests it as a possible object of desire.

This clarifies the *way* in which the *enantia*, the contraries, are given: because the *archē* of *dunamis meta logou* is an *orekton prakton legomenon*, it is related to the contraries in the manner of *orexis* itself, as flight or pursuit. The contraries are thus given not in or as something at hand, such as the end product, but "*in* the production and *for* this." "The care [*Sorgfalt*] which belongs to production unites both in itself: holding to the right path and avoiding going off track" (GA 33: 152; E 130, emphasis added). Thus, the contraries are separated out and thus first given in and through the divisiveness that is at work in the very being under way of force.

And yet something more is implied in the assertion that the *archē* is "two, and yet only one." What can this mean? The *archē* is one that nevertheless is two: it is *orexis* that is one—in each case one single *orexis* that seeks to unfold itself—but that means one that is under way toward itself as such; which is to say, one that must first have become and thus already be other than itself, the other *of* itself, other to itself within itself; and thereby first enable itself as a relating to itself: as being itself. The Being of force constitutes itself as such, in its unity, only in always already having undergone a splitting of itself that is nothing other than its entry into ekstatic temporality: a temporalizing of itself as ekstatic, the *ekstatikon* that is, as *Being and Time* put it, "an originary 'outside itself' in and for itself" (SZ 329).

In this sense, the intrinsic self-divergence of a *dunamis empsuchon* as *orexis* would be due to a structural necessity within the very Being of *orexis* itself. And this indeed is what Heidegger asserts: *every* force is, as such, constituted by an inner, essential finitude (GA 33: 158; E 135). Yet we must be careful here. In the case of the *dunamis meta logou,* Heidegger emphasizes throughout that this force *follows* the *logos:* it accomplishes itself only on the basis of a relation to *logos,* of a divergence, therefore, that accomplishes its own being as a striving that is a striving *after* logos. Here, the *orekton* is always already a *legomenon.* In other words, the manner in which the *archē* is doubled (steps outside of itself so as to be able to return to itself, to gather itself into itself—or let itself be gathered into itself) occurs here as a *legein,* that is, as a "receptive not-having" in which what is not had—the Being of things themselves, including, therefore, the Being of language itself as manifest—gives itself in partially being taken into possession while always remaining other. Thus, the pursuit and avoidance that is the hallmark of all *orexis* is, in *dunamis meta logou,* always already articulated as a *legein.* Yet this implies that what is primarily pursued and at the same time avoided in such *dunamis* is *logos* itself: having *logos,* as a striving relating to *logos,* is grounded in not-having as the more primary phenomenon.[7] And thus, as Heidegger says, *orexis* is "earlier" (GA 33: 151; E 129).

In other words, to say that the *archē* is both two and one does not mean that the two *archai* are *orexis,* on the one hand, and *logos* on the other, such that *logos* would simply get added to the already intrinsically divergent structure of *orexis.* Rather, in a *dunamis meta logou* this divisiveness is unique in that what is avoided is nonetheless held close by, potentially present, latent, in such a way that it constitutes this force (GA 33: 143; E 122; GA 33: 152; E 130). Such *dunamis* follows "in the wake of *logos.*"

If the Being of force is in a being, Heidegger noted, then that being is "split [*gespalten*] into two forces." The "how," the particular path of force, necessarily belongs to force precisely because, as Heidegger puts it, "force as *dunamis meta logou* is from the bottom up [*von Hause aus*] *doubly* directed and *bi*furcated [zwie*gerichtet* und zwie*spältig*]." Such force proceeds within the necessity of the "either-or" because withdrawal and notness (*Nichtigkeit*) belong to the very essence of force, as its "inner finitude"—because, that is, as Heidegger also puts it, the force that is directed by discourse "is *of* the not [*nichtig*] in an originary sense, that is, shot through with this not and no" (GA 33: 157; E 134). Yet this decision belonging to the force of Being is not simply a splitting into contraries but, as Heidegger indicated, a multiplication or originary dissemination that seeks refuge, or takes up home, in force's own, constitutive withdrawal as its innermost recourse. Every force carries within itself and for itself the possibility of sinking into un-force. But in the case of *dunamis meta logou*, this negativum, Heidegger notes, "does not simply stand beside the positive of force as its opposite, but haunts [*lauert . . . auf*] this force in the force itself, and this because every force of this type according to its essence is invested with divisiveness and so with a 'not'" (GA 33: 154; E 132). Every *dunamis meta logou* is *haunted* by the possibility of its own, constitutive, and yet altogether indeterminate impossibility that lies in wait for it as, in the wake of logos, it accomplishes the finitude of its own being under way. Thus haunted, it is *unheimlich*, uncanny through and through, *von Hause aus*.

In Force of Language

A few remarks by way of conclusion. If the human being was determined by the Greeks as *zōon logon echon*, this was not, according to Heidegger, wrong or inaccurate, but it left undetermined or underdetermined the mode of Being of both the *zōon* and, more emphatically still, of the *logos*, which were interpreted along the lines of *ousia* as simply present at hand. What is meant by this "having" *logos*? This living force that the human being is has *logos* in the same way that it has "within" it an *archē* of movement: as an object of desire; it is not the having of some property (*Eigenschaft*, or *ousia*), but, as Heidegger argues, having in the manner of relating oneself to it—a relating in which that which is related to—here, *logos* itself—is itself made known, or disclosed (GA 33: 151; E 129). This *echein*, this having, he says, has the meaning of Being: it means that humans carry and conduct themselves on the basis of this having; it means, indeed, a "disposing over" language, but as a force of language that comes into being and is "above all through conversance (*logos*)" (GA 33: 128; E 108–109). Yet such force, Heidegger will later show, can enact itself—that is, come to itself and come into being, not as something actual but precisely as force—only as the other of itself. It does so in accomplishing, as Heidegger expresses it, a "transition," a transition that is a passing over, not into something else in the sense of something that would on each occasion be present at hand but as a letting itself be guided over into something that "first forms itself in and through the transitioning" itself: into an enactment in and through which force, in forming in advance for itself that which (as the other of itself) can be mastered, forms itself into its own accomplishment, yet in so doing precisely transforms itself—never to return as it once was (GA 33: 191–192; E 164–165).

It is on account of this poietic moment within the very being of force as *dunamis meta logou,* a poietic moment that guides in advance the very gathering of force (and this is the gathering that Heidegger will later name a destining: a gathering that first gathers the human being onto a certain path or way of revealing[8])—it is on account of this poietic moment, no doubt, that Heidegger identifies the originary emergence and origin of language as *Dichtung,* "poetizing": poetizing, not as the business of writers but as "the proclamation [*Ausruf*] of world in the invocation [*Anruf*] of the god." Or, as he also puts it:

> Being in force of language—; language, however, not merely as a means of asserting and communicating, which indeed it also is, but language as that wherein the openness and conversance of world first irrupts [*aufbricht*] and is. (GA 33: 128; E 109, translation modified)

NOTES

1. If, in *Being and Time,* "discourse" or *Rede* was meant to signify the original sense of the Greek *logos* (SZ 165) and was understood as the articulation of understandability—thus, of the projection of possibilities disclosed for understanding—nevertheless both the manner in which such articulation is accomplished and the negativity and finitude implicit in this were not brought to light. The 1931 course takes up this task via its interpretation of *logos* and *dunamis* in *Metaphysics* Θ.

2. It would be instructive here to compare this analysis of *sterēsis* to Heidegger's characterization, in the 1929–1930 course *The Fundamental Concepts of Metaphysics* (GA 29/30), of the animal's "poverty in world" as a "not-having in

being able to have"—all the more so since Heidegger here, in the 1931 course, comes closer than anywhere else to conceding, with Aristotle, that, insofar as *aisthēsis* is a *logos tis*, the animal perhaps indeed has a kind of *logos*, that the *dunamis* of its very being is also subject to a *legein*. See GA 33: 126–127; E 107–108.

3. "This dialogue is the inner unfolding of *logos*, and is itself *logos*. A (silent) deliberation directs the individual steps of producing" (GA 33: 146; E 125, translation amended).

4. This dispersion of Dasein is presumably one and the same as that identified in the *Metaphysical Foundations of Logic* as grounded in Dasein's thrownness, that is, in the happening of an originary *Streuung* or *Mannigfaltigung* that was there said to be "in a quite determinate respect *Zerstreuung*" (GA 26: 173). Origination as multiplication of the "origin" is grounded in the ekstatic constitution of temporality itself, as we shall indicate below in passing.

5. How, and in what way, and to what extent this is the case also in living beings that do not have—or do not appear to have—*logos*, and in particular how the object of desire is also "somehow made known" in and for such beings—these are questions in their own right, questions of which Heidegger's interpretation remains mindful throughout but which are not explicitly taken up or addressed in this essay. The following remarks pertain specifically to the *dunamis meta logou*.

6. On the *psuchē* as the primary *entelecheia* of a natural body having the potential for life, see *De Anima*, Bk. II, 412 a20f.

7. Not-having: that is to say, concealment as withdrawal that announces itself, draws us into its very withdrawal. *Zōon logon echon—mē echon. Echein*: having = being in the force of . . . , being able to . . . ; not having as withdrawal: not being able to speak because of accident/illness; not being able to find the right word—presupposes a standing in the possibility of the word, standing in withdrawal, in a withdrawal that is thus constitutive of that of which it is the withdrawal.

8. See, for example, "The Question Concerning Technology": *Ge-stell*, "enframing," is the antecedent gathering (*das Versammelnde*) that sets upon man, challenging him to reveal the real as standing reserve; this gathering that first brings man onto a given path is the meaning of a "destining" of Being: "'To start upon a way' means 'to send' in our ordinary language. We shall call that sending-that-gathers [*versammelnde Schicken*] which first starts man upon a way of revealing, *destining* [*Geschick*]" (TK 24; E 24).

WORKS CITED

GA 26 Heidegger, *Metaphysische Anfangsgründe der Logik im Ausgang von Leibniz* (Frankfurt am Main: Klostermann, 1978). Translated as *The Metaphysical Foundations of Logic*, by Michael Heim (Bloomington: Indiana University Press, 1984).

GA 29/30 Heidegger, *Die Grundbegriffe der Metaphysik: Welt—Endlichkeit—Einsamkeit* (Frankfurt am Main: Klostermann, 1983). Translated as *The Fundamental Concepts of Metaphysics: World, Finitude, Solitude*, by William McNeill and Nicholas Walker (Bloomington: Indiana University Press, 1995).

GA 33 Heidegger, *Aristoteles, Metaphysik Θ1–3: Von Wesen und Wirklichkeit der Kraft* (Frankfurt am Main: Klostermann, 1990). Translated as *Aristotle's Metaphysics Θ 1–3: On the Essence and Actuality of Force*, by Walter Brogan and Peter Warnek (Bloomington: Indiana University Press, 1995).

SZ Heidegger, *Sein und Zeit*. 15 Auflage (Tübingen: Niemeyer, 1984). Translated as *Being and Time*, by John Macquarrie and Edward Robinson (New York: HarperCollins, 1962).

TK Heidegger, *Die Technik und die Kehre* (Pfullingen: Neske, 1991). Translated as *The Question Concerning Technology and Other Essays*, by William Lovitt (New York: Harper & Row, 1977).

FOUR

The Secret Homeland of Speech: Heidegger on Language, 1933–1934

Richard Polt

> I keep silent in my thinking—not just since 1927, since the publication of *Being and Time*, but *in* that book itself, and constantly before then.[1]

In the fall of 1933, Professor and Rector Martin Heidegger announces to his students that he has overturned his former understanding of language and silence. Whereas *Being and Time* described speaking and keeping silent as two modes of discourse, Heidegger now sees speech and discourse themselves as founded on a deep silence in which the world is disclosed.

Heidegger's next course, his first after stepping down as rector, is explicitly devoted to "logic as the question concerning the essence of language," which he links to the essence of the *Volk*. But many issues here remain implicit and unspoken. In particular, Heidegger draws no connections between his reflections on silence in the first lecture-course and his reflections on community in the second. As regards the political dimension of silence, Heidegger keeps silent.

How telling is this silence? Can we reveal some of what Heidegger keeps concealed? Is it an accident that silence gains importance for him just when he is speaking out publicly to support and interpret the Nazi revolution, yet experiencing friction with elements of the new regime? A short piece that Heidegger wrote for an audience beyond the confines of academia can help us gain some insight into the Heideggerian politics of silence—which, I will argue, suffers from a fatal misunderstanding of the political. Nevertheless, Heidegger's inquiries into language from this period remain pertinent and provocative, as we can see when we ask his questions in new contexts.

Discourse, Language, and Silence in *Being and Time*

Being and Time presents discourse (*Rede*) as a fundamental characteristic of Dasein. Discourse is the tendency of Dasein's being-in-the-world to get articulated, in the root sense of developing limbs and joints. Our lives and environs emerge as possessing a certain physiognomy: certain features are more rigid than others, certain developments tend to occur along certain lines, and a network of significance and purpose—a world—becomes apparent to us in our operations. As we do things, things become meaningful articles in an articulated whole.

Discourse is the basis of language, because "to significations, words accrue" (SZ 161)[2]: language as we ordinarily think of it, a vocabulary and a grammar, responds to the exigencies of the articulation of being-in-the-world. If, as we say, it is the responsibility of language to cut the world along its joints, then language is indebted to the jointure or articulation that discourse achieves.

The phenomenon of keeping silent interests Heidegger here in part because, like many negative or "deficient" phenomena, it points to a deeper structure, serving as an exception that proves the rule. Both language and silence manifest a more fundamental phenomenon: discourse. We ordinarily oppose speech to silence, but Heidegger emphasizes that both can be significant. In fact, silence can often say more (SZ 164). Think of a refusal to answer, a discreet omission, a pregnant pause, a delayed reply. In context, these telling silences can be highly revealing—they can be appropriate ways to cut a situation along its joints. "Reticence" can be a deep form of communication with others (SZ 165) and even with oneself—for one's own conscience addresses one silently (SZ 277).

Because Dasein is being-with, discourse and language necessarily have public and communal dimensions. The interpersonal articulation of the world normally takes the form of "idle talk," the everyday chatter that reinforces truisms (SZ §35). However, Heidegger hints at a deeper political role that language might play: *Being and Time*'s brief but crucial exploration of the ontological basis of authentic politics, section 74, proposes that the people must discover the destiny of a new generation through "communicating" and "struggling" (SZ 384). Such communication could not be idle talk; it would have to break new ground.

Even though *Being and Time* has little to say about the political dimension of language, Heidegger had addressed the issue in earlier texts, such as his 1924 lectures on Aristotle.[3] When he embarks on his own political venture, Heidegger returns to the relation between language and community with renewed passion.

Winter Semester 1933–1934: Silence as the Basis of Language

In his lecture-course of winter semester 1933–1934, *On the Essence of Truth,* Heidegger revisits his 1931–1932 analysis of truth in Plato.[4] As a preface to this analysis, he provokes us to inquire into truth and being with an interpretation of Heraclitus's *polemos* fragment and a significant reflection on language, whose main points we will now consider.

We are open to beings as such and as a whole, Heidegger claims, because we are exposed to the "superior power of Being." This exposure impels us to speak, and also sets us apart from both animals and divinities—for it would be "impossible for a god to 'speak'" (101/80).[5]

These remarks are implicitly political, if we recall Aristotle's famous statement that one who needs no *polis* is either a beast or a god (*Politics* 1.2). We might infer that, for Heidegger, just as Dasein is thrown into being, it must also be thrown into both language and community. In fact, Aristotle himself draws a connection between *logos* and the *polis:*

> That man is much more a political animal than any kind of bee or any herd animal is clear. For, as we assert, nature does nothing in vain; and man alone among the animals has speech [*logos*]. The voice indeed indicates the painful and pleasant, and hence is present in other animals as well; for their nature has come this far, that they have a perception of the painful and pleasant and indicate these things to each other. But speech serves to reveal the advantageous and the harmful, and hence also the just and the unjust. For it is peculiar to man as compared to the other animals that he alone has a perception of good and bad and just and unjust . . . and partnership in these things is what makes a household and a city.[6]

Of course, Aristotle's interpretation of *logos* is not identical to Heidegger's interpretation of language and of the understanding of Being. In this particular passage, a significant difference may lie in Aristotle's reference to justice as a theme for *logos.* As we saw, Heidegger claims in

Being and Time that a generation must work out its shared destiny through struggle and communication, but he does not mention that debates over what is just are at the heart of this process.[7] We will return to this point.

As Heidegger continues his train of thought in 1933, he refers to language as political debate over justice only in passing, as part of his account of the rise of the "logical-grammatical conception of language." For the Greeks,

> speaking, discourse, is speaking with one another, public transaction, advising, assemblage of the people, judicial proceedings; speaking of this kind is having a public opinion and consulting, deliberating, and *thinking*. And in connection with the question of *what* thinking and opining and understanding and knowing are, contemplation arrives at *discourse*, speaking, as what is immediately accessible and in reach of the senses. Discourse is *given* and *is*, just as are many other things; it "is" as the Greeks understood the Being of beings: the available, stamped, durable presence of something. Language is something present at hand. (102/81)

Heidegger's story, then, is that for the Greeks, language or discourse (*logos*) was one present-at-hand entity among others, which could become the object of study (cf. SZ 159). Language, however, is a distinctive present-at-hand entity, from the Greek point of view, because it has the power to attribute a present-at-hand predicate to a present-at-hand object by forming assertions, such as "The stone is hard" (103/81). Greek logic takes such assertions as the paradigmatic expression of thinking, where thinking is understood as theorizing, or ascertaining what is present at hand. Greek grammar, in turn, is dominated by Greek logic. In this way, our traditional interpretations of language are pervaded by the unquestioned ancient interpretation of being as presence at hand (103–104/82).

This narrow interpretation of language, Heidegger protests, "is *a monstrous violation of what language accomplishes*." It cannot do justice to what happens in a conversation or poem, where much more is at work than the assertion of facts about the present-at-hand; "the tone of voice, the cadence, the melody of the sentences, the rhythm, and so on" may convey a way of being-in-the-world or an encounter with being itself, not just beings (104/82). The usual logico-grammatical prejudice would define these dimensions of meaning in a way that takes assertion as the paradigm: they are connotative rather than denotative, sense rather than reference, subjective rather than objective, or artistic embellishments separable from the factual content.[8] Even when Romanticism celebrates subjectivity and imagination, it fails to overcome these hackneyed distinctions. In contrast, Heidegger focuses on how the event of language in its entirety reveals both beings and being, without consigning any part of this event to the merely subjective domain. (We might add here that rhythm depends on pauses between beats, silences between sounds; Heidegger is starting, then, to approach the question of silence.)

At this point he attacks the further prejudice that language is a kind of sign that expresses thought. Such notions are taken for granted by linguistics, which, as the empirical science of language as an entity, is inherently inferior to a philosophical consideration of being (105/84)—such as a reflection on the ontology of language and signs. Such ontological reflection would have to ask a number of questions (106/84): Is language in fact just one species of sign, or are there human signs only because we already exist in language? Do we speak only in order to signify things, or are things available for us to signify only because we can speak—that is, because language first allows beings to display themselves in their proper power? Do we speak in order to express thoughts, or do we speak because we can keep silent? Is silence a negation, or is it something positive and profound, whereas speaking is the negation of keeping silent? Heidegger prefers the second, less obvious alternatives. He turns now to his proposal that "*The ability to keep silent is . . . the origin and ground of language*" (107/84).

Heidegger first distinguishes silence, in his sense, from the quietness of an inanimate object, a beast, or a mute; genuinely keeping silent is the prerogative of someone who is able to speak (107–109/85–86). To avoid a misunderstanding: there is no need to assume that Heidegger favors audible speech over other forms of language. A mute person who knows sign language can speak, in a broad sense, and can keep silent by refraining from gestures; but someone so disabled that no communication is possible is incapable of keeping silent. Here we might also note that German uses one word, *schweigen,* instead of a phrase such as our "keep silent." It is clearer in German that keeping silent is something one does, a verb—so it can be a meaningful event, not a static absence.

But so far, as Heidegger acknowledges, he simply seems to be repeating the claim in *Being and Time* that both language and silence are modes of discourse. Now he wants to go further:

> I did not see what really has to follow from this starting point: keeping silent is not just an *ultimate* possibility of discourse, but discourse and language *arise from* keeping silent. In recent years, I have gone back over these relationships and worked them through. This obviously cannot be explained here. Not even the different manners of keeping silent, the multiplicity of its causes and grounds, and certainly not the different levels and depths of reticence. Now only as much will be communicated as is needed for the advancement of our questioning. (110/87)

As Heidegger remarks earlier, simply keeping silent about silence would be inadequate—it would leave silence unexamined and let it seem to be an emotional, inarticulate, "mystical" matter.[9] But chattering on and on about silence would suggest that one does not understand what one is talking about (107/85). While we can grant Heidegger this point, we can only wish that he had communicated more of his thoughts on silence.

He does, however, convey an essential idea: profound silence is "*the gathered disclosedness for the overpowering surge of beings as a whole.*" Disclosedness, or being opened up (*Aufgeschlossenheit*), does not mean attending to "every random attraction and incident" but being receptive to the arising of what is, as such and as a whole. "Gathering" here does not mean an egocentric domination or taciturn stubbornness but a kind of self-discipline that keeps one wholly focused on the whole of beings: "the gathering of one's entire comportment so that this comportment holds to itself and so is bound in itself and thereby remains properly oriented and fully exposed to the beings to which it relates" (111/87).

The primordial "reticence" (*Verschwiegenheit*) of keeping silent lends sense and coherence to any words that may emerge from it (111/87–88). Words, then, "break silence"—but as long as they do not become uprooted, free-floating chatter, they still bear witness to silence and draw their power from it. The power of silence empowers us to face the superior power of being and empowers words to reveal beings (111–112/88).[10] The primordial gathering of silence enables words to gather beings and disclose them in their gatheredness (114–116/90–91). This gathering power of language is what the Greeks (according to Heidegger) named in the word *logos,* derived from *legein* in the sense of assembling.[11] (Heidegger adds that for the Greeks, *logos* and philosophy retain a connection to *mythos,* the kind of language that indicates and hints rather than grasping the togetherness of beings: 116/91–92.) The gathering power of the word draws on the fundamental power of silence as it assists a being in coming forth.

In less Heideggerian terms, we could say that our words are most telling when we do not presume that they are completely adequate to their task. Deep speech is not self-sufficient but must pause frequently to *listen*—and what we hear when we listen in the right way is not more speech but the silent oneness of the world. We must attend to our pre-linguistic sense of what things mean as we try to find the words that best reveal what *is* in the moment.

This process, Heidegger notes, is not captured by standard notions of the sign. A word does not *signify* a being, as if we encountered them separately and then established a relation between them; instead we find a unified phenomenon, "*the being in the word*" (114/90). (Consider how when English speakers hear an "s" at the end of a noun, they immediately *feel* the plurality of the things in question.) The distinction between signifier and signified is not illegitimate, but it is a theoretical concept that remains dependent on a more basic experience of the disclosure of beings in language. Beings and words emerge together from the unspoken gatheredness of what is.

All these remarks are pregnant but undeveloped, or at least they keep many points tacit. One notable unexplained shift from *Being and Time* is that Heidegger no longer distinguishes discourse from language; he uses the terms *Rede, Sprache,* and *Wort* as near synonyms. The work of articulating being-in-the-world is now done by reticence, not discourse; instead of discourse as the basis for both language and meaningful silence, we have silence as the basis for discourse or language. To silence, words accrue.

It might seem that this is simply a change in terminology: one could argue that if "discourse" in *Being and Time* is prior to language, then discourse in this sense is already silent. However, Heidegger's substitution of "silence" for "discourse" may have a substantive force. The significance of the world is no longer brought out by Dasein's practical pursuits—its articulative appropriation of ready-to-hand articles for the sake of a way in which Dasein can be. Significance comes forth, instead, when we set things aside and listen—in a state not unrelated to the Aristotelian "leisure" that Heidegger mentions in *Being and Time* (SZ 138). There, Heidegger seems unsure whether theoretical disengagement from practice is anything more than a deficiency.[12] Now, however, the non-practical (though not theoretical) reticence that gathers beings as a whole is a positive, founding experience—a deep attunement to being. This emphasis on our thrown exposure to being is central to Heidegger's turn away from transcendental philosophy after *Being and Time:* rather than seeing the structures of our being-in-the-world as conditions of possibility for the being of beings, we must understand ourselves as subject to the event in which being is given to us. Our dependent receptivity is silent.

However, we should not exaggerate the difference between 1927 and 1933 in this regard: Heidegger's discussion of "reticence" in 1933 is akin to *Being and Time*'s account of anxiety (an experience of the nullity of all entities for which "everyday discourse" is inadequate, SZ 187) and the call of conscience (which discourses in silence, SZ 277). Perhaps once we admit that these profound modes of disclosure are wordless, it "has to follow" that silence is the most fundamental phenomenon (110/87).

There is another question that Heidegger leaves unasked in these lectures: *who* is keeping silent? It is easy to get the impression from this text that language ultimately stems from the silent experience of an individual, something akin to the radically solitary experiences of anxiety and the call of conscience. But could a whole community experience primordial silence?

Summer Semester 1934: Language and People

Heidegger's next lecture-course explores the connection between language and *Volk*. Heidegger later portrayed this course as an act of resistance against Nazism.[13] The truth is more complex. His lectures can be seen as engaged in an internal debate within Nazism, siding against biological reductionism but still accepting the premise that a *Volk* needs a strong state, a state that establishes an "order of rank" (165/137)[14] rather than a liberal society grounded on a social contract (143/119). Heidegger's arguments are politically charged and laced with contemporary imagery, such as service in the SA (50/44, 73/63) and Hitler's visit to Mussolini (83/71). But the text rises above the level of propaganda, as Heidegger refuses to let his audience rest content with unquestioned, one-dimensional concepts of phenomena such as *Volk* and race (60–61/53–54, 65/57).

Heidegger's train of thought in these lectures must be understood as a sequence of questions (summarized at 78/67, 97/81–82, 114–115/95–96).

First of all, what is logic?[15] It is normally understood as the science of the formal rules of assertion, and assertions confront us primarily within language (5/4).

Most logicians give little thought to so-called "natural language" and focus instead on developing precise, formal rules for constructing propositions and ascertaining their implications. The enterprise proceeds under the implicit or explicit assumptions that truth is the correctness of a proposition and that thought (or at least clear and meaningful thought) consists of arguments that derive propositions from other propositions. But Heidegger moves in the opposite direction: he shows no interest in symbolic logic, which he considers superficial (6/5), and instead challenges logicians' assumptions about truth, thought, and language. The question of logic is rooted in the question of language (13/11).

But will turning logic into an investigation of language illegitimately restrict logic's universal relevance and meaning? Heidegger retorts that language appears to be a narrow topic only if one accepts the assumption that it is the sciences that make beings accessible; language is then the theme of some specialized sciences, whereas logic regulates all sciences. But beings are, in fact, accessible in a way that precedes and exceeds all science. Philosophy must attend to this revelation that is deeper than science can ever be—and (Heidegger implies) language plays a role in this revelation (15–16/13). Language is not a mere means, a pointer to things themselves, but is indispensable to the emergence of these things in their being (16/14).

Heidegger thus rejects several stock approaches to language. Language cannot be understood by the "philosophy of language" as an academic specialty; this approach subordinates the topic to an overarching conception of philosophy, whereas perhaps "philosophy originates only out of a sufficient understanding of language" (14–15/12–13).

Grammar is another stumbling block for a deeper understanding of language, as Heidegger already asserted in the previous semester. Grammar is based on Greek logic, and thus on the Greek language and on a specifically Greek way of thinking and existing (17/14).

Language is surely not to be found in the dictionary, which is an "ossuary" holding the dead remnants of speech (23/21). But actual speech is not identical to language, either: when people fall into silence, language does not cease to exist (24/22). Heidegger mentions silence directly in only two contexts in this lecture-course: in this brief remark (repeated at 31/29) and in the comment that a great mood is kept quiet in an individual or an artwork, while a petty mood "continually displays itself, be it in wretchedness or dull boisterousness" (130/108).

To make progress in understanding language, we must investigate humanity, for language is distinctive of human beings (25/23). (Heidegger denies that lower animals have true language: 139/115.) To be able to speak is to be human. But what is humanity? To be human is to be a self, an entity whose own being is at stake. A human being is thrown into the question, "Who am I?"—but also, as a member of a community, into the question, "Who are we?" (34/32).

We are a *Volk*, a people, Heidegger finally proposes—but what is a people? Belonging to the people is a matter of decision. We decide to testify that "We are here!" and we affirm the will of a state that wills that the people become its own master (57/50, cf. 63/55).[16]

Here the question of silence returns, indirectly, for Heidegger argues that no one can know with certainty whether someone else has made the decision to stand by the state, or whether his attitude is a front.

> No individual person among you can in any manner ascertain about any individual person how he has decided. Even you cannot say how I myself have held my lecture, whether decisively or simply as a report, or as stock phrases. . . . We are *properly* ourselves only in the decision, namely, each one singly. . . . In willing to be he himself, [the individual] is sent out precisely beyond himself into the belongingness to which he submits himself in the decision. In the decision, each is separated from each, as only a human being can be separated. . . . Despite the fact that individuals are separated in decision, a concealed *unison* takes place here, whose concealedness is an essential one. This unison is fundamentally always a mystery. (58–59/51–52, translation modified)

There is no way to distinguish decisive speech (*Rede*) from a figure of speech (*Redensart*) (58/51) or from idle talk (*Gerede*). Yet the individual decisions that lie behind speech—decisions that are necessarily secret and silent—bind a community together.

Decision brings us into history, Heidegger continues. But what is history? Is history inseparable from humanity? Heidegger considers some objections to this proposition in a passage that has drawn considerable criticism since its publication: What about "Negros like, for example, Kaffirs," who aren't historical (81/69, cf. 83/71)? What about objects such as the propeller of a plane, which becomes historical when it takes the Führer to Mussolini (83/71)? And don't plants and animals have a history (81/69)? Since this last suggestion is clearly one that Heidegger does not endorse (88/75), we should not simply assume that he is making a racist or Eurocentric assertion when he entertains the objection about Africans.[17] We should also remain open to the possibility that some human beings—including Westerners—fall short of authentic historicity, or that they can fall away from history at a certain point, left stranded without a future (84/71). We will return to this troubling question in the closing pages of this essay.

Whatever historicity may be, we can at least say that history is temporal. But what is time? Original time is the future of having-been (118/98), and in this deep sense we must realize that we ourselves are time's "temporalizing" (120/100) or "time-formation" (125/104).

The question of logic, then, has brought us to language, humanity, people, decision, history, and time, with the question, "Who are we ourselves?" as the crux of the whole reflection (97/82).

Heidegger returns explicitly to language only in the closing moments of the lecture-course. After his train of thought, language has become all the more riddlesome, but he ventures this proposal: the world, as the totality of the being of beings, announces itself to us "in the mystery" and "in the primal-event [*Urgeschehnis*] of language" (168/140). Language is thus far more than a means of communication between subjects: it makes it possible for its speakers to be exposed to being and the world. "Language is how the world-forming and preserving center of the historical Dasein of the people holds sway" (169/140, translation modified). Genuine knowledge thus requires mature, creative language (169/141).

Such language, Heidegger suggests in conclusion, is not the degraded language of everyday business but poetic language, which has "world-forming power" (170/141). The true poet is never contemporary but reaches into the past and the future, alerting us to the being that has long been assigned to us, but which we have never yet reached (170/141–142). The conclusion of this lecture-course thus serves as an introduction to Heidegger's courses on Hölderlin, who explores the mystery of the fatherland, the difficulty of the national, and the poetic "peaks of time" when language itself reaches its peak.[18]

The Secret Homeland

There is one clear parallel between Heidegger's statements on language in the two lecture-courses we have reviewed: in both courses, he associates language with the primordial unconcealment of beings in their being—which is why language cannot be considered simply as one entity among others, or subordinated to some unquestioned concept of being. However, in the first course Heidegger attributes the primal event of unconcealment to silent reticence, which nourishes language; the second course says that language itself plays a role in this unconcealment. Are these views compatible? Is our basic openness to the world linguistic, or silent, or somehow both? Of course, there is no need to assume that a worked-out, systematic theory underlies Heidegger's lectures; it is more likely that his views are in development. Still, it can be helpful to our own thought to juxtapose the two lecture-courses and consider what connections might be drawn between them.

This juxtaposition raises other questions as well. Is there a link between the apparent solitude of silence (which is most evident in an individualizing mood such as *Angst*) and the communal dimension of language? As we asked above, can a community experience silence? Does silence have political implications? In sum, how is silence tied to the *Volk*?

One more text from this period can help us find some connecting threads: the radio talk "Why Do I Stay in the Provinces?"[19] In few words, this piece deftly if somewhat kitschily portrays Heidegger's existence among the peasants of the Black Forest. He faces a choice between accepting an invitation to teach in Berlin and keeping his appointment in the town of Freiburg, with its proximity to his mountain cabin at Todtnauberg. Heidegger makes the case that he would be betraying his own vocation if he became a citified professor, for his "work remains embedded in the happening of the landscape" (10/16, translation modified). In the course of his solitary work, Heidegger experiences the events in the countryside not as an observer who talks about them but as a participant.

Heidegger's life in the Black Forest circles around language and silence. His "struggle to mold something into language is like the resistance of the towering fir against the storm" (10/16). This language-work is quite unlike the urban tourist's "long conversation with a peasant";

Heidegger, in fact, mostly says "nothing at all" but smokes in "silence" when he spends time with his rural neighbors (10/17).

In the conclusion of the piece, Heidegger gets advice from a septuagenarian farmer on whether he should accept an appointment in the capital. "Slowly he fixed the sure gaze of his clear eyes on mine, and keeping his mouth tightly shut, he thoughtfully put his faithful hand on my shoulder. Ever so slightly he shook his head. That meant: absolutely no!" (12–13/18). These gestures are language kept at a laconic minimum—language that keeps as close to silence as possible and, for this very reason, carries more weight than any extended argument could.

For Heidegger, the peasants who waste few words live close to the soil, in every sense: they literally know how to work with the earth, and they also are rooted in the unspoken sense of things that is their heritage as members of the *Volk*. There is no need to disturb this visceral feel for the whole with facile chatter that pretends to illuminate things but actually warps them to fit rootless truisms. Since the farmers inhabit a common earth and are each tied silently to it, there is no need for them to talk their way into a mock belonging. Instead, they share in silence.

Does language play no role in opening the world, then? Is Heidegger wasting his time as he writes his manuscripts in his hut? No—he would say—because his language springs directly from the silent rootedness of the people and questioningly articulates what is experienced in this rootedness. Everyday gossip and assertion are superficial, but the rare forms of language that can draw directly on primordial silence have a special role to play in fulfilling a people's destiny. As Heidegger puts it in a reflection on cross-cultural encounters, the "fundamental attitudes and moods of peoples, which usually cannot be spoken at all in an immediate way, gain their definitive form and their power of enticement in great poetry, in formative art, and in the essential thinking (philosophy) of a people."[20] Poetry and philosophy find ways to "say" what cannot be said in ordinary assertions; they indicate a people's basic orientation to being.

That orientation, however, remains elusive and resists all attempts at direct speech. Although Heidegger, to my knowledge, never makes this play on words, we could speak of *die heimliche Heimat*, "the secret homeland" that silently sustains a people. No language has depth unless it pays tribute to the self-concealing mystery of this homeland, a mystery that is both *heimlich* and *unheimlich*—uncanny. Everyday language is shallow because it forgets or abjures its roots. It is thus in perpetual flight from uncanniness; at the same time, it fails to dwell on the familiar.

Both language and silence, then, can participate in primal unconcealment—but this must be creative, poetic language that is capable of reticence. Such reticence is an individual's attunement, but it connects the individual to the shared silence at the roots of a community. The poetic founder of language is in tune with this shared silence and has the gift of finding the words to name a shared destiny.

Could a political movement somehow manage to maintain its connection to the secret homeland? Heidegger's reluctance to move to Berlin already indicates his doubts, which were to grow more serious over the decade of the thirties. As Germany's largest city and the seat of its government, Berlin was a center of language in two senses: it was a place for idle talk about everything and anything, and a place for the official use of language in legislation and orders. Heidegger himself, acting as rector of the University of Freiburg, issued his share of orders and passed on orders from higher authorities.[21] But this uncreative, all too logical use of language could hardly satisfy Heidegger as a philosopher. To choose the most inflammatory example: as rector, Heidegger obediently implemented a regulation that required all professors to fill out a questionnaire about their family background in order to identify the "non-Aryans."[22] But whatever the extent of his anti-Semitism,[23] as a philosopher Heidegger insisted on the ambiguity and obscurity of the *Volk* and its irreducibility to scientific or pseudoscientific notions of race. The secrets of the homeland could hardly be uncovered by the crude categories of a questionnaire, and the marshaling of human and natural resources could not constitute a primal gathering.

Already in 1933–1934, then, Heidegger's collaboration with the regime fit poorly with his insistence on silence, poetry, and philosophy. The later political, and ultimately apolitical, evolution of his thought consists in a growing disenchantment with the reality of the "movement," as opposed to its ever more distant and nebulous "inner truth and greatness."[24]

Language and the Public Sphere

But let us stay with 1933–1934 and critically consider how Heidegger's thoughts on language, silence, and the people are linked to the pathos and pathology of his enthusiasm for Nazism at that time.

As we have seen, the *Logic* course bases belonging to the *Volk* on a mysterious unison among secret individual choices. "Each must himself venture the leap, if he wants to be a member of a community" (GA 38: 19/16). This idea goes back at least to a comment on authentic being-with in *Being and Time* (SZ 122) and can be found in other texts of the rectoral period as well. In a seminar from this time, where Heidegger promotes the *Führerstaat* as the perfect realization of the relation between state and *Volk*, he appeals in a similar way to an inner choice: "The true implementation of the will [of the state] does not depend on force, but on awakening the same will in another—that is, the same goal and the same engagement or activation. . . . This implementation is not a momentary yes-saying, but a decision of the individual."[25]

Heidegger envisions complete unanimity as the ideal: "Only where the leader [*Führer*] and the led bind themselves in common to *one* destiny, and struggle to realize *one* idea, does true order arise."[26] It would follow that any individual decision that contradicts the will of the state, which is identical with the will of the leader, is out of order and amounts to a betrayal of the people. Here Heidegger seems to be expressing the feelings of many at the time who were all too eager to dissolve the rival parties of the Weimar Republic and align themselves with the new regime. He wishes for a shared national mood, a shared silence, not unlike the taciturn rootedness of the pipe-smoking peasants.

But when unanimity is enforced, it is oppressive and totalitarian: obviously, it excludes all genuine debate and imposes silence by raising the specter of punishment for those who express politically incorrect views. In the absence of free speech, thought and questioning are driven into hiding. For a philosopher to support totalitarianism is a practical contradiction, as Heidegger was eventually to realize.[27]

Heidegger's authoritarianism at this time is allied to a quasi-Kierkegaardian inwardness: public utterances and behavior are genuine only if they are supported by the individual's secret, silent decision to support the new state. This decision is invisible to others; it is a matter of conscience. This totalitarian individualism, so to speak, may seem bizarre, but it is in fact necessary: when public discourse does not tolerate dissent, private consciousness becomes a matter of intense interest both to citizens and to authorities, who will do their utmost to penetrate and police the individual mind.

What has been lost in this situation is a genuine *public sphere*—that is, neither a private mind nor a governmental system, but an arena where individuals can express and display themselves. Such a display should not be understood as a sign of a pre-existing inner consciousness; in a vital public sphere, individuals discover themselves and become themselves *in* their public acts. To take a simple example, the vote of a legislator is a public act. Whatever private motivations may lie behind this vote, it would be wrong to insist that the real decision is hidden: the political decision *consists in* the public act of casting a vote. The choice to vote a certain way is fully actual if and only if one *votes*. The same can be said of speech: to take a certain stand in language on the issues of the day is to be, and not merely seem to be, a political actor. Whatever the speaker's silent experiences or unspoken thoughts may be, they are subpolitical or suprapolitical; politics proper happens in public, between people. As Arendt argues in a line of thought directly aimed at the totalitarian error, the specifically political realm is this public arena of free initiative and self-revelation.[28] In Nazi Germany, such a realm was supplanted ever more forcefully by orders and propaganda; any public discussion of political matters was tightly restricted. Heidegger himself surely chafed against the constraints of this impaired public sphere, both in his capacity as rector and in his lectures and publications during the remainder of the regime.

If a healthy public sphere and public discourse are essential to political existence, we cannot agree that a community is ultimately bound by reticence, or by the creations of solitary thinkers and poets. The peasants smoking silently around the hearth certainly share a world, and without a shared world, there is no *polis*. But we cannot conclude from this that public utterance is the original sin, or that silent co-existence is more authentic than discourse. If a dispute arises among the peasants about whether someone's cattle have the right to graze on a certain pasture, words will become necessary in order, as Aristotle says, to discover the just and the unjust. A debate will begin—perhaps a quarrel without end, perhaps a debate involving plenty of idle talk, sloganeering, or self-deception—but nevertheless a public discourse that will bind the peasants more fully, more explicitly, into a community. That does not mean unanimity, or common devotion to a single idea, but participation in a plurality, with all its friction and faction. The specifically political being of a community does not consist in what goes without saying but on its members' readiness to expose themselves through speech in the public realm. Such speech sets the truly political animal apart from pseudo-political animals such as bees. A hive needs communication, or the transfer of information, but it does not need—in fact, it must exclude—*logos* as political debate (not to mention *logos* as poetry and philosophy).

Heidegger is right to ask "Who are we?" But in 1933–1934, he was too quick to lend a hand to a movement that tried to answer this question by inventing enemies of the people.[29] Are persecution and murder necessary to define who "we" are? Do we have to exclude some of "us" in order to define the rest? To put the problem in terms of language: Who will have the right to decide which language is "ours"? How will they decide? Which language would be more authentic: standard *Hochdeutsch* or a local dialect? What about the German words imported from Greek, Latin, or English? How about a dialect of German—Yiddish—that imports words from Hebrew? How do we find translations between "our" language and "others" that neither reduce all languages to an ahistorical, technical vocabulary nor define the other as enemy? Heidegger was eventually to consider some of these issues—particularly in terms of the relation between German and Greek language and thought—but he never thought through the political problem of the internal multiplicity and multivalence of every community and every language.

At the war's end, Heidegger interpreted evil as a hidden, self-disguising force.[30] If this thought has merit, could it follow that evil lurks in the silent core of the speech of every people? Is the secret homeland also the heart of darkness? If so, then the way to fight the evil within a people is not to appeal to silence but to speak out. Speech—and the institution of *free* speech—is a fallible weapon against evil, but it is the deepest weapon, because it counters mute brutality with articulate humanity.

People without History?

Heidegger's thoughts on language and silence in 1933–1934 are thus entangled with his profound misjudgment of the situation at the time and his permanent blindness to the nature of politics. But I do not wish to end with condemnation. The questions Heidegger raises, whether or not he finds his way to satisfactory answers, can arise in situations far distant from Germany under the Third Reich and can still provoke us to thought.

It remains legitimate to ask, with Heidegger, how a people's understanding of being is experienced in silence and incorporated in language.

Consider the small Amazonian tribe known as the Pirahã. The Pirahã have been a focus of controversy in linguistics and anthropology because of their almost unbelievably restricted culture and their extremely difficult language. The tribe seems to do happily without a number of cultural elements that one might assume to be universal: a mythology or tradition of fiction, well-defined rituals, recognized authority, a collective memory that extends back more than a couple of generations, a counting system, and more. In the absence of any long-lasting material constructions, the tribe's culture is invested heavily in its language, which uses a small set of phonemes and tones and can be expressed in four quite different "channels" (normal conversation, humming, whistling, and shouting). The Pirahã language is highly sophisticated in some ways, with sixteen different verbal suffixes that express nuances of meaning, but it does not involve recursion: there are no subordinate clauses, no possibility of nesting one thought inside another ad infinitum. This last feature contradicts one of the fundamental tenets of Chomskian linguistics, which posits the capacity for recursion as a formal feature of human language.

According to Daniel L. Everett, who has lived for decades with the group, the absence of recursion in Pirahã is tied to the tribe's fundamental cultural orientation: the principle of the "immediacy of experience," or a focus on what is present here and now.[31] As Everett sees it, a recursive sentence, such as "The dog with three legs is sleeping," involves a subordinate clause ("dog with three legs") that is not explicitly tied to a present fact but creates a new abstraction. It is far better, from the Pirahã perspective, to make explicit statements about what is currently apparent: "The dog has three legs. The dog is sleeping." The Pirahã's focus on what is present is expressed in the frequent word *xibipíio,* meaning roughly "appearing or disappearing," which the Pirahã apply with pleasure and fascination whenever something new comes into view or someone leaves their territory.[32] The principle of the immediacy of experience has made for a remarkably resilient culture that has resisted linguistic and religious incursions from the West for over two centuries. Reports from Westerners about spatially or temporally distant figures (such as Jesus) are received by the Pirahã with at most passing curiosity, but all interest evaporates when the tribe returns to its habitual, local pursuits.[33]

To raise some Heideggerian questions: Can the Pirahã language be understood formally, in terms of Western logic and linguistics? Or do that logic and linguistics themselves depend on the Greek understanding of being? Must the Pirahã language then be understood, as Everett proposes, in terms of this people's own sense of being? What, then, does being mean for the Pirahã? They seem to have a keen sense of the boundary between the concealed and the unconcealed; whatever passes into concealment soon becomes a matter of indifference, a non-being. Do the Pirahã put this understanding of being into language? The word *xibipíio* may embody it, but there seems to be no Pirahã philosophy or poetry, no concerted attempt to find words for being as such. Instead, the Pirahã have developed subtle ways to illuminate the present *beings* that confront them, using, as Heidegger puts it, "the tone of voice, the cadence, the melody of the sentences, the rhythm, and so on." The Pirahã language richly brings out the being of the beings in the Pirahã world, but the people do not think about being itself—the original gift that makes their experiences of beings possible. In the absence of philosophical discussion of being and truth, has this group of people failed to enter fully into the understanding of being that is given to it? Or does the very absence of such talk constitute the proper reticence needed to receive the gift? Or, perhaps, do these people need a special kind of talk that retains its ties to primordial silence?

We should also ask whether the Pirahã are historical. Of course, they have a long past—but they are ignorant of it, they have no creation myths or stories about their origins, and they simply take their situation for granted.[34] With no care for their heritage, they have no care for their future but take care only of their current needs, planning for one or two days at a time. Are they capable, then, of coming to grips with their own being as a historical issue? What would it take for them to become explicitly historical? Would that require forming a state and developing a new political language—a language of authority and law, in addition to the everyday discussion of their shared concerns in which they already engage? Would this development of historical and political existence be tied to the development of poetic and philosophical language? And would an attempt to initiate all this be desirable at all—or would it simply destroy the tribe, more surely than modernity is destroying the world of Heidegger's peasants?

The Pirahã are a people that do not exist historically. They have not embarked on a voyage of self-alienation and self-creation but feel that they have always already arrived at their destination. Their silent sense of being as immediate presence sustains the subtle language in which they care for the beings in their world—but they do not speak in a way that draws creatively on silence to achieve "world-forming power" (GA 38: 170/141), a power that could revolutionize their world and their sense of being.

Lest we see the Pirahã too readily as a special case, a band of a few hundred "primitives," let us remember that, in Heidegger's view, Westerners do not fully exist historically either. We can legitimately ask, "Are we historical?" (GA 38: 109–110/91–92)—and Heidegger answers that no age has been less historical than our own (GA 38: 114/95). Although the boundaries of presence are broader for us than for the Pirahã, we too, according to Heidegger, have fallen into our busy concern with present beings and have failed to listen to being. We too look for truth in assertions about what is present at hand and have not learned to experience the event of unconcealment itself. If we can open ourselves to that experience and to the ongoing voyage of selfhood, we will perhaps be less tempted to provide simplistic and violent answers to the question, "Who are we?"

At his most apocalyptic, Heidegger goes so far as to write that "Man has never yet been historical."[35] We can take this extreme statement as a healthy antidote against any complacent assumption that we are already familiar with the essence of history, politics, community, language, or silence. Heidegger's flawed but thought-provoking explorations of these themes in 1933–1934 not only foreshadow his later meditations on language but still serve as food for our own thought.

NOTES

1. "Meine Beseitigung" (1946), in GA 16, *Reden und andere Zeugnisse eines Lebensweges*, ed. Hermann Heidegger (2000), 421–422. Perhaps appropriately, this text is a draft of a letter that may never have been mailed. "GA" will refer to volumes of Heidegger's *Gesamtausgabe* (Frankfurt am Main: Klostermann). I would like to thank Gregory Fried, Adam Knowles, and Jeffrey Powell for their thoughtful comments on this essay.

2. "SZ" will refer to the pagination of the 1953 and later editions of *Sein und Zeit* (Tübingen: Niemeyer). The pagination is reproduced in the margins of the English version by John Macquarrie and Edward Robinson (New York: Harper & Row, 1962), whose translation I quote.

3. GA 18, *Grundbegriffe der aristotelischen Philosophie*, ed. Mark Michalski (2002), translated as *Basic Concepts of Aristotelian Philosophy*, trans. Robert D. Metcalf and Mark B. Tanzer (Bloomington: Indiana University Press, 2009).

4. The earlier lecture-course is GA 34, *Vom Wesen der Wahrheit: Zu Platons Höhlengleichnis und Theätet*, ed. Hermann Mörchen (1988), translated as *The Essence of Truth: On Plato's Cave Allegory and "Theaetetus"* by Ted Sadler (London: Continuum, 2002).

5. Within this section, all parenthetical references are to pages of GA 36/37, *Sein und Wahrheit*, ed. Hartmut Tietjen (2001). The pagination of *Being and Truth*, trans. Gregory Fried and Richard Polt (Bloomington: Indiana University Press, 2010) follows the German pagination.

6. Aristotle, *The Politics*, trans. Carnes Lord (Chicago: University of Chicago Press, 1984), 37 (chap. 1.2, 1253a8–18).

7. As Stuart Elden has pointed out, this de-emphasis of justice is apparent even when Heidegger directly and extensively interprets this passage from *Politics* 1.2 in 1924: *Speaking Against Number: Heidegger, Language and the Politics of Calculation* (Edinburgh: Edinburgh University Press, 2006), 33. For Heidegger's interpretation, see GA 18: 45–64, *Basic Concepts of Aristotelian Philosophy*, 32–45.

8. Compare Carnap's remark that metaphysical discourse, such as Heidegger's talk of "the nothing," reflects attitudes toward life that could better be expressed in music: Rudolf Carnap, "The Overcoming of Metaphysics through Logical Analysis of Language," in Michael Murray, ed., *Heidegger and Modern Philosophy: Critical Essays* (New Haven, Conn.: Yale University Press, 1978), 33.

9. Presumably this would be Heidegger's objection to Wittgenstein's *Tractatus*, where all issues other than what can be signified in propositions about the present-at-hand are designated as the "mystical," and one must keep silent about them. Wittgenstein was true for years to the final proposition of the *Tractatus* and kept silent as a philosopher, out of respect for the unsayable. In 1929, he found Heidegger's talk of anxiety suggestive yet thought that Heidegger was "run[ning] up against the limits of language": Ludwig Wittgenstein, "On Heidegger on Being and Dread," in Murray, *Heidegger and Modern Philosophy*, 80. The disagreement between the two philosophers concerns the essence and potential of language; later Wittgenstein draws closer to Heidegger in emphasizing that language can "do" much more than refer to the present-at-hand, while still acknowledging the finitude of language and our inability to put everything into words.

10. Heidegger's embrace of the language of power and empowerment will reach a climax in the *Introduction to Metaphysics* (1935) but will wane along with his enthusiasm for National Socialism, as he eventually concludes that being lies beyond both power and powerlessness: see Richard Polt, "Beyond Struggle and Power: Heidegger's Secret Resistance," *Interpretation* 35:1 (Fall 2007): 11–40. The evolution of Heidegger's attitude to power is one factor that needs to be taken into account when we interpret the evolution of his thought on language.

11. *Legein* then depends on *sigan* (keeping silent)—hence Heidegger's talk in the *Contributions to Philosophy* of turning from "logic" to "sigetic." See GA 65, *Beiträge zur Philosophie (Vom Ereignis)*, ed. Friedrich-Wilhelm von Herrmann (1989), 78–80; Richard Polt, *The Emergency of Being: On Heidegger's "Contributions to Philosophy"* (Ithaca, N.Y.: Cornell University Press, 2006), 128–131.

12. SZ 61 seems to suggest that theory is merely what is left over after practice has ebbed away, but in a marginal note to the passage, Heidegger corrects himself: "Looking at does not occur merely by looking away": *Being and Time,* trans. Joan Stambaugh, revised by Dennis J. Schmidt (Albany: SUNY Press, 2010), 61. At SZ 363, Heidegger emphasizes that theoretical objectification is not merely deficient but requires a distinctive act of "thematizing."

13. "Antrag auf die Wiedereinstellung in die Lehrtätigkeit," in GA 16: 401. In English, "Letter to the Rector of Freiburg University, November 4, 1945," in Richard Wolin (ed.), *The Heidegger Controversy: A Critical Reader* (Cambridge, Mass.: MIT Press, 1993), 64.

14. Within this section, all parenthetical references are to pages of GA 38, *Logik als die Frage nach dem Wesen der Sprache,* ed. Günter Seubold (1998). The pagination of *Logic as the Question Concerning the Essence of Language,* trans. Wanda Torres Gregory and Yvonne Unna (Albany: SUNY Press, 2009), follows the German pagination. The translation has been modified in this case.

15. On Heidegger's ongoing concern with logic, see Alfred Denker and Holger Zaborowski, eds., *Heidegger und die Logik* (Amsterdam: Rodopi, 2006); Daniel O. Dahlstrom, *Heidegger's Concept of Truth* (Cambridge: Cambridge University Press, 2001).

16. Heidegger speaks of *Herrschaftswille* (GA 38: 57); the translation renders *Herrschaft* as "government" (50), but "mastery" is more vivid and appropriate.

17. The term Heidegger uses is *Kaffern.* "Kaffir" is an offensive racial insult when used in South Africa today, but it seems plausible that Heidegger means the term simply as a reference to native black Africans, without any particularly pejorative sense.

18. The lecture-courses in question are GA 39, *Hölderlins Hymnen "Germanien" und "Der Rhein"* (written 1934–1935), ed. Susanne Ziegler (1980); GA 52, *Hölderlins Hymne "Andenken"* (written 1941–1942), ed. Curd Ochwadt (1982); and GA 53, *Hölderlins Hymne "Der Ister"* (written 1942), ed. Walter Biemel (1984), translated as *Hölderlin's Hymn "The Ister"* by William McNeill and Julia Davis (Bloomington: Indiana University Press, 1996). On the mystery of the fatherland, see GA 39: 120–121; on the difficulty of the national, GA 39: 290–294; on the peaks of time, GA 39: 109.

19. "Schöpferische Landschaft—Warum bleiben wir in der Provinz?" in GA 13, *Aus der Erfahrung des Denkens,* ed. Hermann Heidegger (1983), 9–13, translated as "Why Do I Stay in the Provinces?" trans. Thomas Sheehan, in Manfred Stassen, *Martin Heidegger: Philosophical and Political Writings* (London: Continuum, 2003), 16–18. Parenthesized references in this section are to the German text, followed by the pagination of the translation after a virgule. The text dates from fall 1933.

20. "Wege zur Aussprache" (1937), in GA 13: 17.

21. The documents are collected in GA 16: 82–274, and in "Dokumente aus der Rektoratszeit," in Alfred Denker and Holger Zaborowski, eds., *Heidegger und der Nationalsozialismus I: Dokumente,* Heidegger-Jahrbuch 4 (Freiburg/Munich: Karl Alber, 2009), 13–52.

22. *Heidegger und der Nationalsozialismus I,* 13, 17. Heidegger's own questionnaire is reproduced on 240–243.

23. That Heidegger had anti-Semitic views can hardly be doubted any longer: see, for example, his remark on "Semitic nomads," ibid., 82.

24. *Introduction to Metaphysics,* trans. Gregory Fried and Richard Polt (New Haven, Conn.: Yale University Press, 2000), 213.

25. "Über Wesen und Begriff von Natur, Geschichte und Staat" (student protocols from a seminar, winter semester 1933–1934), in Denker and Zaborowski, *Heidegger und der Nationalsozialismus I,* 87. On the *Führerstaat,* see p. 88.

26. Ibid., 77.

27. On Heidegger's later critique of totalitarianism, see Polt, "Beyond Struggle and Power," 24–29. One could argue that the only way to combine philosophy and totalitarianism is to give absolute power to the philosophers themselves—so Heidegger's attraction to Plato around the time of his rectorship is not surprising. However, the concept of philosopher-rulers presupposes that genuine philosophers *possess* knowledge at least as much as they seek it. That supposition is questionable both from a Platonic and from a Heideggerian point of view.

28. See Hannah Arendt, *The Human Condition,* 2nd ed. (Chicago: University of Chicago Press, 1998), especially chap. 5.

29. See GA 36/37: 91/73, for Heidegger's horrifying explication of *Kampf* as the pursuit of the internal enemy of the *Volk*—an invented enemy if need be—to the point of "complete annihilation."

30. GA 77, *Feldweg-Gespräche,* ed. Ingrid Schüßler (1995), 208, translated as *Country Path Conversations,* trans. Bret W. Davis (Bloomington: Indiana University Press, 2010), 134.

31. Daniel L. Everett, *Don't Sleep, There Are Snakes: Life and Language in the Amazonian Jungle* (New York: Vintage, 2009), 131–134, 236.

32. Ibid., 129.

33. Everett himself began as a missionary but ultimately lost his own faith in the face of the Pirahã's contented indifference to his efforts; ibid., chap. 17.

34. Ibid., 133–134.

35. GA 65: 492. For commentary, see Polt, *The Emergency of Being,* 216–227.

FIVE

The Logic of Thinking

John Sallis

From the beginning logic is conceived as the logic of thinking. Already in Greek thought logic is assigned the task of identifying, formulating, and formalizing the laws of thinking. Thus logic is obliged to investigate the ways in which concepts, judgments or propositions, and arguments in the shape of syllogisms are formed. What distinguishes logic from other cognitive disciplines, from other kinds of ἐπιστήμη or science, is that logic considers these various constructions only with respect to their form, that is, without any regard for their content. Thus, whether a syllogism is properly constructed so that the conclusion follows from the premises is purely a matter of the form of the constituent propositions and of the formal relation between them; the validity of the argument has nothing whatsoever to do with the content of the propositions, with what they are about. Because of this disregard or abstraction from content, formalization is already implicit in the very idea of logic. To this extent the modern mathematization of logic represents merely the fulfillment of a tendency that was in force from the beginning.

This classical conception of logic is concisely expressed by Heidegger in his 1934 lecture-course on logic. Here he defines logic as "the science of the basic structures of thinking" and, more specifically, as "the science of the basic formal structures and rules of thinking."[1] Yet these definitions, given at the outset of the 1934 lecture-course, are stated, not by way of reaffirmation but rather as preparation for an *Erschütterung* of logic (as Heidegger calls it) that will have severe consequences for this discipline. This *Erschütterung* is one of several gestures that together may be called the deconstruction of logic.

My primary concern in this essay is to discern precisely what is at stake in this deconstruction of logic—that is, what prompts it, how it is carried out, and what remains to be considered in its wake. Yet this move occurs against the background of a concern with logic that goes back to the very beginning of phenomenology. Already in the *Logical Investigations* Husserl undertakes in a radicalizing way to retrieve and to ground logic. This venture is one that Husserl never abandons, and, in particular, it is powerfully renewed in *Formal and Transcendental Logic*. It is this same venture that is taken up and addressed by Heidegger in his early writings and lecture-courses, initially in its Husserlian form, then in a more independent and eventually deconstructive manner.

(1)

Logic is the science of the formal structures, rules, or laws of thinking. In this conception there is a basic ambiguity. This ambiguity readily gives rise to a misconception. Because of this misconception there arose a certain tendency in modern thought that puts in jeopardy the very status of logic as a pure science. It was in opposition to this tendency that Husserl undertook to retrieve the genuine sense of logic.

The ambiguity lies in the conception of laws or rules of thinking; for they may be taken either as laws by which thinking occurs or as laws by which it ought to occur. They may be construed either as laws that govern actual processes of thinking in the manner that natural laws govern physical processes; or they may be construed as laws that function as norms, laws that prescribe the course that thinking must follow in order to be formally in agreement with its object and hence possibly true or valid.

The tendency that arises in modern thought emphasizes the first of these alternatives. Reinforced by empiricism, the tendency is to regard the laws of thinking as laws that actually govern the human psyche. For example, John Stuart Mill takes the law of non-contradiction to be based primarily on the fact that belief and disbelief are two mental states that exclude one another. Thus, he accounts for this law as arising from the self-observation in which we find that we cannot both believe something and not believe it; this self-observation is, then, according to Mill's account, reinforced by our outward observation that when a certain phenomenon is present its opposite is always absent, as with light and darkness, sound and silence, equality and inequality. The law of non-contradiction he regards, then, as a generalization from all these facts. More generally, he regards all logical laws as merely generalizations based on factual experience, as general expressions of the actual workings of the human psyche. Thus, logic would need to be based on the scientific investigation of the human psyche, that is, on psychology. Such a consignment of logic to psychology is what is called psychologism.

Husserl's *Logical Investigations* begins with a powerful attack on such psychologism. In his "Prolegomena to Pure Logic" Husserl exposes in the most thoroughgoing manner the presuppositions and the consequences of the psychologistic conception of logic. The crux of Husserl's criticism lies in the charge that psychologism is skeptical relativism. This means that in taking the laws of logic to be based on—hence, relative to—the human psyche, this theory in effect undermines the conditions for the very possibility of theory and hence undermines itself. Let me mention only one of the many connections in which Husserl lays out this critique in precise detail. Since psychologism makes the laws of logic relative to the human psyche, these laws, while true for the human species, could be false for members of another species. And yet, the very sense of truth entails that the same content cannot be both true and false. As Husserl declares: "'Truth for this or that species,' e.g., for the human species, is . . . an absurd mode of speech." He continues: "What is true is absolutely, 'in itself' true: truth is one and the same, whether humans or non-humans, angels or gods apprehend and judge it."[2] What is at stake in this, as in all the criticisms that Husserl levels against psychologism, is the difference between the ideal laws of logic and the real laws of empirical sciences such as psychology. What is crucial is the insight that the laws of logic concern not the actual workings of the psyche, but rather the ideal objects of thinking or the ideal connections that hold for these objects. For example, the law of non-contradiction has nothing to do with our inability to think contradictory attributes; many would contend that we can in fact think such contradictions. What the law rules out is the objective possibility of contradictions; what it excludes in principle—that is, ideally—is the possibility of an objective content in which contradictory attributes are combined.

Husserl says that the definitive resolution of the controversy concerning psychologism "depends on the correct discernment of the most fundamental epistemological distinction, namely, that between *real* and *ideal*."[3] Thus the ideal laws of logic have absolute exactness, in distinction from the vague generalizations from experience that empirical psychology puts forth as laws. The ideal laws of logic have a priori validity, unlike empirical laws, which are reached only by induction and which therefore are only probable.

It is against this background that, at the end of the prolegomena, Husserl projects the idea of a pure logic, a logic in which the ideality of its content would have been secured. Such pure logic would remain a logic of thinking, but now in the sense of a logic that would formulate the laws that govern the ideal relations pertaining to the object of thought. Because of the formal and ideal character of its laws, pure logic would display the conditions of the possibility of theory in general; properly conceived, logic would become the theory of theory as such, the science of science.

And yet, Husserl's refutation of psychologism is only a series of prolegomena to pure logic. It is no more than preparation for the radical retrieval and grounding of logic that is Husserl's aim in the *Logical Investigations*. For no matter how vigorously Husserl may refuse to ground logic on empirical psychology, his attack on psychologism does not lead him to seek a purely objective ground for logic. This he indicates already in the prolegomena: "In the dispute over a psychological or objective grounding of logic, I take therefore an intermediate position."[4] Even in the foreword to the first edition, Husserl remarks that he has been pushed more and more toward critical reflections "on the relation between the subjectivity of knowing and the objectivity of the content known."[5]

Thus, once the critique of psychologism has shown that the laws of logic must be characterized by ideal objectivity, Husserl proposes, at the outset of the *Logical Investigations* proper, to turn to the subjective sources of these ideally objective laws. This turn to the sources from which the laws of logic derive is the task assigned to phenomenology, at least its primary task: "Phenomenology discloses the 'sources' from which the basic concepts and ideal laws of pure logic 'arise' and back to which they must again be traced in order to give them the 'clearness and distinctness' needed . . . for pure logic."[6] Though later retracting the term, Husserl initially—in the first edition of the *Logical Investigations*—characterizes phenomenology as "descriptive psychology" and attempts to differentiate this discipline from empirical psychology by construing it as preparatory for psychology proper. Yet it is only in the *Logical Investigations* proper, in the analyses themselves, that Husserl begins to effect the differentiation through which the purity of phenomenology will be secured. This differentiation between phenomenology and psychology, a problem to which Husserl never ceases to return, is clearly required in order to elucidate the character and relevance of the phenomenological turn. Only in this way can it be shown that the turn to the subjective sources of logical laws is the counterpart to the rejection of psychologism and not, as Husserl's early critics charged, a turn to the very position refuted in the prolegomena.

Formal and Transcendental Logic is a powerful work of clarification. Though it comes almost three decades after the *Logical Investigations,* Husserl insists that, granted the clarifications it provides, he still upholds in the later work the project first launched in the "Prolegomena to Pure Logic."[7] But *Formal and Transcendental Logic* also advances this project, primarily by re-situating the problem of a philosophical logic within the developed context of transcendental phenomenology. Within this context the later work acquires the methodological means by which to give a rigorous account of what is involved in the turn from logical idealities back to their subjective sources.

The context is also framed in a way that anticipates Husserl's concern with the crisis of the sciences. He observes that as the sciences have become independent, they have tended to abandon the ideal of radical scientific self-responsibility and to become mere theoretical techniques. Amidst this "tragedy of modern scientific culture," as he terms it,[8] logic has lost its historical vocation; instead of providing a theory of science, logic has itself become a special science. What was formerly "the torchbearer of method"[9] has lagged ever further behind and in recent times has strayed utterly away from its own sense and task.

Framed in this way, the context appears all the more imperative. For underlying the contemporary failure of logic is a radical defect that belongs to logic throughout its history. The defect lies in its inability to carry out its proper task *with respect to the subjective,* that is, with respect to thinking. Its defect lies in its inability to become, in the radical sense, a logic of thinking. To refer logic back, in this radical sense, to thinking and to subjectivity is possible, according to Husserl, only within the context of transcendental phenomenology. Only within this context can a rigorous account be given of the inwardness (*Innerlichkeit*) from which cognition and theory are produced. Thus, Husserl declares: "Only a transcendental logic can be an ultimate theory of science."[10]

Formal and Transcendental Logic traces the way from mere formal logic to transcendental logic. And yet, in the conclusion to the work, Husserl insists that transcendental logic "is not a second logic, but only radical and concrete logic that arises through phenomenological method."[11] Husserl grants even that what he has in mind as transcendental logic is merely traditional, limited logic. Thus, it appears that transcendental logic does not significantly alter the content of traditional logic, not at least beyond the supplements proposed in Husserl's elaboration of formal logic. Transcendental logic is simply formal logic that has been explicitly attached, thematically connected, to its transcendental origin. Transcendental logic is simply formal logic that has been radicalized by being transcendentally grounded.

Thus, in *Formal and Transcendental Logic,* Husserl stresses repeatedly the double directionality that must now be required of logic. Referring to the reform that is necessary for logic, he declares that logic must overcome its phenomenological naïveté. What this requires is that it not lose itself in its idealities but rather carry out a regress from the ideal formations to the consciousness that constitutes them.[12] What is required is a logic that inquires in two opposite directions, turning back, on the one side, to the productive activities and habitualities that constitute, on the other side, results, ideal formations, that afterward persist in their ideal objectivity. Husserl suggests that it is precisely this two-sidedness—that is, the difficulty it poses—that accounts for the fact that logic after millennia has still not entered the course of a truly rational development.[13] The difficulty, he explains, lies primarily in the fact that ideal formations such as judgments are not already there like external things but arise from our thinking activity; yet once they are generated, they persist and thus seem to float obscurely between subjectivity and objectivity.[14] Traditionally they tend to be referred to one side or the other, whereas what is required is an inquiry—transcendentally situated—that proceeds in both directions.

What is required is a double movement, an oscillating, as it were, between the structures of formal logic and the subjective turn that transcendental logic puts in play. On the one side, logic takes up the abiding formations that have been constituted; yet by regressing to the underlying constitutive activity, re-awakening it through a thematizing reflection, logic can secure the identity of the ideal formations against the shiftings and disguisements that result in equivocations in meaning and in language.[15] In this way the movement from formal to transcendental logic turns back upon formal logic so as to instill in it a precision and a rigor of which otherwise it would not be capable.

(2)

Heidegger openly acknowledges the advances made by Husserl in philosophical logic. Indeed Heidegger's own earliest publications are situated within the context of the logical research stemming from Husserl's *Logical Investigations.* Both Heidegger's survey of recent logical studies, "Neuere Forschungen über Logik" (1912), and his dissertation, "Die Lehre vom Urteil im Psychologismus" (1913), refer to the wide-ranging significance of Husserl's work and themselves proceed within the horizons opened by that work. More than a decade later, at the time when he was composing *Being and Time,* he still singles out Husserl's *Logical Investigations* as the only text in which vital questioning in logic is still to be found.[16] Even much later, in the retrospective essay from the 1960s, "My Way into Phenomenology," Heidegger stresses the significance that the *Logical Investigations* had in the development of his thought and recalls that, even after Husserl's work took a somewhat new direction, he himself remained "captivated by the never-ceasing spell of the *Logical Investigations.*"[17]

Thus it is not surprising that Heidegger addresses questions of logic in numerous texts and in various connections. Even in many texts in which logic is not the explicit theme, one easily discerns beneath the surface of the text questions and themes linked to Heidegger's logical studies and even to his appropriation of analyses from the *Logical Investigations.* Yet what is perhaps most striking in this regard is the fact that between 1925 and 1938, Heidegger presented four lecture-courses that are devoted—each in its own way—to logic; in each case this theme is indicated by the occurrence of the word *logic* in the title of the course. Considering that these courses span the decisive period from the time when Heidegger was composing the published part of *Being and Time* to the year in which he completed *Contributions to Philosophy,* it is to be expected that they strike out in very different directions. Indeed even a cursory glance at them reveals that in the sequence there are not only developments but also discontinuities, leaps in which the very sense of philosophical logic undergoes profound mutation.

The first of these lecture-courses is titled *Logik* and bears, in addition, the subtitle *Die Frage nach der Wahrheit;* Heidegger presented it in winter semester 1925–1926, one year before the publication of *Being and Time.* The primary theme in the initial part of the course is Husserl's critique of psychologism. Heidegger offers a succinct account of this critique and draws out certain historical connections (for example, with Lotze) and certain consequences. Though for the most part Heidegger's discussion reaffirms and reinforces Husserl's critique, there are two points where one can discern the beginning of a certain divergence.

The first point concerns the evaluation of traditional logic. In contrast to Husserl, who, even in the more radical framework of *Formal and Transcendental Logic,* largely retains the content of traditional logic, Heidegger has nothing but disdain for the school logic that is the contemporary heir of traditional logic. This logic, he says, is nothing but a matter of comfort (*Bequemlichkeit*) for lazy teachers. It is a mere deceptive construct (*Scheingebilde*) that has lost all connection with philosophy and with questioning. It is a mere repository of propositions, formulas, rules, and definitions to be merely passed along. According to Heidegger, such logic derives from a stage at which philosophy had already lost its productive character; it represents the utterly uprooted and rigidified remains of the originary philosophical questioning that was alive in Plato and Aristotle.[18] The historical reference makes it clear that Heidegger's denigration extends beyond logic in its present-day form to traditional logic as such, as it was codified in Hellenistic philosophy.

Heidegger vigorously distinguishes such logic from philosophical logic. It is a logic that is other than philosophical logic rather than, as with Husserl, a logic that would be rendered philosophical by being transcendentally grounded. As the subtitle of this course already suggests, the primary question that animates philosophical logic, as Heidegger conceives it, is the question of truth.[19] Here especially it becomes evident that, as regards the content and articulation of logic, Heidegger leaps beyond the more traditional conception developed by Husserl. In *Formal and Transcendental Logic* Husserl distinguishes between three levels of logic. The lowest level deals with the pure forms of judgment; it determines and systematizes the fundamental forms and the basic operations. The second level is the logic of non-contradiction, which includes the whole of syllogistics. Only at the third level does the question of truth come into play; as truth-logic, its task is to formulate the formal laws of possible truth. On the other hand, to refer logic immediately and directly to the question of truth, as Heidegger does, is to leap over the first two levels. The question is whether and how, from the question of truth, it is possible to return to those other levels so as to appropriate—or perhaps transform—their traditional content.

The second point that marks the beginning of a certain divergence occurs in Heidegger's discussion of Husserl's critique of psychologism. According to Heidegger, the principal defect of psychologism lies in its attempt to base logical principles on empirical facts, for example, to take the principle of non-contradiction as an assertion about real psychic occurrences and as arising even by generalization from such occurrences. In this connection psychologism proves to be blind to the genuine sense of such principles, namely, that they assert something about *ideal* Being, about the judged content and not about the psychic occurrence of judging. Thus, the basic defect of psychologism consists in its naturalistic blindness to ideal Being, that is, in its failure to understand a basic differentiation in the Being of beings (*im Sein des Seienden*). Heidegger notes that what lies in the background of the entire debate is the question of the meaning of Being (*Sinn des Seins*). More to the immediate point, he says that "this critique of psychologism is governed by the distinction between real and ideal Being." And then—decisively—he adds: "This distinction is nothing other than the Platonic distinction between sensible Being, the αισθητόν, and Being as it becomes accessible through reason, through νοῦς, the νοητόν."[20] This distinction is what provides the positive basis for Husserl's entire critique of psychologism. Indeed, this basis is clearly identified in Husserl's text. For example, in the "Prolegomena to Pure Logic," in a passage in which Husserl is criticizing the relativizing of truth, he writes: "Each truth, however, remains in itself what it is; it retains its ideal Being. It does not hang 'somewhere in the void,' but is a valid unity in the timeless realm of ideas."[21]

This passage makes it clear that Heidegger's account simply underlines what is already evident in Husserl's text. And yet, the implications of Husserl's reliance on the basic Platonic distinction are more far-reaching for Heidegger and will become even more so in the years following the publication of *Being and Time*. For this distinction lies at the very basis of metaphysics; and, as Heidegger's work in the 1930s will show, it is a distinction that, with Nietzsche, proves to have been exhausted. The question looms already on the horizon: what is the implication for logic once thinking twists free of this distinction?

Yet in the 1925–1926 course Heidegger remains within the context of phenomenology and, at most, of the transformation it undergoes in *Being and Time*. Thus, in the course, Heidegger introduces phenomenology as a new kind of research that takes over the role previously assigned to psychology, but now with full awareness of the difference between real and ideal Being. It is a question, then, of just how this difference is to be understood phenomenologically. Heidegger recalls that this is just the old problem of the participation of the sensible in the supersensible. Yet he insists that this conception perverts the problem and contributes nothing to its solution. Here is his caricature of it: "One would take the gap and bridge it; this is about as clever as the advice that in order to make the barrel of a cannon one should take a hole and put steel around it."[22] Over against such strategies, Heidegger poses the conception of the psyche according to which its basic character consists in intentionality. Granted this basic character, it can then be said "that the psychic is in itself something like a relation of the real to the ideal."[23] As intentional, the psyche opens the distinction rather than coming to bridge a gap that is already there. At the most profound level such an opening occurs through what Husserl calls transcendental constitution and describes as the idealizing achievement of intentional consciousness. Thus, even as—in the later parts of this very course—Heidegger's Dasein analytic comes to displace—or at least to resituate—the phenomenological conception of the psyche, he continues nonetheless to draw on that conception. In one recently published text from 1927, he even refers—in a conciliatory gesture perhaps—to transcendental constitution as made possible by Dasein.[24]

But no such conciliatory gestures are to be found in the second of the four lecture-courses. Indeed the difference can already be heard in the title of this course, which Heidegger presented in summer semester 1928, his last semester in Marburg. The course is called *Metaphysische Anfangsgründe der Logik*, and the specific approach that Heidegger takes to this theme is indicated by the supplementary phrase *Im Ausgang von Leibniz*. Thus the course is not addressed primarily to logic as such but to its originary metaphysical grounds as these can be discerned in the thought of Leibniz.

Nonetheless the tone with which the 1928 course begins sounds very much like that of the earlier course. Heidegger observes that logic as currently taught is dry as dust; also it seems to be quite useless and completely disconnected from philosophy. Heidegger declares: "There is need for another logic . . . , because what is called logic is not a logic at all and has nothing in common anymore with philosophy."[25] What is needed, he adds, is that logic become philosophical. If, envisioning this goal, one could clarify the idea of a philosophical logic, then—says Heidegger—it would be possible to render transparent the genuine history of logic. But then—he continues—it will become clear that "the thread of logic's 'development' was already broken with Aristotle and Plato and could not be picked up again—despite all the new impulses that entered logic through Leibniz, Kant, and Hegel, and finally through Husserl."[26] Here the dissonance begins to sound. In Heidegger's effort to render logic philosophical and thus to overcome the decline that it has suffered since antiquity, it no longer suffices, in Heidegger's view, to renew the phenomenological grounding of logic inaugurated by Husserl, nor even to radicalize the Husserlian initiative. Not even Husserl has succeeded in picking up the broken thread of logic; and if logic is to be genuinely renewed, if it is to be rendered philosophical, the effort must move in another direction.

This other direction is precisely what is indicated in the main title of the course, *Metaphysische Anfangsgründe der Logik.* What Heidegger undertakes is no longer the move from logical idealities back to the constitutive performances in relation to which they would be grounded. Rather, the move now is from the laws of logic back to their metaphysical ground. It is a move from traditional logic, for example, from the logic of judgment as formulated by Leibniz, back to such basic problems as those of truth, ground, and freedom. The move is, in Heidegger's words, "a critical dismantling (*Abbau*) of traditional logic down to its concealed foundations."[27] And, as the title of the first major part says, it begins with the *Destruktion* of the Leibnizian theory of judgment down to the underlying metaphysical problems. What is said in these two words, *Abbau* and *Destruktion,* as they are shaped in Heidegger's discourse, is precisely what Jacques Derrida undertook to express in French by the word *déconstruction.* What Heidegger's 1928 course proposes, then, is precisely the deconstruction of logic.

And yet, even at the conclusion of the 1928 course, the question remains: Does this deconstruction of logic have the effect of renewing logic? Does it render logic philosophical? Is the outcome of the deconstruction a philosophical logic? Or does the move back to the metaphysical grounds not simply leave logic behind? Toward the end of the course there are several significant indications. First of all, Heidegger relates logic to the fundamental problems of truth and of transcendence, and then on this basis he declares that "logic itself is metaphysics."[28] It is as if the very move from logic to the metaphysical grounds were such as to draw logic into the sphere of metaphysics. Thus, secondly, Heidegger refers to the "*Radikalizierung der Logik zur Metaphysik*" and even, finally, to "logic as metaphysics."[29] The radicalization and grounding of logic have, it seems, had the effect of assimilating logic to metaphysics. What remains is not a philosophical logic but rather a metaphysical discourse in which logic as such has disappeared.

The third lecture-course on logic was presented in summer semester 1934. Like the first course, its title expresses a definite conception of what logic is. It is called *Logik als Frage nach dem Wesen der Sprache.* As in many other discussions, Heidegger notes that the word *logic* derives from the expression ἐπιστήμη λογική; but now he stresses that, as the science or knowledge of λόγος, logic has pre-eminently to do with language.

Unlike the other courses, this one begins with a review of the structure of traditional logic: Heidegger describes the ways in which logic investigates terms, propositions, and syllogisms; and he shows how, corresponding to these themes, logic involves the principles of identity, of contradiction, and of ground. He stresses also the purely formal character of logic.

It is only after this review of the themes of traditional logic that Heidegger announces the aim of the course: it is neither to ground logic nor to regress to the metaphysical principles that underlie it; the aim is, rather, *to shake* logic. In his words: "We want to shake logic as such from its beginning on and from the ground up, to awaken and make conceivable an originary task beneath this title."[30] Through this shaking of logic, Heidegger undertakes to show that the basic question of logic is that of the essence of language. The goal is, in his words, "the transformation of logic into the general task of the question concerning the essence of language."[31]

Toward the end of the course Heidegger touches again on the prospects for logic and speaks of the still-ungrasped task of renewing logic on the basis of the originary concept of the essence of language.[32] Yet this remains little more than a prospect as Heidegger concludes the course by declaring that the originary essence of language is to be found in the language of poetry (*Dichtung*). The way back from the language of poetry to the renewal of logic remains entirely uncharted.

In the last of the four courses, there is no longer any reference to this way back, and it appears that Heidegger has abandoned entirely the task of renewing logic, of rendering it philosophical. It is significant that in the title of this course, *Grundfragen der Philosophie: Ausgewählte "Probleme" der "Logik,"* the word *logic* occurs only in the subtitle and is enclosed in quotation marks. Heidegger explains the modification indicated by these marks: his intent is to go behind what have been taken—that is, misconstrued—as problems of logic in order that he might discover there the concealed, still-unasked basic questions of philosophy. In the idiom of this course, the word *logic* no longer names a philosophical discipline, not even one still in need of being rendered philosophical. Logic is no longer the logic of thinking but rather precisely that with which thinking must break. For the questions with which thinking would break through to its task at the end of philosophy have remained—even in the most radical case, that of Nietzsche—"caught in the shackles of 'logic.'"[33] Heidegger declares that the task is to go "beyond logic."[34]

In his postwar writings Heidegger seldom returns to the theme of logic. In those instances where he does touch on this theme—always briefly—what he says serves largely to confirm and consolidate the tendency that has been traced in the four lecture-courses.

For example, in the *Brief über den "Humanismus"* (1947), he places logic squarely on the side of metaphysics. But now, rather than leaving logic behind for the sake of metaphysics, Heidegger sets both over against originary thinking. He says: "'Logic' understands thinking as the representing of beings in their Being."[35] Yet this precisely is metaphysical thinking in distinction from the originary thinking of the truth of Being. Only such originary thinking can gain access to the essence of λόγος, which, says Heidegger, "was already obfuscated and lost in Plato and Aristotle, the founders of 'logic.'"[36] Yet such originary thinking of λόγος Heidegger describes, not as a renewal or radicalizing of logic, but rather as what is meant by "thinking against 'logic'" (*"gegen 'die Logik' denken"*).

The text from the 1960s titled "Das Ende der Philosophie und die Aufgabe des Denkens" clarifies the displacement that, from the late 1920s on, prevented Heidegger from adopting the Husserlian strategy for grounding logic. Already in *Being and Time* such a strategy was prohibited by the resituating of intentionality within Being-in-the-world, that is, by the displacement of subjectivity into Dasein. In the later text the sense of this displacement is conveyed by a word that already figures significantly in *Being and Time,* the word *Lichtung.* This word, according to Heidegger, says what remained unthought in phenomenology, in the appeal to the things themselves and in the turn to transcendental subjectivity.

As Heidegger inscribed his deconstruction of logic in the context, first, of fundamental ontology and, then, of the originary thinking of the truth of Being, he became ever more insistent on setting thinking apart from logic or from whatever might remain of logic. Thinking would go beyond logic, would become a thinking against logic, simply leaving it behind in its utter solidarity with metaphysics. The question that remains is that of a return from the deconstruction of logic to a renewal of logic. Once thinking is engaged with the truth of Being, once it is owned over to (*zugeeignet*) Being as *Ereignis,* does it become possible to take up again logic as the logic of thinking and in still unheard-of kinds of schemata to chart the traces (*Spuren*) of originary thinking?

NOTES

1. "die Wissenschaft von den Grundgebilden des Denkens" (Martin Heidegger, *Logik als die Frage nach dem Wesen der Sprache,* vol. 38 of *Gesamtausgabe* [Frankfurt am Main: Klostermann, 1998], 5. "die Wissenschaft von den formalen Grundgebilden und Regeln des Denkens" (GA 38: 11).

2. "'Wahrheit für die oder jene Spezies,' z.B. für die menschliche, das ist . . . eine widersinnige Rede." / "Was wahr ist, ist absolut, ist 'an sich' wahr; die Wahrheit ist identisch Eine, ob sie Menschen oder Unmenschen, Engel oder Götter urteilend erfassen" (Edmund Husserl, *Logische Untersuchungen,* 5th ed. [Tübingen: Max Niemeyer, 1968], vol. 1, 1936, 117).

3. "Endlich und schliesslich hängt die letzte Klärung auch in diesem Streite zunächst [Zitat fängt hier an] von der richtigen Erkenntnis des fundamentalsten erkenntnistheoretischen Unterschiedes, nämlich dem zwischen Realem und Idealem ab . . ." (ibid., 1951, 188).

4. "In dem Streit um psychologische oder objektive Begründung der Logik nehme ich also eine Mittelstellung ein" (ibid., 1943, 164).

5. "so sah ich mich in immer steigendem Masse zu allgemeinen kritischen Reflexionen über das Wesen der Logik und zumal [Zitat fängt hier an] über das Verhältnis zwischen der Subjektivität des Erkennens und der Objektivität des Erkenntnisinhaltes gedrängt" (ibid., vii).

6. "[Andererseits] erschliesst die Phänomenologie die 'Quellen,' aus denen die Grundbegriffe und die idealen Gesetze der reinen Logik 'entspringen,' und bis zu welchen sie wieder zurückverfolgt werden müssen, um ihnen die für ein erkenntniskritisches Verständnis der reinen Logik erforderliche 'Klarheit und Deutlichkeit' zu verschaffen" (ibid., vol. II/1, 3).

7. See Husserl, *Formale und Transzendentale Logik*, vol. 17 of Husserliana, ed. Paul Janssen (The Hague: Martinus Nijhoff, 1974), 109. This work first appeared in 1929.

8. "Tragik der modernen wissenschaftlichen Kultur," ibid., 7.

9. "Fackelträgerin der Methode," ibid., 6.

10. "nur eine transzendentale Logik kann eine letzte Wissenschaftslehre . . . sein" (ibid., 20).

11. "die nicht eine zweite Logik, sondern nur die in phänomenologischer Methode erwachsende radikale und konkrete Logik selbst ist" (ibid., 296).

12. Husserl says regarding logic: "Vielmehr in beständig zweiseitiger (sich dabei wechselweise bestimmender) Forschung muss sie systematisch von den idealen Gebilden auf das sie phänomenologisch konstituierende Bewusstsein zurückgehen" (ibid., 270).

13. See ibid., 38–39.

14. See ibid., 85–86.

15. See ibid., 184.

16. See Heidegger, *Logik: Die Frage nach der Wahrheit*, vol. 21 of *Gesamtausgabe* (Frankfurt am Main: Klostermann, 1976), 24. This lecture-course was given in winter semester 1925–1926.

17. Heidegger, "Mein Weg in die Phänomenologie," in *Zur Sache des Denkens*, vol. 14 of *Gesamtausgabe* (Frankfurt am Main: Klostermann, 2007), 97.

18. See Heidegger, *Logik*, 12–13.

19. See ibid., 18.

20. "diese Kritik des Psychologismus ist am Leitfaden der Unterscheidung von realem und idealem Sein. . . . Dieser Unterschied ist nichts anderes als der Platonische Unterschied zwischen dem sinnlichen Sein, dem αἰσθητόν, und dem Sein, wie es durch Vernunft zugänglich wird, durch den νος, das νοητον" (ibid., 52).

21. "Aber jede Wahrheit an sich bleibt, was sie ist, sie behält ihr ideales Sein. Sie ist nicht 'irgendwo im Leeren,' sondern ist eine Geltungseinheit im unzeitlichen Reiche der Ideen" (Husserl, *Logische Untersuchungen*, vol. 1, 1939, 130).

22. "Man nehme die Kluft und ziehe die Brücke; das ist ungefähr so schlau, wie die übliche Anweisung, man nehme ein Loch und mache darum Stahl, um ein Kanonenrohr herzustellen" (Heidegger, *Logik*, 92).

23. "dass das Psychische in sich selbst so etwas wie eine Beziehung ist des Realen zum Idealen" (ibid., 98).

24. Heidegger writes that Dasein "in sich die Moglichkeit der transzendentalen Konstitution birgt"; also that "die Existenzverfassung des Daseins die transzendentale Konstitution alles Positiven ermöglicht." These remarks occur in Anlage I to a letter of October 22, 1927, that Heidegger wrote to Husserl concerning their joint work on the article "Phenomenology" for the *Encyclopedia Britannica*. The texts are published in *Zur Sache des Denkens*, 129–132.

25. "bedarf es einer anderen Logik . . . , weil die sogenannte Logik gar keine Logik ist und mit Philosophie nichts mehr gemein hat" (Heidegger, *Metaphysische Anfangsgründe der Logik im Ausgang von Leibniz,* vol. 26 of *Gesamtausgabe* [Frankfurt am Main: Klostermann, 1978], 5–6).

26. "dann zeigt sich, dass der Faden ihrer 'Entwicklung' bereits bei Aristoteles und Plato abriss und seitdem unauffindbar geblieben ist—bei allen neuen Impulsen, die durch Leibniz, Kant und Hegel und zuletzt durch Husserl in die Logik kamen" (ibid., 7).

27. See ibid., 27.

28. "dann ist die Logik selbst Metaphysik" (ibid., 281).

29. Ibid., 282.

30. "Wir wollen die Logik als solche von ihrem Anfang an aus ihrem Grund erschüttern, eine ursprüngliche Aufgabe unter diesem Titel erwecken und greifbar machen" (Heidegger, *Logik als die Frage nach dem Wesen der Sprache,* vol. 38 of *Gesamtausgabe* [Frankfurt am Main: Klostermann, 1998], 8).

31. "die Verwandlung der Logik in die allgemeine Aufgabe der Frage nach dem Wesen der Sprache" (ibid., 18).

32. See ibid., 169.

33. "in den Fesseln der 'Logik' gefangen" (Heidegger, *Grundfragen der Philosophie: Ausgewählte "Probleme" der "Logik,"* vol. 45 of *Gesamtausgabe* [Frankfurt am Main: Klostermann, 1984], 11).

34. "über die Logik" (ibid., 8).

35. "Die 'Logik' versteht das Denken als das Vorstellen von Seiendem in seinem Sein" (*Brief über den "Humanismus,"* in *Wegmarken,* vol. 9 of *Gesamtausgabe* [Frankfurt am Main: Klostermann, 1976], 348).

36. "das anfängliche Wesen des λόγος, das [Zitat fängt an] bei Plato und Aristoteles, dem Begründer der 'Logik,' schon verschüttet und verlorengegangen ist" (ibid.).

SIX

Giving Its Word: Event (as) Language

Krzysztof Ziarek

> "What is the word? The soundless voice/tune of beyng. What is called voice here? Not 'sound' but the tuning, that is, letting ex-perience." *Das Ereignis,* 283

Language is not simply one of the topics or issues in Heidegger's vast work. Rather it is the issue *of* Heidegger's work in the literal sense: Heidegger's thinking issues *from* language, from the way-making of language and its signature trait of having always already arrived into signs, into speech and writing, into poetry (*Dichten*) and thinking (*Denken*), as though there has only been nothing before words. Language sets the tone (*Stimmung*) for Heidegger's work, lets its experience unfold, lending it its idiomatic non-metaphysical voice (*Stimme*), at once challenging and annoying to our metaphysically well-trained ears. What English translation of these terms cannot capture is precisely the way in which the tonality of Heidegger's thought—its idiomatic rendering of being and its event *question-worthy* (*Fragwürdig*)—in short, its *Stimmung,* issues into the specific "voice" associated with his texts, especially those after the "turn," from *Contributions to Philosophy* onward. As Heidegger himself repeatedly underscores, it is only from the tonality of thinking that what is at issue in it can be determined (*bestimmt*). Understanding in the sense of conceptual grasp, the determination of the matter at hand and reflection upon it, takes place well only when it happens in tune with the tonality of thinking: *Bestimmung* needs to be in tune with the *Stimmung.* Only then can one say that the text's voice (*Stimme*) is own, proper (*eigen*) to the thinking.

This means that one cannot hear what is at issue in Heidegger's thought—let alone how and from where this thinking itself issues—nor determine its stakes, without primary attentiveness to language: both Heidegger's language and the way it issues from the problematic of language understood as being's event. Certainly no "critique," no *Auseinandersetzung* with Heidegger makes sense or makes any sense *of* his thinking without a careful and alert consideration of language, in fact, without a transformation of our relation to language beyond its metaphysical parameters of signs, differential signification, code, communication, and so forth. As *Contributions to Philosophy* indicates, the question of being, animating all of Heidegger's works, needs to be thought from the event (*Ereignis*). Yet such thinking from the event, or in "the other beginning," is not possible, or is quite simply un-thinkable—in the sense that it already reverts to metaphysical modes of thought—without, as Heidegger puts it in *On the Way to Language,* a transformation (*Verwandlung*) of our relation to language: "In order to pursue in thought the being of language and to say of it what is its own, a transformation of language is needed which we can neither compel nor invent. . . . It touches on our relation to language."[1] And this means a transformation in how the word and saying transpire, how language comes into signs, and thus into speech and writing. It does not, therefore, make sense—or perhaps makes only metaphysical (non)sense—to analyze or critique Heidegger's thought without that very transformation of (our relation to) language.

Yet all too often only scant attention is paid to language in discussion of Heidegger, or else such discussion becomes too quickly limited to consideration of poetry and art. And in the discussions of Heidegger situated between Continental and Analytic perspectives, the matter of language becomes telescoped into the problematic of ordinary language and/or of logic, as though the aim was to try to domesticate Heidegger's thought back into familiar and recognizable categories and terms. As a result, the latter approaches tend to evacuate precisely the very impetus of Heideggerian thought toward a *transformation* of our relation to language, a transformation that specifically requires changing the terms and the ways in which we experience language and ourselves in it.

Though Heidegger does not—at least in the texts published so far[2]—spell out in any one place the specifics of this transformation, with the continuing publication of his writings from the mid-1930s through mid-1940s, it has become possible to understand better the development of this notion of transformation in relation to language beyond what otherwise seems like a surprising turnabout from the notion of *Rede* (discourse) in *Being and Time* to the notions of saying (*Sage*), way-making (*Bewëgung*), word (*Wort*), and signs (*Wörter*), characteristic of Heidegger's later idiom, familiar especially from *On the Way to Language.* What follows attempts to elaborate and push further Heidegger's remarks on word, event, and saying in order to develop more explicitly this notion of transformation in relation to language hinted at in Heidegger's texts ranging from *Contributions to Philosophy* (1936–1938) to *On the Way to Language.*

Already in *Contributions,* Heidegger's approach to language evidences a shift, a new emphasis on transforming our relation to word, which comes to be seen as the movement of giving differentiated from signs. "The word fails. . . . originarily. The word does not even come to word, even though it is precisely when the word escapes one that the word begins to take its first leap. The word's escaping one is event (*Ereignis*) as the hint and onset of being (*Seyn*)."[3] When the word fails, when it does not reach words (that is, signs), the word, as it were, also escapes and frees itself from signs. This escape is the opening of the interval, and as such it is the hint of being, that is, of the endowing with being of what has been brought into words. Specifically, it is the hint of the temporal-spatial play that opens being into the always already given site, that is, its *Da,* its (t)here. It is the leap-origin, and that is why the word, in not coming into the word (sign), fails originarily, that is, in its ur-leap (*ursprünglich*). The word is originarily, which means in how it originates into signs, precisely in this escape from the word understood as sign. By working as a leap and not primarily as a sign, the word abides in being: since being unfolds and grounds by leaping, by having always already brought us "here and now." Similarly, word has always already given (itself) into terms or signs. This is why words taken as signs and conceived first and foremost in relation to their differential play of signification tend to obscure the way in which the word unfolds as a leap, which endows with being.

Later Heidegger will explicitly play on the distinction between words (*Worte*) and terms or signs (*Wörter*), which both function as plural forms of *Wort* (word), which means in turn that, in a way, words and signs can be seen as two dimensions of the complex event of the word. "Terms" refer to words taken as linguistic signs (*Zeichen*) and reflect an understanding of language through the prism of the play of signification. "Words," by contrast, describe a different dimension of language, one that constitutes its originary or originative momentum. This momentum is the leap, the origin (*Ur-sprung*), of language, which, by giving being to beings, makes room for signification and signs. Giving being to beings constitutes the origin of language, that is, the originary leap (*Ur-sprung*) that has always already brought language into the play of signification. The issuing of words marks not only the origin of language but also the opening up of world, which constitutes the clearing of being. As Heidegger puts it in his seminar *Vom Wesen der Sprache*, "the word grounds not only 'world,' but is of being and silently preserves the clearing of the there [*Da*]."[4] As the clearing of the *Da*, which gives being to beings by opening up world, the word is essentially richer than language understood in terms of signs and signification (WS 56). That is why the word taken in this sense of opening up world should not be understood as the singular form of "terms" or signs (*Wörter*), or as a specific single word, but approached instead as constituting "naming, address, and claim, and above all and essentially, it is the word of being, which means the reticence of the decision [*Austrag*] (event [*Ereignis*]), originary clearing" (WS 56). The word in its originative momentum opens the clearing of the there, where signification can arise to begin with. As this enactment of world, the word is to be understood as the attuning stillness (*die stimmende Stille*, WS 70), and this reticent, self-silencing stillness becomes audible, as it were, only when words, this time understood as linguistic signs, reach their limit and break up, opening onto silence. As Heidegger writes in *Vom Wesen der Sprache*, "when the word breaks up—being refuses itself [*versagen*]. But in this refusal, it [being] manifests itself in its reticence—as stillness, as the 'in-between,' as Da" (WS 72). This foregoing of being at the point of the breaking up of words is only seemingly a refusal, for it constitutes in fact a necessary missaying of being into signs, a missaying that marks a specific sense of nearness to being, a *Wesensnähe*, a nearness to the attuning stillness with which being unfolds.

Since a new language cannot be invented, one has instead "to say the language of beings as the language of be-ing" (CP 54). At issue here is precisely a transformed way of saying, which opens a decisively altered relation to the word. This relation to the word in its saying—that is, in its leap/origination into signs—is neither immediate nor in need of mediation. "We can never say be-ing (event) immediately—and thus also never say it mediately—in the sense of an enhanced 'logic' of dialectic" (CP 55). This is the case because for Heidegger, the event opens the very space for the immediate and the mediated, the space of this very distinction, its vicissitudes, movements, sublations, and so forth: "Whenever this reservedness comes to word, what is said is always the event [*Ereignis*]. . . . Saying grounds as reticence in silencing. Its word is not somehow only a sign for something totally other. What it names is what it means. But 'meaning' is owned up to only as *Da-sein* and that means in thinking-questioning" (CP 55). Obviously, the word is understood here in a very specific and circumscribed way, namely as the manner and the movement in which a being is given its being. As Heidegger writes in his essay "The Word," the word endows a thing with being,[5] and thus it conditions the thing, it literally be-things (*be-dingt*) it, by letting a thing be a thing.[6] It is this minimal and yet all opening momentum—the incipient momentum of being and of language—that Heidegger calls the "word" (*Wort*).

Because of the change in our relation to the word (UZS 228), one can no longer relate to words the same way one relates to signs or terms. For signs (*Wörter*) are in a certain way "things," or beings, and one can say of them precisely that they "are," which makes possible describing their manner of being and analyzing their functions. The word, on the other hand, is not any thing; in fact, it is not a thing to begin with, as it does not pertain to the domain of beings but has to do instead with being. "Thus the poetic experience with the word gives us a meaningful hint. The word—no thing, nothing that is, no being" (WL 87). One cannot say, therefore, that the word "is," only that it gives being, that the word means nothing other than this specific way of letting be. "We may never say of the word that it is, but rather that it gives. The word is itself the giver [Das Wort: das Gebende] . . . the word gives Being" (WL 88/UZS 193). The word is the giving but never a *something* given, for the word never "is" as a thing or as a being. Because the word "gives," it is the word of being in a double sense: it both gives "of" being, that is, it lets something be, but it is also itself "of" being, that is, it issues from being. Language thus is the issue *of* being in the double, subjective and objective, momentum of the genitive. Being issues (into) language; and language provides the issue for being—its event—into words as signs or terms in the play of signification.

Examined through the prism of this originative "between" between word and sign, Heidegger's approach to words evidences constant attempts to open words beyond their operation as linguistic signs (*Wörter*). What can be seen as interpreting or laying out (*Auslegung*) of the etymological layers gathered in the sign's lexical resonance—whether in relation to Greek and Latin terms or with regard to the complex deployment of German terminology—can, and in fact I would say needs to, be understood as an opening of signs to the covered-over momentum of giving, to the "between" characteristic of what Heidegger calls the word (*Wort*). As *Das Ereignis* puts it, at issue is a thinking that can sometimes hear in the language signs the word of being: "in den Wörtern der Sprache jeweils das Wort hört."[7] This hearing that enfolds signs back into words is likewise at stake in the hyper-hyphenation to which Heidegger subjects most of the key German terms he employs, alters, or introduces. A much longer analysis would be required here but let me just point to a few key examples: *Ereignis, Da-sein/Da-seyn, Ur-sprung, Ge-stell, An-fang, Auf-riss,* or, in a slightly different key, the play, the invisible hyphen as it were, between *Sein* and *Seyn* on which the "drawer" writings from the decade following the mid-1930s rely. Beyond the generative play of the double etymology of *Ereignis* (*er-eignen* and *er-äugen*) (E 184–185) and debates about which one is more "proper" (*eigen*) to the term in Heidegger's use of it—all crucial and significant in their own right—what is even more interesting and, for me, more important, is the way in which Heidegger, using an everyday German word, breaks it open beyond its signification, beyond its role as a sign, indicating thus the very momentum of giving, which he associates with the word as *das Gebende,* as nothing but the very movement of giving. It is precisely this momentum, a vibration beyond the term's possible play of signification, that is brought forth and emphasized by the employment of the hyphen in *Er-eignis* and the simultaneous spotlighting and heightening by this very hyphen of the enactive capacity of the prefix *er-*.

This breaching of the envelope of the sign, the opening of the sign to its covered silent resonance of the "word," is perhaps even more ingenious in the *Ge-stell,* which turns an ordinary term for rack or frame into the "saying," through the multiple resonances of *stellen,* of the word(s) for the essential unfolding of technicity: *vorstellen, darstellen, herstellen, bestellen, sicherstellen, verstellen.* Again the hyphen plays the same role here: it estranges the sign into word and emphasizes the gathering at work in the prefix *ge-*. It is quite fitting that "word," since it is not a being or a thing like signs, and since as such it does not "exist" as a something and in fact is not an "it" to begin with, is marked precisely by hyphens: the indices of the in-between, of the spacing-temporalizing play opening into the (t)here of Da-sein. Hyphens enact the originative between of the word's giving (into) sign; they recall the momentum of the always already, which tends to be covered over by the sign's lexical spectrum. It is in this sense that I see the force of hyphenation in Heidegger as the index of the transformation of our relation to language; since a new language cannot be invented, hyphens and etymological dis-layerings prompt us perhaps into a changed relation to language: beyond the system of signs and their differential play to words in their originative giving. *Er-eignis* is above all the event of this transformation.

That *Ereignis* "gives" and "is given" into language is made explicit, apart from the essays collected in *On the Way to Language,* in Heidegger's first sustained articulation of the transformation in relation to language that comes in the just published volume 71 of *Gesamtausgabe,* with the eponymous title *Das Ereignis,* or *The Event,* whose manuscript dates from 1941/1942. The most important remarks are contained in chapter 5, "Das Ereignis: Der Wortschatz seines Wesens": "The Event: The Vocabulary of Its Essential Unfolding," though observations on language, word, and saying are scattered throughout the volume. As Heidegger puts it in this chapter, "Das Ereignis ist das anfägliche Wort, weil seine Zueignung (als die einzige An-eignung des Menschenwesens in die Wahrheit des Seyns) das Wesen des Menschen auf die Wahrheit des Seyns stimmt": "The event is the inceptive word, because its dedication [Zueignung] (as the singular appropriation [An-eignung] of man's essence into the truth of being) tunes the essence of man to the truth of being" (E 169). The play of *Zueignung* and *Aneignung* manifests the momentum of the event itself, of the "proper-ing" (*eignis*) reverberating in the German term. The prefix *zu* indicates the way in which the event dedicates its "giving to be" to "man" and in the same move dedicates man's thinking to itself, that is, to the event. This reciprocal dedication, the event's saying itself to the human and the saying by the human "of" the event into words, comes to transpire only because what takes place as and in the event is the rendering of the human "appropriate" (*An-eignung*), that is, alert and attentive to, the truth, the unconcealment, of being. In this way the event "tunes" (*stimmt*) the humans to how being has, in the blink of an eye, always already unfolded in its spatio-temporal leap/origin into the "here and now," that is, unfolded as the moment (*Augenblick*).

The event is a soundless (*lautlose*) word: word before sounds and letters, word before sign, word giving in(to) sign. It is nothing but the movement into signs that gives "being" to what exists, naming and signifying it in signs, in human language. In *Das Ereignis,* word is described by Heidegger as both *Vor-wort* (E 252) and *An-wort,* at once a pre-word or fore-word and a to- or on-word. As that which gives (being), the word precedes words (as signs), it fore-words them. As pre-word, it is not, however, a something that exists before or prior to signs. Rather, the word happens by to-wording, by having always already arrived into and as signs. The word is neither identical nor different from the sign, since it is not of the order of signs, that is, of beings. Just as being is neither different nor identical to beings but rather marks the giving of beings to be, neither separable from nor identical to what beings come to be. The differential operation breaks down here, and for the "simple" reason that this very opening of being onto beings makes possible and marks the activation of difference. It is in this specific way that the word fore- and en-words, giving the resonance of being to what comes to be signified. The word in its resonance as sign is already the word's response to the pre-word ("Das Vorwort in der Antwort des Wortes" [E 263]). This is perhaps how *Stimmung* has to be thought: the word gives the key to signs, it tunes language, and on occasion perhaps even attunes it in such a way that what is given voice (*Stimme*) in language remains attentive to the tuning itself. The link between "tuning" or "key" and "voice" in German allows for a movement of *Stimmung* to transpire precisely as what gives voice, what "sounds" into language. The way in which the event addresses and dedicates humans, rendering them appropriate for, or in tune with, the event, is what prompts human speaking and writing. In this way, the verb *stimmen* in Heidegger does not signify only the tuning or tonality of experience but, and crucially, the movement through which this tuning brings being to the brink of human language, thus allowing experience ("Erfahren lassen"). Heidegger on occasion writes about the soundless voice (*lautlose Stimme*) of words, trying to mark this transition, which has always already happened, from word to sign, and from soundlessness to language. In fact, the German term for language, *Sprache,* indicates this pivot of vocalization, making it the "essence," the way that language unfolds. As Heidegger elsewhere remarks, the fact that language speaks ("*Die Sprache spricht*") or languages is taken by him as the opening onto letters and sounds, writing and speech. There is no room here to elaborate in more detail what should be more fittingly called the pivot of language (as vocalization/lettering) but only to indicate that it is not to be taken too quickly as a privileging of speech over writing, presence over absence, and so forth. The preponderance of terms having to do with sounding and hearing, tuning and saying in Heidegger is linked to the fact that the word in the sense outlined above has less to do with speech as opposed to writing than it does with melody and rhythm, with *melos* and *rhythmos,* understood not simply in relation to language but rather to the rhythm of the unfolding of the world and experience, a kind of *melos* or melody of manifestation. And perhaps like in music, the writing, the score, pre-scribes here the sounding in performance. For the word in its special Heideggerian valence is neither speech nor writing but rather the giving into signs and therefore into speech and writing. *Stimmung* thus performs the tonalization of language in the complex sense of both setting the tone and giving "voice" to the soundless and signless pre-wording addressing itself to language. It is in this sense that Heidegger can write about the word as the inceptually "tuning/voicing voice": "die anfänglich stimmende Stimme: das Wort" (E 169).

It is clear that Heidegger's approach to language pivots on the notion that the giving of being, its event, is itself already a language, a word-less, that is, as yet sign-free language of giving/manifestation, on the way to signs: "Das Ereignis ist das anfägliche Wort." And "das Seyn selbst anfänglich das Wort ist" ("being is itself inceptually the word") (E 172). Human languages are part of this broader sense of language, as they come always already as a response to the giving of being—a hearing-belonging (*hören/gehören*) to manifestation and a bringing of it into words/signs. Human language, its words or signs, its speech and writing, are constituted in response and as a response (*Antwort*) to the word as event. This is why Heidegger can write in *On the Way to Language:* "the being (Wesen) of language: the language of being (Wesen)." Here it is the colon that marks the always already occurred transition or tonalization, which has moved the event as the inceptive word into the words of human language. The colon also indicates that the very being/essence of language, its unfolding or "languaging," is the language of being, that is, the wordless saying of the way being is given to be, that is, the event, always by way of beings and the signs used to signify them.

A few words need to be said here about the sense of inceptuality that Heidegger associates with the event as word.[8] Heidegger employs the term

Anfang (most often translated as "beginning") to differentiate it from *Beginn:* start or mere beginning. *An-fang,* often hyphenated by Heidegger, does not indicate a temporal moment in which something starts or commences, but instead an opening into an initial, inceptual capture (from the verb *fangen:* to capture, catch, seize): a proleptic extension that gives the momentum to what is coming and thus captures it within the tonality set at and by the beginning (*An-fang*). The first beginning of thinking in ancient Greece has thus captured "Western" thought in its peculiar tonality of presence, idea, substance, and so forth, which still resonate today through the key structuring terms of Western thought: representation, subject/object, essence, substance, presence/absence, and so forth. In this sense, Greece, though inescapably Latinized, keeps "beginning" over and over again; or, to put it differently, our thinking, no matter how changed, developed, or evolved from the first beginning, finds itself repeatedly captured by its tonality. Hence Heidegger's investment in the possibility of the other beginning has to do with a different tonality for thinking, which would breach the inceptual enclosure of the Greek beginning and possibly allow thinking to begin otherwise.

To say that the event is the inceptive word is to suggest this initial and initializing capture in a saying that the word brings into signs. "Die Sage ist selbst die Anfängnis des Anfangs. Sage bringt stimmend ins Wort (nicht Wörter) und erschweigt den Anfang" (E 297). "The saying is itself the inceptuality of the beginning. Tuning, saying brings into word (not signs) and keeps silent the beginning." The word is "inceptive" precisely in the sense that it tonalizes (*stimmt*) language (by keeping reticent in signs the saying of the beginning): its signs, grammar, play of signification, social and communicative functions, literary and philosophical use, and so forth. If the word is legible at all it is only as the pitch, the silent saying, it has given to signs, to human language(s). And if the event is the inceptive word, then what this means is that it prompts and perhaps makes possible a transformation in our relation to language, the transformation beyond the capture of the first, metaphysical, beginning. This would mean a difficult transformation in our essentially metaphysical attitude to language: as primarily human language, a differential system of signs and signification, an informational tool. The metaphysical beginning has captured us in the relation to language in which language increasingly and ever more powerfully discloses itself as information, open to and in fact inviting manipulation, change, experimentation, without, however, any transformation in the metaphysical tone in which we have come to experience language. In fact, this metaphysical tone only strengthens and amplifies, drowning out any other possible relation to language as "ineffectual," value-less, unproductive, impractical, unreal. The metaphysical determination of language, culminating in the notion of language as information, discloses being into information, that is, as informational code: from human genome to genetic research and macro-informational and global telematic communications. The informational tonality of language determinative of the information age functions as part and parcel of the power-driven operations of the contemporary world: it secures, via disclosure of beings and their transposition into information, an unprecedented access to being(s), rendering them open to increasingly penetrative deployments of power, manipulation, and processing.

The encounter of being in terms of power is thus coded, one could say "literally," into the prevalence of informational codes as the contemporary conduits of power. It is linked in an essential way to the metaphysical tonality of language, which distills language down to its supposed informational essence. Being does not happen here as event that gives but instead opens up into an informational code, intrinsically predisposed to manipulation, that is, predisposed to be at the disposal of power. Being here has no words, only signs, which, in spite of the multiplicity of languages, appear to be all reducible to two, to the binary code of informational operations. At the time when being appears to be the most loquacious it has ever been, disclosing everywhere and everything into potential informational value and transmitting information with unprecedented speed and on a global scale, it seems to be simultaneously losing its ability to say anything beyond the stutter of 0 and 1. The Janus face of information: information is power affecting all; information says very little, almost nothing, repeating ones and zeros ever more efficiently.

Heidegger hoped that the Janus-faced *Ge-stell* could potentially allow the disclosure of a different way of relating beyond the global *Machenschaft* of power. But this would precisely entail a decisive transformation in our relation to language. At present, this relation is the result of the metaphysically set tone for relations as operations of power, graded and evaluated in terms of effectiveness and conducted today most efficiently by way of information. As information, language is perhaps the most powerful tool the humans could hope for. Yet at the same time, it is so because being today speaks the language of information: being *is* information, to be decoded and recoded with a view to the increase in power and its more thorough circulation. The transformation in relation to language would then be a transformation in relation to power, as it would shift the center of gravity away from humans and from their apparent control of the operations of power. Since the informational coding of language suggests that its primary function is to be of use in conveying and processing information, it gives the humans the position of those who aim to control and profit from this processing. Thus all that exists appears to be there *for* humans and their benefit, informational and otherwise, at their disposal, or at least at the disposal of power that humans aspire to control ever more efficiently. By contrast, in Heidegger's "transformational" view of language, humans are always already in response, their word is never originative but always a response (*Antwort*). This response enacts an originary "responsibility" or responsiveness (*Verantwortung*) of the humans toward the event. This responsibility is of an ontological order, that is, toward being, and, as Heidegger makes clear, is not to be thought of in moral or ethical terms. In fact, only because humans are by way of responding and being responsive/responsible toward the event can there be ethical or moral responsibility. Without the human capacity to be responsive to the event—a capacity that the event itself gives or dedicates to humans in the sense Heidegger calls *Zueignung*—that is, without the human capacity to listen to and bring the word of being into signs, there would be no possibility of ethics.

The transformation here would be from the relation in terms of power to relation as responsiveness. This does not mean that power could be wished away but rather that its operations would be enveloped within responsiveness; its tone would be reset from machination and drive toward more power to that of primary responsiveness, perhaps even responsibility. Information relies on the possibility of grasping the "language" of being as a code and its intrinsic disposition toward processing and manipulation, making language essentially the business of power: signification, representation, knowledge, and so forth. No doubt creative power as well, which means power open to changes, invention, and re-fashioning, but nonetheless conceived of and carried out exclusively on its own terms, that is, without changing the fundamental tone: power. What would be involved in the transformation indicated by Heidegger would be precisely a re-tuning of relation into a tonality not permeated and regulated by power. While signs can be said to be within the domain of power—its alterations, subversions, undoings, re-formulations, and so forth—signs, as Heidegger remarks, are given from the event. "Das Ereignis . . . , als welche die Kehre des Seyns sich stimmend sich ereignet und das Zeigen des Zeichen gewärt" (E 173). The event is the turning of being, which, eventing in a tonality, grants or accords the showing/display of signs. As such the event is the treasure or wealth of words ("Das Er-eignis ist der Schatz des Wortes"; E 173). This wealth of words is to be experienced as the origin of the vocabulary, that is, of signs or words in the usual sense ("der Schatz des Wortes als der Ursprung des 'Wortschatzes'"; E 172).

The leap (*Ursprung*), always already leaped, into signs (*Zeichen*) leaves the mark of the hyphen in signs: it is the mark of the hyphen in *das Ereignis,* which transforms "event" (occurrence, happening, incident) into the full-blown transformative resonance into which Heidegger opens this term. The same can be said of other familiar terms in Heidegger and their estrangement into "words." Therefore what we need to pay more attention to is precisely the valence, the momentum of the hyphen in its thinking/poietic resonance or tonality. For Heidegger, it is the "words" that allow signs to appear, to have language in the sense of human languages. Yet we should not forget this movement of the dispersion and the transfer into signs. It is this movement, the way-making of language, as Heidegger comes to call it in *On the Way to Language,* that maintains itself apart from power while opening onto it and allowing it its full play: it is *macht-los,* released, unrelated to power, in the sense developed in *Besinnung.*

The ability to engage with Heidegger's thought is written into his texts in the form of a call to transforming our relation to language. This means that the possibility of following and confronting critically this thought is predicated upon the switch in the tenor of thinking, a switch essentially related to language, to how experience and thought find themselves in and undergo this relation. I have focused here on the hyphen and its inceptive possibilities in Heidegger's work: from *Er-eignis* and *Da-sein* to *An-fang* and *Ge-stell.* The hyphen and its enacting of the originative in-between (word to sign; saying to meaning; *Stimmung* to *Stimme*) is coupled in its workings to the nexus of prefixes, which from the start play a pivotal role in how Heidegger thinks and writes. It is possible to quickly sketch out Heidegger's approach to language precisely by way of paying attention to four strings of words he uses to give the particular resonance to his remarks: *Wort* (word); *sprechen* (to speak) and *Sprache* (language); *Sage* and *sagen* (saying); *Stimme* (voice) and *Stimmung* (tonality, pitch, mood). I am limiting my remarks here to four word strings, though at least two more immediately come to mind: *Klang* and *Laut*. Obviously Heidegger highlights these terms, in fact he bases the very movement of his writings on language on these words and their derivatives, because they directly "address" matters of language; word, language, speaking, saying, voice. Though it is impossible to illustrate it here, I would suggest that this cluster of words and their derivatives plays in Heidegger's thought in tune with *Er-eignis* and its related words: *ereignen, eräugen, eigen, zueignen, aneignen, übereignen, enteignen,* and so forth. In fact, the various ways in which the event "events," resonant in how the sheaf of words with the root *-eignen* is diffused through Heidegger's texts, take explicitly the tone of language, that is, the event transpires by way of *sagen, sprechen, stimmen,* in short as the relational momentum associated with the word (*Wort*). Briefly, one could say that *Zueignung* unfolds as *Zusprechen* and/or *Zusagen, Aneignung* as *Ansprechen, Anstimmen,* and so forth. While there is no exact mapping, word for word or prefix for prefix, of the way the event "gives" onto the cluster of words explicitly moving language (from *sagen* to *sprechen* and *stimmen*), what strikes one is the precise and sustained deployment of the hyphenated prefixes, which animate much of Heidegger's writing. As I have already stated, this hyphenation and telescoping of attention onto prefixes constitutes in fact the very momentum, the movement, of Heidegger's thinking. This means that, over against whatever gets captured by thinking into signs (concepts, ideas), or foreshortened into propositions, what is at issue in Heidegger's work is precisely what fails to be captured by propositional statements, by signs and their signification, as he indicates explicitly at the end of "Time and Being."[9]

To the extent that Heidegger's texts ineluctably "write" in propositions, they contravene the very transformation his thought is trying to evince. For the transformation at issue here is expressly the transformation of the priority given to statements and thus to words as signs, meaning, concepts, definitions, and so forth. In short, the transformation Heidegger pushes toward will not be captured or performed by way of propositional statements: trying to define it would only effectuate the contrary by re-capturing within the tenor of metaphysical thinking what tries to breach its boundaries. As if against propositional efficiency, the force of this transformation is located precisely in the prefix: *Ver-wandlung.* Unlike the Latinate "trans," the German "*ver*" does not indicate a transition into something new or other, the possibility of a beyond to metaphysics and metaphysical deployments of language. Rather it provokes a twisting and a skewing, a turn or a torsion exposing language to its concealed "verso." In Heidegger's texts, we can track this twisting precisely by way of hyphenated prefixes, which, in a sense, all augment and resonate the torquing force of the German "*ver.*"

This cluster of prefixes singles out, though is not limited to, the following: er-, an-, ent-, zu-, unter-, über-, ant-, ge-, and, of course, ver-. Throughout his texts, Heidegger attaches these prefixes to the four words signaling the movement of language: *stimmen, Wort, sagen, sprechen.* Doing so and, at the same time, frequently hyphenating the attached prefixes allows Heidegger to emphasize the directionality of the ways in which the event eventuates by tuning, saying, wording, speaking, and so forth. The prefixes thus come to form a web of their own, marking the moment, the blink of an eye, in which the breaking open of the relationality constitutes the very (t)here, the clearing, in which beings come to appear. Though "words of being" do not enter signs, for Heidegger they do "say" themselves along with them, with words become signs, as *Basic Concepts* explains.[10] What is thus "said" is only always as pre- or fore-said: a *Vor-wort* or fore-word. Its silent resonance does not need to be directly in sounds or letters, scripted into the network of signs, for, if listened to on the right frequency, as it were, its tonality can still be detected in the operations of language. The exaggerated hyphenation of prefixes lends Heidegger's texts an unmistakable spatio-temporal "tenor," if that is the term to be used here, displaying signs as "words" always already dislocated. This dis-location is a fitting way for words to mark the in-between spanning words and signs in the gesture of opening the spatio-temporal play of signification. It is this in-between that says itself along with signs. The prefixes thus mark the spatio-temporal nexus of relationality, momentaneously opened into what is: a web of relations pre-scribing the movement of being as language.

Being is this pre-scriptive event, spatio-temporalizing into signs. And here the difficulty comes to a head. For this thinking of the event as the inceptive word goes against the metaphysical precepts of experience. Here language and word are no longer human, neither just human nor even primarily and from the first "human." Second, being, metaphysically mute and in need of language, present there to be re-presented, is now called "word" and calls forth language. Not only not mute or immediate, being is the inceptive word, as Heidegger writes in *Das Ereignis* (E 172), its words marking the vectors of relations pre-scripted and echoed through the hyphenated prefixes into the writing, always already human. What is thus pre-scribed and hopefully echoed in signs is the singularity (*Einzigkeit*) and one-timeness (*Einmaligkeit*) of the each time singular sketching out of time-space. This singularness and one-timeness is what silently recedes and withdraws from signs, which operate on the principle of generalizable particularity. At issue is how to register in the repeatability of signs the one-time giving that marks each moment and what is singularly there. The singularity of "es gibt" signified over into signs: both transferred into them and covered over by this transition. The singularity let be outside both the power of signs to signify the meaning and their concomitant powerlessness to say the singular. The "word" of the always one-time singularness of the "there is," given to be heard in the already known meaning of the sign. The third difficulty involves the fact that, while it is possible to outline the transformation, writing about it does not in itself make it possible. Furthermore, even if successfully outlined, the transformation, its conception or "theory," cannot be sprung into action. For this would amount only to the prolongation of metaphysical doing, which assigns priority to making and producing, while the transformation, as Heidegger makes clear, cannot be compelled or manufactured. In short, it is not up to human doing. However, it does require human preparation, and it is in this sense that Heidegger conceives of his thinking as preparatory: preparing for the possibility of letting transformation occur. Even though the transformation at stake cannot be enacted or produced, it will not take place without humans undergoing it, and they can only be ready to undergo such transformation if their being (*Wesen*) is prepared for such letting. Differently put, the preparation makes room for human participation, allows it to happen if called for, without procuring or assuring the transformation itself. What is called for then is a specific, transformed relating to language, which Heidegger signals through the term *lassen*. Yet even to allow this term the resonance fitting to it, the metaphysical binary of doing and not doing, of action and indifference, needs to be loosened, admitting a different way of rendering possible. To experience being as saying, to let it give its word is the prerequisite, or better, the pre-scription Heidegger is looking for. In the words from *Das Ereignis* attached as the epigraph to this essay: "What is the word? The soundless voice/tune of beyng. What is called voice here? Not 'sound' but the tuning, that is, letting ex-perience" (E 283). Evaluated metaphysically, this "word" does not quite make sense, or at least does not make sense yet. It goes against our need to act, our constant mobilization to make it happen, our "human" calling, whether we see it as confidence or arrogance, to effectuate a change. And it is perhaps in this countering, in this metaphysically induced reaction we all experience to such a call, reaction reinforced by "our" language, that we can have a pre-sage, one almost wants to say, playing between English and German, a pre-saying of what would need to be let transform.

NOTES

1. Martin Heidegger, *On the Way to Language,* trans. Peter D. Hertz (San Francisco: Harper & Row, 1971), 135.

2. Vol. 74 of the *Gesamtausgabe,* just published this past year (2010), is titled *Zum Wesen der Sprache,* and will likely add a good deal more material to what we know of Heidegger's approach to language.

3. Heidegger, *Contributions to Philosophy (From Enowning),* trans. Parvis Emad and Kenneth Maly (Bloomington: Indiana University Press, 1999), 26; modified. Subsequent references cited parenthetically, preceded by CP.

4. "*Das Wort gründet nicht nur 'Welt', sondern ist des Seyns und verwahrt verschwiegen die Lichtung des Da.*" Martin Heidegger, *Vom Wesen der Sprache, Gesamtausgabe,* vol. 85 (Frankfurt am Main: Klostermann, 1999), 55. Subsequent references to this edition cited parenthetically in the text, preceded by WS.

5. Martin Heidegger, *On the Way to Language,* trans. Peter D. Hertz (New York: Harper & Row, 1971), 141. Subsequent references to this edition cited parenthetically in the text, preceded by WL.

6. "Das Wort be-dingt das Ding zum Ding." *Unterwegs zur Sprache* (Pfullingen: Neske, 1959), 232. Subsequent references to this edition cited parenthetically in the text, preceded by UZS.

7. Heidegger, *Das Ereignis, Gesamtausgabe,* vol. 71 (Frankfurt am Main: Klostermann, 2009), 173. All translations from this volume are mine. Subsequent references cited parenthetically in the text, preceded by E.

8. See vol. 70 of the *Gesamtausgabe* titled *Über den Anfang* (1941) published in 2005 (Frankfurt am Main: Klostermann, 2005).

9. Martin Heidegger, *On Time and Being,* trans. Joan Stambaugh (Chicago: University of Chicago Press, 2002), 24.

10. Martin Heidegger, *Basic Concepts,* trans. Gary E. Aylesworth (Bloomington: Indiana University Press, 1993), 53.

SEVEN

Heidegger's Poietic Writings: From *Contributions to Philosophy* to *Das Ereignis*

Daniela Vallega-Neu

With Heidegger's failure to complete the project of *Being and Time*[1] and the subsequent turn in his thinking began a relentless quest for words and ways of thinking and speaking that brought the issue of language to the forefront of his concerns. This failure in the project of *Being and Time*—Heidegger calls it a "*Versagen*" in the "Letter on Humanism"[2]—already bears in it this relation to language, since *Ver-sagen* literally means the failure to say, the denying of words. In its common sense, it means the inability to fulfill a demand. For Heidegger, both—the demand to think and say as well as the inability to say what demands to be thought and said—are rooted in the way being itself occurs historically, namely, as a lack, as withdrawal. Because of this historical determination of thinking, Heidegger speaks of the latter, in *Contributions of Philosophy*[3] and the volumes following it, as "*seynsgeschichtliches Denken*," as a thinking of (belonging to) being in its historicality. These volumes contain Heidegger's most radical attempts not to speak *about* being but rather to speak in a way that lets being itself in its historicality eventuate out of the very refusal characterizing its essence. These "works" (I will refer to them as Heidegger's poietic writings[4]) were not written with a specific reader in mind; they contain sections that are dense like poetry, others that are more discursive and somewhat explanatory, while some sections are sketches of themes. We may think of much of what happens in these volumes as meditative exercises, thought experiments, notes, and/or sketches for future elaborations. One may argue (as it has been done) that *Contributions to Philosophy* and the volumes following it[5] are simply personal notebooks that should not be taken too seriously. But I believe that despite the fact that they are difficult to read and at times perhaps incomprehensible, they should not be dismissed as being less important than his more public writings, since they give us access to the main domains as well as to the core activity of Heidegger's thinking. This includes especially Heidegger's struggle with language. It is in his poietic writings that Heidegger develops his thought of *Ereignis* (event), to which he keeps alluding in writings published during his lifetime.

We may compare these poietic writings to the sketches or sketchbooks of an artist who gives free rein to his hands and imagination, searching for a direction, a shape or color pattern that may eventually find its way into a painting. It is in a similar way that *Contributions to Philosophy* is "*Richtscheid einer Ausgestaltung,*" "the straightedge of a configuration," as Heidegger writes in the opening words to *Contributions.* As he says in section 1, they constitute only an attempt to speak "*vom Ereignis,*" that is, "of" in the sense of "out of" the historicality of beyng understood as event. They "are not yet able to join the free conjuncture of the truth of beyng out of beyng itself."[6] Whether Heidegger was ever granted to succeed in such a free joining of words is another issue. Given the care with which Heidegger selects and comments on the title of this earlier work (*Contributions*), when looking at the title of volume GA 71, *Das Ereignis,* one has to wonder whether this volume—at least in Heidegger's view—accomplishes something that *Contributions* could not yet do. However, *Das Ereignis* is the most cryptic of Heidegger's poietic writings and instead of presenting us with the foreshadowed configuration for which *Contributions* were only a straightedge, they seem to defy attempts at configuring and ordering what Heidegger says and also distance themselves precisely from those aspects of *Contributions* that allow us to find a structure in the work.

In the following essay, I would like to address not only what Heidegger writes concerning language in his poietic writings but also *how* he writes (since the two cannot be separated), focusing especially on *Contributions to Philosophy* (1936–1948) and *Das Ereignis* (1941/1942) together with *Über den Anfang* (1941). These last two volumes give the reader some insight into a work with language that we find in Heidegger's later lectures (for instance *On the Way to Language*) and constitute in some way a transition from

Heidegger's texts of the late thirties to those of the fourfold (*Geviert*). However, especially in *Das Ereignis,* his writing becomes more cryptic, more inaccessible, and for the reader the question as to *how* to read this text becomes inevitable. I believe that this volume exposes us to a limit of philosophical thinking and that what Heidegger does there sheds a new and disconcerting light on his indication that the thinking he pursues in his later writings should no longer be called "philosophy."[7]

But let us first take a look at what Heidegger says and does in relation to language in his *Contributions to Philosophy* by beginning with some brief indications as to how this work departs from common conceptions of language as well as from the fundamental ontological thinking of *Being and Time.*[8]

Introduction to the Issue of Language in *Contributions to Philosophy*

We tend to think of language as a human faculty and of words as signs signifying something to which they are arbitrarily conjoined. The word "tree" signifies the thing we call tree, which is something quite different from the word "tree" as well as from the meaning attached to this word, a meaning by virtue of which a tree becomes recognizable for us. Such common understanding of language moves within representational thinking and a subject-object distinction that has marked Western metaphysics. It places language on the side of the human subject, keeps language distinct from things, from beings it names. Speaking is always viewed as speaking *about* something, about an "other" that is the object of speech.

But in another, maybe less explicit understanding, we commonly also experience a revelatory function of language. Something is revealed to us by virtue of its becoming nameable. It is only then that we properly grasp something as *being* such and such, for instance this thing we see on a tree as *being* a living insect. The revelatory function of language is essential also in understanding ourselves. We become aware of a fear we have been nurturing once we are able to express it. We experience this kind of revelatory function of language especially as freeing us toward ourselves while we come to understand aspects of ourselves. Thus language first reveals to us things, a world, and ourselves and frees us to an explicit relationship with things, world, and ourselves.

It is in this revelatory sense that Heidegger understands language in reference to the Greek *logos* and as being constitutive of *Dasein* in the fundamental ontology of *Being and Time.* In section 7 of *Being and Time* he writes: "*logos* as discourse really means . . . to make manifest 'what is being talked about' in discourse."[9] Only "when fully concrete, discourse (letting something be seen) has the character of speaking or vocalizing in words."[10] This understanding of language does not begin with words signifying something but rather with the articulating revealing through which something becomes nameable. Our understanding of language as consisting of words signifying something, as a speaking *about* something, pre-supposes the structuring revealing that occurs in discourse, through which something first emerges for us as something nameable. Thus, in *Being and Time,* Heidegger distinguishes between "language" (as written and spoken words signifying something) and "discourse" (*Rede*) such that language is founded on discourse as "the 'significant' structuring [*Gliedern*] of the intelligibility of being-in-the-world."[11]

In *Being and Time,* neither language nor discourse is grasped as a faculty of human beings (of human entities or subjects), but they are constitutive of the *being* (the *to be* in its "how") of humans, that is, of *Dasein,* which, in its ecstatic constitution, is exposed to and discovers (through discourse) its own being together with the being of other beings.

Still, in *Being and Time,* discourse and thus language remain tied to the existential constitution of *Dasein,* whereas in *Contributions to Philosophy,* Heidegger will understand language more radically as belonging to being itself (not first human being). In the original (incomplete) project of *Being and Time,* the fundamental analysis of *Dasein* was supposed to lead to the analysis of being as such in its temporality, such that the temporalizing of *Dasein* (the projection out of which *Dasein* retrieves its past and comes to be who it is) would occur out of the temporal horizon of being as such. This temporal horizon is what Heidegger will call, in *Contributions,* the "truth of beyng." Thereby he conceives truth as the revealing-concealing out of which we and things in general historically come to be; and he conceives "beyng" (*Seyn,* written in its archaic form with a "y")[12] as the non-representable historical occurrence of being itself, which is presencing and in withdrawal at once.

Heidegger's failure to complete the project of *Being and Time* derives (in his own understanding) from the transcendental-horizonal approach of thinking in this project. Although his notion of *Dasein* as ecstatic being-in-the-world makes significant steps in overcoming subjectivity (i.e., a thinking rooted in consciousness), the language Heidegger uses when he speaks of *Dasein* "transcending" particular beings into the temporal horizon of being as such (even if it is an "always-already-having-transcended"), the designation of being as such as a "horizon," and finally the distinction between being and beings itself (the ontological difference) reinforce a traditional representational thinking. They do this because the relation between *Dasein,* things, and being itself is viewed in such a way that we create a mental picture of some "being as such" as something over against ourselves (vaguely understood in term of human entities), as something we first need to transcend into in order to come back to ourselves in a fuller understanding of who we are.[13] Consequently, the task became for Heidegger to abandon all transcendental-horizonal perspective in an "overcoming of the horizon as such" and a "turn back into the source [*Herkunft*]."[14] The task became for him to think and speak *out of* this source rather than toward it, *out of* the truth of beyng rather than *about* it. This is the famous "turn" Heidegger's thinking performs in the thirties.

To think and speak *out of* the occurrence of the truth of beyng (i.e., out of the *to be* in which we find an originary but finite historical disclosure of a world and of ourselves) is a difficult task since it runs against our common way of thinking and speaking. It is a thinking and saying that maintains itself in what in *Being and Time* Heidegger calls an *authentic* (*eigentlich*) mode of being, which distinguishes itself from our everyday dealing with things as well as from scientific and any other representational modes of thinking, in which we visualize and experience what we think and talk about as something "over against" us, as object.

With *Contributions to Philosophy* begin a series of writings in which Heidegger made his most radical attempts at an authentic, originary thinking and saying of beyng in its historicality.[15] He approaches this task on the one hand within a constant re-interpretation of and confrontation with Ancient Greek thinking ("the first beginning"), such that in this re-interpretation he finds venues for an originary experience and articulation of beyng. On the other hand, he approaches this task in the confrontation with the history of metaphysics (especially in its ending) as a history of the abandonment of beings by beyng and forgetfulness of beyng in its originary occurrence. He thinks that our current age is dominated by machination and lived experience, that is, by calculation and the hunt for always new adventures such that the very possibility of experiencing beyng in its historicality is threatened. Thus Heidegger thinks and experiences in our epoch, the epoch of the end of metaphysics, an extreme distress that, when endured as such, thrusts one back into a more originary relation with the truth of beyng ("the second beginning"). In this more originary dimension of being, beyng is experienced primarily as withdrawal, as lack.

Speaking out of the truth of beyng thus means primarily to attend to the lack of words, to the silence that marks an originary experience with the "to be" in which we find ourselves in the present age. According to Heidegger, when we experience the distress of the abandonment of beings by beyng and when we endure this distress instead of running away from it (for instance by keeping ourselves busy with practical concerns or new adventures), we are disposed, attuned in such a way that a different, more authentic, and at the same time abyssal (groundless) time-space of beyng opens up. By staying in this time-space, one finds oneself responding to a call initiated by the mentioned distress, such that more originary words may accrue and open up this dimensionality of beyng in more enduring ways. The latter is more a hope than a project of Heidegger's, since he believes that for now (in *Contributions*), thinking works only at preparing this time-space, this historical site, which he names *Da-sein,* literally "t/here-being" (now written with a hyphen in order to distinguish it from the notion of *Dasein* in *Being and Time*).[16]

There are some similarities between this transposition into a more originary dimension of beyng in *Contributions* and the call of conscience in *Being and Time* that summons Dasein to a more authentic being. In the earlier work, the silent call of conscience (which is "a mode of *discourse*"[17]) calls *Dasein* away from the everyday fallenness into the "they" and back to its authentic self. Already here, this call has an abyssal dimension; the caller is "no one," it is "Dasein in its uncanniness, primordially thrown being-in-the-world, as not-at-home, the naked 'that' in the nothingness [*Nichts*] of the world."[18] It (the silent call) summons Dasein to be "the ground of a nullity [*Nichtigkeit*]"[19] and it is thus, in the exposure to this nothingness, that the call opens up Dasein to its ownmost potentiality as being-towards-death and with this to being as such, which entails a more authentic being with beings and being with others.

In *Contributions,* the transposition from an inauthentic to an authentic realm of being carries a historical dimension. Thinking is transposed from the abandonment by and forgetfulness of beyng into an experience and thought of the groundless occurrence of beyng as *event* (*Ereignis*). This transposition entails a "leap" (*Sprung*) of thinking such that in this leap, thinking finds itself already responding to the call of beyng (*Zuruf des Seyns*). At the same time, it is *in* this response that beyng first finds a site (*Da-sein*) for its originary occurrence as appropriating event. The truth of beyng as event discloses for us and becomes articulated in this counter-movement of call and response, which Heidegger calls the *turning* (*Kehre*) in the event.[20] For instance, in section 255 of *Contributions* he writes:

> The turning essentially occurs in between the call (to the one that belongs) and the belonging (of the one that is called): the turning is a counter-turning. *The call* to the leap into the appropriation is the great stillness of the most concealed self-knowledge.
>
> Every language of Da-sein originates here and is thus in essence silence.

In section 122 of *Contributions,* Heidegger refers to the turning relation between call and response as the "oscillation" (*Gegenschwung*) between the appropriating throw (*Wurf*) of beyng and the thrown projection (*Entwurf*) by the one who articulates this event in the response. Although this entails a simultaneity of throw and projection—of call and response (both are required for the event to occur)—the thrownness is experienced as being more originary: "As the projector projects, and speaks thoughtfully 'of the event,' it is revealed that he himself, the more of a projector he becomes, the more he is thrown as the one who is already thrown."[21] Beyng is thus experienced as appropriating event (*Er-eignis*), as an event that brings thought and beings to their own (*eigen*) essential occurrence.

That the truth of beyng occurs as appropriating event (*Ereignis*) only in the response of (in Heidegger's case) thinking means that event and language cannot be separated. The event occurs only through a response, in language. Conversely, language originates precisely in the turning (in the great stillness) as which the event discloses for Dasein. Let us look more closely at how Heidegger thinks language here as well as how Heidegger may accomplish a speaking "of" the event in the sense that it is appropriated by the event.

Speaking of the Event in *Contributions to Philosophy*

For Heidegger, to truly speak "of" (out of) the event in *Contributions* means that thinking is appropriated by the event, which requires "a belonging to beyng and to the word 'of' beyng, a belonging in thinking and saying."[22] How can such a belonging in thinking and saying be accomplished such that the thinker can utter the word "of" being? Whoever believes in the power and necessity of human agency will have the most difficulty with this aspect of Heidegger's thinking. One cannot decide and will to speak of the event, since this speaking is appropriated, "given." There is no technique one could learn. According to Heidegger, one needs above all to be disposed by a grounding attunement (*Grundstimmung*) that oscillates in several dispositions, of which Heidegger names above all shock (*Erschrecken*), restraint (*Verhaltenheit*), and diffidence (*Scheu*, often translated as "awe"). Here is what Heidegger says about these dispositions in section 5 of *Contributions:*

> To be shocked is to be taken aback, i.e., back from the familiarity of customary behavior and into the openness of the pressing forth of what is self-concealing. . . . Shock lets us be taken aback by the very fact that beings *are* (whereas, previously, beings were to us simply beings), i.e., by the fact that beings *are* and that beyng has abandoned all "beings" and whatever appeared as a being, has withdrawn itself from them.[23]

"Restraint is the *center* (cf. below) for shock and diffidence. These latter merely characterize with more explicitness what *originally* belongs to restraint."[24] In restraint, there reigns (though one is still taken aback) a turn toward the hesitant self-withholding as the holding sway of beyng.

> *Diffidence* . . . is not confused here with shyness or even understood in that direction. From diffidence in particular arises the necessity of reticence; the latter is what allows an essential occurrence of beyng as event and thoroughly disposes every comportment in the midst of beings and toward beings.[25]

Attuned by these basic dispositions, thinking is transposed into what Heidegger calls the *other beginning* (*der andere Anfang*) of the history (or historicality) of beyng, however, in such a way that this other history of beyng is still mere possibility of another epoch in the history of beyng. The other beginning in the epochal sense still needs to be prepared or initiated by the grounding of Da-sein, that is, of a concrete historical site (a t/here-being) for beyng's originary occurrence as event. Finding the word appropriated by beyng as event is one way of grounding this site. Other ways of grounding would be, for instance, a work of art[26] or a political deed. But clearly for Heidegger words have a privileged place in the grounding of *Da-sein*, so much that in his essay "The Origin of the Work of Art" (which he wrote at the same time that he was working on *Contributions*) he would say that all art is fundamentally *Dichtung*, poetry (understood here in a larger sense than what we usually call poetry).[27]

The privileged position of words derives from the fact that all grounding of beyng, all opening up of a concrete site of being happens in language, such that language has a more originary sense than uttered words.[28] As Heidegger says in that same essay, "Language, by naming beings for the first time, first brings beings to word and to appearance. Only this naming nominates beings to their Being *from out of* their Being."[29]

This naming (*Nennen*) thus is not a signifying but carries more the sense of "discourse" in *Being and Time*. It is an originating articulation guided by a grounding disposition. The German word for disposition, *Stimmung*, already bears a relation to language, since *Stimme* means voice. When one tunes an instrument, one speaks of the *Stimmen* of the instrument, so that one may translate *Stimmung* also as "attunement." Through disposition, one is attuned to, disposed toward, what is given, appropriated in the event. In *Contributions* Heidegger writes, "the basic disposition *disposes* [*stimmt*] Da-sein and thereby disposes *thinking* as a projection of the truth of beyng in word and concept."[30] One can approach this thought by reflecting on how, in order to write, for instance, a poem (or a philosophy essay), one first needs to find the right disposition, a specific mood, in which words can take shape.

According to Heidegger, the basic disposition of restraint, especially the moment of diffidence belonging to it, disposes thinking above all into reticence, that is, not into speaking but into listening. It is by listening (*Hören*) that thinking belongs to (*zugehören*) the event and responds to the call of beyng. Even in speaking what remains most fundamental is silence, a silence that keeps reverberating in the word as it holds the word in its (the silence's) bind. Heidegger speaks in this context of *Erschweigen*, of bearing silence.[31] In section 38 of *Contributions*, he writes:

> Bearing silence arises out of the essentially occurring origin of language itself.
>
> The basic experience is . . . the holding itself back of restraint against the hesitant self-withholding in the truth (clearing of concealment) of the *plight*. . . .
>
> When this restraint reaches *words*, what is said is always the event. But to understand this saying means to carry out the projection and leap of knowledge into the event. The saying that bears silence is what grounds. Its word is not by any means merely a sign for something quite other. What it names is what is meant. But the "meaning" assigns only as *Da-sein*, i.e., in thinking and questioning.[32]

The necessity to bear silence in speaking derives from Heidegger's experience that beyng itself occurs as withdrawal, that truth occurs as self-concealment. For Heidegger it is essential that thinking *maintain itself in* the openness of the self-concealment and self-withdrawal as which beyng occurs historically precisely as he attempts to articulate being as event. He speaks in this context of *Inständigkeit*, which we might translate literally as "the standing in," but which in German also has the sense of steadfastness. Both meanings (the literal and the common one) resonate in the way Heidegger uses this word.[33]

The thinking-saying of *Contributions* attempts to be steadfast in *Dasein*, to maintain itself in the disposition of beyng's occurrence as withdrawal, bearing silence as it attempts to articulate being in its self-refusal. Is Heidegger successful in this attempt? How could one tell? (As we will see, Heidegger himself will later criticize his first attempt at speaking of the event.) Furthermore, does a word's ability to open up a sense of beyng not depend as well on the reader/listener of Heidegger's words?

Sure. Heidegger is aware of that and he is aware that there never is a guarantee that his words are heard out of the holding sway of beyng itself. He meditates about this in section 41 of *Contributions:*

> Every saying of Beyng is couched in words and namings which, as expressions of beyng, are liable to be misunderstood when taken in the sense of the everyday view of beings and thought exclusively in that sense. . . . the word itself already reveals something (something familiar) and thereby conceals that which is supposed to be brought into the open in thoughtful saying.
>
> Nothing can remove this difficulty. . . . The difficulty must be accepted and must be grasped in its essential belonging (to the thinking of Beyng).[34]

And yet, in that same section, Heidegger speaks of how this insight necessitates a stratagem such that although for a while a word continues to have its common subjective and representational (i.e., metaphysical) sense, all of a sudden a reversal happens, such that this word is understood out of beyng itself. Heidegger gives some examples of this:

> For example, "decision" can and should be meant first of all as a human "act," even if not in the moral sense, yet performatively nonetheless, until it suddenly means the essence of beyng itself—which does not mean beyng is interpreted "anthropologically," but just the reverse: it means man is placed back into the essence of beyng and is released from the fetters of "anthropology." Likewise, "machination" is at first a type of human comportment and then suddenly, and properly, it means the reverse: the essence (non-essence) of beyng, in which the ground of the possibility of "undertakings" is first rooted.[35]

What Heidegger here calls "stratagem" (the German word is *Verfahren,* which means a procedure) should not be understood as a technique Heidegger arbitrarily invents and uses. This would go against every claim he has made regarding the language of beyng. It must, then, be a procedure rooted in the very way Heidegger experiences being and attempts to maintain himself in the disposition of restraint, bearing silence as he attempts to articulate the way he experiences beyng in its historicality. Can we find such a proceeding in Heidegger's language?

Schuback finds one at work in Heidegger's later essay "The Way to Language," and I believe that what she finds there and is able to articulate in her essay (performing herself what she finds at work in Heidegger's text) holds true just as much, if not more, with respect to Heidegger's poietic writings (and, as we will see, especially with respect to *Das Ereignis*). Schuback writes: "Heidegger's way to language can be described as a way of a repeated recitation in a hearing of the doubtful or rhythmical beginning. . . . Language speaks. The 'repeated recitation' is the way of 'learning to unlearn' metaphysics, searching for the adequate words for Being as being Itself within the very grammar and language of metaphysics. Heidegger intends thereby to endure this tedious emptiness of having nothing or too little to say. He listens to this lack and lets the lack be empty and void, that is, he surrenders this lack to the rhythm of its own happening."[36] This "insisted repeated recitation" lets rhythm appear and with it the "action of language," which bears in it a specific temporality, a temporality that gives time to things.[37]

Heidegger's style of writing in *Contributions* is by no means consistent. Some sections could appear as parts of essays ready for publication, others remain fragmentary, still others look like outlines; but what emerges constantly is the repetitive character of the work in a constant renewed attempt to say the same. Over and over again Heidegger speaks and lets the words sink back into a void, which is particularly pronounced in fragmentary sections and incomplete sentences. Over and over again Heidegger traces the movement of the turning as which he experiences the event. Yet as one follows Heidegger's words, the same always appears different, allowing the thought of beyng to appear each time anew and not simply as an empty repetition of an identical same.

What is striking as one reads through the volumes following *Contributions* is that, while the practice of writing retains—and in the latest volumes intensifies—its rhythmic element, new basic words appear, creating new vortexes of rhythmic repetitions of movements of thought and resonances of meanings. To trace the changes of the basic words and themes addressed throughout the sequence of Heidegger's poietic writings will be a task that remains to be fulfilled in a larger project. In the following section I would like to focus especially on *Das Ereignis,* keeping the question in mind of whether here Heidegger was able to speak of the event in ways *Contributions* did not.

From *Beiträge zur Philosophie* to *Das Ereignis*

Das Ereignis re-confirms the importance of *Contributions to Philosophy* as a work that opens up venues of thinking and saying that Heidegger continues to pursue in his paths of thinking.[38] *Contributions* begins a long practice of inventive thinking[39] and saying, in which he attempts to think "of" the event as which being occurs historically, every time anew, without any particular plan or goal that would guide his meditations. As one reads progressively from GA 65 to GA 71, one can notice a stronger shift in language between, on the one hand, GA 66 (*Besinnung*) and 69 (*Die Geschichte des Seyns*) (written 1938–1939) and, on the other hand, GA 70 (*Über den Anfang*) and GA 71 (*Das Ereignis*) (written 1941–1942). The earlier volumes after *Contributions* remain more closely within the horizon of the structuring themes, the junctures (the word Heidegger uses, *Fugen,* reminisces also the fugues in a musical piece, i.e., variations on a theme) that make up this work.

Let me briefly mention the junctures structuring *Contributions.* They are called "resonating," "interplay," "leap," "grounding," "the future ones," and "the last god."[40] Despite the fact that Heidegger says that they should not be understood as a linear progression,[41] and that "in each of the six junctures, a saying of the same about the same is attempted, but in each case out of a different essential domain of that which is called the event,"[42] they do appear to trace a path of thinking. Heidegger himself expresses this path when he articulates the relation between the junctures as follows:

> What is said [in *Contributions*] is questioned and thought in the "interplay" between the first and the other beginning, *out of* the "resonating" of beyng in the plight of the abandonment by beyng, *for* the "leap" into beyng, *toward* the "grounding" of its truth, as *preparing* the "future ones" of "the last god."[43]

Besinnung (GA 66) as well as *Die Geschichte des Seyns* (GA 69) focus especially (but by no means exclusively) on the first two junctures of *Contributions* by meditating on metaphysics, its inception in Greek thinking and its ending in modern subjectivity, and they include extensive sections on machination and power. This focus makes sense if one keeps in mind that during this time Heidegger continues to lecture on Nietzsche such that he places Nietzsche more and more into the position of the one who completes the history of metaphysics by thinking will to power as the will to will. The later volumes following *Contributions* (GA 70 and 71) reveal a more daring enterprise: Heidegger seems to dive more deeply into thinking *of* (*from*) the event (*Ereignis*).

With *Über den Anfang* (GA 70) and *Das Ereignis* (GA 71), Heidegger appears to take a fresh start at the practice of inceptive (*anfänglich*), inventive thinking (*Erdenken*) and saying of beyng as event. I will lay out some of the recurring concepts and movements of his thought in these last two volumes shortly. For now, let me just indicate that over and over, Heidegger thinks the event as beginning (*Anfang*), and that the meditations on language, on *Sage* and *Wort*, recur in a more pronounced way along with extensive sections on the relation between thinking and poetizing. The latter makes sense in view of the fact that at the same time, Heidegger gave his lecture-courses on Hölderlin's "*Andenken*" and "*Der Ister*." Heidegger's attempt to let go of any preliminary structure, direction, or order of thought, and to speak as originarily as possible out of the event, is most pronounced in *Das Ereignis*.[44]

The thoughts gathered in *Das Ereignis* are divided into eleven parts.[45] One may find some similarity between the structuring of *Contributions* and *Das Ereignis,* since the latter starts out with thoughts concerning the first beginning and the end of metaphysics, and after a part titled "*Verwindung,*"[46] progresses to parts with sections concerning the event. In *Das Ereignis* one may see some progression from speaking of the first beginning (I) both in Greek thought and in its completion in the will to will (II. The Resonating) to articulating the difference (between beyng and beings; III), to the "*Verwindung,*" which relates to the overcoming of metaphysics in the "descent" into the abyssal occurrence of beyng as event (IV),[47] to sections on the event (V, VI, and IX), Da-seyn (VII), the other beginning (VIII), and the thinking of the historicality of beyng, as well as thoughts regarding the relation between thinking and poetizing (XI). However, *Das Ereignis* cannot be read, like the six conjunctures of *Contributions,* as a progression from a first resonance of beyng in the experience of the abandonment of beings by beyng to the grounding of the truth of beyng. Already in the first part of *Das Ereignis,* Heidegger speaks more thoroughly from within what he conceives as the experience of the event as beginning. He speaks of the very inception of the first beginning, attempting to think it out of the event as beginning. Consider, for instance, the very first section of this first part of *Das Ereignis,* which bears in it a reference to Parmenides' poem:

> 1. The first beginning
> *Aletheia* holds sway as beginning.
> Truth is the truth of being.
> Truth is "the goddess" *thea.*
> Her home is well rounded, not closed off, never [a] (trembling) disguising heart, but unconcealing and lighting up everything throughout. In the first beginning, *Aletheia* is the concealed one—*truth:* the concealing safe-keeping of what is cleared—of the open span, the granting of the emergence, the allowing of presencing.[48]

Heidegger reads *aletheia* right away as primarily concealing ("the concealed one") and not as unconcealing. This reading of the inception of the first beginning performs the movement that Heidegger emphasizes already in *Über den Anfang:* the downgoing into the beginning (*Untergang in den Anfang*).[49] Along the lines of the thought of *Contributions,* we may interpret this downgoing into the inception of the first beginning as the downgoing into the unthought dimension of the truth of beyng, which is harbored in the thought of the pre-Socratics. This downgoing is the inception of the (not yet fully begun other) beginning: "*Downgoing* is inception of the beginning in its inceptiveness."[50] The German word for "inception," *Anfängnis,* is not part of the regular German vocabulary. In GA 70, Heidegger indicates what this word names: "The inception [*Die Anfängnis*] of the beginnings [*Anfänge*] is the way they begin . . . The inception determines and 'is' the holding sway of the beginning."[51]

The following part of *Das Ereignis,* titled "*Der Anklang,*" also offers a more inceptive meditation on what occurs in the resonating (of beyng as event). In *Contributions,* Heidegger says that the resonating (*Anklang*), together with the interplay (*Zuspiel*) of the first and other beginning, *prepare* for the leap into the truth of beyng.[52] But in *Das Ereignis* the resonating already transposes into the occurrence of the beginning. One may say, then, that resonating and leap are no longer thought as sequential in a transitional thought; rather they occur at once.[53] There is still some similarity in the themes that accompany "the resonating" in *Contributions* and *Ereignis,* since in connection with the resonating, Heidegger thinks the end of metaphysics and the abandonment of beings by being, which disclose only for a thinking that discovers the unthought abyssal ground of metaphysics (i.e., beyng in its truth, beyng as event). But the relation between the end of the first beginning and the moving into the other beginning is different. Whereas in *Contributions* Heidegger emphasizes the necessity to *withstand* the plight of the abandonment by being (*Not der Seynsverslassenheit*) such that this withstanding disposes the thinking that experiences a first opening of the truth of beyng,[54] in *Das Ereignis* the reader is told that the abandonment by being and the resonating of the other beginning *pass by each other,* that is, in a certain sense, they do not touch each other. A certain tension between the experience of the end of metaphysics and the opening of another beginning seems to have been released as thinking finds itself already situated in that other beginning. In *Das Ereignis,* Heidegger speaks of the "*Vorbei-gang*" as "the passing by each other of [on the one hand] the abandonment of beings by being and [on the other hand] the *Seynsverwindung* [the twisting free of being] into the beginning."[55] "*Verwindung*" (twisting free) into the beginning contrasts with what Heidegger calls the "*Entwindung*" (twisting away) into metaphysics. "*Verwindung* is allowance of beyng (not first of beings)" and is "downgoing into the departure

[*Untergang in den Abschied*]."[56] "*Entwindung*" addresses the occurrence by which beings emerge in their presence such that the truth of beyng is concealed, which ultimately leads to metaphysics and "letting being loose into what is without truth."[57]

With the resonating, then, already occurs a downgoing into the beginning as which Heidegger thinks the event in *Über den Anfang* and *Das Ereignis*. Thinking seems to have become more inceptive; more a saying granted out of the abyssal occurrence of beyng. From here, we can understand some of the points of critique that Heidegger offers at the beginning of *Das Ereignis* with respect to *Contributions*.[58] He says that in some places *Contributions* is "too doctrinal [*lehrhaft*]" and leans too much onto the differentiation between "grounding question" and "guiding question." In this work, the event does not yet receive the purely inceptive holding sway of the abyss, and Da-sein "is still thought too unilaterally in the direction of man."[59]

The Event as the Inception of the Beginning (*Anfängnis des Anfangs*)

Part V of *Das Ereignis*, titled "Das Ereignis: Der Wortschatz seines Wesens," begins with the remark "Concerning the introduction to 'Das Ereignis'." It starts with section 184, in which Heidegger meditates on *Ereignis* and words related to *Ereignis*.[60] I will interpret some lines from this part in order to try to elucidate at least to some extent how Heidegger thinks the event as beginning in order then to move to the critical issues I want to focus on, namely Heidegger's language and reflections on language in *Das Ereignis*.

"*The event* names the inception of the beginning that properly clears itself [*die eigens sich lichtende Anfängnis des Anfangs*]. . . . The appropriation that occurs in the event is in itself counterturning [*gegenwendig*] out of the inceptive emerging, which is at the same time downgoing into the abyss."[61] This counterturning motion echoes the way Heidegger describes the truth of beyng in *Contributions*, namely as an unconcealing concealment, as appropriating and withdrawal at once, but now he tries to think even more the "keeping to itself" of the beginning as which the event occurs.[62] In *Über den Anfang* he writes: "Beginning is the taking into safe keeping [*An-sich-nehmen*] of the departure into the abyss."[63] This occurrence is at the same time the occurrence of a difference[64] between emerging and concealing. In the German word for difference, *Unterschied*, resonates the same word as in departure, *Abschied*, namely "*scheiden*," "to divide" or "sever." In the departure into the abyss occurs a differentiation, which I understand to be the articulation of the different "aspects" at play in the turning of the event: beyng and being, beyngs and nothing, beyng and beings, beyng and humans, da-seyn, non-being (*das Unseiende*), and (here comes another new concept in Heidegger's thinking) "the beingless" (*das Seinlose*, literally, "the without-being" or "what 'is' ['is' needs to be crossed out here] without beyng").[65]

In *Das Ereignis* Heidegger says the following concerning the beingless:

> The difference divides being and what is without being. But beinglessness is an event of beyng itself. . . .
>
> Beinglessness (of beings) is the inceptive event of dispropriation [*Enteignung*]; the inceptive dispropriation in the sense of the *withholding*. This dispropriation is inceptive, still unwound essencing back into the groundless beginning.[66]

In *Über den Anfang* Heidegger writes that the beingless is not a being that is abandoned by beyng (this would be the non-being, *Unseiendes*). "Beinglessness is *dispropriation* of beings."[67]

The dispropriation of which Heidegger speaks is not the withdrawal that occurs in the coming to presence of things, it is not the occurrence that leads to the abandonment of beings by being. Rather, it is a more originary negativity (more originary than the nothing that belongs to beyng) at the heart of the event insofar as it occurs as inception. One may say that it is the not yet or no longer begun beginning in the beginning.

Heidegger himself meditates on the difficulty of thinking this "beingless"; he calls it daring (*eine Zumutung* requiring *Mut*) and opposing itself to being thought.[68]

The Question of Interpretation

At this point, a serious question poses itself to me, as an interpreter of Heidegger's thinking in the light of the "experimentation"—we more appropriately may say: attempts or ventures—with language at work in *Das Ereignis*. Up to now, I have presented the thought of *Das Ereignis* in an orderly fashion, which does not quite convey the experience one has when reading this text. I have approached the volume in a preliminary way, with reference to a text I am more acquainted with, namely *Contributions to Philosophy,* and I may continue on this path by attempting to recognize in what Heidegger says the structures of thinking I have been finding in other writings by Heidegger. For instance, I may relate appropriation and dispropriation to the movement of the originary unconcealing concealment as which truth occurs and contrast this with a concealment that conceals the originary unconcealing concealment. For Heidegger, this concealing of the unconcealing concealing is what marks metaphysics insofar as it rests on the primacy of the presencing of beings. Or I might point ahead to what Heidegger writes in *Time and Being* and interpret the inception of the beginning as the *Geschick,* the sending of being. Thus, I would re-translate Heidegger into Heidegger, re-translate Heidegger's strange text into what is more familiar to me and also to most Heidegger scholars.

But would I thereby not be missing precisely what Heidegger attempts to do in *Das Ereignis,* namely a saying of the event as beginning, a saying that does not hold on to pre-conceived structures of thinking but that tries to be a poietic, originary language "of" (out of) the event? So, should one then interpret what Heidegger says *within* the relations of thought and with the help of the words that Heidegger himself "uses"—or rather—finds? In other words, should one do a strictly immanent reading of this volume? Yet, what would the point of such an immanent reading be? Considering that many words and word formations Heidegger finds are not part of the regular German language, considering that he speaks without wanting to mediate and thus "communicate"—where would such an immanent reading take us?

Let us look at some thoughts concerning language that Heidegger offers in *Das Ereignis.* Heidegger attempts to speak "of" the event, to let the event come to words in what he calls the "saying of the beginning" (*die Sage des Anfangs*). In section 335 he says:

> *The saying of the beginning*—its expression and presentation can only be simple. Here, this means: emerging out of the one and the unity of the beginning: in the manner of the event.
>
> Any discovering, any teaching, but also any awakening, any thrusting must stay away; in the same manner any "ordering" of "contents." Only the pure word that rests in itself must resonate. No listener must be presupposed and no room for listening-belonging (*Gehören*).[69]

Heidegger's critique of metaphysics and of the domination of productivity in our contemporary world is powerful and illuminating, but *Das Ereignis* makes me wonder about this space of inceptive thinking that carves out an undercurrent that "passes by"[81] a world abandoned by beyng, a world with (in 1941–1942) a raging devastating war. I begin to wonder if with these repetitive exercises in poietic thinking and saying over so many years, and by holding on to the thought that his thinking prepared the possibility of initiating a new destiny of beyng, Heidegger did not encircle himself into a solitary space of thought, a space that—although daring in its own pursuits—kept him safe from the madness of a world.

On the other hand, simply "psychologizing" Heidegger in this way would be too reductive and would not do justice to a work with language and a sense of being that has opened new venues for thought already. The originating of a poietic language in a listening to nothing is like the attempt at staying with the empty page while writing, the empty canvas while painting, the silence in a room while playing music; it is like waiting for the words or the gesture or the sound to emerge without self-consciousness, without a sense of an "I," freely, like a gift. Creativity needs emptiness of such a kind, it needs a space of non-determination; yet not for the sake of non-determination. It is difficult indeed to let these spaces of emptiness and non-determination be without reading into them senses and meanings that work like a concentric force that structures our thinking. I believe that Heidegger's thought of a history of beyng works like such a concentric force and that this made him blind for concrete happenings.

In light of this latter thought, the first "foreword," that is, the very first words of *Das Ereignis*, are quite striking. They consist in a quote from and interpretation of Sophocles' *Oedipus at Colonos*, verse 73–74:

> And what is, then, of a man who cannot see [*blepein*] the guarantee?
> Whatever we may say, by saying all we "see" [*horan*].

Heidegger adds his interpretation of what "seeing" means in each case: *blepein*, he says, means "blicken": "to have the view of beings, of things, and occurrences. In all this the man sees wrong (*versieht er sich*). He is blind for beings." But *horan* means "*sehen*": "to have the eye for 'being'—the destiny—the truth of beings. This seeing is the sight of the pain of experience. The capacity to suffer down to the suffering of the complete concealment of departure."[82]

NOTES

1. Martin Heidegger, *Being and Time,* trans. Joan Stambaugh, rev. and with a foreword by Dennis Schmidt (Albany: SUNY Press, 2010). In the following cited as BaT. *Sein und Zeit,* ed. F.-W. von Herrmann (Frankfurt am Main: Klostermann, 1977), vol. 2 of the *Gesamtausgabe,* in the following referred to as GA 2. Heidegger never completed the third division of the first part of *Being and Time;* neither did he complete the second part. See the outline of the project of his book on BaT: 37; GA 2: 53.

2. Martin Heidegger, *Basic Writings,* trans. David Farrell Krell (San Francisco: Harper San Francisco, 1992), 231. Martin Heidegger, "Brief über den Humanismus," in GA 9 (Frankfurt am Main: Klostermann, 1976), 328.

3. Martin Heidegger, *Beiträge zur Philosophy (Vom Ereignis),* ed. F.-W. von Herrmann, vol. 65 of the *Gesamtausgabe* (Frankfurt am Main: Klostermann, 1989). In the following referenced as GA 65. All translations of *Beiträge zur Philosophie* are taken from the manuscript of the new translation of this book by Richard Rojcewicz and Daniela Vallega-Neu (Bloomington: Indiana University Press, 2012).

4. I call these writings "poietic" (not "poetic") with reference to the Greek word *poiesis,* which means "bringing-forth," since the "bringing-forth" of (and not simply "speaking about") being as a historical event is Heidegger's main concern in these volumes. See Daniela Vallega-Neu, "Poietic Saying," in *Companion to Heidegger's "Contributions to Philosophy,"* ed. Charles E. Scott, Susan M. Schoenbohm, Daniela Vallega-Neu, and Alejandro Vallega (Bloomington: Indiana University Press, 2001), 66–80.

5. All translations of the following volumes are mine.

GA 66: Martin Heidegger, *Besinnung* (1938/1939), ed. F.-W. von Herrmann (Frankfurt am Main: Klostermann, 1997).

GA 67: Metaphysik und Nihilismus. 1. *Überwindung der Metaphysik* (1938/1939). 2. *Das Wesen des Nihilismus* (1946–1948), ed. Hans-Joachim Friedrich (Frankfurt am Main: Klostermann, 1999).

GA 69: Martin Heidegger, *Die Geschichte des Seyns. 1. Die Geschichte des Seyns* (1938/1940) 2. *Koinon. Aus der Geschichte des Seyns* (1939), ed. Peter Trawny (Frankfurt am Main: Klostermann, 1998).

GA 70: *Über den Anfang* (1941), ed. P.-L. Coriando (Frankfurt am Main: Klostermann, 2005).

GA 71: *Das Ereignis* (1941/1942), ed. F.-W. von Herrmann (Frankfurt am Main: Klostermann, 2009).

GA 72: *Die Stege des Anfangs* (1944), ed. F.-W. von Herrmann (not yet published).

6. GA 65: 4, section 1.

7. See Martin Heidegger, "The End of Philosophy and the Task of Thinking," in *Basic Writings,* 427; "Das Ende der Philosophie und die Aufgabe des Denkens," in *Zur Sache des Denkens* (Tübingen: Niemeyer, 1988), 61–80.

8. For a more detailed discussion about the difference between *Being and Time* and *Contributions to Philosophy,* see Daniela Vallega-Neu, *Heidegger's "Contributions to Philosophy": An Introduction* (Bloomington: Indiana University Press,

2003). For a more detailed discussion of the role of language in *Being and Time* in relation to the later thought of *Ereignis*, see Françoise Dastur, "Language and *Ereignis*," in *Reading Heidegger: Commemorations*, ed. John Sallis (Bloomington: Indiana University Press, 1993). For an earlier discussion of the role of language in *Contributions to Philosophy*, see Vallega-Neu, "Poietic Saying," 66–80.

9. BaT: 30; GA 2: 43.

10. BaT: 31; GA 2: 44.

11. BaT: 156, section 34; GA 2: 216.

12. Heidegger writes beyng (*Seyn*) in the archaic form with a "y" in order to indicate that being (in its verbal sense) is not represented analogously to beings (entities) but rather thought and experienced in and out of its historical occurrence.

13. GA 65: 217 and 450–451.

14. BaT: 37; GA 2: 53. These are Heidegger's marginal notes to the unpublished third division of the first part of the project of *Being and Time*.

15. Heidegger distinguishes historicality, in German *Geschichtlichkeit*, from historiology (*Historie*). Historiology remains tied to representational thinking by viewing history as a series of objectifiable events, whereas historicality and history (*Geschichte*) unite the sense of occurrence (*Geschehen*) and a history that determines how we experience things and ourselves, a history in which we are immersed such that we find ourselves as *being* historical. *Seynsgeschichtliches Denken*, the thinking of beyng in its historicality (sometimes translated as "Beyng-historical thinking") is a thinking that *is* historical and at the same time thinks beyng in its historical eventuation. For a more detailed discussion of this, see Alejandro Vallega, "'Being-Historical Thinking' in Heidegger's *Contributions to Philosophy*," in *Companion to Heidegger's "Contributions to Philosophy,"* 48–65.

16. In *Contributions*, Heidegger understands the "Da" of Da-sein to name the open span of the truth of beyng itself, and the "-sein" of Da-sein as the being of humans insofar as they are steadfast in this openness.

17. BaT: 259; GA 2: 358.

18. BaT: 266; GA 2: 367.

19. BaT: 272; GA 2: 376.

20. Note that the oscillation between call and response is only one aspect of the turn in the event (see Heidegger's note to section 255 of *Contributions*). For a fuller discussion of the event, see Daniela Vallega-Neu, "*Ereignis*: The Event of Appropriation," in *Martin Heidegger: Key Concepts*, ed. Bret Davis (Durham, England: Acumen, 2010), 140–154.

21. GA 65: 239.

22. GA 65: 3.

23. GA 65: 15.

24. GA 65: 15.

25. GA 65: 15–16.

26. See in this context Heidegger's essay "The Origin of the Work of Art" (in *Basic Writings*, 139–212), which pursues the question of the grounding of the truth of beyng in the work of art. German: "Vom Ursprung des Kunstwerks," in *Holzwege*, GA 5, ed. F.-W. von Herrmann (Frankfurt am Main: Klostermann, 1977).

27. *Basic Writings*, 199.

28. This does not mean that language does not need uttered (or written) words. The word understood as a being is required for a concrete historical site of being to disclose. The grounding of the truth of beyng in Da-sein requires, according to Heidegger, the "sheltering" (*Bergung*) of this truth in a being, a word, a work of art, or a deed. (See part e of V. Grounding, sections 243–247 of *Contributions.*) Heidegger tries to elaborate this in part in "The Origin of the Work of Art." This essay brings into play also the role of earth and world in the grounding of truth. One aspect of earth is the "materiality" of beings (I am placing "materiality" into quotation marks in order to indicate that it should not be understood in a traditional sense), which would for instance address the sounding of the word.

29. *Basic Writings,* 198.

30. GA 65: 21.

31. *Erschweigen* cannot properly be translated and is a neologism Heidegger forms using the common verb "*schweigen,*" to keep silent, and the prefix "*er-*," which has the sense of initiating or achieving something. This allows him to use the word in a transitive sense.

32. GA 65: 78.

33. *Inständigkeit* relates to the notion of authenticity in *Being and Time.* To be steadfast in Da-sein means to dwell in an authentic disclosure of being.

34. GA 65: 83.

35. GA 65: 84.

36. Marcia Cavalcante Schuback, "The Poetic of Language: Readings of Heidegger's *On the Way to Language,*" in *Metaphysics, Facticity, Interpretation* (Dordrecht: Kluwer Academic Publishers, 2003), 207.

David Krell also points to the "enhanced rhythmical character" of Heidegger's essays from the 1930s on: *Lunar Voices: Of Tragedy, Poetry, Fiction, and Thought* (Chicago: University of Chicago Press, 1995), chap. 3, esp. 70ff.

37. Krell, *Lunar Voices,* 208ff.

38. An earlier version of the following sections appeared in the *Proceedings of the 44th Annual Meeting of the Heidegger Circle* (2010) under the title "Heidegger's Poietic Meditations in *Das Ereignis* (GA 71)."

39. Inventive thinking translates *Erdenken,* which has the sense not of an arbitrary invention but of a thinking that thinks what opens itself up for thinking *as* it opens itself up for thinking.

40. Anklang, Zuspiel, Sprung, Gründung, die Zukünftigen, der letzte Gott.

41. GA 65: 6.

42. GA 65, section 39.

43. GA 65: 7. Italics are mine.

44. I believe that in many cases, making some sense of what he says in this last volume requires the prior reading of *Über den Anfang,* since here he clarifies much more a number of words and concepts that appear in *Das Ereignis* without any attempts at elucidating them.

45. The eleven parts have the following titles: I. Der erste Anfang; II. Der Anklang; III. Der Unterschied; IV. Die Verwindung; V. Das Ereignis. Der Wortschatz seines Wesens; VI. Das Ereignis; VII. Das Ereignis und das Menschenwesen; VIII. Das Da-seyn; IX. Der andere Anfang; X. Weisungen in das Ereignis; XI. Das seynsgeschichtliche Denken. Denken und Dichten.

46. *Verwindung* usually is translated as "overcoming" or "twisting free," but when one looks at how Heidegger thinks "*Verwindung*," neither of these translations seems to fit.

47. One might think of a similar "function" of the "leap" in *Contributions*, since they mark the point at which thinking finds itself appropriated in the event such that it may begin to articulate the event, but what Heidegger does in the part titled "*Verwindung*" is different.

48. "*1. Der erste Anfang.*

Die *Aletheia* west als der Anfang.

Die Wahr-heit ist die Wahrheit des Seins.

Die Wahrheit ist 'die Göttin' *thea*.

Ihr Haus ist wohl gerundet, nicht geschlossen, nie (erzitternedes) verstelltes Herz, sondern entbergendes Durchleuhten von Allem. Die *Aletheia* ist erstanfänglich die Verborgene—die *Wahr-heit:* die verbergende Wahrung des Lichten—Offenen, die Gewährung des Aufgangs, die Zulassung der Anwesung" (GA 71, 9–10).

49. GA 70, sections 64–87.

50. "Der Untergang *ist Anfängnis des Anfangs in seiner Anfänglichkeit*" (GA 70: 142). This movement of thought is reflected as well in the (in normal German) grammatically incorrect expression "Erinnerung *in* den Anfang," literally translated, the remembering "into" the beginning, which recurs in the first part of *Das Ereignis* (GA 71: 54ff.).

51. GA 70: 13.

52. GA 65: 9.

53. See the only place in *Das Ereignis* where Heidegger alludes to the junctures of *Contributions:* "Every thought of such [inceptive/saying/inventive] thinking already is at once resonating, interplay, leap, and grounding out of the appropriated steadfastness in da-sein" (GA 71: 298–299).

54. This leads Polt to speak of the "emergency of beyng" in Heidegger's *Contributions to Philosophy* (see Richard Polt, *The Emergency of Being: On Heidegger's "Contributions to Philosophy"* [Ithaca, N.Y.: Cornell University Press: 2006]), emphasizing both the aspect of urgency or need and the one of emergence.

55. GA 71: 84.

56. GA 70: 19.

57. GA 71: 115.

58. This is my translation of the six points of critique, which Heidegger presents at the end of the foreword of *Das Ereignis:*

1. In some places, the presentation is too doctrinal [*lehrhaft*].
2. Thinking leans onto the differentiation between "grounding question" and "guiding question" within the "question of beyng," which is legitimate only in a doctrinal way. The question of being itself is still captured more in the style of metaphysics, instead of being thought according to the way of the already grasped history of being.
3. Accordingly, "the beginning" too is still seized out of the performing of the thinker and not in its essential unity with the event.
4. Together with this, the event does not yet receive the purely inceptive holding sway of the abyss, in which is prepared the advent of beings and

the decision over the reigning of the gods [*Göttertum*] and humanity [*Menschenwesen*]. The thought of the last god is still unthinkable.

5. Although Da-sein is thought essentially out of the event, it is still thought too unilaterally in the direction of man.
6. Humanity not yet sufficiently historical [*geschichthaft*] (GA 71: 4–5).

59. GA 71: 4f. This may be the reason why, in *Das Ereignis,* Heidegger begins to write "Da-seyn" with a "y."

60. *Ereignen; Vereignung, Übereignung, Zugeignung; Aneignung; Eigentlichkeit; Eignung; Geeignetheit; Enteignung; Eigentum.*

61. GA 71: 147.

62. See also the way Heidegger describes what "*Anfang*" says in GA 70: 10.

63. GA 70: 11.

64. *Unterschied* is a prominent basic concept in *Das Ereignis.*

65. See GA 71: 122–123.

66. GA 71: 132.

67. GA 70: 122.

68. GA 70: 121–123.

69. GA 71: 297.

70. This brings me again to Schuback's essay "The Poetic of Language" mentioned earlier. Schuback includes reflections precisely on the differential sound resonances within sound repetitions in Heidegger's writing, which create a sense of time such that language allows the temporality of things (being in its verbal sense) to emerge. *Metaphysics, Facticity, Interpretation,* 211–212.

71. 187. "The appropriating event is appropriation and saying (a saying that opens up) of what is most proper. The most proper is what is inceptive in its inception: the stillness of the tending grace is as appropriation the consignment of the appropriated into the domain of what is proper (Da-sein) which thus first comes to be in the saying" (GA 71: 181).

72. 188. "Appropriating event and stir. Stir—the shy touch that does not grab, that barely touches; only stirs" (GA 71: 182). Heidegger here plays with the root meaning of Rühren, which relates to touching in various senses. *Rührung,* which I here tentatively translate with "stir," in everyday German is used in a situation when one feels touched by something emotionally. *Anrühren* means to touch something slightly and *Berühren* means touching in the normal sense.

73. 314. "*The word* (the saying)—the attuning. . . . What is the word? The soundless voice of beyng. What does voice here mean? Not 'sound' but attuning, i.e. to grant an experience. How this?

To attune to the experience of the inception (the latter cannot be experienced itself). Attune by determining.

Determining by thinking the voice of the word of the inception.

Thinking through the imageless saying of the inception" (GA 71: 283). This quote contains a semantic play related to *Stimme* (voice), *stimmen* (to attune, dispose, to tune [an instrument]), and *bestimmen* (to determine, define, designate, destine, etc.).

74. GA 71: 170.

75. "Der Schmerz: der Schrecken des Abgrundes und die Wonne des Abschieds" (GA 71: 211).

76. GA 71: 217ff.
77. GA 71: 218.
78. GA 71: 294.
79. Jacques Derrida, *Marges de la philosophie* (Paris: Éditions de Minuit), 1972, 29.
80. GA 69: 167.
81. I am thinking here of the notion of *Vorbeigang* mentioned earlier.
82. GA 71: 3.

EIGHT

Poets as Prophets and as Painters: Heidegger's Turn to Language and the Hölderlinian Turn in Context

Robert Bernasconi

Heidegger's approach to language from the 1930s onward was dominated by his relation to poetry, and his relation to poetry was dominated by one poet, Friedrich Hölderlin. Indeed, the model for the much vaunted dialogue between thinkers and poets was his reading of Hölderlin, and it was in the course of this reading that his own thinking took the decisive turn that is marked by the difference between *Being and Time* and, for example, *On the Way to Language*, a difference that divides the early Heidegger, who has now been admitted into the mainstream of philosophy, from the Heidegger of the 1950s, who has not. In this essay I will focus on his reading of Hölderlin's poem "Andenken" in an effort to show that what was at stake for Heidegger in this path to language through Hölderlin had already been indicated by him at the end of "The Origin of the Work of Art" when he described Hölderlin as "the poet whose work still stands before the Germans as a test."[1] Hölderlin was for Heidegger the poet who, if the Germans decided in his favor by listening to the language of his poetry, could lead them to another place, a place where Western metaphysics no longer held sway. This is why Hölderlin was for Heidegger not one poet among others but a destiny for philosophy.[2]

The fact that it was in the 1930s that Heidegger seemingly began his attempt to learn from Hölderlin a relation to language different from that which he associated with Western metaphysics raises as a question the degree to which this effort was marked by his association with National

Socialism. Unfortunately there is little or no consensus about when, if at all, Heidegger began to distance himself from Hitler's regime.[3] But we will find that Heidegger's relation to Hölderlin shifted during these years, albeit not as much as his relation to Nietzsche did. And although the suspicion is inevitably raised as to whether this had anything to do with his relation to the Nazi regime, that lies beyond the present essay. Nevertheless, the fact that this issue lies on the horizon should help to explain my concern for chronology, especially as Heidegger in the 1930s and early 1940s often used words that seem to echo those employed by the architects of Nazi Germany.

What led Heidegger to listen to Hölderlin as if he was a kind of prophet? More particularly, why did Heidegger invest Hölderlin's words with such force? Levinas posed the question in the most pointed way when he asked why it was no longer regarded as legitimate to quote the Bible, when Heidegger was allowed to quote Hölderlin and Trakl without objection. Speaking of his own work, and his sense that the Bible had come to be outlawed by certain philosophers under Nietzsche's and Heidegger's influence, Levinas wrote: "Biblical verses do not function here as proof but as testimony of a tradition and an experience. Do they not have as much right as Hölderlin and Trakl to be cited?"[4] In the early 1950s Paul de Man asked more modestly: "Why does Heidegger need to refer to Hölderlin?"[5] As de Man explained, Heidegger had little time for philosophical authorities and, as could be seen from his reading of Rilke, whom Heidegger treated very differently from Hölderlin, it cannot simply have been because Hölderlin was a poet. And yet at the end of the essay de Man seems to have been no closer to an answer. He also concluded that Heidegger had denied to Hölderlin the "critical dialogue" (BI 254) that he "wishes so often for among thinkers" (BI 263).

I will show here against de Man that the dialogic character of Heidegger's reading of Hölderlin only becomes fully apparent when one approaches that reading in the context of its time, which means here not only the political context but also and more especially the readings of Hölderlin that were popular among his contemporaries. Defensive readings of Heidegger's politics have led even some of his most distinguished readers to ignore both of these contexts as if Heidegger wrote in a vacuum. To be sure, there is some philosophical justification for isolating Hölderlin's poetry insofar as Heidegger insisted that a work of art establishes its own context.[6]

It is therefore of considerable interest to find that Heidegger, while trying to enable Hölderlin to open up a world for the Germans, as the temples had done for the Greeks, nevertheless did not refrain from engaging his own contemporaries in debate. If such references are not always clear to us at first reading, they would have been clear to Heidegger's immediate audience. Indeed, it would probably have been what was most clear in Heidegger's texts of this time. That is why a scrupulous reading of Heidegger needs to recall the strength of interest in Hölderlin in Germany in the 1930s. This is all the more important because for over ten years Heidegger was willing to allow his public face to be intimately associated with Hölderlin. From the rectoral address of 1933 until 1941 his only substantial publications were two essays on Hölderlin. Furthermore, if one were to extend the period to 1945 so as to include "On the Essence of Truth," "Plato's Doctrine of Truth," and the postscript to "What Is Metaphysics?" one would also have to add two further essays on Hölderlin.[7]

Heidegger was not hiding behind Hölderlin but engaging other readers of Hölderlin in debate. Philosophers had long entertained readings of Hölderlin that related him to German Idealism. For example, Wilhelm Windelband in 1878 gave a lecture, "Über Friedrich Hölderlin und sein Geschick,"[8] Wilhelm Dilthey included an essay on Hölderlin in *Poetry and Experience*,[9] and in 1931 Johannes Hoffmeister published *Hölderlin und Hegel*.[10] Because of his conception of a kinship between the poet and the thinker, Heidegger had an entirely different relation to the poet in mind than we find in these philosophical interpretations. For Heidegger, the proximity of thinking and poeticizing was already reflected in the title of the poem "Andenken." In his essay on this poem, written in August 1942 and published in 1943 in a volume marking the centenary of Hölderlin's death,[11] he highlighted the poet's remembrance as a thinking forward (GA 4: 83; EHP 108), a thanking (GA 4: 85; EHP 110), and a greeting (GA 4: 96; EHP 119). Furthermore, the poet thinks: "Noch denket das mir wohl." But the importance of this dialogue between poeticizing and thinking for Heidegger is that it was on this basis that he not only adopted another language—the language of the earth, the heavens, the gods the mortals, dwelling, and *Innigkeit*—but also came to relate to language differently.

Heidegger did not always thematize language in his readings of poetry because to thematize language was to distort one's relation to it.

Nevertheless, Hölderlin gave Heidegger an insight into the essence of poetry and thus of language in the final words of "Andenken":

> Was bleibet aber stiften die Dichter.
> But the poets found what remains.

In "Hölderlin and the Essence of Poetry" Heidegger understood this line to say that poetry establishes being in words.[12] The lecture-course on "Germanien" from which that essay is largely drawn explains further what this means: "Our poetry founds and grounds a place of existence in which we are not yet standing, but where poetic saying wants to compel us."[13] That place is said to be the *Vaterland* insofar as Beyng (*Seyn*) is the *Vaterland* (GA 39: 121). To understand what Heidegger is saying with that word here, it is not enough to know the way the term *Vaterland* was used within the politics of his day. One needs also to recognize that the word belonged firmly within the literary discussion of Hölderlin as can be seen in the writings of the group of poets and intellectuals associated with Stefan George, the so-called George Kreis. I will begin with the work of Max Kommerell. The word *Vaterland* retains a political sense in broad terms within Kommerell's work, but it is not the politics of the newsreels.

As a young man Kommerell was part of the George circle, and in 1928, while still only in his mid-twenties, he published *Der Dichter als Führer in der deutschen Klassik*. The importance of Kommerell's book is indicated by the fact that Walter Benjamin in a review proclaimed it to be the Magna Carta of German conservatism, "if there were such a thing as a German conservatism worth its salt."[14] Benjamin entitled his essay "Against a Masterpiece" and suggested, somewhat naïvely as it turned out, that Hölderlin "was not of the breed that is resurrected."[15] Kommerell's study examines such poets as Klopstock, Herder, Goethe, Schiller, and Jean Paul, before culminating in an essay on "Das Volk" that concentrates on Hölderlin. Kommerell there quoted Hölderlin's letter to Böhlendorff of 1801, which proved so important to Heidegger, and argued that it should form the basis for a new patriotic literature.[16] The book ends with a celebration of the people's desire for life and an inner serious dawn, where the youth feel the birth of a new fatherland in shining union and in the lack of weapons that had been buried all too deep.[17] However, one should not exaggerate the novelty of this reading of Hölderlin. Already in 1923 Wilhelm Michel had, in *Hölderlins abendländische*

Wendung, announced that Hölderlin was a German leader (*Führer*), the lawgiver of the German realm.[18]

Heidegger once said that Kommerell was the only literary historian with whom he had had fruitful conversations about the historical vocation of thinking and poetry.[19] Kommerell visited Heidegger in his hut in Todtnauberg together with Hans-Georg Gadamer and Gerhard Krüger in August 1942 and, at Heidegger's specific request, Kommerell posed by letter some questions about the relation between Hölderlin's poetry and Heidegger's philosophy as exhibited in his essay on Hölderlin's "Wie wenn am Feiertage."[20] By the time he met with Heidegger, Kommerell had long since quarreled with George and had also revised his approach so as to sound more like a professor of German literature.[21] But what is so surprising is that Kommerell, who was perhaps better placed than anyone to understand what Heidegger was attempting in his readings of Hölderlin, remained largely mystified by them. Kommerell was troubled by the esoteric nature of Heidegger's commentary and the extent to which it was almost impossible to understand without a knowledge of the transformation within Heidegger's thinking that was available only to his students.[22] However, Kommerell also conceded in a passage that merits attention in the context of the current debate on Heidegger's relation to National Socialism that the enigmatic character of Heidegger's writing on Hölderlin, and the difficulty of seeing its place in his work as a whole, arose from the difficulty of his philosophical situation within Germany at that time.[23]

We have a clear, if relatively minor, example of how Kommerell left his trace in Heidegger's texts. Kommerell conceded to Heidegger that Hölderlin was a destiny, but in a letter he asked Heidegger whether it would not be worthwhile to distinguish between religious prophets, prophets who established religions, and poets who are prophetic in a different sense.[24] Heidegger answered Kommerell directly in the essay "Andenken," and when he explained that the poets are prophetic in the strict Greek sense of foretelling, they are nevertheless not prophets in the Judeo-Christian sense (GA 4: 114; EHP 136–137).[25] That is to say, the poet who is only beginning to learn the free use of what is his own "is not the mighty booming 'prophet'" (GA 4: 138; EHP 160).

At first Heidegger seems to have seen himself as in some ways the heir of Norbert von Hellingrath, who had been on the outskirts of the George circle. Von Hellingrath, who had published an edition of Hölderlin's poems and was the first to publish his translations of Pindar, understood Hölderlin as someone concerned about what it meant to be German and what it might mean for the Germans to become a people. In a lecture he delivered in 1915 as part of the war effort, he presented the Germans as the people of Hölderlin. This is no doubt what Heidegger was evoking when he dedicated his first essay on Hölderlin, "Hölderlin and the Essence of Poetry," to von Hellingrath, although by recalling that he had been killed in action in 1916, Heidegger was also promoting the spirit of sacrifice that was characteristic of his writings in the mid-thirties. In 1940, Kommerell wrote to Gadamer that he thought Heidegger's dedication inappropriate.[26] Perhaps later Heidegger would have agreed, but in the lecture-course on "Andenken" Heidegger interrupts himself to criticize one aspect of von Hellingrath's interpretation while still acknowledging his importance (GA 52: 44–46). Nevertheless, we can assume that both Kommerell and Heidegger would have agreed to reject Kurt Hildebrandt's 1939 book on Hölderlin, *Hölderlin, Philosophie und Dichtung,* which went through three editions. Hildebrandt, who also belonged to the George circle and had already offered a racialized reading of Plato, did the same for Hölderlin.[27] For example, he read Hölderlin's references to the Caucasus and to India as references to the Caucasian race and to the Aryan race, respectively.[28] It is important to remember figures like Hildebrandt if one is to understand both the tenor of the times and the ways in which Heidegger was opposing the more extreme political appropriations of Hölderlin being promulgated at this time.

By establishing this context, we can see that the novelty of Heidegger's reading of Hölderlin did not lie in taking him seriously as a prophet, which was characteristic of the circle around George. Nor did it lie in his attempt to have Hölderlin take a leadership role in shaping the German people as a people, which, as I have shown, was also a widespread belief of the George circle, and particularly of Hellingrath and the early work of Max Kommerell. Heidegger's originality is much more specific and it concerned a transformation in the relation to language.[29]

Language had been a major focus of the first lecture-course on Hölderlin from 1934–1935, parts of which had been distilled into the 1935 essay "Hölderlin and the Essence of Poetry" (GA 39: 59–77).[30] Heidegger's basic philosophical point about language is clear: language is not a tool but is the event (*das Ereignis*) that disposes of the highest possibility of human existence (GA 4: 38; EHP 56). Language makes history possible (GA 4: 36; EHP

54). This is the basis on which Heidegger took up the final verse of "Andenken," which he translated into his own terms to read, "Poetry is the founding (*Stiftung*) of Being in the word" (GA 4: 41; EHP 59, translation modified). Nevertheless, the essay had another dimension. In his remarks on language in this essay Heidegger emphasized its relation to history, to the earth, and to the freedom of decision. The conjunction of these themes made it possible for the essay to receive a positive reception from the Nazi philosopher Bruno Bauch.[31] Furthermore, the fact that Heidegger placed the essay in the journal *Das Innere Reich,* which had been introduced by its editors in its opening issue in 1934 with a statement dedicating the journal to the completion of the revolution around the Germans as a single people, cannot be ignored.[32] This was a journal in which politics and culture were closely aligned with a crude politics of national unity.

The final verse of "Andenken," which Heidegger highlighted in "Hölderlin and the Essence of Poetry" to clarify his new view of language, is so well known today that we are tempted to assume it always was, but, for example, Wilhelm Michel did not refer to it in his discussion of Hölderlin and language. Instead, Michel said that the highest concept of the poet was of the inner connectedness of things. It is on this basis that, according to Michel, the poet experiences the resistance of language that is intent on separation.[33] Heidegger saw things differently. The problem is not separation, but that language can also create the danger of dangers: confusion and the possibility of loss of Being (GA 4: 37; EHP 55). It is that sense of danger closely aligned with a sense of poverty of our relation to language that grows in Heidegger, culminating in the Bremen lectures but also in *On the Way to Language.* Hölderlin's saying about the poets founding what remains finds its other side in Stefan George's line that later also came to obsess Heidegger in *On the Way to Language:*

> Kein Ding sei wo das Wort gebricht.
> Where word breaks off no thing may be.[34]

This sense of the danger of dangers might have been labeled prophetic, if we did not know that in 1935 Heidegger was still sympathetic to the regime.

Most commentators on Hölderlin's "Andenken" seem not to know what to say about the final line of the poem. They leave it standing unexplained.[35] Heidegger's initial problem was the opposite. His reading of the final line of "Andenken" in "Hölderlin and the Essence of Poetry" abstracted it from its context, but already in a posthumously published text from 1939 Heidegger began the task of restoring it to the poem.[36] This latter text is also noteworthy for the way in which he renounced the terms blood, soil, *Volkstum,* and *Reich* as means by which the Romantics concealed the abandonment of the Being of beings, but which had no place in the interpretation of what Hölderlin meant by "the Germans" (GA 75: 8). This gives a clear example of what Heidegger meant by language creating danger. Nevertheless, the very nature of the poem made an even more sustained reading necessary. On the face of it the five stanzas are disjointed and the final verse appears to be at most an afterthought. In the lecture-course on the poem Heidegger set himself the task of reading the poem in such a way that the end was central. He sought to show that the poem is from first to last about poetry and not simply about, for example, memories of a stay in France (GA 52: 23).

The means by which Heidegger integrated into his reading of the poem as a whole the line about the poets founding what remains was by understanding what Hölderlin wrote about the mariners or sailors of the poem as a reference to poets. When he introduced this interpretation it seems abrupt, but the idea is not far-fetched given that Hölderlin frequently described the poet as on a journey, a journey that is for the sake of the homecoming (GA 4: 83; EHP 108). Hölderlin wrote of the sailors that they are like painters:

> Sie,
> Wie Maler, bringen zusammen
> Das Schöne der Erd' . . .
> They,
> Like painters, bring together
> The beauties of the earth . . .

But what does it mean to say that the poets are like painters? The poets are not like painters because they are engaged in representation. That is not how Heidegger views painters either. Neither are like journalists. Rather he distinguished these poets who are like painters, who gather the beautiful (GA 4: 138; EHP 159), and who say the holy (GA 4: 86; EHP 111), from the poets who have returned home, and of whom alone one can say that the poet establishes what persists (GA 4: 144; EHP 165). According to Heidegger, Hölderlin, who comes to us from the future, was pre-eminent among the latter. The poet who writes the poem has already fulfilled the journey into the foreign land and so has met one of the conditions for becoming at home in what is proper to one (GA 4: 96; EHP 119).

In a passage in parentheses in the lecture-course, which probably means it was written later, Heidegger speaks with a clarity that he rarely allows himself: "That the poets are here thought of 'like painters' contains the concealed truth about the essence of the poeticizing (*Dichtertum*) of the poets who have not yet crossed over to the other side. They are poets in the essential realm of metaphysics" (GA 52: 178). In other words, what is at stake in the poem is nothing less than the overcoming of metaphysics and the transformation of language at another beginning. This supplies the background to Heidegger's claim in 1943: "now poetry must be different from the presentation that brings beauty together *like painters*" (GA 4: 137–138; EHP 159). He read the poem in terms of a word that nowhere appears in the poem but that is characteristic of Hölderlin: *das Heimische.* It is impossible to convey in English in an adequate way the way this word speaks in Hölderlin's poetry or in Heidegger's reading of that poetry. The thinker is at home in thinking *das Unheimische,* whereas the commemorative questioning (*des andenkende Fragen*) of the poet poetizes *das Heimische. Das Heimische* recalls *die heimatliche Erde* that Heidegger evokes on at least three occasions in the essay (GA 4: 93, 115, 145; EHP 117, 138, 167). *Das Heimische* is the fatherland, but when he used that word in 1942 it has to be read in the context of his rejection of all forms of contemporary politics: Americanism and Bolshevism, as well as National Socialism.

Heidegger's reading of "Andenken" in the 1941–1942 lecture-course is explicitly directed against three of the dominant interpretations of Hölderlin's turn to the fatherland in his late poetry. First, he rejected Wilhelm Michel's idea of an occidental turn (*abendländische Wendung*) as a turn away from Greece.[37] Secondly, he rejected the idea that the occidental turn was a turn to Christianity.[38] This had also been proposed by Michel, but it was also developed by Paul Böckmann and Heidegger's student, Roman Guardini.[39] The third misinterpretation was far more widespread in Heidegger's time and it employed Hölderlin's own phrase "*die vaterländische Umkehr.*" It was associated with Friedrich Beissner, who highlighted it in 1931.[40] Beissner, drawing heavily on both of Hölderlin's letters to Böhlendorff, presented an interpretation of Hölderlin that rejected the idea of the Germans as a continuation of the Greeks.[41] Furthermore, he did so specifically in opposition to the Kantian conception of Hölderlin proposed by Böhm, who argued that Hölderlin promoted a cosmopolitan conception of history, that is to say, a conception addressing the development of mankind as a whole. In its place Beissner highlighted Hölderlin's conception of the *Vaterland*.[42] This reading had clear political overtones that contributed to its popularity at that time.[43]

Already in 1939 Heidegger had insisted that the *vaterländische Wendung* was not political but was about the gods (GA 73: 277). He repeated this same warning in 1942, and on this occasion referred the *Vaterland* to the holy (GA 52: 141). However, Heidegger was subsequently persuaded by Beda Allemann that his interpretation of the *vaterländische Umkehr* needed modification, and this was reflected in 1959 in his essay "Hölderlin's Earth and Heaven" (GA 4: 158–159n; EHP 206n).[44] But in the early 1940s Heidegger's turn to language was a turn to the fatherland, albeit he highlighted the role of poets—and by implication also thinkers—for their capacity to create. This contrasts with the way that politics was presented in the 1934 lecture-course on Hölderlin where the founder of the state is put alongside the poet and the thinker (GA 39: 51). His commentary on "Andenken" seems to support the possibility that any regime with a deficient relation to language and to its poet cannot found anything. The political is subordinated to the poet because the political is subordinated to the *polis*, which is determined by the holy (GA 4: 88; EHP 112). That is why the poet has had a special place in "the foundation (*Gründung*) of the history of the 'fatherland'" (GA 4: 87; EHP 112), and that is why it is the poet, not the statesman, who founds what remains.

To be sure, Heidegger had his own idea of the political, which emerged in his 1934–1935 lectures on the poet. Presenting Hölderlin as the future poet of the Germans, he wrote: "To contribute to this is politics in the highest and authentic sense so much that whoever accomplishes something here does not need to talk about politics" (GA 39: 214). In this paradoxical gesture Heidegger not only pronounced the word "politics" in order to renounce it but also decreed that any use of the term was a misuse. To be sure, he later on a number of occasions tried to circumscribe the meaning of the word.[45] Heidegger became increasingly dismissive of "the political," but one should beware of accepting Heidegger's own definition of the political at face value.

The following semester in his lecture-course on Hölderlin's "Der Ister," Heidegger criticized "the Anglo-Saxon world of Americanism" for its resolve to annihilate Europe, the homeland, and thus the beginning of the West.[46] Whatever Heidegger meant by this there seems little doubt that in the context of summer 1942, his students would have heard it as a defense of the Nazi regime. To be sure, when he subsequently came to provide his review of the lecture his remarks were restricted to a polemic against the American use of language (see also GA 52: 33), but his conflation of the defense of the German language with the defense of Germany was surely in the context of the times irresponsible. Heidegger conceded its value for technical and practical purposes, but it was clear that his preference was for learning Greek (GA 53: 80–81; HH 66).[47] Underlying this observation was his conviction that "A historical people *is* only from the dialogue between its language and foreign languages" (GA 53: 80; HH 65). To that extent Heidegger would have had to admit a continuing political dimension to his discussion of language.

The suggestion that there should be a dialogue between languages is more characteristic of Heidegger than the suggestion that there should be an exclusion of the foreign in the quest for some kind of artificial purity, although that aspect can be found in his thought because of his opposition to cosmopolitanism (GA 36/37). According to Heidegger, every people has its assignment (*das Aufgegebene*) as well as its endowment (*das Mitgegebene*) (UK 79; OBT 49). Bringing these into an appropriate balance takes place in the dialogue with the foreign. In an essay from 1937, "Wege zur Aussprache," Heidegger had presented the dialogue between the French and the Germans in this light (GA 13: 15–21), but otherwise it was the dialogue between the Greeks and the Germans that attracted Heidegger's attention and his understanding of it was modeled on Hölderlin's letter to Böhlendorff from December 4, 1801. As Heidegger understood the letter, it said that the Germans are endowed with clarity of presentation as what is most proper to them, but they could not take possession of it until they took up their assignment, which is the fire from heaven. Its importance to Heidegger was not limited to its value as a key to deciphering Hölderlin's poetry. It also guided him in his formulation of the task of establishing "another beginning." This beginning would be German, not Greek, but the Germans could only learn who they might become in struggle (*Kampf*) (GA 39: 293) or confrontation (*Auseinandersetzung*) with the Greeks. On this basis Hölderlin supplied Heidegger with a much needed escape from Nietzsche, which is why he was so critical of attempts to join them together (GA 52: 78).[48] In the "Andenken" course Heidegger was clear that Hölderlin, not Nietzsche, was the one who prepared the way for the overcoming of metaphysics (GA 52: 143). This is also why, in the "Der Ister" course, Heidegger repeatedly insisted that Hölderlin's hymnal poeticizing fell outside of all metaphysics (GA 53: 21, 30, 66; HH 18, 26, 53). From this perspective Hölderlin had announced in his first letter to Böhlendorff poetically what Heidegger himself sought to accomplish in thought.[49]

Hans-Georg Gadamer in response explicitly to Beissner, but also one suspects to Heidegger's essay "Andenken," which had recently appeared in a volume to which Gadamer had also contributed an essay, remarked: "What hermeneutical naïveté to base one's views on the letter to Böhlendorff instead of acknowledging the context of the poem as first appeal."[50] But what is the context of the poem? Is it the world that, according to Heidegger, the poem itself opens up (UK 37; PLT 20)? Or is it the circumstances that surrounded the writing of the poem, particularly if those are incorporated into the poem? The latter was the option that Dieter Henrich adopted in his explicit attempt to rescue Hölderlin from Heidegger by using old maps, travel diaries, and lithographs to refer the details of the poem to "the concrete reality of a landscape."[51] However, Henrich aims only at the content of the poem, whereas Heidegger explicitly evokes something else: what is composed into the poetry (GA 4: 82; EHP 107). Subsequently Gadamer himself offered a reading of "Andenken," and unlike many other readings it had the virtue of being organized around the concluding line, which he understood in terms of the overcoming of distance.[52] Nevertheless, even if one were to accept Gadamer's interpretation, that would not diminish the interest in Heidegger's reading following the criteria established by Gadamer himself in "Hölderlin and the Future": it belongs to "the history of his work and its effect" and was written at a time when Hölderlin's poetry was—or at least seemed—"absolutely contemporary."[53]

Even though Heidegger's readings of Hölderlin are almost always directed to whole poems and are, furthermore, line-by-line readings that attempt to disappear in the poem, they are still dialogues in which the thinker not only seeks to learn but also brings something to the encounter. That means not only reading the poem in the light of the task of thinking but also bringing something of his own time. It is in this way that the poetry comes to appear contemporary. This is more visible in the lecture-course on "Andenken" than in the essay, only because by the time of the essay Heidegger had become more successful in making them disappear. That does not mean they are not present. Indeed, it is when this debate with his contemporaries is removed from Heidegger's reading so that it seems that he is attempting merely another reading of the poem, like those of de Man or Henrich, rather than like those of Kommerell or Beissner, that his approach appears ultimately more arbitrary because less motivated.

Heidegger should not be thought of as writing in isolation but as being in dialogue with his contemporaries, whether they were readers of Hölderlin or promoters of a political conception of the *Vaterland*. Heidegger in this context contested the meaning of that word and ultimately that was what was at stake over and above any historical claim about Hölderlin. This means that any approach to the dialogue between the poet and the thinker and any appreciation of Heidegger's turn to language as a way to overcome metaphysics should not lose sight of the context in which these reflections were developed.

NOTES

1. Martin Heidegger, *Der Ursprung des Kunstwerkes* (Stuttgart: Reclam, 1960), 81; *Off the Beaten Track*, trans. Julian Young and Kenneth Haynes (Cambridge: Cambridge University Press, 2002), 50. Henceforth UK and OBT, respectively.

2. For example, see Martin Heidegger, *Beiträge zur Philosophie, Gesamtausgabe* 65 (Frankfurt am Main: Klostermann, 1989), 422; *Contributions to Philosophy (From Enowning)*, trans. Parvis Emad and Kenneth Maly (Bloomington: Indiana University Press, 1999), 297. Henceforth GA 65 and CP, respectively. The idea is not peculiar to Heidegger. It can already be found in F. W. J. Schelling: "But how a new mythology is itself to arise, which shall be the creation, not of some individual author, but of a new race (*Geschlecht*), personifying, as it were, one single poet—that is a problem whose solution can be looked for only in the future destinies of the world, and in the course of history to come." *System des Transzendentalen Idealismus (1800)*, eds. Harald Korten and Paul Ziche, Werke 9 (Stuttgart: Frommann-Holzboog, 2005), 329; *System of Transcendental Idealism*, trans. Peter Heath (Charlottesville: University Press of Virginia, 1978), 232–233.

3. For an indication of my own views on this vexed issue, see Robert Bernasconi, "Race and Earth in Heidegger's Thinking during the Late 1930s," *Southern Journal of Philosophy* 48 (March 2010): 49–66. There is a hint of a possible critique of the racial policies of the Nazi regime, and indeed of the eugenics programs of other countries, in Heidegger's reference to *Bestandsicherung* in the essay "Andenken"

(GA 4: 105; EHP 129). The term refers somewhat generally to the securing of stock or materials but would include the securing of racial stock. See Heidegger's use of this term specifically in the context of a discussion of programs of racial breeding in *Nietzsches Metaphysik, Gesamtausgabe* 50 (Frankfurt am Main: Klostermann, 1990), 56.

4. Emmanuel Levinas, "Sans Identité," *Humanisme de l'autre homme* (Montpellier, France: Fata Morgana, 1972), 96; *Humanism of the Other,* trans. Nidra Poller (Urbana: University of Illinois Press, 2003), 66.

5. Paul de Man, "Heidegger's Exegeses of Hölderlin," *Blindness and Insight,* 2nd ed. (London: Methuen, 1983), 252. Henceforth BI.

6. "Where does a work belong? As a work it belongs uniquely within the region it itself opens up" (UK 37; OBT 20).

7. Heidegger would even select his two shortest essays on Hölderlin, alongside "What Is Metaphysics?" and "The Essence of Truth," to be among his first English-language publications. See Stefan Schimanski, foreword to *Existence and Being* (London: Vision, 1949), 10–11.

8. Wilhelm Windelband, *Präludien. Aufsätze und Reden zur Einleitung in die Philosophie* (Frieburg: J. C. B. Mohr, 1884), 146–173.

9. Wilhelm Dilthey, *Das Erlebnis und die Dichtung,* 4th ed. (Leipzig: B. G. Teubner, 1913), 349–459; *Poetry and Experience,* trans. Joseph Ross (Princeton, N.J.: Princeton University Press, 1985), 303–383.

10. Johannes Hoffmeister, *Hölderlin und Hegel* (Leipzig: Felix Meiner, 1942).

11. Martin Heidegger, "Andenken," in *Hölderlin. Gedenkschrift zu seimem 100. Todestag,* ed. Paul Kluckhohn (Tübingen: J. C. B. Mohr, 1943), 267–323. Reprinted in GA 4: 79–151; EHP 102–173.

12. Max Kommerell to Martin Heidegger, July 29, 1942, in Max Kommerell, *Briefe und Aufzeichnungen 1919–1944,* ed. Inge Jens (Freiburg: Walter Verlag, 1967), 400–401.

13. Martin Heidegger, *Hölderlins Hymnem "Germanien" und "Der Rhein," Gesamtausgabe* 39 (Frankfurt am Main: Klostermann, 1980), esp. p. 115. Henceforth GA 39.

14. Walter Benjamin, *Gesammelte Schriften,* vol. 3, ed. Hella Tiedemann-Bartels (Frankfurt am Main: Suhrkamp, 1989), 252; *Selected Writings, Volume 2, 1927–1934,* trans. Rodney Livingstone (Cambridge, Mass.: Harvard University Press, 1999), 378.

15. Benjamin, *Gesammelte Schriften,* 3, 299; *Selected Writings,* 2, 284.

16. Max Kommerell, *Der Dichter als Führer in der deutschen Klassik* (Berlin: Georg Bondi, 1928), 478.

17. Ibid., 483.

18. Wilhelm Michel, *Hölderlins abendländische Wendung* (1923).

19. Martin Heidegger, "Max Kommerell, Zum Gedächtnis," *Reden und andere Zeugnisse eines Lebensweges, Gesamtausgabe* 16 (Frankfurt am Main: Klostermann, 2000), 364. In 1962, Heidegger flew to Berlin to give a speech at the commemoration of Kommerell as an indication of his high regard for him. Gertrud Heidegger, *"Mein liebes Seelchen!" Briefe Martin Heideggers an seine Frau Elfride* (Munich: Deutsche Verlags-Anstalt, 2005), 345. On Heidegger's relation to Kommerell, see Bernard Zeller (ed.), *Max Kommerell-Wiedererinnert* (Marbach: Deutsche Schillergesellschaft, 1985), 80–91, and Joachim W. Storck, "'Zwiesprache von Dichten und Denken.' Hölderlin

bei Martin Heidegger und Max Kommerell," in *Klassiker in finsteren Zeiten. 1933–1945*, ed. B. Zeller (Marbach: Deutsche Schillergesellschaft, 1983); vol. 1, 345–365.

20. For a useful but brief account of the relation between Heidegger and Kommerell, see Joachim W. Storck, *Max Kommerell 1902–1944*, Marbacher Magazin 34 (Marbach: Deutsche Schillergesellschaft, 1985), 80–91.

21. See Max Kommerell, "Hölderlins Empedokles-Dichtungen" in *Geist und Buchstabe der Dichtung* (Frankfurt am Main: Klostermann, 1940), 255–294; "Holderlins Hymnen in freien Rhythmen" in *Gedanken über Gedichte* (Frankfurt am Main: Klostermann, 1943), 456–481; and, most importantly, his Florence lecture of May 29, 1941, "Das Problem der Aktualität in Hölderlins Dichtung" in *Dichterische Welterfahrung*, ed. Hans-Georg Gadamer (Frankfurt am Main: Klostermann, 1952), 174–193. On Kommerell's quarrel with George, see Robert E. Norton, *Secret Germany: Stefan George and His Circle* (Ithaca, N.Y.: Cornell University Press, 2002), 702–712.

22. Martin Heidegger, *Erläuterungen zu Hölderlins Dichtung, Gesamtausgabe* 4 (Frankfurt am Main: Klostermann, 1981), 41; *Elucidations of Hölderlin's Poetry*, trans. Keith Hoeller (Amherst, N.Y.: Humanity Books, 2000), 59. Henceforth GA 4 and EHP, respectively.

23. Kommerell to Karl Reinhardt, January 19, 1942, *Briefe*, 388.

24. Kommerell to Heidegger, July 29, 1942, *Briefe*, 401.

25. This can be taken as a direct response to Kommerell because it is not found in the lecture-course from the winter semester 1941–1942 on which the essay was based and which Heidegger had already finished delivering before he received this letter.

26. Max Kommerell to Hans-Georg Gadamer, October 26, 1940, in Kommerell, *Briefe*, 353.

27. On Kurt Hildebrandt's racialized reading of Plato, see Charles Bambach, *Heidegger's Roots* (Ithaca, N.Y.: Cornell University Press, 2003), 204–207. Hildebrandt wrote extensively about race. See *Norm und Entartung des Menschen* (Dresden: Sibyll, 1920), 219–246. This volume was republished together with *Norm und Verfall des Staates* in *Norm/Entartung/Verfall. Bezogen auf den Einzelnen/Die Rasse/ Der Staat* (Berlin: Die Runde, 1934). See pp. 227–254.

28. Kurt Hildebrandt, *Hölderlin* (Stuttgart: Kohlhammer, 1940), 245–246.

29. Martin Heidegger, *Hölderlins Hynme "Andenken," Gesamtausgabe* 52 (Frankfurt am Main: Klostermann, 1982), 38. Henceforth GA 52.

30. The essay version was originally published in *Das Innere Reich*, December 1936, III, 2, 1065–1078. Note the additional epigraph included in this version but subsequently omitted which calls on German youth to remember von Hellingrath. I am grateful to Andrew Mitchell for drawing this to my attention.

31. Bruno Bauch, "Review of Martin Heidegger, 'Hölderlin und das Wesen der Dichtung,'" *Blätter für Deutsche Philosophie* 13 (1939–1940): 217–218.

32. Paul Alverdes and Karl Benno von Mechow, "Inneres Reich," *Das Innere Reich: Zeitschrift für Dichtung, Kunst und deutscher Leben*, April 1934, 7.

33. Michel, *Hölderlins Abendländische Wendung*, 57. By contrast, Werner Barrscher cites the closing lines of "Andenken"; Heidegger's Rome lecture on Hölderlin is cited in the bibliography. See *Hölderlin und die deutsche Nation. Versuch einer Wirkungsgeschichte Hölderlin* (Berlin: Junker und Dünnhaupt, 1942), 223.

34. Martin Heidegger, *Unterwegs zur Sprache, Gesamtausgabe* 12 (Frankfurt am Main: Klostermann, 1985); *On the Way to Language,* trans. Peter D. Hertz (New York: Harper & Row, 1971). See Robert Bernasconi, *The Question of Language in Heidegger's History of Being* (Atlantic Highlands, N.J.: Humanities Press, 1985), 49–53.

35. For example, Rolf Zuberbühler, *Hölderlins Erneuerung der Sprache aus ihren etymologischen Ursprüngen* (Berlin: Erich Schmidt, 1969), 114.

36. Martin Heidegger, *Zu Hölderlin, Gesamtausgabe* 75 (Frankfurt am Main: Klostermann, 2000), 10–26. Henceforth GA 75.

37. Wilhelm Michel, *Hölderlins Abendländische Wendung* (Jena: Eugen Diederich, 1923).

38. Michel, *Hölderlins Abendländische Wendung,* 42–46.

39. Paul Böckmann, *Hölderlin und seine Götter* (Munich: Beck, 1935), 367. Roman Guardini, *Hölderlin* (Leipzig: Jakob Hegner, 1939).

40. Friedrich Beissner, *Hölderlins Übersetzungen aus dem Griechischen* (Stuttgart: Metzler, 1931), 147–186. Heidegger cited this book at GA 53: 156–157; HH 126. For a helpful review of Heidegger's relation to the interpretations of Michel and Beissner, see Peter Trawny, *Heidegger und Hölderlin oder das Europäische Morgen* (Würzburg: Königshausen und Neumann, 2004), 85–181.

41. Beissner, *Hölderlins Übersetzungen,* 157.

42. Ibid., 155.

43. See, for example, the section titled "Völker und Vaterland" in Ludwig Friedrich Barthel (ed.), *Das Seher des Vaterlands* (Munich: Carl Gerber, 1944), 107–119.

44. See Beda Alleman, *Hölderlin und Heidegger* (Zurich: Atlantis, 1954). See Martin Heidegger to Hannah Arendt, April 21, 1954, *Briefe 1925–1975* (Frankfurt am Main: Klostermann, 1999), 142. See also Hans-Joachim Kreutzer, "Kolonie und Vaterland in Hölderlins später Lyrik," *Hölderlin Jahrbuch* 22 (1980–1981): 18–46. Heidegger marked this shift in a footnote to "Hölderlin's Earth and Heaven" where he rehearsed his rejection of Wilhelm Michel's notion of a "western turn" and questioned the then current interpretation of Hölderlin's phrase the "Vaterländische Umkehr": "Hölderlin finally left behind him, by overcoming it, that part of the way that he thought through under the title 'patriotic reversal'" (GA 4: 90n; EHP 206n).

45. Most notably in Martin Heidegger, *Parmenides, Gesamtausgabe* 54 (Frankfurt am Main: Klostermann, 1982), 130–144; *Parmenides,* trans. André Schuwer and Richard Rojcewicz (Bloomington: Indiana University Press, 1992), 88–97.

46. Martin Heidegger, *Hölderlins Hymne "Der Ister," Gesamtausgabe* 53 (Frankfurt am Main: Klostermann, 1984), 68; *Hölderlin's Hymn "The Ister,"* trans. William McNeill and Julia Davis (Bloomington: Indiana University Press, 1996), 54. Henceforth GA 53 and HH, respectively.

47. For a more detailed discussion of these passages, see Robert Bernasconi, "I Will Tell You Who You Are," in *From Phenomenology to Thought, Errancy, and Desire,* ed. Babette Babich (Dordrecht: Kluwer, 1995), 301–313.

48. For an example, see Wilhelm Michel, *Das Leben Friedrich Hölderlins* (Bremen: Carl Schünemann, 1940), 561–565.

49. In this way Heidegger's dialogues with Hölderlin transform his relation to Western metaphysics and especially the Greeks, who are now seen as foreign to the Germans rather than as the source of "the" tradition.

50. Hans-Georg Gadamer, "Hölderlin und das Zukünftige," in *Aesthetik und Poetik II* Gasammelte Werke 9 (Tübingen: J. C. B. Mohr, 1993), 28n; "Hölderlin and the Future," in *Literature and Philosophy in Dialogue,* trans. Robert H. Paslick (Albany: SUNY Press, 1994), 176, translation modified. Gadamer recorded in a note that the essay was written in 1943 but that permission to publish the essay was withheld by the Nazi regime because Gadamer closed the essay by quoting from Hölderlin's poem *Der Frieden* ("Peace"). None of the endnotes including this one were included in the original edition: *Beiträge zur geistigen Überlieferung* (Godesberg: Helmut Küpper, 1947), 53–85.

51. Dieter Henrich, *The Course of Remembrance and Other Essays on Hölderlin* (Stanford, Calif.: Stanford University Press, 2007), 235–242. Henrich argues that Hölderlin in "Andenken" "lets loose a range of experiences and a context of meanings that have their own horizons and that must be conceived and appreciated in their own right, on the basis of their 'totality' before one asks how they fit into Hölderlin's work as a whole" (CR 193). This objection repeats Gadamer's objection many years earlier and the book is dedicated to Gadamer. However, the fact that were trees on the promontory, ships going to the Indies, and sailors bringing back goods does not impact Heidegger's reading, especially as Henrich has nothing to say about the introduction of Bellarmin from Hölderlin's *Hyperion.*

52. Hans-Georg Gadamer, "Thinking and Poetizing in Heidegger and in Hölderlin's 'Andenken,'" Richard Palmer (trans.) in *Heidegger toward the Turn,* ed. James Risser (Albany: SUNY Press, 1999), 145–162.

53. Gadamer, "Hölderlin und das Zukünftige," 20 and 22; "Hölderlin and the Future," 88–89.

NINE

Truth Be Told: Homer, Plato, and Heidegger

Dennis J. Schmidt

The question that I want to ask concerns what Aristotle called the "κίνησις του βιου," the basic movement of life. More precisely, I want to ask how we might speak of this movement without losing its elemental unity and its dynamic character. An assumption that I will make, but not defend, is that the language of philosophy—that is, the language of the concept—is poor at following this movement since such language aims at capturing and grasping this movement. But I want to suggest that one finds an interesting answer to this question of the proper way of speaking of this movement of life when one turns to Heidegger's reading of Homer, since in Homer's language Heidegger finds a way of following this movement, this movement of all appearance, that is closed to the less agile, conceptual language of philosophy. What Homer offers that is foreclosed to our philosophical habits—habits that are amplified by the habits of understanding characterizing modernity—is a way of speaking of the real struggle defining this movement of life; namely, that life both shows and hides itself in its movement.

* * *

Heidegger's analysis and argument about the need to move away from a static conception of truth wedded to the ideal of certainty and to move toward an understanding of truth as the movement of ἀλήθεια is well known.[1] It is, however, not well understood since there is a tendency to regard ἀλήθεια, which Heidegger characterizes as the movement of revealing and concealing, as, in the end, the overcoming of concealing. But the matter is much more complex and here Homer can be of help.[2]

Heidegger turns to Homer because he finds in Homer a language prior to the language of philosophy, a language closer as it were to the ways in which what appears can be spoken of. Instead of taking a distance from Homer's language, Heidegger is most concerned with drawing close to that language and hearing it in a register not measured by the language of the concept. His readings of Homer are all shorn of any concern with justice, morality, or didactic purpose. Heidegger does not find "lessons" in Homer; instead, he takes up Homer as celebrating the various ways in which appearances happen. He finds in Homer a language sensitive to the truth that defines appearance before the idea became the measure of truth of appearance, before something apart from the movement of appearances became the standard for speaking the truth. In short, Heidegger suggests that Homer is able to translate us out of our philosophically defined language and into a "thoughtful and thoughtfully uttered word."[3]

One finds an example of how Heidegger explains the way that *we* have been translated out of a language capable of speaking of the movement of life in the following passage. Here Heidegger refers to the decisive moment for us, one found in another translation, namely, the translation from Greek into Latin, in which appearance comes to take on a very different meaning:

> Think back to Homer, who . . . brought to light the presence of what is present. A scene in the homecoming of Odysseus needs to be recalled. When Eumaios leaves, Athena appears in the form of a beautiful young woman. She appears to Odysseus as the goddess. But his son, Telemachus, does not see her, and the poet says: ου γάρ πως πάντεσσι θεοὶ φαίνονται εναρεις (*Od.* XVI, 161). "Not to all do the gods appear εναρεις"—one translates this word as "visible." However, άργός means "gleaming," "shining." That which shines illuminates itself from out of itself. That which shines, essences from out of itself. Odysseus and Telemachus see the same woman. But Odysseus perceives the presence of the goddess. Later, the Romans translated εναρεις, this shining from out of itself, with *evidentia; evideri* means to make visible. Evidence is thought from out of the human being as the one who sees. εναρεις on the other hand is a characteristic of the presencing thing itself.[4]

In other words, the Roman translation and appropriation of the Homeric way of speaking of how things appear changes that sense by rendering it a subjective matter. Or, as Heidegger remarks in another text: "For the Greeks, things appear. For us, things appear to me."[5] Heard properly, then, Homer's language speaks of appearance, of presencing, not as a subjectively defined event but as a character of the world itself. Homer "brought to light the presence of what is present" insofar as he understands this presence as a "shining from out of itself." It is difficult for us to understand such a way of speaking of the world, of understanding that "for the Greeks, things appear," since "for us, things appear to me." As Heidegger reads him, Homer's language is able—so far as the habits of our own language permit—to translate us into an experience and an understanding of the world that have been covered over by the language of philosophy and the translations that have defined Western culture.

* * *

I want to take a close look now at one instance of Heidegger reading Homer as leading to an understanding of the movement of life that is covered over today by our own language and prejudices. It is the passage that tells the story of Odysseus listening to the song that Demodocus sings in the court of King Alcinous. Heidegger's reading of this passage is found in the context of examining the transformation in the essence of truth that begins with the emergence of philosophy in Greece and that is consolidated by the translation of Greek philosophical notions into Latin. This transformation is, as Heidegger describes it, a decline, a fall in which the original Greek experience of the richness of truth—an experience still preserved in Homer—is constricted and ultimately obscured. Heidegger comments on this transformation by suggesting that one sees it most clearly in the way Plato and Aristotle understand the philosophical counter-concept to ἀλήθεια as ψεῦδος, which Heidegger translates as "falsity" and as "lie." With the move into the standpoint of philosophy, this falseness, this ψεῦδος, is what ἀλήθεια is said to struggle against and what it needs to overcome: ψεῦδος stands in opposition to ἀλήθεια. But Heidegger argues that in Homer we find a more original way of speaking of what is decisive for understanding the movement of truth. We find this in the way Homer speaks of how λανθάνομαι —not ψεῦδος—belongs to this movement as the countermovement of ἀλήθεια.[6]

Heidegger notes that the customary translation of λανθάνομαι is "to forget," but he quickly adds that this forgetting is not a subjective act, the failing of an individual, or a mistake. It is an elemental forgetting such as the forgetting that is spoken of in the opening of *Being and Time,* namely, the forgetting of being itself. Such forgetting is not an error or mistake that can be overcome or corrected. It is rather a quite peculiar "hiding," one that Heidegger described by saying simply that one does not forget being the way one forgets one's pocketknife. It is in order to clarify the deepest sense of this word λανθάνομαι that Heidegger turns to the passage from Homer that I now want to look at more closely. More specifically, in this passage Heidegger turns to the word that is used to describe how it is that Odysseus "remained hidden" ("*blieb im Verborgen*"), his face covered by his cloak, as tears stream down his face.

Heidegger sets the scene of the passage in Homer that he wants to address by reminding us that Odysseus has only just arrived at this colony, having been freed from his seven years of being a hostage to Kalypso. Odysseus has yet to reveal his true identity to his hosts. Demodocus sings the story of a quarrel between Odysseus and Achilles. Odysseus is overwhelmed by the memories brought back by the song and the emotions brought to life by these memories move Odysseus to tears. But rather than let those tears be seen, he covers his head with his cloak. It is this gesture of Odysseus covering his face and then the way in which Odysseus is said to be hidden from the others that form the chief focus of Heidegger's interpretation of this passage. The passage follows:

> ταῦτ' ἄρ' ἀοιδὸς ἄειδε περικλυτός: αὐτὰρ 'Οδυσσεὺς
> This the far-famed singer sang, but Odysseus
>
> πορφύρεον μέγα φᾶρος ἑλὼν χερσὶστιβαρῇσι
> grasped the great purple cloak with his well-knit hands,
>
> κὰκ κεφαλῆς εἴρυσσε, κάλυψε δὲ καλὰ πρόσωπα:
> pulled it over his head, and hid his handsome face, for he was ashamed
>
> αἴδετο γὰρ Φαίηκας ὑπ' ὀφρύσι δάκρυα λείβων.
> to shed tears from under his eyebrows in front of the Phaeacians.
>
> ἤτοι ὅτε λήξειεν ἀείδων θεῖος ἀοιδός,
> Indeed, each time the divine singer stopped singing,
>
> δάκρυ ὀμορξάμενος κεφαλῆς ἄπο φᾶρος ἕλεσκε
> Odysseus took the cloak from his head, wiped his tears,

καὶ δέπας ἀμφικύπελλον ἑλὼν σπείσασκε θεοῖσιν:
grasped a goblet with two handles, and made libation to the gods.

αὐτὰρ ὅτ' ἂψ ἄρχοιτο καὶ ὀτρύνειαν ἀείδειν
But each time he began again, and the best of the Phaeacians

Φαιήκων οἱ ἄριστοι, ἐπεὶ τέρποντ' ἐπέεσσιν,
spurred him on to sing since they enjoyed his stories,

ἂψ 'Οδυσεὺς κατὰ κρᾶτα καλυψάμενος γοάασκεν.
Odysseus immediately covered his head and cried.

ἔνθ' ἄλλους μὲν πάντας ἐλάνθανε δάκρυα λείβων,
He went unnoticed there by all the others, shedding tears,
*Da aber vergoß er (*Od.*) Tränen, ohne daß alle anderen es merkten,*
[da aber im Verhältnis zu allen anderen bleib er verborgen als der Tränen Vergießende,]

'Αλκίνοος δέ μιν οἶος ἐπεφράσατ' ἠδ' ἐνόησεν
and Alcinous alone noticed him and understood.
Alkinoos nur sah aufmerksam die Trauer.

ἥμενος ἄγχ' αὐτοῦ, βαρὺ δὲ στενάχοντος ἄκουσεν.
He sat near him and he heard him moaning deeply.[7]

Of this passage Heidegger says: "this poetic scene of Odysseus concealing as he weeps makes clear how the poet experiences . . . the governance of presencing . . . presencing is luminous self-concealing . . . it is the reserved remaining-concealed in front of the nearness of what is present."[8] But what accounts for this hiding, this concealment and forgetting that is, after all, at the heart of what Heidegger contends is said by Homer in ways we cannot understand? Moved to tears and ashamed ("αἴδετο")[9] by these tears in front of his hosts, Odysseus covers his head ("καλυψάμενος") with his purple cloak, hiding his handsome face ("κάλυψε δὲ καλὰ πρόσωπα"). When Demodocus stopped his song, Odysseus would remove his cloak, dry his tears, and offer a libation to the gods. But, as soon as Demodocus began to sing again, Odysseus would immediately cover his head once again. Throughout, Odysseus "remained hidden" ("ἐλάνθανε"). To help clarify how we are to hear this word, Heidegger gives another instance of it in Homer. The passage is from *Iliad,* XXII, where we read of the final battle between Achilles and Hector: ἀνὰ δ' ἥρπασε ἂψ δ' Ἀχιλῆϊ δίδου, λάθε δ' Ἕκτορα ποιμένα λαῶν ("Athena remained concealed from Hector in giving Achilles back his spear"). Heidegger might have added that the same root word is used by Homer to describe how Penelope's "trick" of unraveling each night what she has woven by day goes "unnoticed" by her suitors.[10] While our natural assumption in reading these passages that describe something "hidden" is to assume that this hiding is the result of some deceit carried out by the one who is concealed, or by some inattention or error of others, Heidegger stresses that it is not to be understood as referring to a subjective act, as if Odysseus's tears, Achilles' lance, or Penelope's trick were simply overlooked by others who failed to pay attention. Heidegger is clear when he argues that this "hiddenness," this original sense of "forgetting," is not an error or mistake. Thus, Heidegger says: "Accordingly, the Greek experience in the case of Odysseus does not proceed from the premise that the guests present are represented as subjects who in their subjective behavior fail to grasp weeping Odysseus as an object of their perception."[11]

Admittedly, it is not easy to understand this "remaining hidden" ("*Verborgenbleiben*") if it is not to be understood as a failing of those around Odysseus. One imagines Odysseus, sitting next to the king, covering his face with his cloak and, though in full view, in plain sight, he remains concealed. The difficulty, strangely, is that Odysseus is, in the end, *in full view, in plain sight,* in other words, it seems that we need to find a reason for this oversight. Homer says that Odysseus covers his face and the word that Homer uses at this point—"πρόσωπα"—reminds one as well that the face is a sort of mask—"πρόσωπειον"—that both shows and hides who one is at the same time. It is a word that reminds us that showing and hiding are not necessarily distinct; that which shows, like the face, can be the same as that which hides. But Heidegger is not referring just to Odysseus's face or his tears; "rather, what governs the Greek experience is a concealment surrounding the one in tears, a concealment which isolates him from the others."[12] Furthermore, Heidegger interprets the passage as saying that Odysseus *remains* hidden, as if he always was hidden and that nothing changes, that being hidden was already the way things were—even in the way the situation was revealed. Later, during Demodocus's third song—this one about Odysseus's plan for the Trojan horse that would hide soldiers—Odysseus will again "remain hidden" while shedding tears, but this time he will not cover his face with his cloak.[13] When this is said we realize that the cloak is not the primary reason that Odysseus remains hidden; in some sense, Odysseus's cloak only calls attention to the fact of his hiding. King Alcinous alone will notice ("ἐπεφρασαστ") him, but not because he saw the tears, instead because he "heard him moaning deeply."[14] What the king notices is that he does not understand who is sitting next to him. Hearing his sorrow, Odysseus emerges as a question for the king, who then finally asks Odysseus his name. Odysseus has been in full view all this time and yet, until this moment, not asked to reveal himself.

Odysseus begins his story by announcing his name and thus revealing himself, and from this point on, he takes over the telling of his own story. The first story he tells—about Cyclops, the one-eyed monster he blinds—is a story that turns on Odysseus once again being asked his name. But in this story, he gives a pseudonym and refers to himself as "Nobody."[15] In other words, this time Odysseus conceals himself by means of a deception, a lie. But this deliberate hiding, for Heidegger, rests upon a more original forgetting, a concealing that belongs to the movement of appearance itself, and it is this essential forgetfulness that he wants to address.

Thus, Heidegger says "if, however, for the Greeks the essence of concealment and unconcealedness was experienced so essentially as the basic trait of being itself, must not concealment itself then display a more original essence, for which concealment in the form of ψεῦδος, dissemblance, in no way suffices?"[16] Heidegger points out that there are multiple forms in which the other of ἀλήθεια is named: "nevertheless, to a certain extent we can still recognize and understand different modes of concealment. In fact we must do so, if we wish to recapture the *ability to catch sight of the one mode of concealment* that for the Greeks, over and beyond ψεῦδος, has codetermined the truth, the unconcealedness and unhiddenness, of all beings."[17] Heidegger refers to a number of "everyday" examples of such sheltering (*Bergen*) and concealing (*Verbergen*), but then points to what he calls the "the pre-eminent level of the essence of concealment"[18] in which we see "the essential connection between death and concealment."[19]

This connection between death and concealment defines the original form of forgetfulness upon which all other forms rest. While this connection is difficult to understand, this connection and the way in which it illuminates the character of forgetting and concealing that belongs to the movement of life is also the most basic and in need of attention. The first example of this connection that Heidegger gives is from the passage in the *Odyssey* in which Athena speaks words of encouragement to Telemachus about his search for his father. Speaking of Telemachus's search, Athena says that he has sailed the world looking for the place "ὅπου κύθε γαῖα" ("where Odysseus lies concealed in the earth").[20] The second passage is from the *Iliad;* in this passage Achilles speaks to Agamemnon urging him to gather Patroclus's bones from the funeral pyre and to keep them safe and separate until Achilles himself lies "'Ἄϊδι κεύθωμαι" ("hidden in Hades").[21] Neither passage uses the word "death" even though each refers to someone who is dead. Instead, both passages speak of death as a hiding or a concealing in the earth. Heidegger argues that this manner of speaking is not "simply" a metaphor or some poetic embellishment; rather, in these expressions of the kinship uniting death and hiding we find the original form of forgetting, of concealing, from out of which Homer thought the basic movement of life, the character of all appearance. After noting this kinship between death and concealment, Heidegger comments:

> For the Greeks, death is not a "biological" process, any more than birth is. Birth and death take their essence from the realm of disclosiveness and concealment. Even the earth receives its essence from this same realm. The earth is the in-between, namely between the concealment of what is under the earth and the luminosity, the disclosiveness, of what is above the earth (the span of heaven, οὐρανός). For the Romans on the contrary, the earth, *tellus, terra,* is the dry, the land as distinct from the sea; this distinction differentiates that upon which construction, settlement, and installation are possible from those places where they are impossible. *Terra* becomes *territorium,* land of settlement as realm of command. In the Roman *terra* can be heard an imperial accent, completely foreign to the Greek γαια und γη.[22]

Death and birth—those asymmetrical ends of the movement of life—find their essential natures in this movement of revealing and concealing. Even more: "λανθάνω, I remain concealed, does not signify just one form of human behavior among many others, rather it names the basic trait of every response to what is present or absent—if not indeed the basic trait of presence and absence themselves."[23] But this concealing in its most archaic sense belongs specifically to the earth, so one might also say that death seals our contract with the earth and that out of this relation to the earth our sense of the basic movement of life, of all appearance, emerges.

So, it is out of this sense of a relation to the earth that the basic movement of life is understood; and yet, it is precisely on this point of living on the earth that we find ourselves most foreign to the Greek sensibility.

Heidegger contends that this foreignness, this move away from a living—and dying—relation to the earth begins in the Roman world. The world as we understand it today has only amplified this difference and made the Greek world all the more difficult to understand. Hölderlin made reference to this difference in his letter to Böhlendorf: "Because the tragic for us is that we are silently packed up in some container and taken away from the realm of the living, not that consumed by flames we pay penalty to the flames we could not tame."[24] The difference is clear: Homer thinks death as the concealment of the earth, as a return in which something of the movement of life itself is exposed; we, on the other hand, box up the dead and pack them away into the dead earth. In other words, our world is a sort of mortification of the Greek world: the earth becomes an object, something dried up, something to be conquered, and in life as well as death we are separated from the earth only to ultimately be boxed up and placed into it. And just as the earth becomes an object, we become subjects. Death is then taken as the end of the subject, its ultimate isolation, no longer as a return to the earth. Not just our belonging to φύσις, but φύσις itself as that which κρύπτεσθαι φίλει disappears from our understanding of the movement of life in such isolation. What disappears is the sense that death signals a return to the earth that belongs to the movement of life as a whole. In a strange way, this elemental kinship of death, earth, and concealment lets us understand something ordinary, something simple about all appearance: that concealment, remaining hidden, is not simply a negation of unconcealment, but, even more originally, it is a way in which unconcealment is possible. Concealment is, one might say, "older" than unconcealment. Or, as Heidegger puts it: "the 'concealed' has priority in the experience of beings."[25]

After saying this and after having alluded to the kinship of death and concealment, and after emphasizing once again that an understanding of this original concealment is foreclosed to us today, Heidegger addresses the riddle of the essence of this hiddenness, this concealing, in a new way, this time by referring to the "most beautiful poetic elucidation of its essence" in Pindar, who writes of "λάθας ἀτέχμαρτα νέφος" ("the signless cloud of concealment").[26] The cloud—itself without sign, without indication whatsoever—hides and casts a darkness over all else: it withdraws clarity and relations. But the essential word here is ἀτέχμαρτα—signless—which means that the cloud does not show itself at all. Thus, the concealment named here is an "absent concealment."[27] "In the fact that the cloud of forgetting concealment conceals itself as such, the uncanny character of forgetting comes to the fore."[28] The irony in speaking of this forgetting is that naming this doubled concealment brings it to light. It is this delicate relation to such irony and to such concealment that sets the languages of poetry and philosophy apart.

After discussing the way in which it hides even itself, Heidegger gives an illustration of such a "signless cloud." While one might expect him to speak of Odysseus's gesture of hiding his face with his cloak, Heidegger gives instead another, initially quite surprising, example when he writes that "the typewriter is a signless cloud, that is, a withdrawing concealment in the midst of its very obtrusiveness, and through it the relation of being to the human being is transformed."[29] The typewriter marks an "almost everyday and thus unnoticed and thus signless relation to writing, that is, to the word, that is, to the essential realm of the hand, and that is, of the word."[30] The typewriter illustrates something about the specific character of self-withdrawing concealment in the age of the *Gestell,* but it should be said that such concealment characterizes *all* appearance. Indeed, it is out of—and back into—this concealment that the movement of life is what it is. When Gadamer speaks of "the hiddenness of health" he names yet another way in which this concealment belongs to the elements of appearance. Noting that health resists objectification and definition, that it is known mostly in its absence, and that its presence is self-concealing, Gadamer reminds us that this self-concealment is, in the end, the movement of φύσις itself. It sets in motion the basic movement of life itself. In the words of Heraclitus: φύσις κρύπτεσθαι φίλει. Heidegger himself makes a similar point when he says "Das Leben ist diesig, es nebelt sich immer ein."

* * *

Heidegger turned to Homer in the course of trying to unfold the meaning of truth as ἀλήθεια. What he found in Homer was a sense of the movement of life that reached beyond the objectification of life defining our present historical juncture. He also found a language prior to the language of philosophy, a language that had not yet ossified into the language of the concept but that was still attentive to the movement of concealing and unconcealing. He found, in other words, a language that had not yet subscribed to a sense of truth as in a struggle with falsity, but rather a sense of truth as co-determined by revealing and concealing. Heidegger is clear that what is most difficult in speaking of the truth is speaking of the concealment, the hiding, forgetting, the signless cloud that is not a subjective failing but is rather elemental and original. Heidegger points to many words that mark the counter-movement of ἀλήθεια—λάθας ἀτέχμαρτα νέφος and κρύπτεσθαι are some that receive special attention—but none of these words holds a singular grip on how the elemental concealment proper to experience is to be thought. What is notable about all of these words, however, is that they need to be understood as *poetic* words. But why? And what does the "poetic" mean in these instances?

Here the contrast between the philosophic word, that is, the concept, and the poetic word is helpful. The philosophic word brings into the clarity of light; the concept illuminates, sheds light, lets us see and grasp the general character of what we experience. It is no accident that the word έιδος comes from the word έιδειν, "to see." It is also no accident that philosophical vocabulary has conceived of thinking in terms of light and seeing, so that we speak of "shedding light" on something, finding "clarity," illuminating, and "seeing" what is meant. The poetic word, on the other hand, is defined by its attentiveness to what we cannot and do not see, to that which conceals itself. It is no accident that Homer—the preeminent poet for the Greeks, the very image of the poet—was thought of as blind. We are not even certain that there was "a Homer," but we are certain that Homer was blind (one name for the blind was "Homeros"—"hostage"—which referred to the way that the blind always needed to walk with someone). Any understanding of the passage where Odysseus covers his face while Demodocus sings of him must also take note of the fact that Demodocus too was blind. Poetry is not defined in the first instance as a genre of literature; rather, it needs to be defined as speech that preserves—gently and respectfully—that which we cannot see and thus that which language cannot fully say.[31] In other words, poetic language is language that follows the full movement of truth both as concealing and unconcealing; it is language responsive to that which remains hidden in the dark as well as to that which emerges into the clarity of the light. That poetry has, since Plato, been said to have a special connection with death and mourning only gives further evidence of its attentiveness to what is lost, absent, unseen, forgotten.

* * *

Plato's criticisms of poetry are chiefly directed toward this essential link uniting poetry, concealment, mourning, and death. There are, however, two scenes in the dialogues that echo Homer's description of Odysseus covering his head. I will only briefly mention these scenes, but, in the end, I believe there is much to be learned from a more detailed look at these Platonic passages with Homer.

One scene is found in the *Phaedrus*. Socrates covers his head just before he begins his first speech on *eros*. Phaedrus pressured Socrates to make such a speech despite Socrates' hesitations; Socrates capitulates and begins his speech by saying: "I'm going to keep my head wrapped up while I talk, that I may get through my discourse as quickly as possible and that I may not look at you and become embarrassed."[32] He begins his second speech on *eros* by saying: "Now I, my friend, must purify myself; and for those who have sinned in matters of mythology there is an ancient purification, unknown to Homer, but known to Stesichorus. For when he was stricken with blindness for speaking ill of Helen, he was not, like Homer, ignorant of the reason . . . and so straightway he writes the poem: 'This story is not true' . . . and when he had written . . . the recantation, he saw again at once."[33] What is most notable in this passage, which is about a lie and its recantation, is that when Socrates covers his face he *calls attention to himself as hiding*, indeed he continues to speak even when his face is hidden; so, contrary to Odysseus, who hides and remains concealed as he covers his face, Socrates intensifies his presence by being present in such a strange manner.

The other Platonic passage echoing Homer is found in a quite different context, namely, in Phaedo's story of Socrates' own death. The death scene that Phaedo recounts begins with Phaedo's own admission that as Socrates prepared to die, Phaedo wept for his own misfortune at losing a friend such as Socrates. Phaedo then says that "in spite of myself, tears rolled down in floods, so that I wrapped my face in my cloak ("εγκαλυψάμενος") and wept for myself."[34] After Socrates urged his friends not to cry and to be silent, and after the effects of the poison began to be felt, Socrates lies down on his back as he grows cold. Then Phaedo describes the scene as follows: "The chill had now reached the region about the groin, and uncovering his face, which had been covered, he said—and these were his last words—'Crito, we owe a cock to Asclepius. Pay it and do not neglect it.' 'That,' said Crito, 'shall be done; but see if you have anything else to say.' To this question he made no reply, but after a little while he moved; the attendant uncovered him; his eyes were fixed. And Crito when he saw it, closed his mouth and eyes."[35] Here then Socrates' face is covered, but this time he removes the veil in order to speak his last, thoroughly enigmatic words. After this, his face is covered once again. Much could be said of these words, especially if one reads them in conjunction with the *Phaedrus* where Socrates uncovers his face to recant what he believes has been a lie. But for my purposes I want to focus rather on the significance of the veiling and the specifics of the death scene since this link—of veiling and of death—is, as Heidegger reminds us, the deepest truth of the concealing proper to all appearance. Remembering this can make the already complicated interpretation of Socrates' death scene even more enigmatic. Rather than pursue that point, I simply want to note that it is striking that Plato uses exactly the same words as Homer does to refer to this gesture of covering—this is more than a coincidence. But that is the topic for another paper.

* * *

Let me conclude by returning to my opening question: how should we understand and speak of the basic movement of life?

Heidegger opens *Sein und Zeit* by referring to a forgetfulness that defines us today, namely, our forgetfulness of the question of being. It is a most peculiar sort of forgetting since it is a forgetting of what is always in plain sight, always "there." But this forgetfulness has two forms: one is defined by our neglect, and by the forces of daily life that have concealed this question for us; but the other form of forgetfulness is more original, one might even say that it defines us since it belongs to the temporalizing that we are. It is upon this primordial forgetfulness that other forms rest and are possible. It also cannot be overcome precisely because it belongs to the movement of life that we are: "Das Leben ist diesig, es nebelt sich immer ein." In *Sein und Zeit,* Heidegger argues that it is precisely this movement of life—which is, in the end, the movement of truth—that philosophy has lost the capacity to say. The language of philosophy has calcified, it has lost its capacity to speak of this movement, to follow it without freezing it. Philosophy has also severed this movement from its ownmost roots, namely, from birth and death—and that means as well from the earth. It has, in other words, lost the sense and language for truth.

Heidegger finds in Homer's pre-philosophic language this sense for truth that is for the movement of life. This language, this sense, is what sets Homer apart from philosophers; indeed, it is what makes Homer a poet. Heidegger never ceased arguing that our deafness to such language defines us today and gives shape to the special dangers of our times. He knew that the need to learn to listen is great. Nothing less than our relation to the earth, to birth, and to death are at stake here. Language is the way we enter the world and belong with others. To have the words that open the world and experience as wider than that which is revealed to us—that is, to have the words that yield to that which withdraws and remains hidden—is to take up residence in a world that can be a home—a world, in the end, of secrets.

NOTES

1. The two most significant counterviews have come from Paul Friedländer and Bruno Snell. Snell presents the case for a more "subjective" conception of ἀληθεια in *Wurzbürger Jahrbücher für Altertumswissenschaft* 1 (1975): 1–18. Friedländer's criticisms, which concerned the use of the word "ἀληθεια" in Homer, were articulated in four different versions—published in different editions of his *Platon*, I (Berlin: Walter de Gruyter, 1954, 1958, 1964, 1968). Heidegger responds to these criticisms (both directly and indirectly) in "Hegel und die Griechen," in *Wegmarken* (Frankfurt am Main: Klostermann, 1978), and in "Das Ende der Philosophie und die Aufgabe des Denkens," in *Zur Sache des Denkens* (Tübingen: Niemeyer Verlag, 1976). For a careful discussion of the Friedländer-Heidegger debate, see R. Bernasconi, *The Question of Language in Heidegger's History of Being* (Atlantic Highlands, N.J.: Humanities Press, 1985), 17–23. For another entry into this debate, see H.-G. Gadamer, "Plato und Heidegger," in *Der Idealismus und seine Gegenwart*, ed. U. Guzzoni, B. Rang, and L. Seip (Hamburg: Meiner Verlag, 1976).

2. A list of some of the citations from Homer found in Heidegger's work follows (with the key word discussed in each citation noted when such is clear): *Gesamtausgabe* 40, 133: *Od.* XXIV, 106, λέγειν; *Gesamtausgabe* 54, 32: *Il.* XVIII, 46, τό αψεδος; 34: *Od.* VIII 40ff/83ff* ἐλάνθανε/αἴδετο; 35: *Il.* X, 22/227, λανθάνομαι; 45: *Il.* II, 348, ὑπόσχεσις; 88: *Il.* XXII, 118, *Od.* IX, 348, *Od.* VI, 303, *Od.* III, 16, κεύθω, κρύπτω, κακύπτω; *Id.* XXIII, 244, Ἄιδι κεύθμαι; 188: *Od.* I, 1; *Il.* I, 1; 190: *Il.* XXIII, 358ff.; *Gesamtausgabe* 79, 161: *Od.* I, 56, λόγος; *Holzwege*, 316ff.: *Il.* I, 68–72, ἐόν/ἐόντα; *Vorträge u. Aufsätze*, 253ff.: *Od.* VIII, 83ff*, ἐλάνθανε /αἴδετο; *Gesamtausgabe* 16, 629: *Od.* XVI, 161, εναρεις.

3. Heidegger, *Holzwege* (Frankfurt am Main: Klostermann, 1972), 323.

4. Heidegger, *Zur Frage nach der Bestimmung der Sache des Denkens* (St. Gallen, Switzerland: Erker Verlag, 1984), 16.

5. Heidegger, *Vier Seminare* (Frankfurt am Main: Klostermann, 1977), 67.

6. Among the reasons Heidegger gives that ἀλήθεια—ψεδος does not name an original conflict is that there is not an α-privative which can be formed with the word ἀλήθεια (it is itself already such a privative), whereas one can form a privative with the root ψεδος: τό αψεδος ("*das Unfalsche*"). Here Heidegger refers to Homer's *Iliad*, XVIII, 46 (see GA 54: 32).

7. *Od.* VIII, 83–95. The specific passages that Heidegger addresses are marked in boldface. His translations of those passages are listed as well.

8. Heidegger, *Vorträge und Aufsätze*, 255: "*In der griechisch gedichteten Szene des in der Verhüllung weinenden Odysseus wird offenkundig, wie der Dichter das Walten des Anwesens erfährt. . . . Anwesen ist das gelichtete Sichverbergen. . . . Sie ist das verhaltene Verborgenbleiben vor dem Nahen des Anwesenden. Sie ist das Bergen des Anwesenden in die unantasbare Nähe des je und je im Kommen Verbleibenden.*" English translation, *Early Greek Thinking*, trans. David Farrell Krell and Frank Capuzzi (San Francisco: Harper & Row, 1984) 107–108.

9. On this notion of "shame," see Bernard Williams, *Shame and Necessity* (Berkeley: University of California Press, 1993), esp. 78–80, where Williams remarks that "The basic experience connected with shame is that of being seen, inappropriately, by the wrong people, in the wrong condition. It is straightforwardly connected with nakedness . . . the word αιδοια, a derivative of αίδως ["shame"], is a standard Greek word for the genitals . . . The reaction is to cover oneself or to hide, and people naturally take steps to avoid situations that call for it."

10. See *Od.* 2.104: "ἔνθα καὶ ἠμαρτίν μὲν ὑφαίνεσκεν μέγαν ἱστόν, νύκτας δ' ἀλλύεσκεν, ἐπὴν δαΐδας παραθεῖτο. ὥς τρίετες μὲν ἔληθε δόλω καὶ ἔπειθεν Ἀχαιούς."

11. Heidegger, *Vorträge und Aufsätze*, 254–255: "*Demgemäß denkt das griechischen Erfahren im Falle des Odysseus nicht nach der Hinsicht, daß die anwesenden Gäste als Subjekte vorgestellt werden, die in ihrem subjektiven Verhalten den weinenden Odysseus als ihr Wahrnehmungsobjekt nicht erfassen.*" English translation, *Early Greek Thinking*, 107.

12. Ibid., 255: "*vielmehr waltet für das griechische Erfahren um den Weinenden eine Verborgenheit, die ihn den anderen entzieht.*"

13. *Od.*, VIII, 532.

14. *Ibid.*, VIII, 534.

15. See *Od.* IX, 366: " Οὖτις ἔμοιν' ὄνομα." See also Heidegger's remarks about pseudonyms at GA 54: 52–54.

16. GA 54: 91: "*Wenn aber im Griechentum das Wesen der Verbergung und der Unverborgenheit so wesenhaft als Grundzug des Seins selbst erfahren ist, muß dann nicht auch die Verbergung selbst ein anfänglicheres Wesen zeigen, dem die Verbergung in der Gestalt des ψεῦδος, der Verstellung, keineswegs genügt?*" *Parmenides, Gesamtausgabe* 54, ed. Manfred S. Frings (Frankfurt am Main: Klostermann, 1982). In English, *Parmenides*, trans. André Schuwer and Richard Rojcewicz (Bloomington: Indiana University Press, 1992), 62.

17. GA 54: 91–92: "*Gleichwohl können auch wir in gewissem Umkreis verscheidene Weisen der Verbergung beachten und verstehen. Wir müssen dies sogar versuchen, wenn wir noch imstand bleiben wollen,* die eine Weise der Verbergung

ahnen zu lernen, die im Griechentum außer dem ψεῦδος *die Wahrheit des Seienden, d.h. seine Unverborgenheit und Unverhohlenheit, mitbestimmt hat. . . .Vielleicht gibt es* Weisen der Verbergung, *die nicht nur bewahren, aufbewahren und so in einer gewissen Weise doch entziehen, die vielmehr* in einer einzigen Art Wesenhaftes zukommen lassen und schenken." English, 62.

18. GA 54: 88: "*ausgezeichneten Rang des Wesens der Verbergung.*" English, 60.

19. GA 54: 88: "*der Wesenszusammenhang zwischen dem Tod und Verbergen.*" English, 60.

20. *Od.*, Bk. III, 16.

21. *Il.*, Bk. XXIII, 244. Heidegger might also have referred to *Il.*, Bk. XXII, 482, where Andromache cries out to the corpse of Hector "νῦν δὲ σὺ μὲν Ἀΐδαο δόμους ὑπὸ κεύθεσι γαίηςἔρχεαι, αὐτὰρ ἐμὲ στυγερῷ ἐνὶ πένθεϊ." That is a line repeated at *Od.*, Bk. XXIV, 204, where the souls ("ψυχαί") that are the phantoms ("εἴδωλα") of the dead speak to one another "in the house of Hades, hidden beneath the earth." The same phrase is used by Sophocles; see *Antigone*, 911.

22. GA 54: 88–89: "*Der Tod ist den Griechen nicht, so wenig wie die Geburt, ein 'biologischer' Vorgang. Geburt und Tod empfangen ihr Wesen aus dem Bereich der Entbergung und Verbergung des Untererdigen und dem Lichten, Entbergenden des Übererdigen (des Himmelsgewölbes* ούρανός). *Für die Römer dagegen ist die Erde* tellus, terra, *das Trockene, das Land im Unterschied zum Meer; diese Unterscheidung unterscheidet das, worauf Anbau und Siedlung und Einrichtung möglich ist, gegen das, wo solches unmöglich ist.* Terra *wird zu* territorium, *das Siedlungsgebiet als Befehlsbereich. Im römischen* terra *liegt der imperiale Akzent, wovon das griechische* γαια *und* γη *nichts hat.*" English, 60.

23. Heidegger, *Vorträge und Aufsätze*, 257: "λανθάνω, *ich bleibe verborgen, [meint] nicht irgendeine Verhaltungsweise des Menschens unter vielen anderen, sondern den Grundzug alles Verhaltens zu An- und Abwesendem, wenn nicht gar den Grundzug des An- und Abwesens selbst nennt.*" English, 109.

24. Hölderlin, *Sämtliche Werke und Briefe*, Bd. II (München: Hanser Verlag, 1992), 931: "*Denn das ist das tragische bei uns, daß wir ganz stille in irgend einem Behälter eingepackt vom Reiche der Lebendigen hinweggehen, nicht daß wir in Flammen verzehrt die Flamme büßen, die wir nicht zu bändigen vermochten.*"

25. GA 54: 41: "*das "verborgen" [hat] bei der Erfahrung des Seienden den Vorrang.*" English, 27.

26. GA 54: 110. It should be noted that the word νέφος is a metaphor for blindness. "*dichterisch schönste Wesenserhellung*" and "*der Verbergung zeichenlose Wolke.*" English, 74.

27. GA 54: 121: "*abwesende Verbergung.*" English, 82.

28. GA 54: 120: "*Darin, daß die Wolke der vergessenden Verbergung sich selbst als solche verbirgt, kommt das Unheimliche des Vergessens zum Vorschein.*" English, 82.

29. GA 54: 126: "*die Schreibmaschine ist eine zeichenlose Wolke, d.h. eine bei aller Aufdringlichkeit sich entziehende Verbergung, durch die der Bezug des Seins zum Menschen sich wandelt.*" English, 85.

30. GA 54: 119: "*fast alltäglichen und daher unbermerkten und daher zeichenlosen Bezug zur Schrift, d.h. zum Wort, d.h. zur Wesensbereich der Hand, und d.h. des Wortes.*" English, 81.

31. On this see my "*Was wir nicht sagen können: Reflexionen zur Sprache und Freiheit*," in *Hermeneutische Wege* (Tübingen: Siebeck Verlag, 2000), 161–175.

32. *Phaedrus*, 237a: " εγκαλυψάμενος ἐρῶ, 'ίν' ό τι τάχιστα διαδράμω τὸν λόγον, καὶ μὲ βλέπον πρὸς σὲ υπ' αἰσχύνης διαπορωμαι."

33. *Phaedrus*, 243a: "ἐμοὶ μὲν οὖν, ὦ φίλε, καθήρασθαι ἀνάγκη: ἔστιν δὲ τοῖς ἁμαρτάνουσι περὶ μυθολογίαν καθαμὸς ἀρχαῖος, ὃν Ὅμηρος μὲν οὐκ ᾔσθετο, Στησίχορος δέ. τῶν γὰρ ὀμμάτων στερηθεὶς διὰ τὴν Ἑλένης κακηγορίαν οὐκ ἠγνόησεν ὥσπερ Ὅμηρος, ἀλ' ἅτε μουσικὸς ὢν ἔγνω τὴν αἰτίαν, καὶ ποιει^ εὐθὺς—
οὐκ ἔστ' ἔτυμος λόγος οὗτος,
οὐδ' ἔβας ἐν νηυσὶν εὐσέλμοις, οὐδ' ἵκεο Πέργαμα Τροίας:καὶ ποιήσας δὴ πᾶσαν τὴν καλουμένην Παλινῳδίαν παραχρῆμα ἀνέβλεψεν. ἐγὼ οὖν σοφώτερος ἐκείνων γενήσομαι κατ' αὐτό γε τοῦτο· πρὶν γάρ τι παθεῖν διὰ τὴν τοῦ Ἔρωτος κακηγορίαν πειράσομαι αὐτῷ ἀποδοῦναι τὴν παλινῳδίαν, γυμνῇ τῇ κεφαλῇ καὶ οὐχ ὥσπερ τότε ὑπ' αἰσχύνης ἐγκεκαλυμμένος."

34. Plato, *Phaedo*, 117c: "οὐκέτι,ἀλλ'ἐμοῦ γε βία καὶ αὐτοὺ ἀστακτὶ εχωρει τά δάκρυα ωστε εγκυψάμενος ἀπεκλαον εμαυτόν."

35. Plato, *Phaedo*, 118a: "ἤδη οὐν σχεδόν τι αὐτοῦ ἡν τὰ περὶ τὸ ἠτρον ψυχόμενα, καὶ ἐκκαλυψάμενος—ἐνεκεκάλυπτο γάρ—εἰπεν—ὃ δὴ τελευταῖον ἐφθέγξατο—"ὠ Κρίτων, ἔφη, τῶ Ἀσκληπιῶ ὀφείλομεν αλεκτρυόνα: αλλὰ ἀπόδοτε καὶ μὴ ἀμελήσητε."
ἀλλὰ ταῦτα, ἔφη, ἔσται, ο Κρίτων: αλλ' ορα εἴ τι ἄλλο λέγεις.
ταῦτα ἐρομένου αὐτοῦ οὐδὲν ἔτι ἀπεκρίνατο, ἀλλ' ὀλίγον χρόνον διαλιπὼν ἐκινήθη τε καὶ ὃ ἄνθρωπος ἐξεκάλυψεν αὐτόν, καὶ ος τὰ ὄμματα εστησεν: ἰδὼν δὲ ο Κρίτων συνέλαβε τὸ στόμα καὶ τοὺς οφθαλμούς."

TEN

The Way to Heidegger's "Way to Language"

Jeffrey L. Powell

The final installment to Heidegger's long encounter with the thinking of language is illuminating, influential, and an experiment with another kind of thinking. The shock that precedes this experiment is prepared for by what is called the turning, a turning that results in the attempt to speak from out of beyng. This attempt at such a speaking is thus also an experiment with language, and for Heidegger an experiment that requires undergoing an experience with language. However, the shock that preceded the experiment was not entirely unprecedented, and Heidegger provides us with slightly more than a hint as to where to look for such a precedent. Perhaps we would have been better prepared for the hint had we first read Novalis, had we first read Novalis in the absence of Heidegger. Had we done so, we would have at least been prepared for a bit of the uncustomary and unfamiliar, or at least a different version of it. Heidegger's concern for the experiment as it relates to the question of language culminates in his final essay concerning language, "The Way to Language." While Heidegger's concern throughout "The Way to Language" is to enter into the ways of language, an entrance that is prepared through an appeal to Novalis, my concern here will be to trace Heidegger's way to "The Way to Language" beginning with *Being and Time* and passing through the writings of the late 1930s.

Let us first pause over the beginning of "The Way to Language" in order to draw out even more the strangeness of an essay that is at once both simple and philosophically unusual. In fact, the strangeness to which Novalis gives rise for Heidegger is embedded in the simplicity of language. In the simplest form, what is strange about language is not that we are presumably capable of speaking "about" it, but that to do so we must always already be lost in it. What is doubly strange in the case of Heidegger is that he might find his way into the experiment with language through Novalis's *Monologue*. Why is this strange? The strangeness is not due to the assertion or proposition by both Heidegger and Novalis that language is ill-conceived when taken up in a propositional form. One hardly needs to cite Heidegger on this point. Novalis's way of putting it is to say that if one "wants to speak about something definite, capricious language makes him say the most ridiculous and confused stuff."[1] Nor is it strange that both Heidegger and Novalis would view poetry as a saying that most properly enters into the monologue of language. What is strange is the degree to which Novalis remains true to the self-saying of language, and the degree to which he might offer a corrective to at least one aspect of Heidegger's analysis of language in *Being and Time*. While Heidegger consistently derides a speaking that he characterizes as *Gerede*, as a kind of "idle talk," Novalis celebrates it. Novalis seemingly celebrates the fact that idle talk or chatter is distinguished by an apparent neglect of trying to say something definite, something susceptible to the language of propositions and the assertion. Thus, just as much as Novalis characterizes language as speaking only with itself in his little fragment, he also notices that language shines through, that it can perhaps even become brilliant through a kind of chattering and noisemaking that has been loosened from any attempt to say something universally meaningful. It is as if Novalis has anticipated Celan's late poetry, but set into the everyday world of experience. "Language is such a marvelous and fruitful secret," he says, "because when someone speaks merely for the sake of speaking, he utters the most splendid, most original truths." On the other hand, those who speak most seriously, those intent on expressing themselves in a definite and clear manner, "notice its [language's] mischief, but not the fact that the chattering they scorn is the infinitely serious aspect of language."[2] In this case the seriousness is due not to the subject who speaks, whether that subject be always already outside in the "there" or not, but to the speaking of language.[3]

While this would appear to indicate a certain imaginary quarrel between Novalis and Heidegger, I believe it would better serve as a corrective to how we might understand what Heidegger calls *Gerede*. "Idle talk" or *Gerede* suffers from being reducible to propositional language, a taking up of positions available and understandable to all without being claimed by what is addressed in speaking. While it is indeed the case that Heidegger derides *Gerede,* despite his warning to the contrary at the beginning of section 35, we must remain ever alert that such derision remains an example of *Gerede* insofar as we believe ourselves capable of joining in and cheering along as we if we all know what we're talking about, as if what is being addressed as *Gerede* is immediately apparent to all readers of Heidegger simply by being readers of Heidegger. "Idle talk," it would seem, is not so much characterized by being what we and Novalis might call "chatter," but by the already interpreted nature of what is said in such chatter, by the already determined nature of what is understood in the chatter. If one were to simply peel away what is proposed and determined in the chatter at least two items would be revealed to which Novalis, Celan, and Heidegger would appeal. For Novalis, what is revealed is the speaking of language. For Celan, what is revealed is the source of poetry, the that it is, or what Heidegger in *Being and Time* calls formal indication. For Heidegger, what remains is double. What remains is a language of the world, or what calls for speaking; and what remains is an openness for the discourse between speakers, what we might otherwise call communication.[4] Thus, through language what remains is an essential relation to beings, Daseins and otherwise, or world.

Nevertheless, a proper addressing of the question of language in Heidegger still requires a proper understanding of *Gerede.* At the very least, without such an understanding the mere appropriation of the language of Heidegger can easily pass as an achievement when all that has been accomplished will have been the setting of a different set of terms into a preexisting framework meeting all the conditions of *Gerede.* At the risk of being too reductive those conditions might be arguably reducible to one, albeit one that was included among many in *Being and Time.* With specific regard to the question of language, Heidegger is much clearer in this regard in a late-1930s seminar treating language in the context of Herder. What is implied in the seminar is that the already determined character of what is talked about in the form of *Gerede* is reducible to the following: "The development of the human being as subjectum is the presupposition of the philosophy of language proper."[5] The philosophy of language is no different from any other theoretical investigation in this regard, in which case all philosophical reflection that takes up an object for its reflection falls under the scope of *Gerede.* This is not to say that any and all discourse that sets out from such a theoretical attitude is bound to remain in that attitude, for there remains the possible forging of a way toward another origin than that of the subjectum. That is to say, it always remains possible to forge a way toward an other beginning. This other possibility, of course, would be a speaking directly from such an other beginning. Heidegger's concern, at this moment in history, is directed toward this other possibility. His own assessment is as follows: "Our reflection [*Besinnung*] is no philosophy of language, and it is also no philosophy of the word. In general, philosophy has no 'about which' as object—not even beyng, especially as beyng-historical thinking.

"Furthermore, it 'is' from beyng."[6]

If *Gerede* is essentially characterized through the appeal to an origin in the subject, this appeal is prepared by means of an understanding of world that arises in an interpretation and modification of the "as." It is due to the interpretation of the "as" and its appeal to the subject that philosophy becomes not only an analysis of statements or propositions but also becomes understood under the force of representation. That is, if language is reducible to the subject, then all language can possibly achieve is a representation of that to which it would presumably refer, a collection of objects over against a representing subject. Unless we are simply to succumb to the various ways in which we might account for representation, the "as" that is the ground of representation must be submitted to a phenomenological analysis. This is precisely what Heidegger performs in *Being and Time,* and even more thoroughly in his 1929/1930 lecture-course translated as *The Fundamental Concepts of Metaphysics: World, Finitude, Solitude.*[7] Let us provide a facsimile of this analysis.

Whenever we encounter something in the world, we encounter it *as* something. We might initially think what comes after the "as" as a series of predicates that determine the subject of an assertion or proposition; for example, the hammer *as* heavy, or the hammer *is* heavy. If the proposition, and the various forms of it that might make it true, becomes either the focus of our attention or the sphere to which our view of language is restricted, then the something to which the "as," so to speak, refers, will be nothing more than the form of propositions. In that case, all analyses will be doomed to one of a number of forms of idealism, as if the internal consistency of a series of propositions can determine the truth of an object for which any means of access has been denied through the interpretation of the "as" as both logical order and the propositional form (which is also why

Heidegger says again and again that this is ultimately reducible to a transformation in the notion of truth from ἀλήθεια to *veritas* or correspondence). The problem with the form of the proposition as the sole sphere of investigation for the problem of language—and thus the absence of an object or referent—can be resolved through interpreting the "as" as designating the present-at-hand object. However, this interpretation of the "as" comes at a price, for the interpretation leaves a bare, extant object as the referent of the apophantical statement, a price that becomes inflated due to the previously mentioned problem of representation. What is more this correction does not resolve, or adjust to, the formerly mentioned transformation of truth. In *Being and Time,* this is discussed in the treatment of *Gerede* and its interpretation of the "as" as a closing off and interpreting of things of the world as extant and measurable.

The present-at-hand would appear to be the result of what Heidegger thinks as formal indication. If formal indication is thought as the pointing out of that to which the "as" refers, then the "as" becomes limited to something like an intended object, a kind of noema. But this cannot be the case, if for no other reason than the objective of the analysis cannot be the present-at-hand. But the question remains: What is the significance of the difference between the formal indication of something present-at-hand and what the present-at-hand indicates as that from which it is to be distinguished? In short, what is revealed is the very limitation of such a rendering of formal indication, a rendering that makes explicit an essential feature of formal indication that has been omitted in our analysis, albeit an omission that is itself revealing. That is, what has been omitted is the factical worldly condition of what is indicated in formal indication, which is to say that what is pointed out through the something "as" something is that the something is always already situated in a worldly relation, in a totality of relations.[8] Such a severing of the something from its worldly relations, *as if* the something were encountered as an instance of formal indication, is, in fact, an abstraction from the formal indication included as a moment of the "as-structure." In Heidegger's words, "When we just stare at something, our just-having-it-before-us lies before us *as a failure to understand it* any more. This grasping which is free of the as is a privation of *simple* seeing, which understands; it is not more primordial than the latter, but derived from it."[9]

It would seem, then, that the resolution to this difficulty would amount to a thematizing of the totality of relations in a meaningful way.

True, but what might we mean by a meaningful way? Is it to transmit what we mean or how we define what it is we might be talking about? Is it to make clear what we intend through the use of a word or term? All of this would certainly help, but it would not be sufficient. If we take what Heidegger calls *Rede,* discourse, *Reden,* discoursing, in *Being and Time* as our guide, then we might follow him when he says "Discoursing is the 'significant' [*bedeutende*] structuring [*Gliedern*] of the intelligibility of being-in-the-world, to which being-with belongs, and which maintains itself in a particular way of heedful being-with-one-another."[10] Said in a different way that is often invoked in discussions concerning discourse in *Being and Time,* discourse or discoursing is the articulation of intelligibility or understandability. What is involved in this articulation is a situating of an understanding of world as the condition of possibility for a world that makes sense. It is tempting to think such a condition of possibility along Kantian lines as a transcendental condition of possibility, but relinquishing to such a temptation would be terribly misleading for a number of reasons. Most importantly, the articulation of intelligibility provided by discourse is neither conceptual in any proper sense (as in the Kantian categories), nor is it a priori in the Kantian sense (as being independent of experience). To venture a word that has received a good deal of attention in circles often, but not exclusively, critical of Heidegger, I would call the articulation of intelligibility of discourse *immanent.* A salient expression of what I mean here is provided by Len Lawlor in his *The Implications of Immanence: Toward a New Concept of Life.* In commenting on a passage from Heidegger's "What Is Metaphysics?" in which Heidegger invokes a future thinking that attempts to address the "'outside itself' [*Auseinander*] of the opening of Being itself,"[11] Lawlor remarks: "This *Auseinander* is the completion of immanence. But here, as in Deleuze, immanence does not mean the 'immanence of consciousness or spirit.' We can speak of immanence here because what Heidegger is speaking about is an interior of the outside. In other words, immanence is the 'outside of one another,' the outside that is the abyss."[12]

To provide a brief summary of what we have too briefly attempted to discern, the as-structure indicates the totality of relations in which a something is situated when experienced "as" something. That totality of relations is at all times, or always already, addressed in discourse or *Rede* (even in *Gerede,* even if only by way of a turning away). The totality of relations addressed by discourse is the articulation of intelligibility that is constitutive of the being of the *Da*, or clearing, of *Dasein*. Discourse is that to which the human being responds in the speaking of language, and thus the speaking of language requires the silence of which Heidegger speaks in order that discourse might be heard. Discourse, as the speaking of the totality of relations, is the already outside in which Dasein is situated and to which Dasein relates in an immanent manner. As such, the totality of relations to which the as-structure corresponds, the experience of something *as* something, is accessible or always already accessed by Dasein in an everyday manner (although its interpretation may certainly vary). The "as" and its interpretation is thus not some transcendental domain abstracted from experience; rather, it is the domain of experience, the domain in which experience is situated, the domain otherwise referred to as world, the outside.

To characterize the outside or world in such manner, even in its simplicity, gives rise to a difficult thing to think. This difficulty can be characterized in a number of ways, but we might first approach it with regard to Dasein. That is, Dasein is not to be thought as the internal identity of the human being—be it in the casual manner of the everyday way of conceiving identity or the transcendental identity of the Kantian subject, or even through a Hegelian act of *Erinnerung*—that is then externalized in going out into the world, the outside. This is not possible, for according to Heidegger, Dasein is always already outside. But does this characterization help? Does it make sense to say that Dasein is not an inside to be externalized and still to conceive of Dasein as outside? If Dasein is outside, then outside of what, or outside with respect to what? But it is precisely here that what Heidegger has to say, and what he has to say very early on, demands something different, a different analysis, a different way of conceiving the world, a different way of addressing the world. For it is from here on that it is no longer permissible to speak of a subject of language, or at least no longer permissible to speak of a subject of language in the same way as before. As if Nietzsche were whispering in our ear, we must now say that the subject, some "I" that purportedly speaks, is no more than an effect of the grammar of a language. We might say this in at least two different ways. First, we could think the "I" as fulfilling, not only a need of grammar, but a need of language, a need that is required for the purposes of indication, a need to be fulfilled for no other purpose than that what is "pointed out" in formal indication be pointed out. Second, the grammatical "I," what Foucault at some later point calls "no more than a grammatical fold,"[13] is a requirement fulfilled by grammar for yet another reason, another purpose, for the purpose of providing a transition or crossing (*Übergang*) to that other language called *Rede*, λόγος, the language of the world. To engage in the philosophical enterprise as Heidegger understood it in 1929/1930, or to engage in what was later called thinking, was to undergo an experience with language, was to be drawn, so to speak, to the outside; furthermore, to do so was to "understand that *what philosophy deals with only discloses itself at all within and from out of a transformation of human Dasein.*"[14]

To return more concretely to Heidegger's 1929/1930 course, we should now add a few details concerning the as-structure and totality of relations. In that course, Heidegger repeatedly insists that the as-structure always concerns a relation. In the experience of something "as" something, the "as" is the relation connecting the two terms. But, as Heidegger also repeatedly points out, the "as" is not simply a word we might investigate independently of the two terms, for the "as," as much as it might function similarly in different languages, is simply an indicator of what the two terms in their turn indicate. That is to say, the "as" is itself a kind of formal indication that relates two terms of formal indication, or two formally indicative terms. However, as the relation that it is, the "as" is irreducible to identity and difference. That is, the "as" is specific to Dasein, the world "as" such is specific to Dasein, in indicating the multiplicity through which any given thing is given to Dasein as a something universal (in the form of a word or concept, for example). What is more, the "as" also provides the something in terms of formal indication; that is, it provides for the pointing out of something in its singularity or identity, a singularity or identity that is not to be surmounted through any conceptual machinery. Nevertheless, there is a danger when considering the "as" as a relation, the danger of considering the "as" itself as some present-at-hand thing that the "as" sets out to overcome. Rather than some present-at-hand thing, the "as" might be better characterized as a movement between the two relational terms that it holds together; "it is a relation which moves from one term to the other—something as something," says Heidegger.[15]

This movement, to which we will turn later in the essay, draws attention to something more essential about the "as," something more essential that should counter the urge to think the "as" under the sign of the present. That is, if the "as" is to be viewed as a movement between terms, then there must be some domain within which it moves and within which the relation is situated. This domain Heidegger calls a dimension (*Dimension*). While dimension is not to be thought as a container within which the relational terms are related through the "as," it is nevertheless the case that the dimension is the ground of such relation. As the ground of that relation, there is the tendency to think the ground in a manner similar to what it grounds. That is, since the relational terms are typically thought under the sign of the present, the ground of those terms is itself also subject to such a thinking; this urge must be constantly undone, and language frequently serves such a purpose. In any case, the condition for thinking the "as" as a relation between terms is the concealing or suppression of the dimension within which the relating occurs. Thus, while the dimension is the ground of the relational terms, it is a concealed ground in which and through which the identity and difference of the terms come to presence. As the concealed ground of difference, then, the dimension is at once both ground and what it grounds, although both the ground and what it grounds are engaged in the strife of revealing and concealing. But, once again, according to Heidegger, this is also misconceiving, for just as there is the previous tendency to view the relational terms under the force of the present, there is an equal tendency to view the dimension itself in the same manner, that is, under the force of the present.

This tendency is largely due to the conceptual manner in which we attempt to render both the relational terms and the dimension. That is, whenever we attempt to allow the positing of the concepts to do all the work, then what is rendered is brought under the language of metaphysics and posited in the grammar of the language of metaphysics. Thus, in such a rendering, something has been forgotten. That something is the formal indicative nature of the concepts through which the analysis is conveyed, which is to say that the concepts only formally indicate what is a matter of existence and time and not simply an epistemological problem through discursive means. When conceived in the latter form, as a problem of epistemology, then all relation is viewed in the same manner, and all relation is thus viewed as being equivalent. What is more, then, when the ground of such relation is revealed in its dimension, that dimension is also viewed in the same equivalent manner, that is, as a conceptual problem. In Heidegger's analysis, on the other hand, when the dimension in which the relational terms is revealed, a proper relation to what is revealed (the dimension) "directs us toward our proper relation and peculiar task."[16] Heidegger then continues by saying: "That is why I speak of *formal indication* in connection with such a characterization of the 'as.'"[17] At this point, to enter into the dimension that is the essence of the "as," the dimension in which the relational terms are brought into relation by the "as," is to be claimed by what is pointed out in formal indication. But, in order to be so claimed, one must be open to being claimed, to being claimed by language in the form of the "as." However, this being open to being claimed by the "as" requires nothing short of a transformation; a transformation through which the "I," formerly taken to be the subject of language, the subject of speech, has effectively been erased through the movement to the outside. Being drawn into the "as" through formal indication is to be drawn into the dimension, an openness, in which Dasein is both transformed and brought into relation with the things of the world; that is, transformed and drawn into the web of identity and difference through which Dasein, things, and world—being-in-the-world—are maintained in a relation to being. To engage in such a transformation, of course, requires, at the very least, a crossing over from Dasein as the *subject* of metaphysics to Dasein as the subject *of* language.

Although the transformation is already in place in *Being and Time,* the transformation from the subject of metaphysics to the subject of language, the seizing of the transformation is more gradual, becoming further and further radicalized until it reaches what appears to be a point of no return in 1935 with the delivery of "The Origin of the Work of Art." The biographical reasons for such a radicalization are certainly obvious, even if a reductive account of them is unclear: the political mess in which Heidegger became entwined due to his own workings, naïveté, practical blindness, sheer evil, and so forth; the more focused encounter with the thought of Hölderlin, first brought publicly to bear in the 1934/1935 lecture-course concerning "Germanien" and "Der Rhein"; and following "The Origin of the Work of Art," the encounter with the thought of Nietzsche. Of course, such biographical reasons are anything but simple, and what they indicate are more thoughtful encounters. Aside from what might be revealed through a biographical contextualization of Heidegger in the mid-1930s, it is nevertheless clearly the case that the transformation he emphatically pursues is an extension of the very first page of the first introduction to *Being and Time*. When Heidegger writes that the history of metaphysics is founded and erected upon a forgetting of the question of being, then the pursuit of this question will eventually require the hunting down of a different history than the one founded on that forgetting. Not that Heidegger had his entire career in his head while writing *Being and Time*, but the turn toward the other beginning that is relentlessly tracked throughout the late 1930s would seem to be inevitable. In a convenient retrospective glance, it would seem that the goal of *Being and Time* was the resurrection of the perplexity introduced by its epigraph drawn from Plato's *Sophist*.[18] The resurrection having been accomplished, and the attention re-directed toward a beginning different from that of the metaphysical tradition, the task in the late 1930s is then to speak from that other beginning, what is typically termed "inception" or "commencement" (*Anfänglich*). The thinking associated with the "inceptive," rather than the "beginning" which is associated with the metaphysical tradition, is called beyng–historical thinking (*seynsgeschichtliches Denken*).[19]

However, beyng–historical thinking is not to be achieved by the simple adoption of a new position or even a new language, a position reached by means of a leap beyond metaphysics and its respective language. "Everyday language, which is ever more comprehensively used up today and degraded through idle chatter, does not allow the truth of beyng to be said. Can this truth be said immediately, if all language is indeed the language of beings? Or can a new language be invented for beyng? No."[20] Rather, the other beginning, the inceptive, is bound up with the metaphysical tradition, if in no other way than through its very covering up, through its having withdrawn from the metaphysical tradition; in fact, the metaphysical tradition can only come to presence through the withdrawal of the other beginning. According to Heidegger, the beginning of the metaphysical beginning, rather than its inception, maintains a relation to the other beginning insofar as what it names and thinks through the language of metaphysics has its inceptive beginning elsewhere. In thus speaking of the familiar, it is always already bound to that other beginning. Said differently, "the words themselves [of metaphysics] already reveal something (something familiar) and thus conceal that which is supposed to be brought into the open in thoughtful saying."[21] Giving voice, then, to the inceptive, giving voice to the other beginning, speaking from the inceptive, is only possible in and as the movement from the language of metaphysics to a different relation to language.

Although intimated already in *Being and Time*, this different relation rules in Heidegger's work from the 1930s. Heidegger even begins and ends what is arguably his most speculative work, *Beiträge zur Philosophie (Vom Ereignis)*, through an appeal to language, an appeal that assumes that relation. However, the renewed relation to language first requires an exposition or revealing of the non-relation of the former relation to the word. As such an exposition, the renewed relation to the word is not achieved through an act of determinate negation but through an appeal to that other relation that serves the exposition. This exposing of the metaphysical relation to the word and language has been noted many times by Heidegger, and by many following in his wake. Heidegger expresses it most poignantly in 1946 (some eight to ten years after the *Beiträge* in his "Letter on Humanism").[22] The failure of metaphysical language is there related to what Heidegger calls an "other thinking" required by what in *Being and Time* concerned "projection," an "other thinking that abandons subjectivity." Such an other thinking was to have determined the path of the withheld third division of *Being and Time*, a third division that was to track the turning from being and time to time and being. "The division in question was held back because thinking failed in the adequate saying of this turning [*Kehre*] and did not succeed with the help of the language of metaphysics," says Heidegger.[23] Although this is abundantly clear by 1946, by the time of the *Beiträge*, Heidegger had already gained a full appreciation of the extent to which his project must founder due to that language. In fact, the *Beiträge* ensues with a full awareness of this inevitable failure. On the very first page, Heidegger alerts us of the desert in which we discover ourselves even in the attempt to provide a title to such a work. The title must provide the appearance of being scholarly and purporting to provide some progress for the discipline of philosophy. These appearances are due specifically to our relation to language. Thus Heidegger begins this work in the following manner: "Philosophy can be officially announced in no other way, since all essential titles have become impossible through the exhaustion of every fundamental word and the destruction of the genuine relation to the word."[24]

Similar to the transformation we have just addressed, the *Beiträge* likewise calls for a transformation. In Heidegger's words, insofar as language is an issue, it "amounts to an essential transformation of the human being from 'rational animal' (animal rationale) into Da-sein."[25] This transformation into Da-sein, which is also the transformation from out of the ruinous relation to the word into a new relation to the word, is prepared through a reconsideration of the clearing of the *da* into which Dasein was viewed as having been thrown in *Being and Time.* Whereas in *Being and Time,* the *da* was to be considered the outside, as discussed previously, in the *Beiträge* and its associated texts Dasein is considered as having been projected into the between, the between in which Dasein is captured in the *Ereignis* attributed to the truth of beyng. In being thrown or projected into the between, a thrownness from which Dasein is inseparable as the thrower ("What is meant is always only the projection of the truth of beyng. The thrower itself, Da-sein, is thrown, ap-propriated, by beyng"[26]), Da-sein is discovered in time-space (*Zeit-Raum*). Time-space, which Heidegger first addresses in his Kant lecture-course from the winter semester 1935/1936 and later published as *Die Frage nach dem Ding,* functions as the abyssal ground of the metaphysical notions of time and space. However one might come to think of time-space, what is clear is that it is both what is called the in-between and the foundation for all thinking of time and space. As such, the in-between and its time-space are both pre-spatial and pre-temporal, before space and before time. This is most clearly expressed in *Besinnung,* where Heidegger writes that "The in-between of the *Da* is to be taken as *pre*-spatial and *pre*-temporal, if 'space' and 'time' mean the objective sphere of the present-at-hand and its pinpoint place and time re-presentations."[27] However, as pre-spatial, the in-between at once makes way and makes time for space and time; it makes a path within which time and space might be traversed. Again, *Besinnung:* "The in-between wherein strife and countering cross the paths between one another, and safeguardedly radiate everywhere into the clearing."[28]

Now, it is only insofar as Da-sein has been transformed by being thrown into the in-between that Dasein might make the transition in crossing from the first to the other beginning, which is also to say to another relation to the word. If language is to speak from within the crossing, then the in-between must be vigilantly maintained; otherwise, the way will have been made only as the transition into the metaphysics of the first beginning, or stated differently, there will have occurred a turning toward beings (or, alternatively, a turn away from the in-between, which is at once also a turning away from being). It is only in the sustainment of the in-between, the open, that a relation between being and beings can be maintained. This sustaining is addressed in *Die Geschichte des Seyns* and elsewhere under the sign of *Austrag,* often obliquely, sometimes not: "*Ereignis* as sustainment [*Austrag*]: the in-between."[29] If a different relation to the word is to take place, then this will only occur as a speaking by the transformed Da-sein from out of the sustainment of the abyss as time-space, as the in-between. Thus, still in accord with *Being and Time,* what is crucial is not what is said but that the speaking or saying be preserved from out of the clearing. The preservation of such a speaking presumably leaves a trace or traces of such speaking that will have been removed from presence, removed and yet preserved as the ways in which the pre-spatial and pre-temporal time-space have been crossed by the transformed Da-sein.[30] Thus Heidegger says of time-space that it "is the propriated sundering of the turning paths [*Kehrungsbahnen*] of *Ereignis,* the sundering of the turn between belongingness and call, between the abandonment by being and intimation (the trembling of the oscillation of beyng itself)."[31] I would suggest that the turning paths that make up time-space, the in-between, are comprised insofar as Da-sein has been propriated by the truth of beyng in the crossing from the first to the other beginning, in the crossing from the beginning as metaphysics to inceptive or beyng–historical thinking.

Heidegger returns to Novalis near the end of "The Way to Language," a return wherein he at once appeals to the statement of Novalis concerning the "monological character" of language and marks an insufficiency in Novalis due to his allegiance to both subjectivity and absolute idealism.[32] What is most problematic about Novalis is that his allegiances prevent his addressing of language in *Monologue* from coinciding with what Heidegger calls *Aufriß.* Presumably, this is due to the engine behind absolute idealism and its underlying subjectivity, which is a dialectical method that operates in a manner other than what is called for by the *Aufriß.* The problem, then, is the insufficiency of the dialectical method for an encounter with the unity attributed to the *Aufriß.*[33] That is to say, the unity of the *Aufriß* of the essence of language is a unity to which we are always already bound, a unity that grants to us the very ability to speak. It is in this sense that whenever we speak, we have already responded to language as in Heidegger's famous formula from the essay simply titled "Language":

> Language speaks.
> The human being speaks insofar as he cor-responds to language.[34]

It is only insofar as we are claimed by language that we might remain in the grips of that claim, so to speak, and thus speak in a corresponding response to language. By being so claimed, it is not possible for us speakers to adopt a position outside language and offer pronouncements about it; it is not possible for us to achieve a unity through a series of determinate negations whereby we might believe ourselves to have comprehended language, as would be the case in the absolute idealism to which Heidegger refers. Thus Heidegger writes that "The essence of language does not submit to our circumspection, inasmuch as we—we who can say only by reiterating the saying—ourselves belong within the saying."[35] What is more, even if we pretend to adopt a position outside of language, such a pretending is still yet a co-responding to language and thus also monologue, even if the pretending relies on a different relation to language than the one called for by Heidegger from even before *Being and Time*. Finally, the unity to which Heidegger appeals is prior to all determinate negation, even if this unity is anything but simple.[36]

The unity of the *Aufriß* is comprised of the saying of language. The saying of language, according to Heidegger, is more properly a showing, a pointing out, the formal indication of the as-structure, if you like, albeit one that is even more removed from a kind of speaking of the subject (or, more properly, Dasein) characteristic of *Being and Time* and the 1929/1930 lecture-course. As showing, the saying of language unfolds as the ways in which the things of the world show themselves, and the *Aufriß* is the gathering and unifying of those ways. This showing of the *Aufriß* is contained in the word itself, the word that sounds as the co-responding to the saying of language. Heidegger thus writes that "*Riss* [*rift*] is the same word as *ritzen* [to notch, carve]."[37] In a gloss of the names *Riss* and *ritzen*, Heidegger denotes the manner in which humans are comported to these names in the saying of language, as well as the manner in which what has come to presence is linked to these names. *Riss* is employed to denote "a crack in the wall"; "plowing a field, drawing furrows through it" is denoted by *aufreißen* and *umreißen*. *Aufreißen* means to tear up, to rend, while *umreißen* is to turn over, as in turning over the soil. Both of the terms, Heidegger says, "open up the field."[38] *Aufriß* would mean the totality of elements and relations that saying-showing renders as an opening-up, as a tearing asunder, as a carving and notching. We could say, then, that rift-design indicates, points to, all those ways and paths of the essence of language as way-ings (*Bewëgungen*) in and of language. *Aufriß* would consist of the totality of the way-ings of language as brought into relation and, as brought into relation by *Aufriß*, brought into unity and cohesion. "The rift-design is the totality of traits in the kind of drawing [*Zeichnung*] that permeates what is opened up and set free in language."[39]

The kind of drawing (*Zeichnung*) that comprises the totality of traits in the rift-design would thus be the carving, notching, opening-up, and way-ing (*be-wëgen*) of the rift-design. Crossing the open expanse of time-space, the speaking, saying, and pointing of language—that is, the showing of language, language as showing—is such that the way of language unfolds or essences. In Heidegger's words, "in language as the saying, something like a way essences [*west*]."[40] In such a saying, the nature of this way consists of the self-showing of beings whose upsurgence requires the site of the in-between. It is thus only insofar as Dasein enters or is drawn into the in-between that it is able to hear the saying of language, which is to hear or undergo an experience of self-showing of the things of the world. The saying of language, which is nothing short of the self-showing of things, thus points to what shows itself through either coming to presence or withdrawing into absence and mystery. Thus Heidegger says that "*The essential unfolding of language* [Das Wesende der Sprache] *is the saying as pointing.*"[41] The saying of language, the pointing adjoined to self-showing, thus traces the ways comprising the rift-design, even if the tracing of such traces withdraws in the tracing. If we, the speakers of language, respond to the saying of language, we do so only in response to what is heard/pointed out in language's saying.

If the drawing of traits comprising the *Aufriß* consists of the various pointings to what has shown itself from within time-space, the abyssal ground of the truth of beyng, then this ground must be grounded. The grounding of the abyssal ground of the truth of beyng is allotted to Dasein, allotted to Dasein only inasmuch as Dasein is always already bound to language as saying, bound to the *Aufriß* in the manner in which Dasein shows itself, which is through speaking. As speaking, Dasein is attuned to the in-between, attuned to the abyss, through which beings show themselves and do so in relation to being. This is why

Heidegger ends section II of his essay concerning the way to language by saying, "Language does remain unmistakably bound up with human speech. . . . Language needs human speech."[42] How does speech achieve such grounding? Not through the utterance of propositions "about" things, but by means of an attunement, by means of a *Stimmung*, an attunement through which the abyssal ground is held open for the showing of beings in relation to beyng. That is, through what Heidegger in 1959 calls listening, a listening that in Heidegger's long encounter with the question of language stretches back to at least section 34 of *Being and Time*.[43] Furthermore, it is through listening that humans are capable of being open for what shows itself as what is propriated through the event of propriation.

But, the *Aufriß* as the unifying of the totality of traits emerging in pointing is not the result of some differentiating process that has become stabilized. Rather, "The rift-design is the drawing of the essence of language,"[44] what was above called tracing of the traces comprising the *Aufriß*. We might say this another way by saying that the essence of language is the saying of language in the tracing of the ways that draw us into language, the ways that allow for the speaking of language through our speaking. Our speaking, then, is not only a speaking that responds to language through the hearing of language's tracings, but a speaking after the ways of language, a speaking after what has been opened up by language in the providing of our way to it. Thus all language, all speaking, is a tracing of the ways of language. These ways are attributable to what Heidegger calls *Be-wëgung*, the way-making movement of language through which all the various relations to language are drawn into the circle of language, drawn into the monologue. In the simplest form, Heidegger thus writes that "The way-making movement [*Be-wëgung*] brings language (the essence of language) as language (the saying) to language (to the resounding word)."[45] To follow the way-making movement of language is to follow or be drawn into a different relation to language, it is to be drawn into the clearing of the "as." Furthermore, to be drawn into the way-making movement is to be drawn into the crossing from the first to the other beginning, to be drawn into the way-ing of the crossing. But, being so drawn is to be claimed and propriated as speakers by a very different relation to language. This is realized at one point in Heidegger's Herder seminar from 1939, which compels two telling questions: "Could we *then,* if we attempt the crossing thereto, still talk in general about 'language'? Must we not then try hearing [*er-hören*] the crossing word itself—in its singularity?"[46]

If speaking is to be just—that is, with the ways of showing—then it must do so in a way that preserves showing in all its singularity, which requires the preserving or sheltering of self-showing. If language as metaphysics has been the language of representation, then a different response to language as showing or saying, to the way-making movement, a response that speaks from out of being drawn into the *Aufriß,* calls for what is no longer philosophy.[47] If Heidegger is relegated to the dust heap of philosophy, such a judgment is at least partially accurate; however, that same judgment stems from a tired, well-worn—worn-out, even—relation to language. If there remains a promise in philosophy at all, and if that promise is not to be aborted from the very beginning (by the first beginning) due to the relation it holds to language, then it must stretch its ties to philosophy to the breaking point, to the very edge, to the point of running the risk of no longer being philosophy at all. To set out on such a path is to venture being drawn into the peculiar way-making movement of language.

To run the risk of non-philosophy, to run with that risk, was an experience from which Heidegger did not turn away. At the very beginning of *Die Geschichte des Seyns,* Heidegger characterizes the thinking from beyng, or the thinking with which Heidegger associates from at least 1935 onward, as something far different than philosophy. "What speaks here is neither a 'philosophy of philosophy,' nor indeed a philosophy at all."[48] Rather, modest as it may sound, what is called for is simply the preparation for a way that is to be heard, the preparation of a crossing, the preparation for a way-ing of the crossing that is language.

NOTES

1. Novalis, "Monologue," in *Philosophical Writings,* trans. and ed. Margaret Mahoney Stoljar (Albany: SUNY Press, 1997), 83.

2. Ibid.

3. Celan makes a similar point concerning the speaking of Lucille in Büchner's *Danton's Death* in his "The Meridian Speech." See my "Spiritual Death / Poetic Death" in *International Studies in Philosophy* 36, no. 4 (2004): 89–101.

4. See my "Heidegger and the Communicative World" in *Research in Phenomenology* 40, no. 1 (2010): 55–71.

5. Martin Heidegger, *Vom Wesen der Sprache: Zu Herders Abhandlung "Über den Ursprung der Sprache," Gesamtausgabe,* vol. 85 (Frankfurt am Main: Vittorio Klostermann, 1999), 51. Hereafter referred to as GA 85.

6. Ibid.

7. Martin Heidegger, *Der Grundbegriffe der Metaphysik: Welt—Endlichkeit—Einsamkeit, Gesamtausgabe,* vol. 29/30 (Frankfurt am Main: Klostermann, 1983). In English, *The Fundamental Concepts of Metaphysics: World, Finitude, Solitude,* trans. William McNeill and Nicholas Walker (Bloomington: Indiana University Press, 1995). All citations will be given as GA 29/30, followed by the German, then English, page numbers.

8. It is in this sense of the "as" that Heidegger maintains a difference between Dasein and the animal. "It is this quite elementary *'as'* which—and we can put it quite simply—is refused to the animal" (GA 29/30: 416/287). Aside from the problems resulting from this distinction indicated by Derrida and those writing in his wake, I have always been surprised that Heidegger has not invoked Herder in any of his analyses treating the animal, not even in his seminar devoted to Herder's essay on the origin of language. Herder's essay is remarkably close to Heidegger in the manner in which he distinguishes the human being from the animal. Herder asserts the animal is a more refined artist than is the human being, by which he means the animal has a more refined techné insofar as the animal is restricted in its relation to the world by its techné, its inborn skill for survival, otherwise referred to as its instincts. The world of the animal, according to Herder, is limited by its instincts, its techné; what lies beyond the reach of its techné is not part of its world. The human being, on the other hand, is essentially characterized by its *Besinnung,* translated, by a stroke of genius, by Michael N. Forster in the most recent Cambridge edition as "awareness." What this means for Herder is that the human being, while being techné poor, poor in instinct, is thrown into the world in such manner that it is aware of the entire world, both the visible and the invisible, even if such a world is not explicitly pondered. Because of being bodily situated in the world in such manner, the human being is bound by necessity to interpret the world so as to calculate its movements. The animal, because of its art, has no need for such an elaborate interpretive mechanism, for it has its art from the beginning, so to speak.

9. Martin Heidegger, *Sein und Zeit,* 15th ed. (Tübingen: Max Niemeyer, 1979), 149. In English, *Being and Time,* trans. Joan Stambaugh (Albany: SUNY Press, 2010), 145. Hereafter referred to as SZ, followed by German, then English, page numbers.

10. SZ 161/151.

11. Martin Heidegger, "What Is Metaphysics?" in *Pathmarks,* ed. and trans. William McNeill (New York: Cambridge University Press, 1998), 284.

12. Leonard Lawlor, *The Implications of Immanence: Toward a New Concept of Life* (New York: Fordham University Press, 2006), 7. Lawlor spells all this out and, as it relates to Heidegger, in a clearer form in a recent essay, "Further Questions: A Way Out of the Present Philosophical Situation (via Foucault)," in *Journal of French and Francophone Philosophy* 19, no. 1 (2011): 91–105, see esp. 95–97.

13. Michel Foucault, "La pensée du dehors," in *Dits et écrits,* vol. 1 (Paris: Quatro Gallimard, 2001), 565. In English, "The Thought of the Outside," in *Essential Works of Foucault 1954–1984,* vol. 2: *Aesthetics, Method, Epistemology,* ed. Paul Rabinow (New York: New Press, 1998), 166.

14. GA 29/30: 423/292.

15. GA 29/30: 424/292.

16. GA 29/30: 425/293.

17. Ibid.

18. That this perplexity, this *aporia*, has been neglected since Plato and continued up through Husserlian phenomenology is reaffirmed in GA 65: §94: "since Plato, the *truth* of the interpretation of 'being' has never been questioned. Representational correctness and its validation by means of intuition were merely carried over, in a movement from the representation of beings back to the representation of the 'essence'; most recently in pre-hermeneutical 'phenomenology.'"

19. See Alejandro Vallega's "'Beyng–Historical Thinking' in Heidegger's *Contributions to Philosophy*," in *Companion to Heidegger's "Contributions to Philosophy,"* ed. Charles E. Scott, Susan M. Schoenbohm, Daniela Vallega-Neu, and Alejandro Vallega (Bloomington: Indiana University Press, 2001), 48–65.

20. GA 65: §36.

21. GA 65: §41.

22. Heidegger, "Letter on Humanism," Frank A. Capuzzi (trans.), in *Basic Writings*, 2nd rev. and expanded edition, ed. David Farrell Krell (New York: HarperCollins, 1993), 217–265.

23. "Letter on Humanism," 231.

24. Martin Heidegger, *Beiträge zur Philosophie (Vom Ereignis), Gesamtausgabe*, vol. 65 (Frankfurt am Main: Klostermann, 1989), first unnumbered page. In English, *Contributions to Philosophy (From Enowning)*, trans. Parvis Emad and Kenneth Maly (Bloomington: Indiana University Press, 1999). Translation altered. Future references to this text will be provided by section number. The translations are frequently altered.

25. Ibid.

26. GA 65: §182.

27. *Besinnung, Gesamtausgabe*, vol. 66 (Frankfurt am Main: Klostermann, 1997), §41.

28. GA 66: §91. This is similarly expressed in *Die Geschichte des Seyns, Gesamtausgabe*, vol. 69 (Frankfurt am Main: Klosterman, 1998), §14: "The strife itself must be comprehended from out of the crossing-through of their countering [*Entgegnung*], and both must be comprehended from out of *Ereignis*."

29. GA 69: §23.

30. This expression, "will have been removed," is determined by a reading of Derrida and his concern for a past that was never present.

31. GA 65: §239.

32. Heidegger, "*Der Weg zur Sprache*," in *Unterwegs zur Sprache*, 6th ed. (Pfullingen: Verlag Günther Neske, 1979), 265. In English, "The Way to Language," in *Basic Writings* (see n. 22), trans. David Farrell Krell, 423. Hereafter referenced as WzS, followed by German, then English, page numbers.

33. One should see here David Krell's "Is There a Heidegger—or, for That Matter, a Lacan—Beyond All Gathering?" in this volume.

34. Heidegger, "Die Sprache," in *Unterwegs zur Sprache*, 32–33. One should note here the proximity of all these terms, a proximity that is only partially preserved in the English:

Die Sprache spricht.

Der Mensch spricht, insofern er Sprache entspricht.

35. WzS 265/423.

36. And this, of course, requires a grappling with that difficult relation, if relation can even be used here, between language and death. Heidegger's quarrel with German idealism would appear to be mainly a quarrel with Hegel, and that quarrel is already implied on the very first page of *Being and Time* where Heidegger recalls the history of metaphysics having been constructed from out of the forgetting of being, a forgetting that "has been preserved in various distorted and 'camouflaged' forms down to Hegel's *Logic*" (SZ 2/1). Heidegger's position with regard to Hegel is made clear in "What Is Metaphysics?" and it concerns the difference between the two regarding the nothing. This position never changes.

37. WzS 252/407.

38. WzS 252/408.

39. Ibid.

40. WzS 256/413, translation slightly altered. Krell translates the passage "In language as the saying, something like a way unfolds essentially." Krell's translation might well be the preferred one, for it is unquestionable that Heidegger is concerned with the unfolding or creating of a way, the creating of a way by language that draws speakers in to its way. Nevertheless, I have altered the translation to retain, in English, the verbal quality of essence that is part of Heidegger's incessant work on the notion.

41. WzS 254/410, translation altered.

42. WzS 256/412.

43. One of Petzet's "dialogues" with Heidegger leaves no doubt about this. The dialogue dating from April 17, 1959, is recounted as follows: "I take this opportunity to bring up something that has preoccupied me for days—namely, that what is said in *Being and Time* on language shows itself in another way in the lecture on language, as though we were just dealing with another version of the same thing: What you speak about here as the 'having-already-heard' that occurs prior to all 'speaking'—isn't this the same as the 'being-always-already-along-with' mentioned in *Being and Time,* that is, in the existential constitution, the sudden recognition of which came over me in a flash thirty years ago?" Heidegger stops walking, turns to me, and says, 'It is splendid that you say this. We don't even need to talk about it, since you have noticed it. Basically it is no different from what I tried to show forty years ago. But who pays attention? Read section 34 of *Being and Time*!'" Heinrich Wiegand Petzet, *Encounters and Dialogues with Martin Heidegger, 1929–1976,* trans. Parvis Emad and Kenneth Maly (Chicago: University of Chicago Press, 1993), 87–88. Krell also notes the connection to section 34 in a footnote to his translation. The point is also made in Heidegger's conversation with the Japanese friend in "A Dialogue on Language," in *Unterweg zur Sprache,* 137/41–42.

44. WzS 252/408.

45. WzS 261/418, translation altered.

46. GA 85: §51.

47. For a different version of this, see Sallis's "The Logic of Thinking" in this volume.

48. GA 69: §3.

ELEVEN

Is There a Heidegger—or, for That Matter, a Lacan—Beyond All Gathering?

διαφερόμενον in Heidegger's "Logos: Heraclitus B 50" as a Possible Response to Derrida's Disquiet

David Farrell Krell

Is there a Heidegger beyond the seemingly omnipresent gesture of gathering? Is there a Heidegger who resists the unifying force of the One, τὸ ἕν, and who acknowledges the disseminating force of the many, τὰ πάντα? A number of Heidegger's translators have suggested that there is indeed such a Heidegger. Yet let it be said at the outset: translators of Heidegger, and especially of Heidegger's "Logos" article, are a mad bunch at best, and are certainly not to be trusted. I am thinking of course of Jacques Lacan, who translated the "Logos" article of Heidegger into French decades ago.[1]

One wonders what could have drawn Lacan to such a text. Perhaps he was attracted to Heidegger's "Logos" by its early remarks on reason and unreason, the rational and irrational, both of which our tradition, according to Heidegger, equally neglects in their essential provenance: *irraison* and *déraison* would be, as it were, Lacan's home territory in the Heideggerian landscape; the relation of these words to *raison* could constitute the very ethics, or at least the ethos, of psychoanalysis, which takes the book of reason so seriously that it attempts to swallow it whole.[2] Or could Lacan have been excited by the notion of an irresistible *gathering* that occurs in and through language, a *Versammlung* in and through a unique unifying One—the Ἓν of Heraclitus's fragment B 50, as read by Heidegger? Or, quite to the contrary, could he have espied in Heidegger's reading, in spite of the unique-unifying-One, a force of resistance or interruption that disrupts all gathering of the Πάντα? In any case, must not Jacques Derrida have been troubled by Lacan's attraction to this essay, inasmuch as almost everything in Lacan and a great deal of what is in Heidegger—above all, the insistence on gathering, *versammeln*—disquieted him? Perhaps Derrida felt that Lacan's translation of Heidegger's "Logos" was just another case of the psychoanalytic postman gathering up the truth of desire and conducting it to its final destination, delivering the logos to the door of the École Freudienne? For even if, in Lacan's view, the truth of desire is unconscious, is not the unconscious structured as a language? Everyone, it seems, except for Derrida, knows what language is.

Thought-provoking questions or suspicions—to which I have no replies and no anodynes. Here I can say little about Lacan, and very little, and only very indirectly, about Derrida. The focus will be on Heidegger's pervasive notion of *Versammlung* as the gathering of beings in their presencing, with the "Logos" essay as my text. Yet that text is not *merely* about gathering. There is also something of a differing and a deferring there, or at least a moment of hesitation, expressed initially by the word Πάντα in Heraclitus's fragment B 50, and above all by the word διαφερόμενον, which Heraclitus employs several times in other fragments. Logos as gathering, yes, but also as something very much like difference, deferral, dissemination—perhaps even dispersion and scattering.

Heidegger begins the "Logos" essay by noting that the path most needed for our thinking of ὁ Λόγος "stretches far ahead," or so says the translator into English, bless his pitter-pattering heart. Yet when Heidegger says that the path *ist weit*, he may mean that we are not yet on it—the path may be far off to our left or right, or far ahead or far behind us, still remote from our position no matter where we may be wandering in our wasteland; we may still be *wide of* the path, or *far off* the beaten path, as English says so beautifully; the path may lie on a remote horizon, a horizon that has 360° with which to beguile us, each degree opening upon an infinite number of possible directions. Heidegger is fond of quoting Novalis when it comes to language, and one of Novalis's favorite words is *mannigfach*, as in the opening sentence of *The Apprentices at Saïs*, "Manifold are the paths that human beings tread," *Mannichfache Wege gehen die Menschen* (CHV 1: 201).[3] Full of twists and turns is each of our many paths, and each path opens upon the most diverse objects (*mannichfache Gegenstände:* CHV 1: 204); but there is *more than one path* in any case, even if one can identify the one that is "most needed." For Novalis, nature is myriad, or "thousandfold," and the conversations and activities that are pursued in the halls at Saïs are themselves *mannichfach;* if only a human being could learn to *feel* as well as to *think*, says Novalis's apprentice, "the stars would rise in him or her, and each would learn to feel the entire world, feel it more clearly and multifariously [*mannichfaltiger*] than the eye that confronts mere boundaries and superficies" (CHV 1: 218–219). The word *mannichfaltig* appears in manifold places further on in Novalis's text, but let me get back to the path—the path that we may not yet be treading, the path for which we are so far merely searching.

Human beings walk many paths, but the path "most needed" for thinking the logos is "far." Heidegger's sojourn on the path, or toward it, is less circuitous than the route he takes toward "The Anaximander Fragment." Recall that in that remarkable final essay of *Holzwege* Heidegger starts at the end, with ἀδικία, "injustice" or *Un-Fug*, tragic disjunction and disorder. In the tragic thinking of Anaximander, ἀδικία comes first and last. By contrast, the stations on Heidegger's way in "Logos: Heraclitus B 50" are more orderly, although hardly linear and sequential, hardly the perfect measuring out of a *Nebeneinander*. Heidegger pursues the eleven words that he acknowledges as authentic in Heraclitus's fragment (Diels-Kranz B 50) in the following seven steps:

4 5 1 2 3 6 7

Οὐκ ἐμοῦ ἀλλὰ τοῦ Λόγου ἀκούσαντας ὁμολογεῖν σοφόν ἐστιν Ἓν Πάντα. Unfortunately for the present essay, the most salient word is the very last one, and Heidegger does not consider it until far down the line, although, as we shall see, not at the very end of his path. Why insist on the Πάντα? and why on διαφερόμενον, which does not appear in B 50, but which Heidegger invokes in his commentary on "the many," "the manifold," or "the all" in that fragment? If we can anticipate a bit we may say that what is intriguing here is the possibility that the "many" that are "carried out" or somehow "settled" in the Greek word διαφερόμενον, which nonetheless in some sense remains a "differing," may not be so readily recoverable in an all-encompassing "One"; furthermore, the German word *Austrag*, which in Heidegger's text means the "carrying out" of unification, may be read in a way that challenges every sense of "the One" and of "gathering" as such. If we pursue such a reading, Πάντα may turn out to be a word for Derrida. And Lacan's position in the Heideggerian landscape? Somewhere, maddeningly, between settlement and a radical deferring/differing.

The very first step on Heidegger's path, presuming now that he is on it, determines the logos as the laying that gleans and gathers: ὁ Λόγος λέγει. The German verb *legen* clearly derives from the Latin *legere,* which for once does justice to the Greek, an epochal achievement in itself that should give us pause; indeed, language seems to have gone out of its way to preserve the word that designates its own modus vivendi in cognates that the ear can appreciate over the ages and across the epochs, λέγειν, *legere, legen,* laying. Lacan, for example, is able to find the word *lèguer,* "to bequeath, hand down, pass on," as in the noun *legs,* "legacy, heritage, bequest," in order to render at least some senses of the *legen* in logos. In any case, it is clear that Heidegger is referring to a laying that *lets* things lie before it, a laying that gleans and gathers without violent manipulation, as it were: *Versammlung,* "gathering," turns out to be the crucial sense of Λόγος, although Heidegger arrives at it only by virtue of the adverb *beisammen. Beisammen vorliegen lassen:* language lets (beings) lie together before us (in their being), gathering whatever presents itself in presencing, assembling all in its colloquy, safeguarding all that comes to presence in a kind of revelation or a kind of concealment—it is difficult to say which, and, indeed, one must truly say both. *Entbergen, bergen,* and *Unverborgenheit* express the great mystery of language, which reveals only by safeguarding in concealment, which discovers not by ripping off the cover but by letting-be, and which manifests by eschewing manifestos and hearkening to the pure if cryptic word of poesy. The gesture of *Gelassenheit,* from Meister Eckhart through Böhme, Baader, and Schelling, is preserved here in Heidegger's "Logos" essay, as it is throughout his work.

Lacan translates Heidegger's *legen* as *mettre-à-reposer,* "to set down before," "to place in repose," and perhaps even "to put to bed"; Heidegger's *zum Liegen bringen* he translates as *porter à gésir,* "to carry toward repose," "to bring to a reclining." Indeed, the bed, *le lit,* will play an important role in Lacan's rendering of the laying that gathers. When Heidegger writes that *Legen ist Lesen,* whereby *Lesen* is both reading and gleaning in general, Lacan translates, ingeniously, though not ingenuously, *Mettre en ce lit est donner à lire,* "To put to bed this way is to give to read." Reading in bed? Yes, that would have been Lacan's preference;

anything else would have meant surrendering the symbolic to the imaginary. True, Lacan leaves his bed for a while in order to follow Heidegger's path toward the vineyard. Yet he will return to it for certain.

The gesture of laying down and before, of gathering together and assembling, is what Heidegger thinks in the phrase *die lesende Lege*. What is this *Lesen*? To the contemporary German ear, it is clearly "reading," scanning the newspaper or gleaning the sense of an essay on Heraclitus. Heidegger does not say much about such "reading," perhaps because Socrates, the purest thinker of the West, never wrote, so that wherever "thinking" is the matter in question there is nothing "pure" to read. (In this, Derrida would surely concur; he remains always and everywhere a thinker of impurities.) Yet the meaning of *Lesen* does not end with "reading," unless one is surveying the label on a bottle of wine: for *Lesen* invokes the entire operation of viniculture and its vintages, from the preliminary selection of the grapes to be picked through the gathering performed by the harvesters, the collection of the fruit in baskets and bins, the trip back to the press, the barreling of the lively liquid in oak or stainless steel, and, both before and after the bottling, the storing away from sunlight in the cool dark of the cellar. All these phases of gathering constitute what will come to be called *wine*. For Heidegger, no doubt about it, language cannot be thought outside of the cultivation of the grape and the production of fine wines—say, a Saint-Joseph from Burgundy, which was his personal favorite, or the long-lived Barolo from northern Italy, the sturdy Rioja of Spain, the convivial Vin Santo of Santorini, the peppery Carmenere of Chile, and the velvety Pinotage of South Africa. Nor is the vinicultural vocabulary of *Lesen, Auslese, Spätlese* a mere "example" of the logos, as though it could just as well be a matter of a pair of shoes or a Roman fountain or a Greek temple. Wine is of the essence. *Mannichfache Wege gehen die Menschen,* to be sure, but since the days of King Gilgamesh of Uruk and his friend Enkidu, whose beautiful temple-priestess taught him to drink wine, eat bread, and make love, and thus to become human, the ways of language pass through the vineyard. It is as though language were the gift not of Apollo but of Dionysos, so that, in spite of the young Nietzsche's worries, music and the word need not strive against, but may accompany and mutually grace, one another.

Lacan, for his part, savors all the words of the French vineyard and allows his readers to get mildly high on Heidegger's "reading": *vendange, l'émondage, ramassage, moisson, récolte, réserve, cueillette*—the therapist smacks his lips over Heidegger's text, which he clearly savors. Whether Lacan's *mettre-à-reposer* puts the meaning of Heidegger's *lesende Lege* to bed, however, is difficult to say; some will certainly dispute his choice of words for the most telling phrase in Heidegger's "Logos." Yet even the harshest critic will bow before the Lacan of viniculture: the good doctor has found and used the essential words of the vintage, especially *récolter, vendenger, glaner,* and therefore shows that he knows the essence of *Lese.*

It is clear that for Heidegger the meaning of λέγειν as *Legen* is an *Ereignis* of the greatest importance:

> The saying and talking of mortals comes to pass [*ereignet sich*] from early on as λέγειν, laying. Saying and talking occur essentially [*wesen*] as the letting-lie-together-before of everything which, laid in unconcealment, comes to presence [*anwest*]. The original λέγειν, laying, unfolds itself early on and in a manner ruling everything unconcealed as saying and talking. Λέγειν as laying lets itself be overpowered by the predominant sense, but only in order to deposit the essence of saying and talking at the outset under the governance of laying proper. (212/63)

Why the laying that gathers acquiesces in the usurpation by saying and talking is an arresting question. So too is the question of the secret governance of *Legen,* concealed throughout the epochs of metaphysics and linguistics, yet somehow "deposited," *hinterlegt,* in a secure space and time, waiting only for a Heidegger to draw upon it and bring it to the light of day. Later on in the essay there will be talk of a "safety-net," a *Rücklage,* a kind of "savings" or "deposit" account that one can draw upon in destitute times. Derrida would surely want to know about such a safety-net or savings account, held secure and in suspension through all the epochs of metaphysics—metaphysics being all about securities, as Heidegger well knew, securities of sanctity and certitude. Yet let us not get sidetracked so early on our way. Only one more diversion, this one concerning Lacan's translation in general, before we move on to the second step.

If one were to stop teasing Lacan about his translation, and if one were to risk condescension, one would have to say that it is almost always remarkably precise and everywhere thought provoking. There are only one or two moments when Lacan takes a surprisingly free and daring step, and those are the steps that will be highlighted in what follows. The most daring step, or series of steps (since *dispersion* is the matter in question), occurs with the phrase we have been considering, Heidegger's *die lesende Lege,* the laying that gleans and gathers, for which Lacan attempts multiple solutions. We will turn to them in a moment.

The second step along or toward Heidegger's path has to do with *hearing* what is said and being talked about. It involves those who are listening, those who are ἀκούσαντας. By now, readers of Heidegger, if they have anything at all between their ears, are familiar with the *hearkening* to which he is always harking back, the *horchen* that since *Being and Time* has haunted Heidegger's thinking. Lacan renders Heidegger's *gehört,* "having heard," which for Heidegger always remembers its affinity with *gehören,* "to belong," in a particularly effective way: "*Nous avons ouï,*" he says, "*quand nous* sommes en entente." We hear when we are in accord, in cordial alliance, as it were, with what addresses us. We do not hear because we have ears, Heidegger loves to say; rather, we have acoustical apparatus because we hear. It is as though Heidegger were the last surviving Lamarckian. Heidegger along with Freud, to be sure. A Heideggerian of the looser persuasion once went so far as to quote (or to paraphrase) the Bible, "Who has ears to hear, let him ear!" Heidegger's embarrassment in the face of the ears, as it were—at least if we recall Dawne McCance's *Medusa's Ear*—has something to do with his discomfiture in the presence of the human body as such, that "most difficult problem," as he remarked to both Medard Boss and Eugen Fink.[4] Still more disturbing to Heidegger than the ears is the tongue, that γλῶσσα by which the Greeks sullied the very name of language, presumably at the moment of usurpation of λέγειν by saying and talking. Whereas Derrida everywhere celebrates the glossary of eating, vomiting, kissing, and speaking—from his 1974 *Glas,* through his 1989 lecture-course on *The Rhetoric of Cannibalism,* to his later interview with Jean-Luc Nancy, "How to Eat Well"—Heidegger shudders over it; on the positive side, Heidegger does concede that our apprehending of spoken or written language can live only by being embodied, that *das Vernehmen nur lebt, indem es leibt.*[5] The embarrassment or discomfiture that Heidegger experiences in and with the human body may have something to do with strewing or bestrewal, the *dispersion* that haunts the transcendental power of a sexed being—readers of Heidegger will recall that abstruse and somehow tortured discussion in §10 of the lecture-course on Leibniz of "the mightiness of Da-sein" viewed "also" as a sexual being, and they will also recall Derrida's reading of that section in his "Geschlecht I."[6] At all events, whether with or without the ears, "listening," or "hearkening," is of the essence. Of what, and to what end?

In order—and this is the third step—to say the same, ὁμολογεῖν. To let the one, *Eines,* lie before us as selfsame, *als Selbes.* Which one? Not necessarily the henological One of gathering proper, not just yet. Rather, any one being that lies before us, this one or that one. But *which* one, I hear my readers insisting, precisely in the way that Heidegger insisted at the outset of both *Being and Time* and *Introduction to Metaphysics,* and I hear Heidegger taking his fourth step. Yet before Lacan lets him take that step, he is there to remind us of the re-affirmation in Heidegger's text of Λόγος as λέγειν. Lacan reminds us by going back to (the) bed. Logos, writes Heidegger, "essentially unfolds as *das reine versammelnde lesende Legen*" (215/66). The English translation says, rather lamely and inelegantly, "In this fashion Logos occurs essentially as the pure laying which gathers and assembles." Lacan, more intriguingly, writes: *Tel est essentiellement le Logos comme le pur lit de ce qui se lit dans ce qu'il recueille,* which would be something like, "Such is essentially the Logos as the pure bed [or layer] of that which is embedded in what gathers." Many beds and embeddings here, many layings and layerings, although each of them is pure. Heidegger's neologism *Lege,* built on the model of *Sage,* "saying" or "saga," Lacan translates with an obsolete word that is homonymous with *legs,* namely, *lais.* The latter word, he tells us, is from *laisser,* "to let." Thus Lacan would elide the German *lassen* with *legen: lais* would be the letting-lie-in-repose, the embedding, of what is gleaned. And since what is gleaned is chosen, selected or elected, from all the fruit that lies on the ground, Lacan can say that Logos is *le lais où se lit ce qui s'élit,* meaning something like "the letting-lie in which what is chosen is embedded." Yet Lacan's is a phrase that has to be sung rather than merely read, inasmuch as the words are selected, or elected, more as homologous signifiers than as signifieds. Lacan's are words given by the tongue rather than by the brain—if one may make such a naïve distinction. Heraclitean *homologein* as homology. More on this musical selection in a moment.

Heidegger's fourth step is Heraclitus's first step, and it is a prohibition: "Not to me" should you hearken, οὐκ ἐμοῦ. Not to this person or that person, not to Heraclitus and not to Heidegger, and certainly not to Lacan, not even to Derrida, not to any one authority in particular should you listen.

"But," and here in rapid succession is the fifth step, which takes us back to the first, you must listen to the logos as the laying-that-gleans-and-gathers, that is, to the gleaning of whatever is coming to presence *in* its presencing. For this presencing of what is present is the twofold (*Zwiefalt*) that commands Heidegger's entire engagement with the early Greek thinkers, perhaps most strongly in his "Moira" essay on Parmenides, but really everywhere. It is as though this twofold of presencing, the (1) presencing of (2) what presences, were his, Heidegger's own, destiny, and as though such a twofold were quite different from the One.[7]

And that indeed is the sixth and penultimate step, σοφόν ἐστιν. The "wisdom" of saying the selfsame as the logos goes beyond the normal wisdom, for it follows the direction of destiny. Saying the selfsame requires the skill that comes from a sending of being; it is a *Geschick* that enables a gatherer to be *geschickt*.[8] The epoch in which Heidegger finds himself living calls for the selfsame saying in which he is now engaged—he is held in suspense by an epoch of being, namely, the one that he and we call "the end of metaphysics." Yet that saying of the selfsame is less a "what," less the response to a metaphysical question, than the response to a "how" question. It involves not so much *what* the logos says as the *way in which* it lays down together before us whatever comes to presence. And what way is that?

The seventh seal is now breached, the seventh step broached: Ἓν Πάντα. *Eins Alles.* Or, reading also from right to left, as the early Greeks often do, *Alles Eins. Eins: Alles, Alles: Eins.* Yet even if one should write and read boustrophedon, the gleaning in the present case is all one, by the One and for the One. For the commanding word in Heraclitus's saying, as Heidegger hears it, is "the unique-One as the unifying," *das Einzig-Eine als das Einende* (220/70). And here is where the word *Versammlung*, "gathering," gathers all the words of the fragment most forcefully:

> Ἓν is the unique-One as the unifying. It unifies by gathering. It gathers when, in gleaning, it lets lie before us whatever lies before us as such and as a whole. The unique-One unifies as the laying that gleans. This gleaning-laying unifying gathers the unifying in itself in such a way that it *is* this One and *is* as such the single One. The Ἓν Πάντα named in Heraclitus's saying gives us the simple clue as to what the Λόγος is. (220/70)

Here the "how" question, whether wittingly or not, collapses back into the "what" question, which would be (Derrida would say) the classic metaphysical gesture. The seventh step has now been taken, the words of the fragment exhausted. Heidegger's essay might well have ended here. Yet it does not end here, not by any means. Instead, there is a caesura at this point, a pause, followed by a return to the beginning. As it happens in Heidegger's essay, we are only three-quarters of the way along the path that is "far."

The path? Have we been on it all the while? Presumably, although only presumably, even if Heidegger's next paragraph begins with this question: "Do we wander off the path if . . . ?" If what? If we think the logos as the laying that gathers or gleans, as we have been doing right from the start. Yet something new enters on the scene, to wit, a new and unexpected attention to the word Πάντα, as though in Heraclitus's fragment we could emphasize that final word rather than the one (the One) preceding it. What this word Πάντα means, according to Heidegger, Heraclitus tells us in another fragment, namely, B 7: Εἰ πάντα τὰ ὄντα . . . , "If everything (namely) that which presences . . ." (220/70). Yet nothing about the unifying presencing of what is present is clear, not as we proceed ever more inextricably into the end of metaphysics. Nothing about the Πάντα is clear, either, in spite of its association with countless beings, manifolds, multiples, and the Novalisian *mannichfach*. For example, it is unclear why Heidegger capitalizes the word. In Diels-Kranz (1: 161) neither the ἓν nor the πάντα is capitalized—the Greeks were not big on capitals—and Heidegger generally respects DK in philological matters. Furthermore, if one of the two should be capitalized, then surely it is the unique One as simply and singularly unifying. Everything else should be merely everything else, and set in the lowercase: that would mark the ontological difference between beings-as-a-whole and their being; that would differentiate the fateful twofold of *Anwesen* as such. Yet everything—indeed, Everything—after the caesura in Heidegger's "Logos" essay, Everything after the seven completed steps, speaks to the concealed power and even the mystery of τὰ πάντα.If we skip ahead for just a moment beyond the discussion of διαφερόμενον to the end of the essay, we may become convinced of this upsurgence of "Everything" as a mystery. At first, what I am contemplating here about the eminence of the Πάντα seems nonsensical. Heidegger cites the first words of fragment B 32, Ἓν τὸ σοφὸν μοῦνον, which he translates as *das Einzig-Eine Alles Einende ist das Geschickliche allein*, "the unique-One unifying all is alone that which is destinal." We seem to be forever cast back to the One, which in fact we never will have abandoned. Yet the remaining words of fragment B 32 soon loom, and they alter this appearance considerably. Meanwhile, there is talk of lightning, the lightning that steers all. Fragment B 64: Τὰ δὲ Πάντα οἰακίζει Κεραυνός, "Lightning-bolt steers All Things," with All Things again capitalized in Heidegger's text (222/72), albeit not in Diels-Kranz; or, as Heidegger has it, "But lightning steers the All (of what presences into presencing)." Lightning-bolt is of course the *epitheton* of Zeus, so that the fragment, according to Heidegger, tells us about "the godhead of the god." Surely, if anything is One, it ought to be the one and only Zeus, or Zas, the Living One, whose very name suggests the power of the redoubling prefix, ζα-. Yet those missing words of B 32 now appear, in order to disconcert us:

> Ἓν τὸ Σοφὸν λέγεσθαι οὐκ ἐθέλει καὶ ἐθέλει Ζηνὸς ὄνομα'. One, the alone Wise, does not want and yet does want to be named Zeus.

The "not," *nota bene*, comes first, as in the case of fragment B 50, "Not to me." The One, which is capitally Wise, does *not* want to be called Zeus, is *not ready* to receive the name of Zeus. Does the negation have its pre-eminence in the matter itself? asks Heidegger. That question is reminiscent of the question he posed back in 1929 in his inaugural lecture at Freiburg, "What Is Metaphysics?" There negation pointed toward some far more obscure and far more drastic and primordial nihilation. Now, in 1951, we find another form of harsh nihilation, the kind that Heidegger in 1929 called "rebuke." The rebuke comes in the form of Heraclitus B 43:

> Ὕβριν χρὲ σβεννύναι μᾶλλον ἢ πυρκαιήν. Measureless pride needs to be extinguished sooner than a raging fire.

Measureless pride, *Vermessenheit*, results in the failure to take adequate measure of Everything, that is, of beings as a whole in their presencing-absencing. Heidegger's Heraclitean condemnation of such failure, and of our measureless pride in dreaming that such measuring could succeed, appears on the first and last pages of his "Logos" article, whether in the shorter 1951 or in the longer 1954 version. The last page of the longer version tells us that a thinker's word has no authority, even if that word should be *being*. We should not go running blindly after any such word, even if the path to it seems endlessly long and therefore boundlessly alluring. And on the very first page of his article Heidegger talks about the most dubious supposition we today can have when we approach the fragments of Heraclitus, namely, the supposition that *anything* Heraclitus might have uttered will be adequately grasped by our johnny-come-lately "everyday understanding." Clearly, we will never gather Everything; more likely, we may not even gather Anything. With these negations and warnings at our heels or hanging over our heads, we may return to that part of the path I am calling the caesura. For it is here that the Derridian word διαφερόμενον, or *Austrag*, falls. From the start of his career, Derrida's worry is that Heidegger is claiming too great a proximity to the matter of his thinking, too great a propriety, propinquity, or appropriateness of Dasein to being. Even if Heidegger is careful to pose the question of *Zugang* or access to the phenomenon of Dasein, and even if he is careful to hold "thinking" in modest regard, announcing that the path is "far," Derrida worries about the privilege that is always claimed for such access and for such thinking. Derrida's disquiet touches the "Logos" essay most directly when in *Of Spirit* he sees all four of his main threads—(1) the question of the question as the piety of thinking, (2) the putatively non-technological essence of technology, (3) the presumptive essence of animality, and (4) the suppressed teleology of Heideggerian epochality—gathering into a knot or a weft that is *gathering* itself, *Versammlung*.[9] In other words, the *Geflecht* or knot of issues that concerns Derrida in Heidegger's work bears the name "Gathering." As Derrida insists throughout the *Geschlecht* series, Heidegger's *bête noir* is dispersion, *Zerstreuung*, and his principal remedy for it is gathering, assembling, encompassing within a One whatever threatens to disperse and scatter. Why should Derrida worry about gathering as a remedy for dispersion? Because, in his view, such gathering is always and everywhere violent. In *Archive Fever* he writes:

> From the moment there is the One, there is murder, laceration, traumatism. *The One guards itself against the other.* It protects *itself* from the other, but in the movement of this jealous violence it bears within itself, and thus preserves within itself, alterity or difference from self (the difference of the with-itself) that constitutes the One. "The One deferring/differing from itself." The One as the Other. At once, within the same time, but a time out of joint, the One forgets to recall itself to itself, preserves and effaces the archive of this injustice that it is. It forgets the violence that it perpetrates. *The One does violence to itself.* It violates itself, works violence upon itself, but it also institutes itself in such violence. It

> becomes what it is, violence itself—which is what it does. Auto-determination as violence. The One protects itself from the other *in order to do violence to itself* (*because* it does violence to itself *with a view* to being violent toward itself).[10]

Derrida's worry is surely well founded. We find dozens of passages in Heidegger's works from *Being and Time* to "Time and Being" that celebrate the gathering, celebrate it without a thought to its dangers. The "Logos" essay alone provides evidence enough of that. Yet the strangest moment in this essay, to repeat, comes in the pause that enables or compels Heidegger to reflect on the Πάντα of "Εν Πάντα'. And on the possibility of hybris. Here one of Heidegger's oldest themes comes to the fore, namely, truth as unveiling, ἀλήθεια, here written in the Heraclitean form ἀληθέια. Truth as unveiling, we know, is itself obscured behind a veil. The River of Forgetfulness, Λήθη, silts all, and only thus do the banks of truth rise. Truth is turbid. Allow me to cite Heidegger's "Logos" at length:

> All disclosure [*Entbergen*] releases what is present from concealment [*enthebt Anwesendes der Verborgenheit*]. Disclosure needs concealment. Ἀ-Λήθεια rests in Λήθη, drawing from it, laying before us whatever remains deposited in and through Λήθη. Λόγος is *in itself and at the same time* a revealing and concealing. It is Ἀλχηθεια. Unconcealment needs concealment, Λήθη, as its deposit [*Rücklage*], upon which disclosure can, as it were, draw. Λόγος, the laying that gleans, has in itself this revealing-concealing character. As soon as we can see in the Λόγος the way in which the Ἕν essentially occurs as unifying, it becomes equally clear that the unifying that occurs in the Λόγος remains infinitely different from what we tend to represent as a connecting or predicating. The unifying that rests in λέγειν is neither a mere comprehensive collecting nor a mere coupling of opposites that equalizes all contraries. The Ἓν Πάντα lets lie together before in one presencing things that are usually separated from and opposed to one another, such as day and night, winter and summer, peace and war, waking and sleeping, Dionysos and Hades. Such opposites, borne along the farthest stretch [*äußerste Weite*] between presence and absence, διαφερόμενον, let the laying that gleans lie before us in its entire bearing. Its laying is itself that which carries things along by bearing them out [*ist das Tragende im Austrag*]. The Ἕν is itself a carrying out [*ist austragend*]. (220–221/71)

To be sure, there is much to worry about here. Above all, this: as long as the lethal is viewed as a safety-net or a security deposit box, as long as the lethargic is celebrated as an energetic source and resource, and as long as the River of Oblivion is taken to be the pool for a refreshing draught and a clear reflection, the force of concealment and nihilation in Heidegger's own thinking is deflected—though not overcome. If safeguarding (*Bergen*) removes what presences into some flimsy shelter that is a mere simulacrum of concealment, if the gathered wines are kept in some shabby makeshift that possesses neither the cool nor the dark of a proper cellar, all talk of preservation is vain self-deception. Heidegger's criticism of predication does not suffice. It is in fact a mere feint. Nor can the διαφερόμενον be a mere matter of delineating the opposites in a new way, subjecting them all to what still seems to be a mere dialectic of revealing-concealing, or perhaps some reassuring *coincidentia oppositorum*. Rather, we must submit revealing-concealing itself to the most sustained scrutiny, one that resists the happy end (the determinate third) of dialectic. And not even scrutiny suffices. How could one hide from a sun that never sets? Concealment has to be taken more earnestly than that; one has to worry about how truly cavernous and deep the cellar must be. Both Hades and Dionysos occupy that space, which is not dug to our specifications. For revealing-concealing is a matter of life and death, and wine a matter of Hölderlin's "Bread and Wine," which is to say, of the essence of poetry. Nothing here gets "drawn upon," especially in destitute times. No safety-net, no savings account.

How, then, to think the *Austrag*? In everyday German, an *Austrag* is the "settling" of some matter, especially of a dispute; a court "ruling," or a "settling out of court"; it is a judicially guaranteed payment of a monthly sum to a farm owner who has turned over his farm to another; it is a competition's having come to a successful end in the rise of a victor; finally, when a mother is able to carry the fetus until it is fully developed, the child is said to have been *ausgetragen*, born only after having been "borne to full term." However, is the *Austrag* merely the cyclical equilibrium or the successful alternation of day and night, the unity and balance of opposites? Heidegger himself seems to deny it. For is there anything that unifies and holds in equilibrium the mystery of the *Urphänomen*, of revealing and concealing "as such"? Are revealing and concealing opposites at all? Is not the entire effort of Heidegger's later thinking an endeavor to show that this is not the case; that, rather, these two are imbricated in a way that baffles? For what could that primal "settlement" between revealing and concealing be? It would not be ready to receive the name of the Ἕν itself, which gathers into presencing; it might be more prepared to receive the double appellation Ἓν Πάντα, heard as a harmony, taken well-nigh as a single word, indeed, as a single verb. Or if that seems still too much of a gathering, what would Πάντα itself look like and sound like as a verb? What would this "everything-ing" be that occurs in the laying that gleans? "Everythinging," in gentle parody of Heidegger's "Das Ding," seems even more outrageous than Leopold Bloom's "I am almosting it"; it seems to be a word from and for *Finnegans Wake*. In any case, the emphatic, verbal Πάντα would look nothing like a "settlement," inasmuch as Lethe can never be dragged into court. To put it in the terms of Heidegger's thinking in *Being and Time*, Dasein never plumbs the ground of the nullity that it is, inasmuch as the nothing can never be brought to account. The nothing of nihilation does not barter and chop. When the initiates at Trophonios emerge from the underground spring of Lethe they are immediately given water from the fount of Mnemosyne to drink. Gradually, they come to their senses. Even so, it takes them about three days, on average, before they learn to laugh again and are allowed to go home. Settlements with Lethe are dicey. Some, they say, slip into Lethe never to return.

What, then, can we say more positively of the force of διαφερόμενον? Heidegger does not cite the source for the word, an omission that is itself remarkable inasmuch as he is quick to cite the form λεγόμενον (208/60). Yet we are reminded of fragment B 8, which speaks of "the coincidence of that which strives against its other, the most beautiful harmony resulting from that which disperses," ἐκ τῶν διαφερόντων (DK 1: 152). Furthermore, the word in the particular grammatical form that Heidegger cites is found in fragment 10 (DK 1: 153), in a quotation passed on to us by Aristotle, who comments on the way in which both nature (in the coupling of the sexes) and art (in the combination of tones in music and of letters—namely, of vowels and consonants—in speech and writing) mix the opposites, "making connections, whole with part, among things that go together and things that do not go together," συμφερόμενον διαφερόμενον. (Compare Lucian's formulation, associated with the child at play, at DK 1: 190, l: 22.) Connections or synapses of things that go together and things that do not go together—what sorts of synapses are these? Do they combine or separate? One thinks of the "one" sphere of

Empedocles, in which the two forces, Love and Strife, strive against one another: they "belong" to the same sphere, and yet because the two *strive* against one another—Strife *striving* against Love, Love *striving* against Strife—the "one" sphere exhibits more of Strife than Love. We may certainly agree with Heraclitus B 51, which says that we fail to understand "how what is borne apart [διαφερόμενον] can come together: a unity that strives against itself, as in the case of the bow and the lyre" (DK 1: 162, ll: 2–4). This we fail to understand; we do not gather it.

The harmony of revealing-concealing is a hidden harmony. If concealment harbors a deposit, then it does so not as a readily available bank account but as an ore too deep to mine. If concealment is a safety-net, we remain uncertain of the size of the holes between the threads. Harmonies of the lyre, sweet; but harmonies of the bow that is both life and death? Are hidden harmonies ever to be "drawn upon"? Are hidden governances ever at our "disposal"? The Heidegger who entertains such questions and suffers such severe doubts is the Heidegger beyond all gathering. If we take Heraclitus's image of the weaving of vowels and consonants—and in an essay on "Logos" we may dare to do so, even if gleaning rather than weaving is the primordial sense of λέγειν—are we remiss if we recall Saussure's disconcerting insistence that C-A-T has meaning only if each consonant and the vowel that conjoins them are differentiated from every other letter and every other combination of these particular letters? And if we begin to think of all the differentiations of signifiers in all the languages from Babel onward, from Enkidu to Lacan, are we not introduced to a concealing that runs very deep indeed? When we contemplate the thoroughgoing contamination of meaning, the unavoidable crossing of the lines in day/night, peace/war, free/slave, and all the rest, not as markedly either present or absent but as maddeningly interlaced, are we not aware of a certain *dispersion* of sense in the very mystery of language itself, a kind of wild sowing of sense and nonsense that so troubled the Plato of *Phaedrus*? One can patiently pare down the concept, as Hegel thought himself to be doing; one can cut the logos diacritically over and over again, as the Eleatic Stranger of Plato's *Sophist* does; but does that stop the proliferation of sense? Does it not accelerate it? Does the diacritical method rescue either Theaetetus or the purest thinker of the West from death? And will the noise of the glottal stop that the word *logos* only barely manages to suppress, the *gl-* that so offends both Hegel's and Heidegger's univocal ear, ever be silenced? Who will bring to a halt the writing that spaces its words across the page with the scratch of a pen, scratchings that Melville's Isabel (in *Pierre; or, The Ambiguities*) hears as "the busy claw of some midnight mole in the ground"?

Let us take a moment—as we slip into our conclusion, as though under the covers—to recall what Lacan does with some of the key words of Heidegger's text. These words, on the unique unifying One, appear once again immediately prior to our own central passage, the passage concerning διαφερόμενον. Astonishingly, however, Lacan introduces a new word for his translation of the "gathering," *die Versammlung*, or the unifying One. The One that unifies *indem es versammelt* Lacan translates now as the One that unifies *en même temps qu'il répartit*. What can that mean? *Versammlung* as *répartition? Répartir* is "to share out, distribute, allot, divide, spread," anything but "to gather." What is Lacan doing here? Is he mad? Mad he may be, but there is method in it, for what he is doing is reading right through Heidegger's resistance to dispersion. Heidegger is so busy gathering that he can gather no more than the One as gathering. Lacan, perversely, polymorphously, maddeningly insightfully, hears resistance at work, and he decides to take the prefix *Ver-*, not as positively and emphatically verbal, but as a kind of negation, expressing a kind of botching, as in the word *vertan*, "mistaken," "failed." *Ver-sammlung*, as Lacan here translates it, would mean a botched or bitched gathering, a gathering that fails to unify. The subordinate conjunction *indem*, which can be understood either instrumentally or temporally, he hears as "all the while," "whereas," or "meanwhile," as though the right (conscious) hand never really knows what the left (unconscious) hand is gathering or scattering. Unifying, in other words, *must* confront a primordial condition of ungatheredness, a kind of chaos, or *Chose*, that waits upon the redeeming One. Lacan, who has translated so precisely and so faithfully up to now, reads through the veil of Heidegger's logos and gleans what ought to be there, reads what desire wants to have been there all the while, even though it is not there. Lacan inverts the two clauses of Heidegger's next sentence but retains his perverse translation of *versammelt* as *répartir*. The repetition is even more astonishing, inasmuch as Heidegger writes, *Es versammelt . . . als solches und im Ganzen*, bringing the gathering to the whole of beings. Lacan retains this reference to the whole: *il le répartit en son entier*, the One "distributes [or: spreads and shares out, allots and divides] in its entirety." Heidegger gathers into a whole, whereas Lacan wholly parcels it out. Heidegger now writes *Das Einzig-Eine eint als die lesende Lege,* "The unique One unifies as the laying that gleans," and this gleaning-gathering laying, almost predictably now, brings Lacan back to his reading: *L'Uniquement-Un unit en tant qu'il est le lais où se lit ce qui s'élit,* "The uniquely one unifies by being the *lais* where the elected is read." *Lais,* to repeat, is said to be an old French word, homophonous with *legs,* which derives from *léguer* and which therefore stands in relation to the German *Legen.* The French equivalents of "delegation" and "relegation" and all their legatees will soon become words for Lacan's Heidegger. Yet the *lais* itself derives from *laisser,* the German *Lassen,* so that Heidegger's *Beisammen-vorliegen-lassen* becomes the single French expression *lais.* And this "letting-lie" soon enough evokes from Lacan *le lit,* "the bed," even though for the speaker of English or German that connection is more difficult to bring over the lips. It seems as though these liquid signifiers have a power of their own in French, even there where thought is of the logos, and the logos is of thought. Lacan now writes *Ce fait ici d'unir ce qui dans ce lit se lit, répartit en soi ce qui unit jusqu'au point qu'il* est *cet un-ci,* which is difficult to render, but says something like this: "Here the deed that unifies what is read [*se lit*] in this bed [*dans ce lit*] shares out in itself that which unifies to the point where it *is* this one." These words are meant to render Heidegger's sentence, "*Dieses lesend-legende Einen versammelt in sich das Einende dahin, daß es dieses Eine und als dieses das Einzige* ist."

Now, it is clear, if anything here is clear, that Lacan is not talking about reading in bed. To translate his French this way is to announce that one's French is as bad as my French *is.* What Lacan means by allowing his tongue to glide liquidly from *s'élit* to *se lit* to *ce lit* is the gleaning-gathering *lesende Lege* that the Logos is . . . *as signifier.* The liquorous noises of lingual language here decide. Here one does not elect to read in bed. Here one sleeps in the bed that language has made for thinking—which, of course, now has to proceed in French, even when Germans do it. And language makes its bed out of sounds and signs. Don't take my word for it. Listen to Lacan, who decides to allow *Versammlung* to become a dividing up or sharing out, a *répartition,* no matter how much it may astonish. It is the sort of outrageous behavior he engaged in toward his patients, if one is to believe all those stories about his therapy sessions, behavior for which he used to charge a considerable amount of money. His gesture is hard to forgive but impossible to forget. Gathering as dispersing or dispensing? With this translation of gathering as sharing out, Lacan has anticipated everything that Heidegger will almost-but-not-quite-have-said in our central passage. For διαφερόμενον, if it is anything, is closer to dispersal than it is to gathering.[11]

Having made his outlandish gesture, Lacan can now return to a more conservative translation: for *hinterlegt* he elects *relégué,* "relegated"; for *Rücklage, la réserve,* "the reserve." As though Lethe could be dammed up and used for water supply, as though concealment—and for a psychotherapist!—could be a safety-net or savings account, a piggy one could bank on. Only after the reference to διαφερόμενον does Lacan take us back to bed: Heidegger's *läßt die lesende Lege in seinem Austrag vorliegen* Lacan renders as *le lais où se lit ce qui s'élit le laisse se présenter dans sa rétribution. Austrag* as retribution? The price for going to bed, it seems, is to be paid in moral currency. Not even the *laisse* that is aligned with the *lais* can soften this judgment. For Heidegger's final two sentences in the paragraph, "*Ihr* [referring here to *die lesende Lege,* Lacan's *lais*] *Legen selber ist das Tragende im Austrag. Das En selber ist austragend,*" Lacan has: *Il se délègue lui-même à être ce qui porte le jugement distributif. Le Hen lui-même est rétribuant.* The distributive judgment sidles up to Kantian retributive justice. Payback time! Retribution pronounced upon he who pronounces the name of Jehovah in vain! And yet. Lacan's *le jugement distributif* might be taken as a reference back to that distribution or sharing out, that *répartition,* by which he so perversely translates *Versammlung.* Retribution may in fact be a motion for retrial, a scattering of judgment to the winds, anything but a "settlement." It is difficult to decide. And so let us leave the translators to their madness.

If there is an affirmative Heidegger for Derrida, and there is, it is the Heidegger who does not settle for settlements. Could such an affirmative Heidegger entertain a very different—and a very differentiating—sense of the logos? Could there be a Heidegger beyond all gathering, who in uttering the Ἓν Πάντα emphasizes not the One but the Many? *Hen* Panta? As though, to repeat, that second word were a verb? Not the unique-One unifying all but the multitudinous and multifaceted Many doing everything it can to frustrate the unities?

In the end, if we along with Heidegger should feel free to say ὁ Λόγος λέγει, we will have to affirm that in its essential unfolding this phrase means nothing other than ὁ Λόγος διασπέιρει. Language disperses and disseminates, and *is* dispersed and disseminated in its diaspora. Language differs and defers; language *is* differentiated and deferred. Language is both scattering and scattered, διασπειρέντος. Our friends Charles Scott and John Llewelyn would both insist, however, and they would be right to do so, that σπείρω has to be said or written in the middle voice: ὁ Λόγος σπείρασθαι, meaning that seed sometimes lets itself be sown but often is simply strewn, disseminated in multitudinous engenderings that are irrecoverably beyond human calculation and control, sown sometimes across a carefully cultivated vineyard or field, yes, but at other times cast into the wild—which is where language dwells.

Don't take my word for it, I repeat, don't listen to me, but hearken to the Λόγος. Hear and understand its repetitions, its *s'entendre-parler*, its *vouloir-dire*. Go to bed with it, if it be willing. For if Heidegger's worst nightmare, haunting him his life long, is *Zerstreuung*, "dispersion," his most transcendent hope is *Streuung*, "bestrewal," and it is impossible to say precisely where and when the exaggeration, marked by the prefixes *Zer-* or ζα-, occurs, impossible to separate out Heidegger's nightmares from his vision of the mightiness of Da-sein. Such separating out, διαφερόμενον, which occurs in and as language itself, does not yield to any mortal or moral gathering. Allotment is of μοῖρα. But don't take Heidegger's word for it, either. Listen. Listen to all the Λόγοι.

NOTES

1. Lacan's translation of Heidegger's "Logos" appears in *La psychanalyse*, no. 1 (1956): 59–79. His translation ends three pages before the German text (as published in *Vorträge und Aufsätze*, 1954) comes to a close: to be sure, Heidegger added these final pages to his earlier text for the *Festschrift für Hans Jantzen*, written and published in 1951. What makes the situation strange, however, is that Lacan's translation, in the endnotes, refers several times to the more complete version in *Vorträge und Aufsätze*, without mentioning the additional pages at the end. What makes the situation even more odd is that the translator of Heidegger's "Logos" into English nowhere mentions the difference between the Jantzen piece and the later text which he is translating; he seems to have been entirely ignorant of the discrepancy, as though he had to wait for a deceased Lacan to inform him of it. For Heidegger's text, see Martin Heidegger, *Vorträge und Aufsätze* (Pfullingen: G. Neske Verlag, 1954), 207–229. The only English version of Heidegger's essay that I know of appears in a book that is now out of print: Martin Heidegger, *Early Greek Thinking*, 2nd ed. (San Francisco: HarperCollins, 1984), 59–78. I will cite Heidegger's text in the body

of my article by the page numbers in these German/English editions. My thanks to Jeff Powell for the invitation to write this piece and for sending me both Lacan's translation and the 1951 (Jantzen) version of Heidegger's "Logos."

2. See the closing lines of Jacques Lacan, *Éthique de la psychanalyse*, Seminar 7 (Paris: Seuil, 1986), 375.

3. I cite Novalis (Friedrich von Hardenberg, 1772–1801) by volume and page, according to the following edition: Novalis, *Werke, Tagebücher und Briefe*, ed. Hans-Joachim Mähl and Richard Samuel, 3 vols. (Munich: Carl Hanser Verlag [hence the code letters CHV], 1987).

4. See Dawne McCance, *The Ear of Medusa: University Foundings from Kant to Chora L* (Albany: SUNY Press, 2004), esp. chap. 4, "Who Has Ears to Hear?" For Heidegger's remark to Medard Boss, see Martin Heidegger, *Zollikoner Seminare*, ed. Medard Boss (Frankfurt am Main: Klostermann, 1987), 293 and passim. On "the most difficult problem," namely, the human body, allow me to cite a long passage from the Heidegger-Fink *Heraclitus Seminar* of 1966–1967 [*Heraklit* (Frankfurt am Main: Klostermann, 1970), hereafter Hk], a passage that is quoted in the introduction to my *Daimon Life: Heidegger and Life-Philosophy* (Bloomington: Indiana University Press, 1990), 25–26:

> *Fink:* . . . The human being differs from all beings. . . . It possesses a double character: on the one hand, it is itself placed in the clearing, and on the other, it is imprisoned in the underground of all clearing.
>
> *Heidegger:* That will become comprehensible only through the phenomenon of the body,
>
> *Fink:* as in the erotic mode of understanding.
>
> *Heidegger:* "Body" is not meant ontically here
>
> *Fink:* and not in the Husserlian sense, either,
>
> *Heidegger:* but rather in the way Nietzsche thinks the body—even though what the body properly signifies for him remains obscure.
>
> *Fink:* In the section "On the Despisers of the Body," Zarathustra says, "Body am I wholly and entirely, and nothing else besides." Through the body and the senses human beings are close to the earth.
>
> *Heidegger:* . . . Can we isolate darkling understanding, which defines our corporeal belonging to the earth, from our being placed in the clearing?
>
> *Fink:* To be sure, darkling understanding can be addressed only in terms of the clearing. But it can no longer be brought to language by way of a nicely articulated jointure.
>
> *Heidegger:* . . . Human beings body forth only if they are alive [*Der Mensch leibt nur, wenn er lebt*]. That is the way to understand "body" in the sense you are using it. At the same time, "to live" is meant in an existential sense. Ontic nearness does not mean any sort of spatial proximity between two things, but a reduced openness [*eine herabgesetzte Offenheit*], hence an ontological moment in human beings. Nevertheless, you speak of an ontic nearness.
>
> *Fink:* Back in the days when you first came to Freiburg, you said in a lecture course: the animal is poor in world [*das Tier ist weltarm*]. At that time you were on the way toward the kinship [*Verwandtschaft*] of human beings with nature.

Heidegger: The phenomenon of the body is the most difficult problem. (Hk, 232–234)

5. That important concession of *leben/leiben,* let it be remarked, Heidegger makes in many places: it is clearly one of his favorite German folk wisdoms, and it compensates to some extent for his failure to think the human body in its "abysmal bodily kinship with the beast." But only to some extent. See Heidegger, *Wegmarken* (Frankfurt am Main: Klostermann, 1967), 326; *Nietzsche I* (Pfullingen: G. Neske, 1961), 119 and 565; *Gesamtausgabe* vol. 29/30, 329, and the seminar with Eugen Fink, Hk, 234; and, surely, elsewhere. Lacan translates accurately Heidegger's phrase, *nur lebt, indem es leibt,* based on the common German expression *wie man leibt und lebt,* albeit without particular esprit: *encore que ce qui est de percevoir ne prenne vie qu'autant qu'il soit d'un corps,* "even if whatever perception may be it comes to life only insofar as it is of a body."

6. For Heidegger's remarks on the *Geschlechtlichkeit* of Dasein, see Martin Heidegger, *Metaphysische Anfangsgründe der Logik im Ausgang von Leibniz, Gesamtausgabe* vol. 26, Marburg lecture-course, summer semester 1928 (Frankfurt am Main: Klostermann, 1978), section 10. For Derrida's "Geschlecht I," see now Jacques Derrida, *Psyché: Inventions de l'autre* (Paris: Galilée, 1987), 395–414.

7. On the destined twofold, *Zwiefalt,* of "presencing," see Martin Heidegger, "Moira (Parmenides VIII, 34–41," in *Vorträge und Aufsätze,* 231–256, esp. section IV; *Early Greek Thinking,* 92–95.

8. Lacan tries his hand at *Geschick/geschickt,* in which the German fuses the destined with the skilled, but all he can come up with is a mandate: *mandat/mandaté.* The fittingness or suitability of saying-the-same, as both gift and gifted, skilled, is not really retained in the French. There are after all some things that the German language keeps to itself.

9. Jacques Derrida, *De l'esprit: Heidegger et la question* (Paris: Galilée, 1987), 24. I will not even begin to cite the vast number of texts in which Derrida articulates his worries about both Heidegger and Lacan, attention to each of which would occupy a tome or two.

10. Jacques Derrida, *Mal d'Archive: Une impression freudienne* (Paris: Galilée, 1995), 124–125.

11. See Hans-Dieter Gondek, "*Logos* und Übersetzung: Heidegger als Übersetzer Heraklits—Lacan als Übersetzer Heideggers," in *Übersetzung und Dekonstruktion,* ed. Alfred Hirsch (Frankfurt am Main: Suhrkamp, 1997), 263–348, which offers an excellent detailed account of Lacan's translation of Heidegger's essay—against the background of the vast question of the hermeneutics of translation in general. Gondek appears to remain quite calm about Lacan's outrageous translation of *Versammlung,* remarking that "*répartir* means *verteilt* [distributed] and not *versammelt* [gathered]," as though Lacan had made a minor mistake (307). Yet this is no Freudian slip on Lacan's part, nor even a Lacanian *lapsus.* Rather, it is the mark of the subject rent by desire, the subject who never passes the bar, as it were; it is the mark of the phallus as signifier, which works its effects only in and through dispersion and absence. Gondek is in fact well aware of this: the question of difference (that is, of the *diapheron*) dominates his article right from the start (280–281), and the second half of his essay responds to the riddle of gathering as *répartir.* Difference has less to do with the oppositions of day and night, peace and war, and

more to do with the concealment of revealing as such: "Because of the *diapheron*, the *Hen Panta* is not to be understood as the universal unity in which everything is to be dissolved. As the laying that gathers, the *legein* also has a diacritical function" (283; cf. 304–305). Following Elisabeth Roudenesco, Gondek affirms that Lacan's strategic "translator-boldness" is Mallarméan in its inspiration. For it is the infinite—infinitely dispersing—domination of the signifier over the signified that makes it so. Lacan's translation, devoted to the truth of desire, if not of being, thus challenges Heidegger's confidence in his own reception of the call from being (303). Lacan's inspiration for *répartition* thus has to do with the insights of Heidegger's "Moira," that is, it pays heed to the endless process of allotment and apportioning, to the ceaseless cycles the ontological difference (306–307). Gondek writes: "That Lacan here no longer speaks of 'gathering' could readily be explained by the fact that signifiers, which stand in a relation of absolute difference to one another, cannot 'gather'; they cannot form a whole, a unity, or a totality, but only a 'distribution' [*Verteilung*]. A supremely transitory one. In which difference, as an 'apportioning judgment,' is endlessly in process."

I am grateful to Gerhard Richter for the reference to Gondek.

TWELVE

Heidegger and the Question of the "Essence" of Language

Françoise Dastur

Logik als Frage nach dem Wesen der Sprache: such is the title of Heidegger's lecture-course from the summer semester 1934,[1] in which *Wesen* should be understood in the new meaning that Heidegger gave to it in the mid-1930s. As he explained in 1936–1938 in *Contributions to Philosophy,* this word should no longer be taken in the generic meaning of *koinon* or *genos* but understood rather as "the happening of the truth of Being" (*Geschehnis der Wahrheit des Seins*),[2] and as he emphasized once more in his 1953 lectures on *The Question of Technology* and *Science and Meditation,* the word *Wesen* should now be understood on the basis of the old verb *wesen,* which is the same word as *währen,* to last.[3] *Wesen* should therefore no longer be considered as the expression of the permanence or invariability of an *eidos* and be taken in a nominal sense as the "essence" or "quiddity" of something, but in the sense of the old verb *wesen,* as the temporal unfolding of the being of something.

From this lecture-course whose manuscript had apparently been lost and subsequently published only in 1998 on the basis of notes taken by students who attended, Heidegger said, first in his 1951–1952 lecture-course on *What Is Called Thinking?*[4] and a second time in his 1954 dialogue with a Japanese interlocutor,[5] that it constituted a decisive moment, the moment of the transformation of logic into the question of the *Wesen der Sprache,* of the unfolding of the being of language. This allows us to understand that what Heidegger names in this course "the necessary task of the shaking (*Erschütterung*) of logic"[6] was a task that remained oriented toward a definite conception of language, that is, the conception of language that was prevailing in *Being and Time,* where language is defined as *Hinausgesprochenheit der Rede,* the oral exteriorization of discourse.[7] It is with such a definition of language, which opposes the articulation of discourse to the vocal resonance of speech, that will have led Heidegger to the mid-1930s break, because such a definition remained under the dependency of the Husserlian distinction between signification and expression, as shown in a passage from section 18 where it is said that significations "found the possible being of words and language."[8]

It seems nevertheless that Heidegger, to a certain extent, refused to consider that a clean break took place between *Being and Time* and the period of the so-called *Kehre* concerning the question of language. In the already mentioned 1954 dialogue with a Japanese interlocutor, he acknowledges that his questions "circled around the problem of language and Being," and that the reflection on language had determined his path of thinking from early on. He mentions as proof the title of his 1915 dissertation "'Duns Scotus' Doctrine of Categories and Theory of Meaning' . . . 'doctrine of categories' is the usual name of the discussion of the Being of beings and 'theory of meaning,' means the *grammatica speculativa,* the metaphysical reflection on language in its relation to Being."[9] He concedes then that this relation between language and Being was not clear for him in this early period and he explains that today he knows that "because the reflection on language and Being has determined my path of thinking from early on, therefore the discussion of them has stayed as far as possible in the background," but he also recognizes that "the fundamental flaw of the book *Being and Time* is perhaps that I ventured forth too far too early."[10] However, when his Japanese interlocutor emphasized the fact that in *Being and Time* the *Erörterung,* the discussion, about the site (*Ort*) of language remained "quite sparse," Heidegger advised him "to read section 34 in *Being and Time* more closely,"[11] implicitly repeating the retrospective judgment he had already passed upon this section in 1946 in his *Letter on Humanism* where he declared that it contains "a reference to the being dimension of language [*Wesensdimension*]," because it "touches upon the simple question as to what mode of Being language as language in any given case has."[12]

This judgment comes from Heidegger's retrospective view of his own work, which constitutes what has been legitimately called his "self-interpretation" in which his own path of thinking is understood as a process that includes a "turn," but not a brisk interruption, necessitating a new point of departure. Nevertheless, the question remains for us to decide if Heidegger's leading theme of thought is, as he seems to acknowledge in 1954, "Language and Being," and not, as it was at first, "Being and Time," and if there is a way leading from this first theme to the second one, from his 1927 book *Being and Time* to his 1959 book *On the Way to Language*. It has to be recalled that in 1927 Heidegger's plan consisted in showing that time is the transcendental horizon of Being, in other words that Being is intrinsically "temporal," which means that it should be thought in a verbal manner and always in relation to time. This goal was not reached in the published part of *Being and Time*, a book that remained unfinished, as Heidegger refused to publish the famous third division of his book, which suggested in its title "Time and Being" that the relation between Being and time is overturned, time being no longer only the fundamental dimension of the being of man but of Being itself. This meant, he says in his *Letter on Humanism* that "the adequate execution and completion of this other thinking that abandons subjectivity" could not be brought to its end, since "thinking failed in the adequate saying of this turning and did not succeed with the help of the language of metaphysics,"[13] which gives to the thought that the old words "transcendence" and "horizon" finally appeared to be no longer appropriate for naming the relation between time and Being.

It became clear, therefore, that another language than the language of the philosophical tradition was required. But, as Heidegger stresses in *On the Way to Language*, the required transformation of language does not consist in the coining of new words or phrases,[14] as if the question would be to give better names to things and to change the structure of our statements in order to express the phenomena in a more adequate way. If this were the case, then it would mean that Heidegger had remained imprisoned in the logical and grammatical conception of language, a conception that the commentators of Wittgenstein's *Philosophical Investigations* legitimately call the Augustinian image of language, that is, a nominalistic conception of language for which words are merely names and language a mere lexicon.[15] The required transformation of language is not so much the transformation of language itself than the transformation of our relation to language. This means that we have to go through an experience of language that could teach us to give up our usual understanding of the relation between word and thing as a connection between two already constituted objects,[16] which implies the destitution of the logicist conception of language that remained prevalent since the constitution of formal logic in the Aristotelian schools. Already in his 1934 lecture-course, Heidegger made a distinction between words (*Worte*) and terms (*Wörter*)[17] and put the emphasis on the fact that language (*Sprache*) "can be found only there where it is spoken, i.e. amongst human beings."[18] Afterward, in his texts of the 1950s period, this distinction, which has become a fundamental one, allows him to show that words, in opposition to terms, which consist in phonemes or graphemes, are not beings and cannot be substituted for the things they designate, but are what originally gives them presence and being, so that speaking considered thus as the dimension of saying is the source of Being.[19]

Breaking in such a way with what can be named, following Wittgenstein, the "pictorial" conception of language, which is nothing else than the logicistic conception of language, we are led to leave aside the metaphysical opposition that has always prevailed in the Western tradition of thought between "being" and "becoming," and that has led to understanding being as something already present, as *vorhanden*, so that the question was to try afterward to express it. As soon as we attempt to inhabit language instead of using it as a mere means of communication, we leave aside what can be named the "metaphysics of presence," but in a meaning other than the one Derrida has provided for this expression, because it has to be understood here as the metaphysics of *Vorhandenheit*, of presence conceived after the model of substance. In his last writings, Heidegger gives the name of "onto-theo-logy" to this metaphysics that conceives being at the same time as a substantial presence and as the present ground of beings instead of seeing in it the advent of the clearing, of *aletheia*, which can only happen on the basis of *lethe*, that is, of an abyssal oblivion or occultation. We are thus opening ourselves to another conception of being, to being as *Ereignis*, insofar as this word, which we will not try to translate for the moment, names what defines the co-belonging of time and Being.

Language and *Ereignis:* this would be the name of the real theme of Heidegger's thought, a theme that does not replace the first one, "Being and Time," but expresses it in a more original manner, in the sense that it makes more explicit its central problem: the problem of the relation between the human being and Being. This is the hypothesis proposed here. But in order to verify this hypothesis, it is necessary to retrace in its major steps the itinerary of the Heideggerian questioning of language, which means that we have to go back to section 34 of *Being and Time.*

* * *

In this section, "Da-sein and discourse. Language," discourse is understood as a constitutive element of being-in-the-world, that is, as a specifically human mode of being. In this respect, Heidegger does not hesitate to rely upon the Greek definition of the human being as *zōon logon ekhon,* a definition that he nevertheless considers insufficient. However, this definition does not mean for him that the human being is a being able to speak in the sense of producing vocal sounds, but rather a being able to be open to itself and to the world. For Heidegger the subject-object relation is secondary, since what allows a subject to meet an object is the preliminary establishment of a soil common to both of them. World is this common soil; it comes before the object, since it is not, as says its traditional definition, the totality of beings but a structure of Dasein. World is neither the totality of all possible objects nor a structure of the subject, it is neither purely objective nor purely subjective; it is the structure of *Bedeutsamkeit,* of significance, on the basis of which there can be an intentional relation between subject and object. Heidegger shows in *Being and Time* that the being opened to the world of Dasein is not the result of an intellectual act but rather depends upon what is traditionally called "affectivity." In this respect, the existential to which Heidegger gives the name of *Befindlichkeit,* disposition, plays a fundamental role.[20] It is the fact of finding oneself and feeling oneself in the world, in the double, passive and active meaning of the pronominal verb *sich befinden,* which characterizes in an originary manner the existent being that can only first meet the individual thing on this basis. The fact that Dasein is always already opened to the world constitutes for him the true meaning of the "past," which is not once and for all accomplished and does not take the form of a substantial substratum, but on the contrary remains present in the sense that it is constantly taken up again by understanding whose projecting character constitutes being-in-the-world itself.[21] It is certainly possible to see in these two existentials,

Befindlichkeit and *Verstehen,* disposition and understanding, two new names of these separate sources of knowledge that are for Kant *Sinnlichkeit,* sensibility, and *Verstand,* understanding; but what is precisely new in Heidegger's existential analysis is the thinking of their co-originality, that is, of their intertwining, which implies, from a temporal standpoint, that past and future, thrownness and project, passivity and activity, cannot be separated and refer to each other.

But to these two existentials, Heidegger adds the existential of *Rede,* discourse,[22] which allows the articulation of the two first existentials, because existing involves essentially in itself the possibility of expliciting itself in a discourse about itself and the world. However, it is necessary not to identify discourse as existential structure and statement (*Aussage*), which is a derivative mode of discourse corresponding to the proper theoretical attitude and to the ontology of *Vorhandenheit,* of given presence. There is indeed a more originary explicitation than statement and that makes it possible. Explicitation (*Auslegung*), according to Heidegger, is the development of understanding,[23] that is, its concrete actualization, and is characterized by the "as-structure," which can become effective either through action or through discourse. At this originary level, we have to do with the "abilities" of what is at hand (*das Zuhandene*), with what Plato named *dunamai,* without any reference to the subject or substratum of these *dunamai,* since the tool (*Zeug*) is nothing outside these abilities: the hammer is immediately "understood" as useful for hammering, the nail as useful for hanging, and so forth. Explicitation can therefore be accomplished outside language, at the antepredicative level. It is only with the statement, that is, predication, that the subject or substratum is posited. But this requires a change, a modification, of our relation to world, which means that we have now to do with mere things and no longer with tools.[24] Nevertheless this change is not a complete break with the level of "taking care of" (*Besorgen*) that remains the fundamental mode of our relation to world; it is only a modification of this primary level, a modification of our "interest," to use here a Kantian concept, which becomes merely "theoretical." Therefore, taking care of becomes reduced to a mere look, it separates the individual being from all the others, posits it as a substratum or subject, to which defined "qualities" have to be added.

What is therefore opened in this way is the predicative realm, the "logical" realm in the Aristotelian sense of the word. This new level is precisely the level of the intentional relation of consciousness to the object, which is the result of a complete reversal of the relations governing everydayness. The explicitation of the tool was constituted by its abilities and usage, whereas now it is the thing as substratum that constitutes the basis of its predicates. Such a reversal reflects itself in the conception of language: language is now identified with the statement and the statement itself is considered as something *vorhanden,* something presently given. This explains why in the philosophical tradition, and already for the late Greeks, language is understood on the basis of *phōnē,* of the given presence of sound, of its "materiality," so that all language theory is at first a phonology. Heidegger shows that such a conception of language as a sum of given elements and as substance is the origin of the classical theory of truth defined as *adaequatio rei et intellectus,* as adequation between thing and intellect, since both of them are defined as two beings that have to be supposed as possessing the same ontological value.

The Greek word *logos* does not originally mean language, but discourse in the sense of *deloun,* making manifest.[25] In 1927, Heidegger put the emphasis on the fact that "the Greeks do not have a word for language," because "they 'at first' understood this phenomenon as discourse."[26] It seems that Heidegger understands the word *Rede* (discourse) on the basis of its etymology in connection with the Indo-European root **ar,* whose meaning is joining, articulating together, which corresponds up to a certain extent to the meaning of the word discourse that implies the articulation of several elements in a whole.[27] He defines it in fact as "the articulation of what can be understood,"[28] but this does not mean that discourse follows understanding as a kind of post-structuration of what has already been understood. On the contrary, understanding (*Verstehen*) is already in itself articulated, and in the same way, disposition (*Befindlichkeit*) always implies understanding. The three existentials that constitute Dasein's disclosedness, understanding, disposition, and discourse, are not based upon each other but are equi-original.[29] By contrast, language (*Sprache*) is not considered in *Being and Time* as an original phenomenon, but as a phenomenon based from an existential-ontological standpoint on discourse (*Rede*). This explains why the phenomenon of language could be analyzed in the form of the statement (*Aussage*) in section 33, that is, before language could be thematized: statement can be considered as an "extreme derivative of explicitation" because explicitation, as the development of understanding and as appropriation of what has been understood, is possible only on the basis of discourse.[30]

Discourse is therefore the condition of possibility of language and language is the worldly being of discourse, its vocal exteriorization, so that we have to say that "significations expand into words" instead of "word-things are provided with significations."[31] Language is therefore discovered inside the world as if it were a being at hand, that is, a mere instrument, whereas discourse, which does not necessarily need to be formulated, possesses the existential possibilities of hearing and keeping silence. For hearing cannot be identified with acoustic perception and in the same manner keeping silence cannot be identified with speechlessness. The perception of mere sounds is only possible on the basis of hearing, as speech is only possible on the basis of discourse, for hearing always means the understanding of a being at hand inside the world and not the interpretation of the internal sensations of a subject having only a mediate relation with the world. Keeping silence does not mean that the capacity for speaking is missing, but on the contrary pre-supposes the capacity for saying, that is, for showing, so that silence has to be seen as this originary mode of discourse that can even be given to understanding better than speech itself. It is therefore necessary not to identify the constitutive elements of discourse with those of speech and language: the first are existential characters, the second merely ontic ones.

But after this brief recapitulation of the analysis of discourse developed in section 34, the question remains: how could Heidegger retrospectively find in this section, in which only a subordinate position is assigned to language, "a reference to the *Wesensdimension,* the being dimension, of language"?[32] It is in fact only at the end of this section that Heidegger asks the question of the mode of being of language. Since the spoken or written words are discovered inside the world, they can be considered as beings at hand, so that language could seem to be a mere instrument of communication. But are handiness and instrumentality the proper mode of language? Is not language rather a mode of being of Dasein, an existential element similar to discourse, and not a mere existentiell and ontic phenomenon? Or has language neither the mode of being of an instrument nor the mode of the being of Dasein? If this were the case, then it could not be included among the different modes of being, but referred to Being itself in its unity. Heidegger does not develop, as is done here, the implications of this question, but he nevertheless finally declares that, because the object of the science of language remains obscure and undecided from the ontological viewpoint, time has come for philosophy to cease seeing in language the particular domain of the "philosophy of language" and to begin questioning the "things themselves," and this means to let the phenomenon of language show itself as itself.[33]

* * *

Through this re-reading of section 34 of the 1927 work, we have become aware of, in spite of the scarce indications relative to the phenomenon of language contained in it, the importance dedicated to discourse, which is not only a specific existential structure but one that is related to Dasein as a whole. Language itself, and not only discourse, can only become essentially thematized when it is no longer understood on the basis of the phonetic utterance of words, but when understood, just as discourse, on the basis of showing, that is, as saying. In section 7 of *Being and Time*, Heidegger, in accordance with Aristotle, understood the Greek *logos* as discourse and gave it the meaning of "making manifest what is in question in discourse."[34] In the following period, he developed his analysis of *logos* and undertook the "shaking" of traditional logic in order to lead *logos* back to its foundation, that is, to its initial meaning. He was then led to think language itself no longer as a purely phonetic process of expression and communication—this is in fact the traditional and metaphysical conception of language that is still prevailing to some extent in *Being and Time*—but as a showing and as the advent itself of the clearing. As he declared in 1946 to Jean Beaufret: "In the unfolding of its being (*Wesen*), language is not the utterance of an organism; nor is it the expression of a living being. Nor can it ever be thought according to the unfolding of its being (*wesensgerecht*) in terms of its sign-character, perhaps not even in terms of the character of signification. Language is the clearing-concealing advent of Being itself."[35]

In the second of the three lectures he gave in 1957 again under the title "*Das Wesen der Sprache,*" "The Unfolding of the Being of Language," when commenting on a verse from Stefan George that says that "Where word breaks off no thing may be," Heidegger stresses that precisely this relation between thing and word, which "is among the earliest matters to which

Western thinking gives voice and word . . . assaults thinking in such an overpowering manner that it announces itself in a single word," the word *logos,* which "speaks simultaneously as the name for Being and for Saying."[36] In his lecture-courses from the beginning of the 1940s, especially those dedicated to the pre-Socratic thinkers, Heidegger had in fact already begun to go back to a more originary meaning of *logos* than the Aristotelian one. He explained that what happened in the beginning of Western thinking with Heraclitus, with regard to the leading word *logos,* is the experience of the being of language as *die lesende Lege,* the gathering laying. Language thus means: "to gather what is present and let it lay in front in its presence." To this Heidegger adds: "The Greeks *dwelt* in this unfolding of the being of language. But they never *thought* it, not even Heraclitus."[37] This explains why, when they tried to define the nature of language, they at first understood it as based on a phonetic process. Language was therefore defined by Aristotle as a *phōnē sēmantikē,* as a sound that signifies, and since then language has constantly been seen in this perspective, as is still shown in the title Husserl gave to his first *Logical Investigation:* "Expression and Signification." The superiority of the Greek language, which was stressed by Heidegger already in 1935 in his lecture-course *An Introduction to Metaphysics,*[38] and later in his 1955 Cerisy lecture on *What Is Philosophy?*[39] has in fact nothing to do with a specific quality that would only belong to the Greek idiom and would make it more proper than any other idiom to say Being. It is necessary in this respect to recall Heidegger's statement in "The Saying of Anaximander," a text written in 1946: "Being speaks everywhere and always through all languages. The difficulty is not so much to find in thinking the word for Being, but it is rather to purely retain the found word in proper thinking."[40]

The superiority of the Greek language comes merely from the fact that the Greeks *dwelt* in their language, which means that, by means of the Greek's words, they were put in relation with the "things themselves" instead of remaining prisoners in a realm of arbitrary signs. They did not possess a language superior to all the other ones, but they had a different relation to their language, a relation of dwelling and not a mere instrumental one. This is the reason why they invented philosophy: because dwelling in their language did not mean for them to be in a complete familiarity with it and be able to dominate it totally, but on the contrary to be opened to its strangeness and be forced to appropriate it, that is, as Heidegger emphasizes in his 1942–1943 lecture-course on Parmenides, to translate Greek into Greek, as is always the case for each thinker with regard to his own idiom.[41] For, as Heidegger explains in his "Letter on Humanism," when commenting on Heraclitus's fragment 119, "*ēthos anthrōpōi daimōn*," authentic dwelling, which is named in Greek *ēthos*, does not imply only to be familiar with the world in which one dwells but requires also and above all else the capacity for perceiving the unfamiliar (*das Ungeheure*) in the familiar (*im Geheuren*), the *daimōn* in the *anthropos*, that is, the divine in the human being and the stranger in the friend.[42] Dwelling means in fact to be able to maintain distance inside proximity and to make room for strangeness (*Unheimlichkeit*) in one's own native place (*in der Heimat*).

But following the Greeks who have shown, without, however, being able to think it, that language is a dimension of Being, Heidegger is led to completely inverse the definition that has at first been assigned to language in the Western tradition. Whereas the human being behaved up to now as if he was the creator and master of language, it seems that on the contrary it is language that now reigns over him.[43] The instrumental relation that the metaphysical man has with language seems thus to be diametrically reversed, in the sense that it is now language that "needs" man and "employs" him (*braucht*).[44] However, such a reversal from the metaphysical viewpoint could only lead, as Heidegger himself remarks in connection with Sartre's existentialism in his "Letter on Humanism," to a new form of metaphysics rather than to its destitution, because "the reversal of a metaphysical statement remains a metaphysical statement."[45] This would therefore only mean the return of the metaphysical chimera in the form of a language completely separated from human speech, thus elevated "into a fantastic, self-sustained being which cannot be encountered anywhere as long as our reflection on language remains sober."[46] The risk of the return of metaphysics is clearly implied in the tautological statements by which Heidegger formulates the new being of language: "language speaks" (*Die Sprache spricht*),[47] "language is language."[48] It is also involved in the goal he assigns to himself in *On the Way to Language:* to reflect on language itself and only on it, since "language itself is language and nothing else."[49] The attempt to show that language has no other basis than language itself could lead to idealize language and to a new kind of Platonism. This is a risk that is implied in the phenomenological way of thinking, that is, the

Greek mode of thinking, as became clear when the reproach of a "realism of essences" was directed against Husserl after the publication of *Logical Investigations.*[50] But if it can be shown that the Husserlian essence is not a Platonic hypostasis, because it is not similar to a real being, as Plato himself also explained, this does not mean that Husserl did not remain a Platonist in a deeper sense in his eidetic mode of thinking. Heidegger breaks in a more decisive manner with the eidetic mode of thinking and therefore places himself "beyond" the Greeks and their understanding of what is philosophy, that is, as a *matter of vision,* as he stresses in one of his last lectures.[51] This explains why, after having shown that in order to think the being of language, "it is needful that language vouchsafe itself to us," he undertakes to reverse the phrase "*Wesen der Sprache*" (the being of language) into "*Sprache des Wesens*" (the language of being), stressing that the word *Wesen* does not have the same meaning in both phrases, since in the first one it has the traditional meaning of *essentia,* whereas in the second one *Wesen* is heard as a verb, and means "to perdure and persist."[52] What Heidegger now means by "*Wesen der Sprache*" is no longer the "essence" of language, understood as its non-historical "aspect" that appears to the human being from which, as a mortal, he is therefore separated, but the "advent of language," the unfolding of its being that in itself requires human speech. This transformation of the understanding of what is *Wesen* is therefore already in itself the thinking of *Ereignis.*

Since the publication of *Beiträge zur Philosophie,*[53] we know that under the name of *Ereignis,* Heidegger developed from 1936 onward a new conception of Being that is no longer considered the ground of beings, but on the basis of an abyssal occultation, the advent of a clearing, which is not the result of man's projection but in which he stands. In the perspective of this new conception of Being, the human being is no longer considered as the thrown ground of the clearing but as the being that remains exposed to it and receives from it his own being. Whereas in 1927 man's projection and transcendence is at the origin of the clearing of Being, it is now understood as this clearing in which man stands and to which he has to correspond (*ent-sprechen*). *Das Verhältnis,* the re-ference between Being and man, should not be understood as a mere relation between two separate entities but as the manner according to which Being withdraws itself in the letting be of Dasein. In his 1957 lecture on "The Principle of Identity," Heidegger names *Er-eignis,* the advent of propriation, this co-belonging of

Being and man, which is neither coincidence nor dialectical relation but being for each other and the con-stellation of Being and man.[54] He explains there that *Ereignis* cannot be considered an event taking place inside the world, as the ordinary meaning of this word suggests, but as *singulare tantum,* as what happens in a unique manner and is nothing else than the opening of the clearing in which all beings can appear and come to what is proper (*Eigen*) to them. But this *Er-eigen,* this propriation is not a process that could take place from itself; on the contrary, it essentially requires man's participation. Propriation should therefore be understood, according to the true etymology of the word *Ereignis,* which does not come from the word *eigen* (proper) but from the word *Auge* (eye), as the call of Being's look addressed to man: *das Ereignis er-aügt den Menschen—Ereignis* calls man in looking at him.[55] In his 1959 lecture on "The Way to Language," Heidegger declares that *Ereignis* "grants to mortals their abode within the unfolding of their being (*Wesen*), so that they may be capable of being those who speak."[56] *Ereignis* unfolds itself therefore as language. From there, it becomes possible to understand that language is not only a human capacity. It is true that language has been represented for a very long time on the basis of speech as a corporeal and sensible phenomenon, as shown in the terms *glossa, lingua, language,* as well as in the term *Mundart,* the German word for dialect, which means literally "mouth's manners." However, for Heidegger the question is not to oppose language and speech and consider the vocal utterance as a secondary phenomenon, as did Saussure, the founder of modern linguistics, but to wonder if explaining in a physiological way what belongs to corporeality in the phenomenon of language can be sufficient, and if it is possible to reduce it to the metaphysical domain of the sensible as opposed to the intelligible.[57] What constitutes for him what is proper to the voice is the fact that it belongs to the earth, as Hölderlin stresses when he suggests seeing in language "the flower of mouth," in which "the earth blossoms toward the bloom of sky."[58] What resounds in the voice and constitutes the terrestrial element of language should therefore be understood on the basis of the co-belonging of earth and sky, which are no longer opposed in a metaphysical way as the sensible and the intelligible but refer to each other as the Open dimension (the sky), which requires the obscurity of what withdraws into itself (the earth) in order to appear. The advent that Heidegger calls the *Geviert,* the fourfold that is world, that is, the face to face of sky and earth, of mortals and divinities, opens itself and is in itself a silent advent, but it is precisely to this *Ereignis der Stille,* the advent of stillness, that the mortals that we are belong.[59] For it is only as mortals, that is, as beings able to experience death, and only as such beings, that we have to respond to it and to let resound our voice. It is therefore this *Gelaüt der Stille,* this ringing of stillness, which makes of human language *die Sprache des Wesens,* the language of the unfolding of Being.[60]

But here, Heidegger stresses, "The relation of being (*Wesensverhältnis*) between death and language flashes up, but remains still unthought."[61] What remains to be thought is the fact that death as the shelter of being[62] and the nocturnal source of all light is what grants to world its realm and to the human being its existence and speaking capacity. For it is as if it were on the lips of death itself that, as Hölderlin says, "words like flowers leap alive,"[63] words whose sonorous blooming lets appear, rather than breaking it, the boundless silence from which it is born.

NOTES

1. Martin Heidegger, *Logik als Frage nach dem Wesen der Sprache, Gesamtausgabe,* vol. 38 (Frankfurt am Main: Klostermann, 1998). In the following referred to as GA 38.

2. Martin Heidegger, *Beiträge zur Philosophie (Vom Ereignis)* (Frankfurt am Main: Klostermann, 1989), §165, 287.

3. Martin Heidegger, *Vorträge und Aufsätze* (Pfullingen: Neske, 1959), 38 and 50.

4. Martin Heidegger, *Was heisst Denken?* (Tübingen: Niemeyer, 1954), 100.

5. Martin Heidegger, *Unterwegs zur Sprache* (Pfullingen: Neske), 1959, 93. In the following referred to as US. See *On the Way to Language,* trans. Peter D. Hertz (New York: Harper & Row, 1971), 8.

6. GA 38: §4.

7. Martin Heidegger, *Sein und Zeit* (Tübingen: Niemeyer, 1963), §34, 161. In the following referred to as SZ. We will refer to the English translation by J. Stambaugh, *Being and Time* (Albany: SUNY Press, 1996), which we will modify on some points.

8. Ibid., §18, 87.

9. US, 91ff., trans. 6.

10. US, 93, trans. 7.

11. US, 137, trans. 41–42.

12. Martin Heidegger, *Basic Writings,* 2nd ed., ed. and trans. David Farrell Krell (San Francisco: Harper & Row, 1993), 222.

13. Ibid., 231.

14. US, 267, trans. 135.

15. See L. Wittgenstein, *Philosophische Untersuchungen* (Frankfurt am Main: Suhrkamp, 1967), 13. The first section of the book is a quotation from Augustine, *Confessions,* 1, 8.

16. US, 170, trans. 66.

17. GA 38: §7, 23.

18. Ibid., §8, 24.

19. US, 169, trans. 66. Heidegger defines there the poet's vocation as the vocation to the word as the source, the bourn of Being. See also the famous passage of *Was heisst Denken?* 87–89, about the distinction between *Worte* and *Wörter.*

20. See SZ §29. We choose to translate *Befindlichkeit* as "disposition" rather than "attunement" as does the English translator, because this word can be heard in the same double, passive and active meaning as the German *Befindlichkeit.* Attunement could in fact be considered a better translation for *Stimmung* than "mood," because the primary meaning of the word is "tuning."

21. Ibid., §31, 145.

22. Ibid., §28, 133.

23. Ibid., §32, 148. We choose to translate *Auslegung* as the neologism "explicitation" rather than "interpretation" as does the English translator, because the verb *auslegen* means originally to lay out, to display. Heidegger himself uses (§42, 149) the word *Ausdrücklichkeit* (explicitness) to define the structure of *Auslegung.*

24. We choose to translate *Zeug* as "tool" and not as does the English translator as "useful thing," in order to stress the fact that a *Zeug* can never be identified with a thing. The translation as "tool" is however not completely adequate, because this word originally means something indefinite that can be used to produce (*zeugen*) something else.

25. Ibid., §7, 32.

26. Ibid., §34, 165.

27. Discourse comes from the Latin verb *discurrere,* and the original meaning is to run here and there.

28. Ibid., §34, 161.

29. Ibid.

30. Ibid., §34, 160–161.

31. Ibid., §34, 161.

32. *Basic Writings,* 222.

33. SZ, §34, 166.

34. Ibid., §7 b, 32.

35. *Basic Writings,* 230, translation modified.

36. *On the Way to Language,* 80.

37. "Logos," *Vorträge und Aufsätze,* 228. This lecture, held in 1951, takes up again a thematic developed in 1944 in a lecture-course dedicated to Heraclitus. In English "*Logos* (Heraclitus, Fragment B 50)," in *Early Greek Thinking,* trans. David Farrell Krell (New York: Harper & Row, 1984), 77.

38. Martin Heidegger, *Einführung in die Metaphysik* (Tübingen: Niemeyer, 1953), 43.

39. M Heidegger, *Was ist das—die Philosophie?* (Pfullingen: Neske, 1956), 20: "The Greek language, and only it, is *logos.*"

40. Martin Heidegger, *Holzwege* (Frankfurt am Main: Klostermann, 1950), 338.

41. Martin Heidegger, *Parmenides, Gesamtausgabe* 54 (Frankfurt am Main, Klostermann, 1992), 17.

42. *Basic Writings,* 256 sq.

43. See "Building Dwelling Thinking," *Basic Writings*, 348: "Man acts as though *he* were the shaper and master of language, while in fact *language* remains the master of man."

44. US, 260, trans. 129.

45. *Basic Writings*, 232.

46. US, 255–256, trans. 125.

47. Ibid., 254, trans.124. See also "Die Sprache," US 12, 20. (text of a 1950 lecture that has not been included in the English translation).

48. Ibid., 12–13.

49. Ibid.

50. See E. Husserl, *Ideas Pertaining to a Pure Phenomenology and to a Phenomenological Philosophy*, trans. F. Kersten (The Hague: Marinus Nijhoff, 1983), §22: "The Reproach of Platonic Realism. Essence and Concept."

51. See Martin Heidegger, "The End of Philosophy and the Task of Thinking," in *Basic Writings*, 448, where it is said that *aletheia* has to be thought "above and beyond the Greek" as "the clearing of self-concealing."

52. Ibid., 201, trans. 94–95.

53. *Beiträge zur Philosophie (Vom Ereignis)*, a text written between 1936 and 1938, was published in 1989 (see n. 2, above).

54. Martin Heidegger, *Identität und Differenz* (Pfullingen: Neske, 1957), 24 and 28–29.

55. Ibid., 28–29.

56. US, 259, trans.128.

57. Ibid., 204, trans. 98.

58. Ibid., 206, trans. 99.

59. Ibid., 214, trans. 106.

60. Ibid., 216, trans. 108.

61. Ibid., 215, trans. 107.

62. "Das Ding," in *Vorträge und Ausätze*, 177.

63. F. Hölderlin, "Bread and Wine," in *Poems & Fragments*, trans. Michael Hamburger (New York: Cambridge University Press, 1986), 249.

THIRTEEN

Dark Celebration: Heidegger's Silent Music

Peter Hanly

> You mustn't cry
> Says the music.
> Otherwise
> No-one
> Says
> Anything.
> —INGEBORG BACHMANN

We shall begin with a letter. It dates from the winter months of 1950 and is addressed from Heidegger to Hannah Arendt.[1] The letter reflects, as such a letter might, on the passage of time, on renewed affections, on political circumstances. But at the top of the letter, before it is even begun, before its addressee's name is inscribed, are the following words:

> Beethoven, op. 111, Adagio, Conclusion.

Just that, no more: then, the letter itself. It is almost as if the music, summoned by its inscription, were hovering over the discourse of the letter. As if the music might enclose the words that are to be thought. Beyond and before those words, the music might be both their source and their destination—a presence both silent and resounding, enfolding everything that is spoken. From out of this possibility, a question looms up: a question about music itself, about the kinds of connections it might maintain with language. More specifically still, we might find a way to pose a question regarding the status of music in Heidegger's discourse, of its presence or absence, its elision or its inclusion.[2]

Immediately, the evidence marshals itself against such an undertaking. If we wanted to summarize the objections, we might listen to Philippe

Lacoue-Labarthe, who tells us that "Heidegger's attention to music is, *we know,* practically nil," and continues: "allusions and references to music are extremely rare, and mostly conventional."[3] Now, the assertion concerning the absence of extended discussion of music in Heidegger's work is undeniably correct: after all, even his most massive contribution to the understanding of the artwork makes only the most meager and fleeting direct references to music. Further, and more compelling still, the longest and most specific of these apparently rare and slight engagements would seem to speak with unequivocal negativity of a dominance of music within the field of art. In the Nietszche lectures, and in sympathy with Nietszche's rejection of Wagner, Heidegger writes with a kind of fury of "the domination of art as music, and thereby the domination of the pure state of feeling—the tumult and delirium of the senses . . . the plunge into frenzy and disintegration into sheer feeling as redemptive."[4] If one were to conclude, as Lacoue-Labarthe does, that, insofar as it represents Heidegger's lengthiest explicit address to musical experience as such, this passage is clear evidence of Heidegger's negative attitude to music in general, then no amount of anecdotal support, it would seem, can resist the conclusion that music simply does not play a significant role in Heidegger's thinking.

Certainly, our endeavor must recognize this silence. From the outset, the absence of explicit engagement must be acknowledged. Music is not "addressed" by Heidegger as a topic, as a realm of human experience: it never becomes the subject of a discourse. Lacoue-Labarthe suggests that for the history of philosophy music has played the role of "rebel object par excellence . . . continuously and silently indicating a limit to philosophy, a secret menace to its full deployment."[5] In that sense, to refuse to engage music would be simply to play out again structures laid out by ancient ambivalence. The question, then, becomes the following: is Heidegger's lack of engagement simply another manifestation of that kind of suspicion, a holding-at-arms-length, a necessary blind spot?

The force of the "no" with which we intend to answer that question can be supplied by a moment from one of Heidegger's own texts: a passage crucially overlooked by Lacoue-Labarthe.[6] Toward the end of the lecture-course *Der Satz vom Grund,* Heidegger addresses directly a new "tonality" (*Tonart*) with which he invites us to listen to the words "*nichts ist ohne Grund*" such that a different inflection might occasion a "leap" (*Sprung*) into a different kind of hearing, one that might allow the *ist* and the *Grund* to play in resonance with one another. It is only, says Heidegger, if we are able to push through the polyvalence of the word *Satz,* such that it includes its *musical* sense (*Satz* as musical "movement"), that we might "achieve for the first time a full relation to the *Satz vom Grund.*"[7] A kind of thinking is to be made possible in this hearing, then, a thinking that is possible only in and through a kind of music. There is an intimacy of thought and music, here, that steps beyond "influence" or "inspiration." It is not that, under the influence of music, one might be provoked to think different kinds of thought, which could be then detached from their musical inspiration. Rather, an utterly new possibility of thinking is engendered here, one that cannot be detached from the resounding together (*Einklang*) of the words themselves, one in which thinking is not so much to become musical, as music is to become a kind of thinking.

If music is to make possible a kind of thinking, then clearly the relation of thinking and music will not be such that music can ever become a "subject" of that thinking. Rather, if music is to be uncovered, is to be found at work in Heidegger's texts, its operation will be brought to light only in pointing to a kind of play, an oscillation in which one might glimpse, briefly, the movement of a changing register of thought.[8] This will mean stepping beyond merely "exposing" the absence of an explicit engagement with music in Heidegger's thinking, and then attributing this lack either to accidental oversight or inadequate consideration. Rather, music will belong to thought precisely in such a way as to preclude its becoming an object of that thought. The silence that governs the presence of music in Heidegger's thinking will, then, belong to the very core of that presence. It is within the reflections on language that the play of a modality governed by the silent presence of music might be brought to light. What will be addressed here, then, are certain operations within the texts that seem to gesture toward an opening within which this play can be seen. And the first and most transparent locus of such an opening will be the emergence of *song.*

Song

What is song? What does it mean for the word that it is changed into song? Stretched out along the time of its utterance, drawn out of itself into a resonance that overwhelms the opposition of sound and sense, the word that shifts register into song undergoes a transformation that reaches toward a fundamental experience of voice, toward the encounter of language and time. Heidegger's sense of this transformation is manifest at different moments within his reflections on Rilke, on Hölderlin, on Stefan George. The shift is witnessed in each case from within the idiom of the dialogue Heidegger has engaged; the transformation of word into song is encountered, not imposed. Hence, the context of each encounter must be understood within the structure from which it emerges. The contextual immanence of these moments renders impossible any project that would seek to articulate a unitary understanding of this transformation, to extrapolate a single sense from its different occasions. Rather, what would be demanded is that we allow the different senses of this transformation to play in resonance with one another, precisely to echo and resound together.

Such a resounding can orient itself around the transformation of word into song that is explicit in Heidegger's reflections on Stefan George. The shift is occasioned by a particular experience of the word, echoing out of a narrative poem, "*Das Wort.*" The experience is one of collapse: the disruption, the dislocation of a rhythm that sustains the relation of word and thing. The poet-narrator of George's verse is one who experiences a kind of process in this relation: the process of naming. He speaks, in mythic voice, of "wonders from afar or from dreams" that he brings to the "border" (*Saum*). An impatient waiting is described, a hovering at the limit, at the edge of language (and we must hear, in this border/limit, Heidegger's sense of *Grenz,* πέρας: that from out of which thought gathers itself), as he offers his dark treasure to the "grey norn," the source of names. But this process, the rhythm of this naming, is suddenly interrupted, dislocated. In George's narrative the poet returns from a journey with a "treasure rich and delicate," for which no name can be found. In this disturbance of the rhythm of searching, attending, naming, Heidegger writes: "another, higher, rule (*Walten*) of the word glances abruptly at the poet."[9] Why? Because in the absence of word, the treasure itself vanishes, precipitating an utter disorientation, one that shatters the rhythm of his relation to language, that brings him face to face with "the terrifying . . . the undreamed-of." The poet, whose connection to language is bound up in the process of discovery, retrieval, and naming, must abandon this prior orientation. He must suffer the de-stabilization of the link between word and thing, which becomes inverted in such a way as to bind them together with a wholly unexpected force. Suddenly, word becomes something other than a name for what is already present. In the treasure's vanishing is revealed a different order: "no thing," he learns, "may *be* where word breaks off." The poet will henceforth speak from out of this disorientation, this fracture, out of an experience of the word that is bound up with loss, with mourning (*Trauer*), with "abandonment" (*Verzichten*). And to speak from out of such a loss is to *sing*:

> Because the word is shown in a different, higher rule, the relation to the word must also undergo a transformation. Saying attains to a different articulation, a different μέλος, a different tone.... *For this poem is a song.*[10]

It is thus that a kind of music enters the scene: in the face of an abyssal disruption of language as naming, a new kind of utterance is engendered, an utterance in which the familiar orientations of sound and sense are displaced and re-configured. Song is the locus of this displacement, an utterance that speaks out of fracture and loss. Music will enter into language, as song, at the instant in which the relation of word and thing hesitates, falters. And this appearance will have consequences: the irruption of music will be that around which the oppositions of sound and meaning, speaking and listening, voice and silence, will gather, coalesce, and collapse.

The Hölderlin readings, too, and in particular the reading of "*Wie Wenn am Feiertage*,"[11] equally engage a fractured correspondence of word and thing. The poet, here, is one who is always both with and beyond what he names, echoing, re-sounding, and anticipating what Hölderlin calls "*die wunderbar Allgegenwärtig*," the "wonderfully all-present."[12] In Heidegger's reading, the poet belongs, co-responds (*ent-spricht*) to this "omnipresence" to the extent that this presence—Hölderlin's "nature"—is always, precisely, in anticipation of itself. Once again, the classical mechanics of poetic response—description, representation, imitation—are displaced in this anticipatory belonging-together, in which the poetic utterance—the naming—is intertwined with the unfolding of natural process. Hölderlin's lines become exemplary in this respect:

> But now the day breaks; I waited and saw it come.
> And what I saw; holy be my word.[13]

The poet names nature in its unfolding, and in so doing co-responds with the event of that unfolding, with that awakening. Co-respondence, here, is the name for an abyssal disruption of a logic of precedence that would insist on the priority of either word or thing in the generation of the poetic utterance. If the utterance of the poet is to co-respond with and to this unfolding, then that utterance will be subject to the same "upheaval," the same disordering (*Aufruhr*) that the event itself is exposed to. "The awakening," in Heidegger's appropriation of Hölderlin, "happens in 'storms' that 'drift on between heaven and earth.'"[14] In utterance, the poetic word is exposed to the same trauma of awakening, and experiences what Heidegger calls an *Erschütterung*, a shudder that echoes out of Kant[15] in subtle and complex ways. The exposure of the word to this "shock" is an exposure to the richness, the abundance of an inceptive moment (*Reichtum des Anfänglichen*), which, says Heidegger, "grants (the) word *such an excess of meaning as can scarcely be uttered*."[16] It is out of this excess, and this improbability, that song is born—a fragile thing, the barest possibility that an utterance might resonate with the shock of inception:

> Song must spring from the awakening of nature . . . If it shares in this way the "awakening inspiration," then the breath of the coming of the holy drifts in it.[17]

In the George readings, song had rung from out of a gesture of abandonment (*verzichten*), of renunciation, that embraced a fractured longing. Within the sway of Hölderlin, song shudders forth from an unstable correspondence of event and name, a disruptive instant in which the word is overwhelmed in a gesture of excess. "The singer is blind," remarks Heidegger, in the reading of *Heimkunft*—a beautiful remark, born of Hölderlin, that captures the traumatic complexity of dazzlement and loss that occasions song. The "scarcely utterable excess of meaning" from which song is born in "*Wie Wenn am Feiertage*" becomes, here, the blindness of the singer, the shudder of whose song is so saturated with loss and longing that it sings entirely beyond, without words: "*ein wortloses Lied*." The singer reaches so far into this loss that his song twists free of the word altogether:

> Poetic "singing," because it lacks the proper, the naming word, remains still a wordless song—a string-music.[18]

Sound

It is only in relation to *sound* that a transformation, a slippage from word into song, can be conceived. Even if the song never achieves utterance, even if one were to imagine a "silent singing," it is only in relation to sound that such an imagining could occur. Thus, the relation of language to its sounding must be central to this movement. Heidegger, in fact, goes further: it is only in the instant of its utterance, in its enaction, that word becomes song: "the song is sung, not after it has come to be, but rather: in the singing the song begins to be a song."[19] Song does not emerge out of language by taking up words in their pre-given fullness and transforming them. To describe such an operation would be to "fail to understand the higher meaning of song," to reduce it to a merely "retroactive setting to music of what is spoken and written."[20] Heidegger will emphasize often the necessity of *listening* to the poem, in a way that cannot be separated out from its performance, its sounding: indeed, *Time and Being* opens precisely with an appeal to just such a listening: "if it were possible right now to have Georg Trakl's poem *Septet of Death* recited to us, *perhaps even by the poet himself.*"[21]

The transformation of word into song leads us, then, necessarily, to confront the question of voice, of voicing. But what will determine voice, here, is a conception that will radically displace the classical opposition of sound and sense. It is precisely Heidegger's intent to render impossible the determination of language as the "manifestation in sound of inner emotions."[22] Such a classical determination would revolve around the notion of language as "expression," and render utterance subordinate to intention. What must be effected, then, is clearly not a reversal of this hierarchy: to invert the determination of language as "vocal expression" in order to emphasize intelligibility and intention would be merely to re-iterate and reconstruct the classical opposition of inner and outer. He writes: "it should in no way appear that we wish to belittle vocal sounds as . . . the mere sensuousness of language, in favor of what is called the meaning."[23] Quite the contrary: "it belongs to language to sound and ring and vibrate, to hover and tremble, just as much as it does for what is spoken to carry meaning."[24] The sounding of language, then, will re-emerge as central but can do so only within a deconstruction of its metaphysical opposition to sense, to intelligibility. Sound must be involved, must be stitched into the fabric of language in a wholly new way.

If song, too, belongs to the voice—to the instant of a transformative utterance—it must equally do so in the orbit of a thinking that refuses easy recourse to a vocabulary of "expression." It must be clear, however, that, in that song utters the dislocation of language exposed to the fracturing of the relation of word and thing, this kind of utterance cannot be understood as a recourse to the "merely sensuous." Song can never be in opposition to language in such a way as to restore or renew the opposition between sound and sense. If music emerges from a dislocation of language, such an emergence must not be determined as a sort of sonic rarefaction, a "musicalization" of language. Within this kind of structure, the "affinity (*Verwandschaft*) of song and speech" can be thought only in terms of the "melody and rhythm of language,"[25] as if these might be some kind of ornament, an unnecessary addition to a plenitude of meaning. But equally, a simple reversal of this supplementarity will be inadequate: a conception of word that prioritizes its pure aural resonance, its "musicality," leaves intact the opposition to meaning, merely re-organizing the hierarchy. Instead, the displacement from out of which the music of language—song—emerges will mean that the entire conception of the relation of sound and language will have to be re-thought.

How, then, is the event of sound in language to be understood? "Language is the flower of the mouth,"[26] writes Heidegger, citing Hölderlin, and in so doing ensures that whatever understanding of the sounding instant of language we may reach will not be separate from the body, from a corporeality that directly pertains to the human. But this is not a corporeality that locates the body as the repository of an interior expressive plenitude. Rather, the *Mundarten* that Heidegger recalls are the loci, not of modes of expression, but of a relation that binds the instant of utterance to the earth: "body and mouth belong to the earth's flow and growth," he writes.[27] The sounding of language becomes the event of this bindedness; not as something to be grasped, to be used, but as the happening of a relation. We might here, perhaps, listen to Jean-Luc Nancy, as he describes the "listening subject," who is, says Nancy, "perhaps no subject at all, except as the place of resonance, of its infinite tension and rebound, the amplitude of sonorous deployment and the slightness of its simultaneous redeployment."[28]

To the event of the sounding word (which means, also, to listening), to its irruption (Heidegger will call this the *Aufriß*—in which one must hear more the incision, cut, the tearing of language than its "design") belongs an excess that gathers and hovers around it:

> What it says wells up from the once spoken and the as yet still unspoken saying that flows through the tear (*Aufriß*) of language.[29]

The excess is the excess of the soundless, of soundless-ness, which belongs to the event of the sounded word. The poet will be he who listens to this excess—waiting, attending—in the co-respondent expectancy determined from the Hölderlin readings. The *singing* of the poet, then—belonging, as it does, utterly to a transformation in the sounded word—must belong in an equally originary way to this sense of the sounding of language. It will be the event of the sounding of language that keeps closest to the absence that emerges out of the failure of the name. It must belong, too, within the embrace of the soundless. *Aufriß*—the cut, the tearing of the word—and *zerbrechen/zerschlag*—its breaking, its shattering—become the twin axes of the constellation within which song emerges and collapses:[30] a song, says Heidegger, "shattered even in its sounding (*im Klang schon zerschlug*)."[31]

"*Step* (that is, way), and *call* and *breath* vibrate around the rule of the word," writes Heidegger, in an extreme recension of the opening poem of George's *Das Lied*.[32] And these three will be addressed in turn, and seen, each one, to circulate around a relation to the soundlessness that both belongs to and determines the possibility of song. *Breath* speaks to the silent undergirding that draws language into the corporeality of the *Mundarten*. George sings of the "secret breath of melancholy": the systole and diastole, the give and take, the silence in which I catch my breath, the silence of a respiration that belongs to the occasion of song—"*ein Hauch um nichts*."[33]

Call responds to the re-situating of listening that flows through *Unterwegs zur Sprache:* "we let the soundless voice come to us, claiming, reaching out and calling for the sound that is already kept open for us."[34] The rethinking, the re-configuring of the relation of sound to language involves, with equal intensity, a re-structuring of the relation of speaking and listening. No longer will the listening that belongs originarily to language be a listening that "accompanies." Rather, we listen, necessarily, in advance of our words: "speaking . . . is a listening, not *while*, but *before* we speak."[35] *Call,* then, expresses the polyvalent senses of a listening that is at once an attending, a being-called by language, and a reaching out into language, a calling-to, stretched toward the possibility of the sounded word.[36]

If speaking is to fold into a listening, if speaking is, precisely, to *be* a listening, then Heidegger must articulate the silence of listening as the very essence of the spoken, as the dark wellspring of the word. But this silence must be one that reaches beyond an opposition to sound. "Silence

(*Schweigen*)," writes Heidegger, "is already a corresponding (*Entsprechen*)":[37] a simple opposition cannot sustain the interweaving of the spoken with the unspoken. "In no way merely the soundless,"[38] the originary, impossible absence to which both the spoken and the unspoken always already correspond is named by Heidegger "*die Stille*": the stillness. The abyssal beyond of the opposition of sound and silence, "stillness" will escape any determination as simply a more originary undergirding of the sounding of language. The stillness itself rings, resounds, resonates. Language does not stand in opposition to this stillness, as if to once more re-establish a metaphysical opposition at a more originary level. Rather, language *is* the resonance of this stillness: "Language speaks as the ringing of stillness (*Geläut der Stille*),"[39] says Heidegger. Once again, we confront the inadequacy of the determinations of sound in language in terms that would restrict it to an acoustical phenomenon:

> The phonetic-acoustic-physiological explanation of the sounds of language does not experience their origin in ringing stillness and even less how sound is determined/voiced (*Be-stimmung*) by that stillness.[40]

Sound, then, the sounding of language, of voice, will emerge from the ringing, the resonance, the resounding of a stillness that it must paradoxically break precisely in order to be itself. The "sounding, and vibrating, and ringing"[41] of language, and thus of poetry, of song, is the breaking, the shattering, of the stillness to which it belongs.

Rhythm

In Heidegger's three-word recension of George's *Lied*—"step (that is, way), and call, and breath"—it is "*step*" that ventures in the most radical direction. Described, in context, simply as a "journey through the domain of Saying," the seemingly casual, parenthetical association of *Schritt* with *Weg* in fact opens onto an entirely new dimension. Addressing the sense of *Weg* that determines the title of the last essay of his reflections on language, Heidegger insists on an archaic inflection of *Weg* that makes of it the product of a transitive verb: *Weg*, in other words, not as a directional structure, but as a process, *Be-wëgung* (*way-making*). And it is *Be-wëgung* that comes to determine the movement within language to which the irruption of the sounded word belongs:

> The way-making brings *Sprache* (the essence of language) as *Sprache* (saying) into *Sprache* (into the sounded word).[42]

The circular, re-iterative structure of this formulation insists on a refusal, here as elsewhere, of a simple directionality within the *Bewëgung* that would risk returning the sounding of the word to a process of externalization. Language, here, is always—completely, and at once—all of its different moments: it is both the stillness and its shattering, both the sounding and the silence. But how, nonetheless, to resist locating a single point of origin for the way-making that is language? How to avoid describing *die Stille* as, again and again, a plenitude that functions as originating source for an utterance that "exteriorizes" itself in the sounded word? Precisely by uncoupling the opposition of motion and rest, by making of stillness itself, not the source of movement (*Bewegung*), but the very movement itself.[43] "What is stillness?" asks Heidegger. And, in refusing a simple equivalence with soundless-ness ("merely the lack of the movement of sounding"), and the consequent invocation of a "restfulness" (*Ruhe*) that would "precede" such a movement, Heidegger answers that, indeed, stillness is rest, but:

> As stilling of stillness, rest is, properly thought, always more moving (*bewegter*) than all movement (*Bewegung*) and always more active than any agitation.[44]

To install movement at the heart of absence, agitation (*Regung*) at the heart of what is most at peace (*Ruhig*), is to defer indefinitely the question of origin. The way-making in which word comes to sound can no longer be a movement that originates out of the pure repose of a stillness. Such a structure would again re-articulate an opposition. *Bewegung,* rather, will be constitutive of language in such a way as to dislocate any sense of a directionality moving from soundless-ness into sound, silence into the spoken word. Rather, what is exposed is a radical instability, an an-archic configuration (*Fügung*). And what is most crucial, here, for us, is that it is the same configuration that underpins Heidegger's conception of *rhythm,* which will thus become determinative of his thinking of language.[45]

Commenting on a lyric of George's, Heidegger writes:

> Rhythm, ῥυσμός, does not mean here flux and flowing, but rather form/arrangement (*Fügung*). Rhythm is what is at rest (*das Ruhende*), what

occasions (*fügt*) the moving (*Be-wegung*) of dance and song, and so lets it rest within itself.[46]

The passage points, with precision, toward the same chiasmic intertwinement of movement and rest, sounding and stillness, that we have seen to be already operative in the *Be-wëgung* constitutive of language. The brief glimpse of a conception of rhythm that the passage offers us becomes more significant when it is allowed to echo out of parallel indications that punctuate Heidegger's work, echoes that resound both forward and backward. The seminar text of 1940 on φύσις in Aristotle's Physics B1 already identifies ῥυθμός with "form," with the "character of articulating, impressing, fitting and forming," not with pure fluidity.[47] As late as 1966, in the Heraclitus seminar, Heidegger will again return to the question of rhythm, here refusing the traditional etymology of ῥυσμός as a derivative of ῥέω, to flow, insisting that, instead, "it must be understood as *imprint*." Nonetheless, it is clear from the sense generated in relation to the interpretation of George above, that "form" or "imprint" cannot mean pure stasis but rather must always be thought out of and in relation to movement.

In order to understand better this intertwinement, we can appeal, if only briefly, to the analysis of Émile Benveniste.[48] Writing in 1951, Benveniste does not reject outright the derivation of ῥυθμός from ῥέω, which he finds "morphologically satisfying," but refuses adamantly the conventional assumption that links its origin to the flow of water: "ῥυθμός is never used for the movement of the waves," he claims. Furthermore, "if ῥυθμός means 'flux,' 'flowing,' it is hard to see how it could have taken on the value proper to 'rhythm.'" By contrast, Benveniste, like Heidegger, points to uses of ῥυθμός that indicate an entirely different sense. In particular, he points to the identification that Aristotle makes (*Metaphysics* 985b 16) between ῥυθμός and σχῆμα ("form," dispensation). Nonetheless, unwilling to abandon entirely the morphology that attaches rhythm to a sense of flow, ῥυθμός to ῥέω, Benveniste insists on a conception that brings both of these senses together. His formulation of the belonging-together of these seeming opposites is breathtakingly pertinent to our endeavor. He writes that "ῥυθμός designates the form in the instant in which it is assumed by what is mobile and fluid . . . It is the form as improvised, momentary, changeable."[49] And then, more decisively still:

> We can now understand how ῥυθμός, meaning literally "the particular manner of flowing," could have been the most proper term for describing "*dispositions,*" "configurations," *without fixity* or natural necessity and arising from an arrangement which is always subject to change.[50]

It is in this interlacing of disposition and flux, in the sense of form ("imprint") insofar as it belongs to what is changeable, that we come close to Heidegger's conception of rhythm:[51] the "resting in itself" of the *Bewegung* that constitutes language. And if the involution of rest and movement belongs deeply to this conception, then so, equally, must the intertwinement of sound and the soundless, of stillness and its breaking, of the irruption and collapse of the word. The conception of *Be-wëgung* is introduced to refract indefinitely the directionality of the emergence of the sounded word, to defer impossibly the question of source, of origin, to leave indefinitely open the question that Heidegger himself leaves unanswered close to the opening of *Unterwegs zur Sprache:* "On what does the ringing stillness break? How does the broken stillness come to sound?"[52] If we are now able to call the intertwinements, the interlacings that constitute the "way-making" of language *rhythm,* then to rhythm must belong the shattering of the word. Rhythm—the form, the configuration, the imprint of what is in motion—is *interruption.* It is the interruptive and the interrupting, the hiatus that makes possible the sounded word. It is perhaps this that prompts Marcia Sá Cavalcante Schuback to write, most beautifully, that: "*Rhythm* is *discontinuity in continuity.* What in music is called rhythm is properly an unrhythm, that is, a 'break,' an interruption, a rift (*Riß*), a breathing or caesura of and in continuity."[53]

Rhythm, thus, takes on a centrality within language that entirely displaces its position within a metaphysical structuring. As with the μέλος of song, rhythm is dis-engaged from any possible containment in the language of Aesthetics, for which the "rhythm" of words, like their song, are always separable from, and in opposition to, the structures of meaning. Further still, we must point to the radicality of harnessing rhythm to the sounding of the word: any aesthetics, whether of language or of music, will need to insist on a distinction between sound and its occurrence, between *timbre* and temporality. In fusing the two, Heidegger ensures that wherever music is to be uncovered, however it is to be understood, that uncovering, that understanding is only to be gained by addressing the occasion of language itself.

In Heidegger's reading of Stefan George, music entered the scene, became possible, from out of a disorientation, a disordering of the relation between word and thing. In this disordering a space opens up: the expectant attention with which the poet waits for the "treasure" to find its name is replaced by another kind of silence. This is no longer the silence of an "unspoken" that, as it were, waits upon the spoken. This is the silence of an abyssal disruption, into which the "treasure" slips as the collapse of the structure of naming looms. The poet, remaining always within language, sings the loss of his "treasure," sings his abandon; the language that belongs to this de-stabilization *is* precisely song. The effect of this de-structuring was a kind of irruption of music into language, taking the form of a relation to the word that cannot be detached from the mode and instant of its utterance.

But how is such a music to be conceived? If song belongs to language precisely as the articulation of a disruption, then it is clear that the music into which this language enters is not one that can be detached from this mode of its appearing. Music, in other words, cannot be considered as a "phenomenon" in its own right. To situate music within its own phenomenal region is merely to re-cast it in opposition to the intelligibility of language: it is to re-engage the language of Aesthetics. Outside of, and in opposition to, the intelligibility of language, music would then become merely a sonorous exploration of endless reservoirs of feeling: leaving language intact, music will become the celebration of a kind of powerlessness, a beautiful cry that remains always subordinate to the "real work" of meaning. The dominance of such a music, then, would—far from freeing music into new possibilities—emphatically reinforce the metaphysical oppositions that govern the determination of art as aesthetic experience. And this, precisely, is the perspective from which Heidegger's negative assessment of Wagner's project becomes intelligible. It is not that, in this reading of Wagner, music is afforded too much power. Rather, it is the opposite: in attempting to unchain music, to unleash it into a realm of pure "states of feeling," Heidegger's Wagner condemns it instead to a renewed impotence in the face of metaphysics.[54]

To separate music, then, into its own domain, its own phenomenal region, is necessarily to place it, in a sense, opposite language, as the discursive is opposed to the sensuous. What will be required, rather, in order to sustain and rigorously pursue the deconstruction of the opposition of sound and meaning, is that language and music be yoked together in a wholly new way. Music, emerging from and within the destabilization of the hierarchies of meaning, does not present itself as an alternative, as a possibility of language that can then be opposed to a newly recovered discursive dimension. Music, precisely, *is* the destabilization, the slippage of language, always within, but in a certain way equally beyond it. And thus it is that Heidegger can claim that:

> Song is not the opposite of discourse (*Gespräch*), but rather the most intimate kinship (*innigste Verwandtschaft*) with it; for *song is language.*[55]

Song belongs to *Gespräch,* and *Gespräch* to song. Song is not a separable, optional mode that one might or might not attach to discursive language. They are bound together in an intimacy that leaves neither one intact. The music that plays within the disorientation of the relation of word and thing, that haunts the dislocations and interruptions of language, is welded into language in an insoluble bond. Or perhaps, to put it more simply: language *is* music.

Music

Heidegger's readings of Trakl speak precisely from out of this intimacy of song and discourse. Indeed, his most sustained engagement is itself described as a *Gespräch*—that between poet and thinker. The true *Gespräch,* we are told, can only be between poets, but here, Heidegger will attempt to engage an improbable dialogue, reading Trakl wholly from within, from inside the resounding of the words themselves, in a way that reaches beyond what is attempted in the readings of Stefan George. The essay "*Das Wort,*" for example, seeks a corroborative reading, George's language supporting, resonating within Heidegger's philosophical discourse. Thus it is, perhaps, that song can be addressed directly in that reading: song, music, becomes thematic precisely because of the distance that Heidegger maintains from George's words themselves. *Die Sprache im Gedicht* travels much further, travels even recklessly—impossibly, perhaps—toward a place, a site, *ein Ort,* within which language speaks as music. What the essay will attempt to do is to read, to listen, to think Trakl utterly beyond "allegory and symbol," beyond metaphysical opposition. The music of language will be so close, here, that the essay can no longer—even for an instant—become a discussion of or about song. The reading will instead perform a re-iterative movement—echoing, repeating, recalling—that tugs at the threads of Trakl's polysemic utterance, but always from within. We will be able, here, to trace out only one thread from this fabric but will try to glimpse in its weave the operation of a kind of music.

The discourse, the conversation (*Gespräch*) between poet and thinker, then, is possible from out of the prior determination of the intimacy of song and discourse, of music and language. Because it is music that carries language through and beyond its metaphysical determinations, a kind of listening becomes possible, one that entirely eschews the externality of commentary, of interpretation, but can yet strive for an "*Erläuterung*," a speaking that clears, that clarifies. The *Erläuterung* belongs to an *Erörterung*, from out of which Heidegger hears resonate the *Ort*, the locus. Allowing these words to resonate together, Heidegger can say that what is to be aimed at, in the *Erläuterung*, is a clarification of the *Ort* that plays within the difference between the two terms. But how is the *Ort*, the locus, to be understood? Not, clearly, as a guiding meaning, an overarching principle to which the intentions of Trakl's poetry would be subordinate. Rather, the *Ort* will be itself a kind of gathering, a collecting (*Versammlung*) around which Trakl's words will tend to coalesce.

The "*Ort*"—the locus around which the words of Trakl's utterance gather—is what holds within itself the abyssal emptiness that appears only in the breaking, the rupturing that is the happening of language. To name this emptiness is the work of the *Gespräch* between poet and philosopher. The *Ort* is what remains unspoken within the poet's work: it is only from out of the play of the *Gespräch* that such a name might resonate. But such a resonance must necessarily acknowledge its impossibility—acknowledge the risk that to name what lies outside the words of the poem might fall back upon the authority of a metaphysics, in which the philosopher is to provide the "meanings" for which the poet has no name. Which is why, when Heidegger finally comes, hesitantly, to "name" the unspoken *Ort* within which Trakl's words resound, he does so only in invoking a figure of deep absence: "*Abgeschiedenheit*."

The questions that resonate around the determination of *Abgeschiedenheit*—in which we must hear continually the melancholy movement of *Abschied* (leave-taking) ringing through the different senses of the verb *scheiden*—are posed by Heidegger himself. He asks: "how is *Abgeschiedenheit* to gather a poetic saying to itself as its site, and determine it from there?" And again: "how can *Abgeschiedenheit* start a saying and a singing on its way?"[56] The question, for us, will invoke the entire range of displacements we have hitherto encountered: the intertwinements of discovery and loss (George), of plenitude and absence (Hölderlin), of sound, rhythm, and silence, of speaking and of listening.

The gesture of parting—of having-already departed—that belongs to *Abgeschiedenheit* generates a vocabulary of "following," of "coming-after," which will co-ordinate the coming-to-be of song. The singer will be the "friend," he who is left behind, following always after what has already gone. Once again "step" (*Schritt*), path (*Pfad*), way (*Weg*) are decisive, but are so by being folded into a listening, into a responding, into gestures of mourning that parallel the *Verzichten* of the George readings, that echo the fate of the blind singer in Hölderlin. The friend will follow by listening, tracing his way along the wake:

> A friend listens after the stranger. Listening after, he follows the departed (*Abgeschiedenen*) and becomes himself a wanderer, a stranger.[57]

And how *is* this listening? How does it occur? Not as silence, but as a listening once more wrapped up in song: the friend, we are told, "listens, *in that he sings of death*."[58]

It is in this distance of listening, this *Nachsagen* (saying-*after*), that the singing of the poet is born. It is this gap, this rent, in which coalesces all the different senses of fracture and loss we have encountered already, that generates the movement that "moves the poetic saying toward language."[59] Heidegger describes a kind of wave, a surging forth, as if the poet's words might seem to flow out from and at the same time back into this gathering point. *Abgeschiedenheit,* the "site," the *Ort* of Heidegger's reading of Trakl, is the figure of loss that generates this movement (*Bewegung*), the loss in which language recognizes its own impossibility. The movement, says Heidegger, is one that "within a metaphysical-aesthetic conception, might appear as rhythm."[60] To talk of the "rhythm" of words, here, would risk awakening once more the ghost of a metaphysical distinction that separates out the "musicality" of language from its content. The ghost is indicated here, to be sure, gestured toward—perhaps the *Gespräch* cannot take place without such a gesturing—but only so that it can continue to be pushed away, held out at arm's length. This spectre looms up out of the pure flow of Trakl's words, their resounding, resonating in and around one another as they circulate around the blank space of their gathering. The movement that is generated within the *Ort* of Trakl's words is not a flow of resonance but the movement of "way-making" (*Be-wëgung*) we have described, the movement to which belongs the rupture (*Aufriß*) of the word. It is in this sense that Heidegger points to the *Ort,* etymologically, as the *Spitze des Speers,* the tip of the spear, the point toward which the poet's words gather, but equally the point that rends, that shatters the stillness, bursting apart the seams of sound and silence.[61] It is here, in the Trakl readings, that this rending is brought closest to the loss, the abandonment from which we tracked the happening of song, and where we will discover its most powerful occasion.

To move further, we must confront a question, one that raises itself precisely at the moment in Heidegger's text at which *Abgeschiedenheit* is identified as the locus of the poet's listening, the absence after which his song reaches. Heidegger writes: "To sing means to praise, to watch over the praised in song."[62] Would the sense of praise, accorded here to song, not point toward its origin in celebration, not in affective loss? And there are more examples that suggest such an interpretation—in an earlier text on Hölderlin, for example, we read: "ὑμνεῖν: to sing, to praise, to glorify, to celebrate, to consecrate."[63] And yet again, from the essay on Stefan George: "a jubilant homage, a eulogy, a praise: *laudare.* Laudare is the Latin name for song."[64] Indeed, this understanding of song as celebration has been emphasized by Derrida, among others. He writes: "the necessary path would lead from speech to saying, from saying to poetic saying, from *Dichten* to song, to the accord of consonance, from this to the hymn and thus to praise . . . It is merely a question of pointing to a problematic . . . in which these meanings appear indissociable."[65]

However internally consistent this trajectory appears, it nonetheless runs roughshod over the contexts from out of which its different elements emerge. Within the discussion of Trakl, the gesture of "praise" that belongs to a singing cannot be dissociated from the *Nachsagen,* the saying-after, the listening that listens to what has departed, that sings of what is dead. And this, too, is a kind of praising, a watching-over (*hüten*), the protection of an absence. If the celebratory emerges, then, in the event of singing, it is not to be thought in terms of a pure consonance, a plenitude of joy. Song, rather, will be what holds, what binds together praise and loss, celebration and abandonment, joy and mourning. It is this holding-together (*Gefüge*) that must concern us now.

Pain

In the Trakl reading, the figure of the friend, the listener that sings the departed (*Abgeschieden*), emerges from lines of Trakl's "*An einen Frühverstorbenen*" ("To One Who Died Young"). The lines are as follows:

> And in the garden, the silver countenance of the friend remained behind,
> Listening in the leaves or among ancient stones.[66]

It is from these lines that the pathos of distance is generated; it is here that song is cast as a longing for what has been lost. The lines open the space, the rent, the gap in which the movement of the *Ort* is initiated. But this is not their first appearance in the text. Earlier, the same lines make a seemingly unwarranted and unexpected appearance in the context of a reading of a stanza from "*Heiterer Frühling.*" In the midst of a detailed, line-by-line description, Heidegger pauses to say that "the entire stanza corresponds (*entspricht*)" to the lines above. The correspondence is not obvious, nor is it clarified in Heidegger's text. The stanza with which Heidegger wishes to indicate this correspondence runs as follows:

> So painfully good and true is, what lives,
> And softly an ancient stone touches you:
> Truly! I shall forever be with you.
> O mouth! that trembles through the silvery willow.[67]

Resonating deeply within these lines is another text of Heidegger's, another reading of Trakl, where we can locate the thematic that draws this obscure but crucial "correspondence" together. The echo has to do with the relation between stone and pain, which resounds out of Heidegger's reading of "*Ein Winterabend,*" and the line in question runs:

> *Schmerz versteinerte die Schwelle* [Pain has turned the threshold to stone].[68]

The discussion of this line, strikingly repeated four times in the text of "*die Sprache,*" focuses on the idea of threshold, which functions within the narrative of the poem as the connective instant that binds the "wanderer," the stranger—he who is apart, outside (*abgeschieden*)—to the intimacy of the home, an intimacy both welcoming and alien. Decisive, here, is Heidegger's understanding of "threshold" as what both separates but also joins, what keeps apart but also holds together: "the threshold bears the between."[69] Nothing itself, the threshold both determines and is determined by what it keeps apart; impossible, here, to even outline the context of the emergence of "threshold" in this essay, its function in the configuration of "world" and "thing." But the re-occurrence of the conjunction of pain and stone in "*Die Sprache im Gedicht*" more than suggests that the "between-ness" of the threshold, its function as pure difference (dif-ference, *Unter-schied*),[70] is equally operative in this second context: that the *Unter-schied* and the *Abgeschiedenen* can be seen to play within the same orbit.

In Heidegger's reading of Trakl we have already identified the gap, the rent—the distance between stranger and friend—as the generative force of poetic utterance, that which makes of song always a song of absence. And this force of loss corresponded, too, to the gesture of abandonment, to the failure of the name, which emerged in the readings of George and of Hölderlin. Music was to have arisen as, and in, the fracture of a language exposed to loss, a language intimate with its interruption, its collapse; a language forced to sing its own limits. Now, in the context of "*ein Winterabend*" the senses of fracture, of interruption, and of absence are to be determined as "threshold." And the urgency of this determination is its identification with *pain*. "Pain has turned the threshold to stone," repeats Heidegger, and understands, here, not merely an affective transformation. Rather, it is in and *as* pain that the threshold itself emerges, becomes possible—that it is "made stone." Pain, then, is crucially identified, not merely with the rent, the fracture (*Riß*) itself but as that which binds together what is torn, what holds them in intimacy (*Innigkeit*):

> Pain rends (*reißt*). It is the rift (*Riß*). But it does not just tear (*zerreißt*) into dispersive fragments. Pain indeed tears asunder, it separates, yet so that at the same time it draws everything to itself, gathers it to itself . . . Pain is the joining agent in the rending that divides and gathers. Pain is the joining of the rift. The joining *is* the threshold.[71]

Pain, then, carries the ambivalence, the play, the togetherness of joy and sadness. It is the between space that holds opposites in proximity to one another. The celebration, the joy of affirmation belongs within the sadness. Song belongs always in the vicinity of loss, but always as a gesture of abandon, in its manifold senses. And it is thus that when Heidegger comes to describe Trakl's *Heiterer Frühling,* he can say of the stanza that it is "*the pure song of pain.*"[72] Song is occasioned in the very play that Heidegger calls "pain," the very togetherness of joy and loss: as such, it is, *always,* the "pure song of pain." Music is such that, *in voicing itself, it voices pain*—fundamentally and essentially. The "pure song of pain," then, would be the purest expression of the essence of music itself, an essence that does not exclude the celebratory, the joyful, but that draws its abandon from exposure to a deep absence.

To "sing of death," to listen after what has been lost, is to hold together a language fractured at its core. What is sung across this fracturing is ecstatic celebration *and* deep loss, with all the fragility and vulnerability to which that exposes us. Moving across the *Riß,* reaching for what is *abgeschieden,* the singer is the voice of this gathering, this holding-together. Music, which sings always in and around language, *is* the fracturing, the *Riß,* but also that which joins what is apart (*geschieden*): music is the pain of language, the painful ἁρμονία of joy and sorrow, a celebration of absence.

Writing of the resonance of Trakl's words, the way in which they play, echo, within a polyvalence that cannot be reduced to their "meanings," Heidegger writes that "the polysemic sounding (*mehrdeutige Ton*) of Trakl's poetic utterance comes from a gathering (*Versammlung*), that is, a unison (*Einklang*) which, meant for itself alone, remains unsayable."[73] The play in which these words are held, then, revolves around a silence, a space in which they ring together in a unison so perfect as to collapse all difference, all sounding, into itself:

> The rigorous unison (*Einklang*) in which the many-voiced language of Trakl's poetry speaks—and this means also: is silent—corresponds to *Abgeschiedenheit* as the locus (*Ort*) of the poetic utterance (*Gedicht*).[74]

The locus around which Trakl's poetry gathers comes to language as the figure of absence, of one who has departed, who has always already left. But this absence corresponds (*entspricht*) to the absence around which all language plays. It is the fracture, the *Riß* that opens in a language exposed to the dislocation that belongs to poetry, to words abandoned to the slippage that comes with the de-stabilization of the name, the disruption of presence. We have called this fracture, this dislocation, "music," and watched for its implicit operation in Heidegger's thinking. The *Einklang* that merges into silence, the *Ort* of Heidegger's own thinking of language: this is music. Not, perhaps, a music that one can know, that one can recognize, or even identify as such. *That* music blossoms out of a more originary kind: it blossoms out of a music that sounds in the deepest recesses of the language that we speak, that makes of language always more than the meanings we express: a music that echoes in the space of a play that enjoins us to speak, and speak again, in the rhythm of a dark celebration.

NOTES

The epigraph is from *Du sollst ja nicht weinen,/Sagt eine Musik./Sonst/sagt/niemand/etwas.* Ingeborg Bachmann, from "Enigma," in *Darkness Spoken,* trans. Peter Filkins (Brookline, Mass.: Zephyr Press, 2006), 622–623.

1. Hannah Arendt and Martin Heidegger, *Letters, 1925–75* (Orlando: Harcourt, 2004), 74.

2. An earlier version of this paper was presented at the annual Meeting of the Nordic Society for Phenomenology at Södertörn University, in Stockholm, in April 2010. I am endlessly indebted to the quality of listening in evidence at that event.

3. Philippe Lacoue-Labarthe, *Musica Ficta (Figures of Wagner)* (Stanford, Calif.: Stanford University Press, 1994), 91, my emphasis.

4. Martin Heidegger, *Nietszche, Vol. 1. The Will to Power as Art,* trans. David Farrell Krell (San Francisco: Harper & Row, 1979), 86.

5. Lacoue-Labarthe, *Musica Ficta,* 86.

6. The passage in question has, however, received invaluable attention recently from Dennis Schmidt, in *Lyrical and Ethical Subjects: Essays on the Periphery of the Word, Freedom, and History* (Albany: SUNY Press, 2005), 61–64.

7. Martin Heidegger, *Der Satz vom Grund* (Tübingen: Verlag Günther Neske, 1957), 151.

8. In this connection, Krzysztof Ziarek has described this changing register as one in which words play around one another in an "infold," which exerts a counterforce to the logic of difference that appears to dominate Heidegger's texts. See K. Ziarek, *Inflected Language: Towards a Hermeneutic of Nearness* (Albany: SUNY Press, 1994). He writes that, in this mode, "insights are disclosed not so much by the mode of presentation itself or its argumentative rigor but instead by the exactitude of his verbal exploits and accomplishments" (p. 42). The notion of "infold" is a telling one, provided that one does not assume that the "counterforce" it presents operates outside the logic of difference. Rather, it is precisely the radicality of this "logic" that allows it to *include* strategies which would undermine any attempt to construe difference as a "structure." Difference itself is never undifferentiated.

9. Martin Heidegger, *Unterwegs zur Sprache* (Pfullingen: Neske, 1959), also GA 12: 146. English translation available as *On the Way to Language,* trans. Peter D. Hertz (San Francisco: Harper & Row, 1971), except for the first essay, *Die Sprache,* of

which a translation appears in the volume *Poetry, Language, and Thought*, trans. Albert Hofstadter (San Francisco: Harper & Row, 1971), 187–211. Although the standard translations have been usefully consulted throughout, they have been frequently emended here.

10. *Unterwegs zur Sprache*, 228; *On the Way to Language*, 147.

11. Heidegger, *Erläuterungen zu Hölderlins Dichtung*, GA 1: 4, 49–79. English translation in *The Heidegger Reader*, ed. Günter Figal, trans. Jerome Veith (Bloomington: Indiana University Press, 2007), 151–177. Hereafter, German pagination will precede English.

12. *Erläuterungen*, 53; *Heidegger Reader*, 159.

13. *Erläuterungen*, 72; *Heidegger Reader*, 172.

14. *Erläuterungen*, 66; *Heidegger Reader*, 168.

15. Cf. Kant, *Critique of Judgment*, §47.

16. *Erläuterungen*, 66; *Heidegger Reader*, 168.

17. Ibid.

18. Ibid.

19. *Unterwegs zur Sprache*, 182; *On the Way to Language*, 77.

20. *Unterwegs zur Sprache*, 229; *On the Way to Language*, 148.

21. Martin Heidegger, *On Time and Being*, trans. Joan Stambaugh (Chicago: University of Chicago Press, 1972), 1, my emphasis.

22. *Unterwegs zur Sprache*, 15; *Poetry, Language, and Thought*, 193.

23. *Unterwegs zur Sprache*, 204; *On the Way to Language*, 98.

24. Ibid.

25. Ibid.

26. *Unterwegs zur Sprache*, 206; *On the Way to Language*, 99.

27. *Unterwegs zur Sprache*, 205; *On the Way to Language*, 98.

28. Jean-Luc Nancy, *Listening*, trans. Charlotte Mandell (New York: Fordham University Press, 2007), 22.

29. *Unterwegs zur Sprache*, 255; *On the Way to Language*, 124.

30. Christopher Fynsk writes, tellingly, that "only a broken stillness imprints mortal speech—breaking and imprinting are in fact indissociable." They are unthinkable beyond their intertwinement. Fynsk suggests that this intertwinement, the interplay of breaking, tearing, imprinting that circulates around the instant of utterance in Heidegger's text, might be considered as the play of a kind of "noise" that must surround the event of the spoken word. See the essay "Noise at the Threshold," in Fynsk, *Language & Relation: . . . that there is language* (Stanford, Calif.: Stanford University Press, 1996), 28. One might, here, despite the compelling eloquence of Fynsk's analysis, want to express some slight reserve at the use of the word "noise," a reserve that one might find addressed by Paul Valéry, when he writes: "Noise gives ideas of the causes that produce it, dispositions of action, reflexes—but not a state of imminence of an intrinsic family of relations" (Valéry, *Cahiers II* [Paris: Gallimard, 1974]. Quoted in Nancy, *Listening*, 15). Or perhaps the reserve might be expressed as follows: where Fynsk hears noise, might one not rather hear *music*? It is in the direction of this possibility that this essay attempts to move.

31. *Wozu Dichter*, in Heidegger, *Holzwege* (Frankfurt am Main: Klostermann, 1963), 292. Translated as "Why Poets?" in Heidegger, *Off the Beaten Track*, trans.

Julian Young and Kenneth Haynes (Cambridge: Cambridge University Press, 2005), 238.

32. *Unterwegs zur Sprache*, 235; *On the Way to Language*, 153.

33. *Holzwege*, 293; *Off the Beaten Track*, 238.

34. *Unterwegs zur Sprache*, 255; *On the Way to Language*, 124.

35. Ibid.

36. In this context, Christopher Fynsk writes that "correspondence presupposes . . . a kind of reserve, (but) this reserve must be ready . . . to anticipate upon the command of difference." Fynsk, *Language and Relation*, 27.

37. *Unterwegs zur Sprache*, 262; *On the Way to Language*, 131.

38. *Unterwegs zur Sprache*, 29; *Poetry, Language, and Thought*, 206.

39. *Unterwegs zur Sprache*, 30; *Poetry, Language, and Thought*, 209.

40. *Unterwegs zur Sprache*, 252; *On the Way to Language*, 122.

41. *Unterwegs zur Sprache*, 205; *On the Way to Language*, 98.

42. *Unterwegs zur Sprache*, 261; *On the Way to Language*, 130.

43. This twisting of the opposition of repose and movement echoes first from out of "The Origin of the Work of Art": "Where rest includes motion, there can exist a repose which is an inner concentration of motion, hence the highest state of agitation." Heidegger, "The Origin of the Work of Art," in *Poetry, Language, and Thought*, 48. Also GA 5.

44. *Unterwegs zur Sprache*, 29; *Poetry, Language, and Thought*, 207.

45. David Farrell Krell, in a marvelous essay—"The Source of the Wave" (in Krell, *Lunar Voices* [Chicago: University of Chicago Press, 1995], 60)—asks: "does rhythm lend repose precisely in the way that all metaphysical ideas 'beyond' the sensuous word offer solace and rest? The suspicion cannot be readily quelled." No indeed, except perhaps by insisting on the chiasmic involvement of movement and rest in these texts, on their incessant resistance, their refusal to come to rest within the structure of any opposition whatsoever; a refusal to which the opposition of rest and movement is not an exception, but of which it is, rather, almost a paradigm (if a paradigm were possible).

46. *Unterwegs zur Sprache*, 230; *On the Way to Language*, 149.

47. See Krell, "The Source of the Wave," 57–58 for an invaluable discussion of the function of this initial conception of rhythm in relation to Aristotle.

48. See "The Notion of Rhythm in Linguistic Expression," in Benveniste, trans. Mary Elizabeth Meek, *Problems in General Linguistics* (Miami: Miami University Press, 1971), 281–288. A valuable analysis of Benveniste's article can be found in an essay of Henri Maldiney: "*L'Esthetique des Rhythmes*," in the collection *Regard, Parole, Espaces* (Paris: Amers, 1994), 147–172.

49. *Problems*, 286.

50. Ibid., my emphasis.

51. "The wave of rhythm does not just simply flow by; it entwines, links, forges, and inscribes," as Krell puts it (Krell, *Lunar Voices*, 62).

52. *Unterwegs zur Sprache*, 31; *Poetry, Language, and Thought*, 208.

53. "The Poetics of Language: Readings of Heidegger's *On the Way to Language*," in *Metaphysics, Facticity, Interpretation*, eds. Dan Zahavi, Sara Heinämaa, and Hans Ruin (Dordrecht: Kluwer, 2003), 195–217. Schuback focuses, interestingly,

on the endlessly re-iterative, repetitive movement of Heidegger's own text, and on his preoccupation with the grammatically punctual.

54. The question of whether or not this representation of Wagner's achievement is accurate, and even whether this perspective can be thought of as Heidegger's last word on Wagner, is here left in abeyance. Whatever may be the status of Wagner's project, he is here considered by Heidegger purely as emblematic of a certain possibility of music. One should, perhaps, consider writing "Wagner" in inverted commas, to emphasize this emblematic quality.

55. *Unterwegs zur Sprache*, 182; *On the Way to Language*, 78, my emphasis.

56. *Unterwegs zur Sprache*, 67; *On the Way to Language*, 186.

57. Ibid.

58. Ibid., my emphasis.

59. *Unterwegs zur Sprache*, 73; *On the Way to Language*, 191. To risk again a parallel, we will cite Nancy, who writes that "to be listening is to be inclined toward the opening of meaning, hence to a slash, a cut in un-sensed (*in-sensée*) indifference." *Listening*, 27.

60. *Unterwegs zur Sprache*, 38; *On the Way to Language*, 160.

61. My gratitude to Claudia Baracchi for this reminder.

62. *Unterwegs zur Sprache*, 69; *On the Way to Language*, 187.

63. Heidegger, *Hölderlin's Hymn, Der Ister, Gesamtausgabe* 53, 1, trans. William McNeill and Julia Davis (Bloomington: Indiana University Press, 1996), 1.

64. *Unterwegs zur Sprache*, 229; *On the Way to Language*, 148.

65. Jacques Derrida, *Of Spirit: Heidegger and the Question*, trans. Geoffrey Bennington and Rachel Bowlby (Chicago: University of Chicago Press, 1989), 127–128.

66. *Unterwegs zur Sprache*, 68; *On the Way to Language*, 186.

67. *Unterwegs zur Sprache*, 64; *On the Way to Language*, 183.

68. *Unterwegs zur Sprache*, 26; *Poetry, Language, and Thought*, 203.

69. *Unterwegs zur Sprache*, 27; *Poetry, Language, and Thought*, 204.

70. Writes Fynsk, eloquently (*Language and Relation*, 25): "it is a figure of the threshold that is language itself, inasmuch as language is defined as the articulation of difference by which difference comes about."

71. *Unterwegs zur Sprache*, 27; *Poetry, Language, and Thought*, 204.

72. *Unterwegs zur Sprache*, 64; *On the Way to Language*, 183.

73. *Unterwegs zur Sprache*, 75; *On the Way to Language*, 192.

74. *Unterwegs zur Sprache*, 76; *On the Way to Language*, 193.

FOURTEEN

Heidegger with Blanchot: On the Way to Fragmentation

Christopher Fynsk

Maurice Blanchot never masked the importance of Heidegger's thought for his own trajectory of thinking and writing. Nor did he dwell on a relation that grew increasingly indirect in the later years, and whose public face was devoted to questioning regarding Heidegger's debt to the metaphysical tradition and an even more severe condemnation of Heidegger's political and ethical compromises. Taken in the context of an almost obligatory distancing of French thinkers from their Heideggerian legacy over the past three decades, this overt resistance has perhaps had the general effect of inhibiting sustained attention to Blanchot's relation to Heidegger and to the question of how Blanchot's thought of "*le neutre*" interrupts the Heideggerian motif of *Ereignis* and sends his thinking on a profoundly divergent path. How do we assess that divergence and to what exigencies for thought does it introduce us? The questions remain vital, and they are immense.

Clearly the topic of language is of special importance for this question—for intrinsic reasons, of course, but also for the fact that Blanchot is one of a very small number of thinkers who engaged Heidegger's thinking on this topic at a level commensurate with Heidegger's own effort to think from language toward the limits of language (as designated with the motif of *der Brauch*).[1] For this reason alone, Blanchot's engagement with Heidegger, his astonishing accompaniment of a path of thinking from which he so markedly dissociated himself, is invaluable to those of us who still seek to open paths to (and from) Heidegger's text. The difficulty, once again, is that the relation designated here somewhat ironically as "accompaniment" remains so latent in the later works. Even Blanchot's early text *for* Heidegger was marked by a singular indirection, and the indirection only grew in the subsequent years. Thus, one is constantly challenged in every effort to establish a connection, even quite apart from issues of authorial intent. And yet, the echoes and resonances remain insistent. Even where Blanchot's text appears indifferent to a possible linkage, relation seems to suggest itself. For example, when Blanchot evokes, in apparent reference to his own path of thinking/writing, a long "*cheminement*" in *The Step Not Beyond,* and then thematizes this "*cheminement*" in an allegorical mode in a conversation that evokes rivers, a growing wasteland, and then a city of fear, it is very hard not to find in these pages a *devastating* response to key Heideggerian motifs.[2] It might be argued that one does not need a reference to Heidegger to follow this course of the conversation, even if the turn it takes raises intriguing questions for Heidegger's thinking about language. But, can one say the same of the conversation in *The Infinite Conversation* that *The Step Not Beyond* apparently takes over in a kind of *reprise*? *The Infinite Conversation* (to restore the text's original title[3]) takes a course that brings what instigates it and constantly unsettles it—an event in/of language—to speech. If, as I would like to suggest, this fragmented conversation takes over a Heideggerian schema in its manner of being under way to language, can we ignore, as readers of Heidegger, as readers of Blanchot, the possible implication of this instance of accompaniment? This question seems all the more pertinent if we consider that the neutral relation thus brought to language engages the motif of releasement, while giving us this engagement itself to be thought along lines that perhaps evoke the Heideggerian schema of usage, *der Brauch.* The text's manner of bringing language (a certain language) to language is so strong that an avoidance of the question of Blanchot's relation to Heidegger is, in this instance, an avoidance of what the text demands of us—at least "we" who have taken Heidegger seriously and find ourselves before an experience of language that does not just bring forth the strangeness of our relation to language ("*the neutral, the neutral, how strangely this sounds for* me" [IC xxi/XXII]) but also gives this relation as fundamentally disrupted. One might choose simply to leave aside such an experience with language. But one might also see it as a vital opening for thought. My purpose in the pages that follow is to evoke some of the questions presented by this opening.

I have quietly alluded to Heidegger's famous conversation, "Conversation on a Country Path,"[4] and it is from the rapid formulation of the notion of usage we find there that I would like to approach *The Infinite Conversation.* I will presume (throughout this essay) the reader's familiarity with this brief text by Heidegger and simply focus on a lapidary formulation of the notion of usage that arrives late in the conversation—that is to say, well after a definition of the willful character of representational thinking and its transcendental horizon has been displaced by the thought of a waiting releasement into that which "regions." Thus, the "teacher," taking over the scientist's shorthand designation of "that which regions" as *truth* and his own reference to the notion of usage ("human nature is given over to truth, because truth needs man" [*Discourse,* 84]), offers the following:

> The essence of humankind is released to that-which-regions and accordingly used by it for this reason alone: because humankind for itself has no power over truth and the latter remains in-dependent of it. Truth can come into its essence independently of humankind because the essence of humankind as releasement to that-which-regions is used by that which regions in regioning and for the preserving of determining. The independence of truth *from* humankind is clearly a relation *to* the human essence, a relation which rests in the regioning of human essence into that which regions. (*Discourse,* 84)

Truth can only come about in its independence from humankind because the essence of humankind, already appropriated to truth in its releasement, allows truth to occur. Humankind lends itself to truth in its very powerlessness, offering it something like a site, or more precisely, a freeing, open relation.

Might the enigmatic fatigue of the interlocutors in *The Infinite Conversation* be understood as precisely the experience of such a powerlessness? This arresting theme of fatigue or weariness, offered in a beautifully poised prose, has provoked considerable fascination on the part of Blanchot's readers, some of whom have responded quite eloquently.[5] Its force in this text derives in part from its inherent ambiguity. On the one hand, it is introduced initially as a quite physical, quite "human" affliction evoked with playful gentleness. In the opening sequence, it appears as a failing in vital spirits that calls for a mutual solicitude on the part of the two who gather in conversation. But this fatigue, while in some respects indistinguishable from life, even in reaching beyond its limits, proves to be something less than "real" fatigue and is not occasioned by some burden or lapse relating to vital interests. It is excessive in relation to those interests, deriving from exposure to something that the interlocutors cannot initially bring to speech, or that they can only bring to speech via their fatigue in the course of the conversation—not merely because fatigue would lower thresholds of resistance or inhibition but also because this fatigue is in itself an exposure. Commenting upon the ambiguity of fatigue in a later section of *The Infinite Conversation*, Blanchot notes that one can never quite distinguish between the fatigue that can afflict the powers of speech and conversation in a negative fashion, and another fatigue that opens and occupies a void:

> When the power of speech is interrupted, one does not know, one can never know with certainty, what is at work . . . When, for example, interruption arises out of fatigue, out of pain or affliction (all forms of the neutral), do we know to which experience it belongs? Can we be sure, even though it may be sterilizing, that it is simply barren? No, we are not sure (and this, moreover, adds to the fatigue and the affliction). We sense as well that if pain (fatigue or affliction) hollows out an infinite gap between beings, this gap is perhaps what would be the most important to bring to expression, all the while leaving it empty, so that to speak out of fatigue, out of pain or affliction, could be to speak according to the infinite dimension of language. (IC 78/111)

This other fatigue, like the affliction Blanchot will describe at length in *The Step Not Beyond*, is an experience of an im-possible over which a willing subject has no power. Fatigue would appear to be the suffering of a powerlessness that is perhaps not even a suffering in that it would open, in its very indifference—its weary, indifferent "truth" (IC xvii/XVII)—beyond passivity.

But the suspension of will in this indifferent weariness extends to such a degree in the narrated dialogue that the subject in the hold of this fatigue cannot even affirm of it that it would release him into, or allow him to approach, the neutral (another voice will have to do this). Even *supposition* lapses in this relation, faltering and remaining suspended, in its attempted act, over the rupture of the "transcendental horizon." That there should be an event of writing that fragments the horizon, that he should be called into what is perhaps a game by this strange form of event, that his fatigue should be implicated in this writing—these efforts at supposition lend to no judgment because "he," the weary, putative subject of this judgment, is not able to separate himself or locate himself in relation to his "circumstances":

> *He recalls in what circumstances the circle was traced as though around him—a circle: rather, the absence of a circle, the rupture of that vast circumference from come the days and nights.*
>
> *Of this other circle, he knows only that he is not enclosed within it, and, in any case, that he is not enclosed in it with himself. On the contrary, the circle being traced—he forgets to say that the line is only beginning—does not allow him to include himself within it. It is an uninterrupted line that inscribes itself while interrupting itself.*
>
> *Let him admit for an instant this trace traced as though in chalk and certainly by himself—by whom otherwise?—or else by a man like him, he does not differentiate. Let him know that it disturbs nothing in the order of things. Let him sense, nevertheless, that it represents an event of a particular kind—of what kind he does not know, a game perhaps. Let him remain motionless, called upon by the game to be the partner of someone who is not playing . . .*
>
> *And sometimes addressing himself to the circle, saying to it: Try once, indifferent circle, if only for an instant, to close up again, so that I know where you begin, where you end.*
>
> *Be this circle—the absence of a circle—traced by writing or by weariness; weariness will not permit him to decide, even if it is only through writing that he discovers himself weary, entering the circle of weariness—entering, as in a circle, into weariness.* (IC xviii/XVII–XVIII)

What "going toward" or "nearing" could be thought in this spiralling, if it is indeed possible to think together releasement and writing?

But we jump ahead of ourselves in relation to the narrative by turning so immediately to the event of writing. For the account just cited appears to require, for its generation, a passage *in conversation* whereby a shared understanding and a shared waiting open upon the latent speaking that holds this conversation and the disclosure of a third instance (that is in fact multiple). Let us return to opening steps of *The Infinite Conversation.*

The conversation takes its departure from the topic of fatigue and the fact that this fatigue appears to require a deferral of the promised discussion. The interlocutors are accordingly preparing to separate when one, apparently confronting the silence of a library (the time, as we will shortly learn, is that of an accomplished history that leaves only the supplemental task of saying this end), asks how the two will manage to "disappear." The answer, taking its pitch from the gathering night (despite the fact that it is daylight), evokes some unidentified but obvious path—"*It would suffice*" (could this be dying?)—that is immediately refused: "*No, it would not suffice*" (IC xiv/XII).

What follows, in the immediately succeeding section, is the statement that an event of language has occurred.

> *From the instant that this word—a word, a phrase—slipped between them, something changed, a history ended; an interval should be placed between their existence and this word, but the word always comprises this very interval, whatever it may be, and also the distance that separates them and separates them from it.* (IC xv/XII)

Is the reference here to the preceding expression of discord? The discord may have re-marked, in some fashion, the event in question, but "the word, the phrase" of this event appears to have preceded it inasmuch as it has determined the long post-history of this conversation. For even in periods of interruption ("*when they stop seeing each other completely, when the city assigns them rounds of life that do not risk bringing them back together*" [IC XII/xv]), the word, the phrase, remains between them as a kind of latent, disturbing element that makes it impossible for them to avoid returning. It will not be brought to the conversation until the question that provoked the preceding discordant exchange ("*What will we do to disappear?*") returns in a form that is both more neutral and more poignant in its expression of distress: "*I don't know what is to become of me*" (IC xvi/XIV).

What has happened that the host is so reluctant to address the source of his fatigue? Twice he is urged to speak of what has occurred, and it is only after the second expression of distress just cited that something of an answer reaches his guest, no less neutral in its formulation: "What had to happen, something that does not concern me" (IC xvi/XIV). This is, as the guest notes, "just a phrase," and in light of the host's expressed anxiety about the conditions of his visit, he cannot resist asking whether this thing might in fact concern him. To which an answer comes that underscores the neutral character of this event: "This concerns neither the one of us nor the other" (IC xvi /XIV). Here, it would seem, is the word, the phrase, that has intervened, returning again.

A subsequent meditation on this sentence (to which we will return) strengthens the supposition that the intervening word of this *entre-tien* has been brought into their exchange. But as soon as this word comes to language, the exchange ceases to be entirely *theirs:*

> *The silence has a character to which he does not attend, given up entirely to the impression that a threshold has been crossed, a force of affirmation broken, a refusal thrust aside, but also a challenge issued—not to him, the benevolent interlocutor, but impersonally, or—yes, it is strange—to someone else, to the event in which precisely neither one is involved.* (IC xvi/XIV–XV)

The word has been spoken, as we see, as a *counterword* (Heidegger would call this a "*Gegenwort*") in a conversation that has moved to an entirely different level, or has now become the "absence" of a conversation. It is spoken by the suffering interlocutor as a challenge to some other for whom, as was noted at the very outset of the conversation, one might assume a place had been left (IC xviii–xiv/X). This other will come to receive the designation "*il*" in Blanchot's writing, and as a *relay* of the other—the neutral/the neutre—in language, it is a neutral saying of language itself.[6] One could well play with formulations such as "The neutre of language: the language of the neutre,"[7] but Blanchot will employ a simpler expression in referring to what he calls "a word too many." Of course, it is a deceptively simple formula for the fact that the insistence of "*il*" cannot be isolated in the play of signification as some pronominal indicator or even as a pleonastic remainder; its play (as we will already have glimpsed in an earlier citation) belongs to the tracing of the indifferent circle that does not allow the speaking subject to locate himself and that afflicts all his speech (or writing).

But what is most striking in the immediate context of the conversation is the breach that opens between the two interlocutors. Having expressed considerable distress in bringing to language something he did not want to say to his friend (not only was it never a matter of a *vouloir dire:* he did not want to compromise this other in relation to something that did not concern him), the host is no longer prepared to recognize a *common* responsibility, or what the guest proposes as a common "engagement":

> *"Engaged together?"—"Engaged in the same discourse."—"True, but it is also for this that we must take heed. I am aware of my responsibilities."—"As I am also, in regard to you."—"You are, it would be unfriendly not to recognize it, but up to a certain point." He questions himself about this*

> *limit, then he ceases to question: "You mean, inasmuch as we speak. That's right, speaking is the last chance remaining for us, speaking is our chance."— "You would not listen to me, if I spoke."—"But I listen."—"I too listen."— "Well, what do you hear?"* (IC xvii/XV–XVI)

Their *entente*—their understanding, their hearing—has met a decisive limit. Indeed, there is no real sign that the scission that occurs here will ever quite be overcome, though it will give way to another relation Blanchot names "friendship."[8] The one cannot assume, will not assume that the other is prepared to attend to a speaking that would occur, perhaps has occurred, in the neutral. Retreating from this break to their customary solicitude for one another, they suggest that it is perhaps just weariness speaking. But there will be no return, or no more than a return to what was the latent truth of their relations from the very outset, to which the host points when he voices a concern about a friendship that is extended only to weariness itself ("*The thought came to me that the reason for your friendship, perhaps its sole reason—and I could never say enough how constant, how disinterested it is—is what is most particular to me, my privileged part. But can one become attached to a weary man and only by reason of his weariness?*" IC xx/XXI).

We rejoin at this point the passage cited earlier, in which one—but is this now the host, is it the guest?—recalls the circumstances of the advent of a "writing" that breaches what Heidegger termed in his "Conversation" the transcendental horizon. The experience of this writing suspends any willing relation, as we have seen, even any supposition (in the mode Heidegger names *Vermutung*). No resolution, not even a self-location, seems possible in the spiralling circling of fatigue. There is no "in-dwelling" here, no countering orientation via some nearing.

Nevertheless, there is a form of beginning ("*Everything began for him*" begins a section that is followed by another with the words: "*Everything begins for him*" [IC xviii/XVIII]): the opening of a relation to something that comes about without gathering itself in a determinate point. This is the opening of a "simulated" course of reflection and the opening of a kind of passage that will be given form in a decision forcefully thematized in the concluding paragraphs of the text. There, the narrating voice (through most of the dialogue, this has apparently been the guest) expresses astonishment at this step of one who has chosen to separate from the common discursive space. The scission noted above, where the one separates from the other in denying their common engagement, their common *entente,* has become an assumed act:

> He was listening to the speech of the everyday, grave, idle, saying everything, holding up to each one what he would have liked to say, a speech unique, distant and always close, everyone's speech, always already expressed and yet infinitely sweet to say, infinitely precious to hear—the speech of temporal eternity saying: now, now, now.
>
> How had he come to will the interruption of discourse? And not the legitimate pause, the one permitting the give and take of conversation, the benevolent, intelligent pause, nor that beautifully poised waiting with which two interlocutors, from one shore to another, measure their right to communicate. No not that, and no more so the austere silence, the tacit speech of visible things, the reserve of those invisible. What he had wanted was entirely different, a cold interruption, the rupture of the circle. And at once this had happened: the heart ceasing to beat, the eternal speaking drive stopping. (IC xxxiii/XXVI)

But from whence would have come the impetus for this departure, and into what "region" would the interlocutor have stepped, if this is not simply into death?

It would not be uncharacteristic of Blanchot to describe this as a space for dying (*The Step Not Beyond* provides this figure in its evocation of a city of fear). But the course of the conversation suggests clearly that the passage in question is not a perishing. On the contrary, it seems that what the interlocutor has willed is an impetus given in the conversation itself. Shortly before the end, we read the following:

> *Interruption: a pain, a weariness.*
>
> *While speaking to someone, he comes to feel the cold force of interruption assert itself. And strangely, the dialogue does not stop; on the contrary, it becomes more resolute, more decisive, yet so hazardous that their relation to the common space disappears between them forever.* (IC xxii/XXIV)

So there is, in fact, resolve in the space of this other, interrupted conversation, and it belongs to the now infinite conversation itself. Heidegger, as we will recall, suggested that the passage to a thought released from any kind of will would require a negative moment, a willing not to will, or a renunciation. But a thought so released might also entail, as the "scholar" adds in Heidegger's conversation, a "higher acting" that would be linked to what was termed in *Being and Time* "resoluteness" (*Discourse,* 81). The development of this resolve with the motif of waiting in

Heidegger's conversation brings us perhaps close to what is attributed to the infinite conversation in Blanchot.[9]

But to understand what has released this resolution in Blanchot's narrated conversation, we should follow closely the experience of interruption that is described in the text. To do so, it is instructive to compare a subsequent passage in *The Infinite Conversation* that appears to comment directly on this experience. There, in an essay titled "Interruption" that gives an important place to the topic of fatigue, Blanchot summarizes a key motif of the early essays in his volume by suggesting that the interruption of the ontological horizon he seeks to think from Levinas's notion of the neutral presence of *autrui* must be thought from the manner in which it is borne by speech (we have no relation to it otherwise). He emphasizes here that the occurrence of writing in the neutral, from the neutral (in relation to "*il*") can never be a matter of a conceptual play or the marking of a mere gap or silence. It is a matter of renouncing the force of discourse, of writing differently, and even of fragmenting language. Nevertheless, with this renunciation, there is accession to a power of speaking that proceeds from a fundamental change in the very structure of language and invites the thought of a *crossing:*

> A change such that to speak (to write) is *to cease thinking solely with a view to unity,* and to make the relations of words an essentially dissymmetrical field governed by discontinuity; as though, having renounced the uninterrupted force of a coherent discourse, it would be a matter of drawing out a level of language where one might gain the power not only to express oneself in an intermittent manner, but also to allow intermittence itself to speak: a speech that, non-unifying, is no longer content with being a passage or a bridge—a non-pontificating speech capable of clearing the two shores separated by the abyss, but without filling in the abyss or reuniting its shores: a speech without reference to unity. (IC 77–78/109–110)

The reader of *The Infinite Conversation* cannot fail to recognize here a repetition of a description of the one who has begun to write: "*Such is the situation: he has lost the power to express himself in a continuous manner . . . Still, in compensation, he believes now and then that he has gained the power to give speech to intermittence*" (IC xxi/XXII–XXIII). And here again the question of the event recurs: "*What has happened then? He asks himself this, and from time to time he hears the reply: something that does not concern him*" (IC xxi/XXII–XXIII).

There is a description of a form of *disabling* here, rather than renunciation, and the wait is all but suspended by the fatigue. There is, however, an accruing power, though it is not entirely clear *who* possesses this power.[10] For the one who speaks in intermittence is not *immediately* the subject of this speaking (or at least so it appears when he reflects on the position from which he speaks); another answers when he addresses himself, just as another answered for him when he declined to affirm that weariness might give him access to the neutral. This displacement of his position of enunciation is beautifully captured in the succeeding section:

> *The non-concerning. Not only what does not concern him, but what for itself is of no concern. Something illegitimate insinuates itself that way. As once, in the sadness of a knowing night, he could have evoked the foreign spirit simply by modifying a few terms; now he is himself evoked by a simple change in the play of words.* (IC xxi/XXIII)

In his "Conversation," Heidegger asked how we accede to the essence of thought if we have the presentiment that this essence lies in something like releasement to "what regions." We can have such a presentiment, or such a presentiment can come to us in waiting, he suggests, for the fact that thought has already been called into releasement through the "destining" that occurs in the usage by which the essence of humankind is appropriated to the saying of language in *Ereignis*. But to approach this usage, and thus the human share in the destining of *Technik* and whatever new beginning might be thought at its historial limits (the "line" Heidegger attempted to evoke in that exchange with Jünger to which Blanchot attended so carefully[11]), an experience with language is required, even though this usage drives us to the limit of language itself. What calls for thought, Heidegger added, withholds itself in its call, or remains, as we read in the "Conversation," independent of any human doing (at least as conceived in the form of an actualizing). Truth requires, it seems, something on the order of a relation without relation that would be given to thought via an experience with language.[12]

We might well turn to the echoing construction of the phrase cited above ("the neutral, the neutral") that Blanchot transcribes at least three times in the course of *The Infinite Conversation* for a reflection of such an experience and a hint of the estranging character of "evocation," of being used for the saying of "*il*." But the narrative also offers, immediately after its reference to a "simple change in the play of words," another transcription of the phrase that has already emerged, and proceeds to submit it to a kind of examination. Here, it is described as "easy to receive," but gradually weighing in the manner of a *sentence* that enjoins and invites in its insistence, though without requiring assent or lending to refutation in its immobile, neutral presence. "What does not concern" is beyond the interest of any willing relation (thus "independent") and without any enclosing or delimiting horizon: it does not con-cern. But it impels and invites. In the flat insistence of the sentence that transcribes the relation it enjoins, it invites to interruption.

> *He comes to understand that the sentence [phrase]—which sentence is in question?—is there only to provoke intermittence, or through this intermittence to make itself signify, or give this intermittence some content; so that the sentence—is it a sentence?—besides its proper meaning, for it must surely have one, would have as its other meaning this intermittent interruption to which it invites him.* (IC xxii/XXIV)

From this simple change in the play of signification, it seems, dialogue can become something resolute. The interlocutor who has known this usage will assume the exilic implication of this development and thus refuse, from the ground of a peculiar responsibility (which can never prove faithful or sufficient), the claims of a law—*la règle d'airain* [IC xxii/XXV])—that is offended by this event. Indeed, in the concluding sections of the narrated conversation, the one who assumes interruption faces a veritable interrogation in the name of the *one* law of the logos for whom this interruption will remain forever illegitimate ("*You know very well that the only law—there is no other—consists in this unique, continual, universal discourse*" [IC xxii/XXIV]). But in the light of the preceding account of his gaining the power of giving expression to interruption, we recognize that the decision to refuse the law and to will the interruption of the discourse has proceeded from the assumption of the "cold" force of another interruption. A releasement (to and by interruption) has thus enabled the willing of releasement (from the horizon of discourse) and passage into the resolute space of an infinite conversation. The circling that began with fatigue might appear to reverse the movement evoked by Heidegger (where willing not to will releases a resolute thinking that is no longer a willing), but as in Heidegger, there would be no crossing at the line had another engagement not already given the impetus for this movement.

Where does this leave us? Blanchot has clearly invited us into a space (of fragmentation) and a time (of return) that irremediably disrupts any gathering in anticipation. Judging from what this space becomes in *The Step Not Beyond,* as Blanchot traces and re-traces an event of exposure that calls to further exposure, its implied topology is both more complex and more spare than Heidegger's "fourfold." The movement is one of *going out* into an ever-expanding wasteland, an ever more severe disappropriation. At the same time, it is true that Blanchot envisions this movement as the tracing of the conditions of another kind of opening to other beings—a radical hospitality and even a radically different relation to what he continues to call life. After the inscription of the "sentence" received by the writing subject in *The Infinite Conversation,* we read the following:

> *There are various ways of responding to this situation. Some say: we must live as though living did not concern us. Others say: since this does not concern, we must live without changing anything about life. But then others: you are changing, you are living non-change as the trace and the mark of that which, not concerning, could not change you.* (IC xxi/XXIV)

It is hard to employ the term "dwelling" for anything proposed here (particularly as regards the last option, which seems to describe an enigmatic relation of living *from* the neutral, or *en différence*). But can we so simply oppose a moving *into* the relation of nearing and a movement *out* toward encounter with the other if we recognize both movements as transpiring in relation to a life whose inevitable resistance ("life" being always inauthentic in some measure, always obscure in its becoming) such releasement must also affirm? Of course, on the one side, the one shore, we have a nomadic affirmation (always haunted by a yearning for peace), and on the other the thought of a gathering appropriation, earthly, yet never quite free of a certain *Unheimlichkeit* and forever unsettled by a dis-junction—a fragmentation?—that also belongs to usage.[13] On one bank a thought of friendship and a community of the question, to borrow a phrase proposed long ago by Jacques Derrida in relation to its Jewish inspiration (this is the community of *les uns . . . les autres,* and in *The Step Not Beyond,* where this will become a central theme, *des gens*).[14] On the other, a strange failure to carry through a thought of hospitality worthy of the text. In the one hemisphere, as at the end of Heidegger's conversation, the night's nearing of stellar distances, a vision proper to "the child in man"; in the other space, without sidereal comfort, a dis-aster for a child and a form of survival that implies a vigilance without anticipation.

One can go very far in enumerating these fundamental differences in *ethos* (to use another shorthand that is not meant to exclude Levinasian ethics and the ethico-political thought that follows). And there is no question that these differences are profoundly *telling,* that they must inevitably shape the decisions taken in that "resolute" conversation to which Blanchot points (in a *fundamental* sense, and not simply as determining considerations for ethical choice). We must not avoid acknowledging, and to some extent, assuming, the determinations or attitudes they imply (both authors told us this in their respective ways), even as we recognize that such oppositional thinking is also profoundly comforting in relation to what we might call "ideology," and perhaps equally inevitable for this reason. But if, in the task of reading these texts, we indulge too eagerly in *figuring* for ourselves the traits of the spaces into which these respective paths of thinking/writing open, we risk passing right by that abyss that lies between them, consigning it to oblivion as we go. For the real proximity or distance between these authors has to be thought from what their texts bring to language of language, inasmuch as both tirelessly seek to convey to us that it is only on this path that we can glimpse the strangeness of our relation to language, and open thereby to its limits and an *other* relation.

From a language so fore-grounded, we might begin—*begin*—to ask about the motif of naming (the significance of Blanchot's reflection on the name of God for the Heideggerian motif of the lack of holy names, for example), or about the presuppositions that allow Blanchot to stipulate that another word "too many" such as "I'm afraid" might bring a fear to language from which it could never wholly recover in the gathering, metaphoric movement that would restore a subject and a meaning to this disruption. How does Blanchot's attempted disruption of metaphor in *The Step Not Beyond* pertain to Heidegger's work with a phrase such as "words like flowers"? These are questions for a philosophy of language that must be prepared to read the relation between Blanchot and Heidegger from the tradition they share and that is marked by names such as Hegel, Hölderlin, Humboldt, Nietzsche, and Mallarmé, not to mention their own. But before—and while—leaping into the conceptual exposition required by engagement with such a history, we must constantly recall that neither author wrote, at the limit, in a representational or conceptual mode. Neither of them gave themselves to metaphor in a classical sense of the term. Indeed, they shared an insistent tendency to think from language in posing their questions about language. The point of the present contribution is simply to draw forth how Blanchot's *cheminement,* like Heidegger's, proceeds from an engagement with language, and to urge us to recall that we do not begin to get under way in a conversation or confrontation between these thinkers from any other site.

NOTES

1. I will give special attention to this motif of "usage" in order to link this discussion to my past work on Heidegger's thinking on language in *Language & Relation: . . . that there is language* (Stanford, Calif.: Stanford University Press, 1996).

2. Drawing, here, on the Latin "*devastare.*" The reference to "a very long process" appears on p. 2 of the translation of *The Step Not Beyond* by Lycette Nelson (Albany: SUNY Press, 1993) and what I have loosely termed an allegory runs throughout.

3. The text was originally published in *La Nouvelle Revue Française* with this title in 1966. In *The Infinite Conversation,* it bears no title and is not even mentioned in the table of contents. It thus opens the collection after a note and several epigraphs. Since it lends the collection its title, one could well say that *The Infinite Conversation* opens *from* it (though in view of its status in the table of contents, one could also say it opens without it). I offered a translation of this text in *Enclitic* some years ago (3, no. 1 [1979]: 48–81), but I will cite here the translation by Susan Hanson with only occasional changes ([Minneapolis: University of Minnesota Press, 1993], xii–xxiii]. References will appear in the body of this text with the abbreviation IC; the first page reference will be to the English edition, the second to the French ([Paris: Gallimard, 1969], IX–XXVI). I might add that the present reading of *The Infinite Conversation* will appear in a more lengthy form in a forthcoming volume on Blanchot that currently bears the title *Last Steps.*

4. Part 2 of *Discourse on Thinking,* trans. John M. Anderson and E. Hans Freund (New York: Harper & Row, 1966).

5. See, for example, "Weary Words: *L'entretien infini,*" in *Clandestine Encounters,* ed. Kevin Hart (Notre Dame, Ind.: University of Notre Dame Press, 2010), 282–303.

6. The motif of "*il*" appears prominently in *The Infinite Conversation.* For this paragraph, I condense quite a bit of material from the opening pages of *The Step Not Beyond* (3–6); see also pp. 72–76 for the "neutral" presence of language, as well as pp. 303–306 and 311–313 of *The Infinite Conversation.* See also "The Narrative Voice" in *The Infinite Conversation* (the "he," the neutral) for its articulation of "*il*" and *le neutre.* It seems clear that the notion of *le neutre* develops significantly Blanchot's earlier reflections on the *il y a.* But the references to *le neutre* bring with

them, frequently, a more interruptive, fragmenting, and dispersing force than does the *il y a,* while retaining the latter's haunting insistence as the presence without presence of alterity. But this topic requires very extensive development that cannot be pursued here. Even the question of translating "*le neutre*" as "neutral" or "neutre" must be postponed inasmuch as it would take some pages to explain why it is neither quite the one nor the other.

7. I am pointing here, of course, to Heidegger's generation of a phrase that he claims not to be his own in his essay "The Essence of Language" in *On the Way to Language,* trans. Peter D. Hertz (New York: Harper & Row, 1971), 77. The subject of the enunciation of the guiding phrase of the present text will prove to be equally problematic.

8. This is an important Blanchotian motif that receives its most important development in the memorial essay on Bataille in Blanchot's volume *Friendship,* trans. Elizabeth Rottenberg (Stanford, Calif.: Stanford University Press, 1997).

9. The reference to a wait that opens in conversation is given special emphasis in Blanchot's essay on Bataille in *The Infinite Conversation:* "The Limit-Experience," 202–229.

10. I echo, here, Blanchot's brief essay in *Who Comes After the Subject,* trans. Eduardo Cadava (New York: Routledge, 1991), 58–60.

11. See "Reflections on Nihilism," in *The Infinite Conversation,* 136–150.

12. One of the more intriguing aspects of Heidegger's thought of *der Brauch* concerns the way he attempts to release this relation from any notion of causal determination, production, grasping, or even desiring appropriation (for there is also an erotics of usage). It is in light of Heidegger's appeal to Hölderlin's attribution of an "excessive self-sufficiency" to the gods in "The Rhine" and to the dynamics of the sentence from *What Is Called Thinking?* (which I translate somewhat severely as "the most thought provoking is, that we are not yet thinking") that I am prompted to speak of this as a relation without relation and to link the non-concerning relation of the neutral with the independence of truth (see, for these points, *Language and Relation,* 108–110).

13. Recalling Heidegger's interpretation of Anaximander's fragment: "Usage conjoins the dis-" ("The Anaximander Fragment," in *Early Greek Thinking,* trans. David Farrell Krell and Frank A. Capuzzi [New York: Harper & Row, 1975], 13–58).

14. I am referring here to Derrida's remarkable opening paragraphs in "Violence and Metaphysics," in *Writing and Difference,* trans. Alan Bass (Chicago: University of Chicago Press, 1978).

CONTRIBUTORS

Robert Bernasconi is Edwin Erle Sparks Professor of Philosophy at the Pennsylvania State University. He is author of *The Question of Language in Heidegger's History of Being* and *Heidegger in Question: The Art of Existing.* He has also published numerous articles in nineteenth- and twentieth-century continental philosophy and in critical philosophy of race.

Walter Brogan is Professor of Philosophy at Villanova University. He is author of *Heidegger and Aristotle: The Twofoldness of Being* and editor of numerous volumes concerning continental philosophy, as well as editor of the journal *Epoché: Journal of the History of Philosophy.* He is co-translator of Heidegger's *Metaphysics Theta 1–3: On the Essence and Actuality of Force* and has authored many articles focusing on ancient Greek philosophy and contemporary European thought.

Daniel O. Dahlstrom is Professor of Philosophy at Boston University. In addition to translating Heidegger's first Marburg lectures, *Introduction to Phenomenological Research* (Indiana University Press, 2005), he is the editor of *Interpreting Heidegger: Critical Essays* and *Gatherings: The Heidegger Circle Annual.*

Françoise Dastur is Honorary Professor of Philosophy, Archives Husserl de Paris (ENS Ulm). She is author of *Heidegger and the Question of Time; Telling Time; Heidegger et la question du temps; Heidegger: La question du logos,* and many other texts treating Heidegger, Hölderlin, Husserl, and others.

Christopher Fynsk is Professor of Modern Thought and Comparative Literature at the University of Aberdeen, where he is Director of the Centre for Modern Thought. His books include *Heidegger: Thought and Historicity; Language & Relation: . . . that there is language; Infant Figures;* and *The Claim of Language: A Case for the Humanities.*

Peter Hanly is a PhD candidate at Boston College and a concert violinist. He is currently completing a dissertation on Heidegger and Novalis. His publications include articles on Blanchot, Kant and Hölderlin, and Hegel and the voice.

David Farrell Krell is Emeritus Professor of Philosophy at DePaul University in Chicago and Guest Professor at the University of Freiburg. He is the author of *The Tragic Absolute: German Idealism and the Languishing of God* (Indiana University Press, 2005); *The Purest of Bastards: Works of Mourning, Art, and Affirmation in the Thought of Jacques Derrida; Daimon Life: Heidegger and Life-Philosophy* (Indiana University Press, 1992); *Intimations of Mortality: Time, Truth, and Finitude in Heidegger's Thinking of Being;* and numerous other philosophical texts. He is the editor and translator of Martin Heidegger's *Basic Writings; Nietzsche;* and *Early Greek Thinking.* His most recent academic book is an annotated translation into English of Friedrich Hölderlin's *The Death of Empedocles.*

William McNeill is Professor of Philosophy at DePaul University, Chicago. He is author of *The Glance of the Eye: Heidegger, Aristotle, and the Ends of Theory* and *The Time of Life: Heidegger and Ethos.* He has also translated or edited a number of Heidegger's works.

Richard Polt of Xavier University, Cincinnati, is the author of *Heidegger: An Introduction* and *The Emergency of Being: On Heidegger's "Contributions to Philosophy."* He edited *Heidegger's "Being and Time": Critical Essays* and is co-translator with Gregory Fried of Heidegger's *Introduction to Metaphysics* and *Being and Truth.*

Jeffrey L. Powell is Professor of Philosophy at Marshall University. He has published numerous essays concerning Heidegger as well as Kant, Hegel, Nietzsche, Freud, Husserl, Levinas, Derrida, and Foucault. He is currently translating (with Will McNeill) Heidegger's *Die Geschichte des Seyns* for Indiana University Press.

John Sallis is Frederick J. Adelmann Professor of Philosophy at Boston College and a regular Visiting Professor at Staffordshire University (UK) and Universität Freiburg (Germany). He is the author of more than twenty books, including, most recently, *Transfigurements: On the True Sense of Art* and *Logic of Imagination: The Expanse of the Elemental.*

Dennis J. Schmidt is Liberal Arts Professor of Philosophy, Comparative Literature, and German at the Pennsylvania State University. He is the author of *Idiome der Wahrheit; Between Word and Image* (Indiana University Press, 2012); *Lyrical and Ethical Subjects; On Germans and Other Greeks* (Indiana University Press, 2001); and *The Ubiquity of the Finite.* He has edited, introduced, and revised the translation of Heidegger's *Being and Time.*

Daniela Vallega-Neu is author of *Heidegger's "Contributions to Philosophy": An Introduction* (Indiana University Press, 2003) and of *The Bodily Dimension in Thinking.* She also co-edited *Companion to Heidegger's "Contributions to Philosophy"* (Indiana University Press, 2001) and is co-translator of a new translation of Heidegger's *Beiträge zur Philosophie (Vom Ereignis)* (Indiana University Press, 2012). Currently she is Visiting Associate Professor at the University of Oregon.

Krzysztof Ziarek is Professor of Comparative Literature at the State University of New York at Buffalo. He is the author of *Inflected Language: Toward a Hermeneutics of Nearness; The Historicity of Experience: Modernity, the Avant-Garde, and the Event;* and *The Force of Art.* He has recently completed a book manuscript titled *Language After Heidegger* for Indiana University Press.

INDEX